UNLOCKING
THE ENGLISH
LEGAL SYSTEM

5th edition

Rebecca Huxley-Binns,
Jacqueline Martin and
Tom Frost

WIT
FROM
UNIVE

D0549792

Routledge
Taylor & Francis Group

LONDON AND NEW YORK

100640414

Fifth edition published 2017
by Routledge
2 Park Square, Milton Park, Abingdon, Oxon OX14 4RN

and by Routledge
711 Third Avenue, New York, NY 10017

Routledge is an imprint of the Taylor & Francis Group, an informa business

© 2017 Rebecca Huxley-Binns, Jacqueline Martin and Tom Frost

The right of Rebecca Huxley-Binns, Jacqueline Martin and Tom Frost to be identified as authors of this work has been asserted by them in accordance with sections 77 and 78 of the Copyright, Designs and Patents Act 1988.

All rights reserved. No part of this book may be reprinted or reproduced or utilised in any form or by any electronic, mechanical or other means, now known or hereafter invented, including photocopying and recording, or in any information storage or retrieval system, without permission in writing from the publishers.

Trademark notice: Product or corporate names may be trademarks or registered trademarks, and are used only for identification and explanation without intent to infringe.

First edition published by Hodder Education 2005
Fourth edition published by Routledge 2014

British Library Cataloguing in Publication Data
A catalogue record for this book is available from the British Library

Library of Congress Cataloging in Publication Data
Names: Huxley-Binns, Rebecca, author. | Martin, Jacqueline, 1945- author. |
Frost, Tom (Lecturer in Law) author.
Title: Unlocking the English legal system/Rebecca Huxley-Binns, Jacqueline Martin, Tom Frost.
Description: Fifth edition. | New York, NY: Routledge, 2017. | Includes bibliographical references and index.
Identifiers: LCCN 2016052444| ISBN 9781138228405 (hardback) | ISBN 9781138228412 (pbk.)
Subjects: LCSH: Law–England.
Classification: LCC KD661 .H89 2017 | DDC 349.42–dc23
LC record available at https://lccn.loc.gov/2016052444

ISBN: 978-1-138-22840-5 (hbk)
ISBN: 978-1-138-22841-2 (pbk)
ISBN: 978-1-315-39266-0 (ebk)

Typeset in Palatino
by Wearset Ltd, Boldon, Tyne and Wear

Visit the companion website at: www.routledge.com/cw/huxley-binns

Printed and bound in Great Britain by
TJ International Ltd, Padstow, Cornwall

Contents

KT-366-653

100640414
349.
42
HUX

CONTENTS

Acknowledgements

The authors and publishers would like to thank the following for permission to reproduce copyright material: extracts on p 176 from 'Jury trials in the dock once more' by Joshua Rozenberg, *Daily Telegraph*, 1 April 2004 © Telegraph Media Group; tables on pp 291 and 295 © The Law Society © Crown copyright material is reproduced with permission of the Controller of HMSO and the Queen's Printer for Scotland.

Every effort has been made to trace and acknowledge ownership of copyright. The publishers will be glad to make suitable arrangements with any copyright holders whom it has not been possible to contact.

Guide to the book

In the *Unlocking the Law* books all the essential elements that make up the law are clearly defined to bring the law alive and make it memorable. In addition, the books are enhanced with learning features to reinforce learning and test your knowledge as you study. Follow this guide to make sure you get the most from reading this book.

AIMS AND OBJECTIVES

Defines what you will learn in each chapter.

SECTION

definition
Find key legal terminology at a glance

Highlights sections from Acts.

ARTICLE

Defines Articles of the EC Treaty or of the European Convention on Human Rights or other Treaty.

CLAUSE

Shows a Bill going through Parliament or a draft Bill proposed by the Law Commission.

CASE EXAMPLE

Illustrates the law in action.

JUDGMENT

Provides extracts from judgments on cases.

Indicates that you will be able to test yourself further on this topic using the Key Questions and Answers section of this book on www.unlockingthelaw.co.uk.

QUOTATION

Encourages you to engage with primary sources.

ACTIVITY

Enables you to test yourself as you progress through the chapter.

KEY FACTS

Draws attention to essential points and information.

SAMPLE ESSAY QUESTIONS

Provide you with real-life sample essays and show you the best way to plan your answer.

SUMMARY

Concludes each chapter to reinforce learning.

Preface

The *Unlocking the Law* series is an entirely new style of undergraduate law textbook. Many student texts are very prose-dense, and have little in the way of interactive materials to help a student feel his or her way through the course of study on a given module.

The purpose of this series, then, is to try to make learning each subject area more accessible by focusing on actual learning needs, and by providing a range of different supporting materials and features.

All topic areas are broken up into 'bite-size' sections, with a logical progression and extensive use of headings and numerous sub-headings. Each book in the series will also contain a variety of charts, diagrams and key facts summaries to reinforce the information in the body of the text. Diagrams and flow charts are particularly useful because they can provide a quick and easy understanding of the key points, especially when revising for examinations. Key facts charts not only provide a quick visual guide through the subject, but are useful for revision purposes also.

The books have a number of common features in the style of text layout. Important cases are separated out for easy access and have full citation in the text as well as in the table of cases, for ease of reference. The emphasis of the series is on depth of understanding rather than breadth. For this reason, each text also includes key extracts from judgments, where appropriate. Extracts from academic comment from journal articles and leading texts are also included to give some insight into the academic debate on complex or controversial areas.

Finally, the books also include much formative 'self-testing', with a variety of activities ranging through subject-specific comprehension, application of the law and a range of other activities to help the student gain a good idea of his or her progress in the course.

Note also that for all incidental references to 'he', 'him', 'his', we invoke the Interpretation Act 1978 and its provisions that 'he' includes 'she' etc.

English legal method and the English legal system are important as they underpin understanding of the development and practice of all substantive areas of law. This book starts with an outline of the sources of law, followed by detailed consideration of the operation of judicial precedent and statutory interpretation. There are also additional exercises on these topics. The court structure in England and Wales is then explained, together with how cases are funded. Chapters 8–11 concentrate on the personnel, both professional and lay, in the legal system. Finally, there is a chapter on sentencing. The book should provide students with a clear understanding of our legal system.

This fifth edition has been updated throughout to include developments in the law since the publication of the last edition. In particular it includes the developments to the legal aid system under the Legal Aid, Sentencing and Punishment of Offenders Act 2012 and the impact of the Criminal Justice and Courts Act 2015, as well as details on the new Combined Family Court.

The book is designed to cover all of the main topic areas on undergraduate and professional syllabuses and help provide a full understanding of each.

The law is stated as we believe it to be on 1 October 2016.

Rebecca Huxley-Binns,
Jacqueline Martin and
Tom Frost

List of figures

Abbreviations

ABSs	alternative business structures
ACAS	Advisory Conciliation and Arbitration Services
ADR	alternative dispute resolution
AJA 1999	Access to Justice Act 1999
ALAS	Accident Legal Advice Service
ARM	automatic referral to mediation
BME	black and minority ethnic
BPTC	Bar Professional Training Course
BSB	Bar Standards Board
BTDCs	Bench Training and Development Committees
CAB	Citizens Advice Bureau
CABx	Citizens Advice Bureaux
CCRC	Criminal Cases Review Commission
CEDR	Centre for Dispute Resolution
CFAs	conditional fee agreements
CILEx	Chartered Institute of Legal Executives
CIPA	Chartered Institute of Patent Attorneys
CJEU	Court of Justice of the European Union
CLACs	Community Legal Advice Centres
CLSA 1990	Courts and Legal Services Act 1990
CNR	cell nuclear replacement
CPE	Common Professional Examination
CPR	Civil Procedure Rules
CPS	Crown Prosecution Service
CrimPRs	Criminal Procedure Rules 2005
DJ(MC)	District Judges (Magistrates' Court)
DPP	Director of Public Prosecutions
ECHR	European Convention on Human Rights
ECtHR	European Court of Human Rights
ELS	English legal system
FRU	Free Representation Unit
GDL	Graduate Diploma in Law
HRA 1998	Human Rights Act 1998
IPReg	Intellectual Property Regulation Board
IPS	ILEX Professional Standards Ltd
IT	information technology
ITMA	Institute of Trade Mark Attorneys
JAC	Judicial Appointments Commission
JCPC	Judicial Committee of the Privy Council
JP	Justice of the Peace
LASPO 2012	Legal Aid, Sentencing and Punishment of Offenders Act 2012
LETR	Legal Education and Training Review
LSB	Legal Services Board
MNTI1	Magistrates New Training Initiative 1998
MNTI2	Magistrates National Training Initiative 2004
ODR	Online Dispute Resolution

OLC	Office for Legal Complaints
PCMH	plea and case management hearing
PDS	Public Defender Service
PI	personal injury
QC	Queen's Counsel
SDT	Solicitors Disciplinary Tribunal
SI	statutory instrument
SRA	Solicitors' Regulation Authority
TEU	Treaty on European Union
TFEU	Treaty on the Functioning of the European Union
VRR	Victims' Right to Review

Table of cases

Tables of statutes and other instruments

TABLES OF STATUTES AND OTHER INSTRUMENTS

1

The sources of law

AIMS AND OBJECTIVES

After reading this chapter you should be able to:

- Identify the main sources of English law
- Distinguish common law and equity, and common law and legislation
- Distinguish primary and secondary legislation and understand what controls exist on the latter
- Recognise the difference between the European Union and the Council of Europe
- Explain the difference between the Human Rights Act 1998 and the European Convention on Human Rights
- Form an opinion concerning how laws are reformed

1.1 The English legal system

What is the English legal system (ELS)? Well, it isn't so much a system as an amalgamation of various agencies, processes and institutions, and the term often includes the personnel involved in the resolution (formal or informal) of legal disputes too. It is certainly more about procedure than the substantive law of, say, contract law or land law, although there is a degree of overlap, as Cownie and Bradney point out:

QUOTATION

'Legal systems are there to determine what will happen when people have disputes. Legal rules are also there so people can order their lives in such a way as to avoid such disputes.'

F Cownie and A Bradney, English Legal System in Context
(2nd edn, Butterworths, 2000), p 6

There is no agreed definition for the term 'English legal system' or for the required content of the subject taught on an undergraduate law course, but, as Bailey, Gunn, Ormerod and Ching warn:

QUOTATION

'Some [students] even have the misguided belief that the study of the institutions and processes of our law does not carry the intellectual challenge of other legal subjects. Yet a failure to understand the English legal system will make much of what the student learns of those other subjects either incomprehensible or misleading.'

S H Bailey, M Gunn, D Ormerod and J Ching, Smith, Bailey and Gunn on the Modern English Legal System (4th edn, Sweet & Maxwell, 2002), p 1

The subject is dealt with differently in the numerous texts available all called *English Legal System*, or *English Legal Process*, and the module is taught and assessed differently in university law schools, because the schools have the freedom to choose the subject content of the modules. However, all texts and courses do, to some extent, cover aspects of the personnel, the law-making machinery and the rules governing each of them, which we proceed to do throughout this text.

There is also an important historical perspective to the study of the ELS, because we can understand how the system operates today only by having a sense of how it developed. Hence, we start by looking at the sources of English law.

First, a note on the terminology. When we refer to the '*English* legal system', we are usually deliberately not referring to Scotland, Northern Ireland, the Isle of Man and the Channel Islands, which have separate legal systems; but to England and, on the whole, Wales. According to context, however, we might use the terms 'Great Britain' or the 'United Kingdom' (UK) where relevant, especially when considering the broader sources of law, such as the European Union (EU) and the European Convention on Human Rights (ECHR), each of which has affected the UK as a whole.

Second, a brief note on Welsh law. Under the Government of Wales Act 2006, the National Assembly for Wales may pass primary and secondary legislation under devolved responsibility (these laws are known as Assembly Measures) on areas including agriculture, education, food, housing and town planning. English laws continue to apply to Wales, unless Welsh law has been passed which conflicts, so some commentators regard Welsh law as a branch of English law. That said, some laws which apply in England do not apply in Wales, and some laws apply in Wales which do not apply or even exist in English law.

1.2 The sources of law

Where does the law come from? The obvious answer is the law-makers. The key law-makers in the ELS are:

Parliament	Parliament is the principal law-maker in the ELS because of the doctrine of **parliamentary sovereignty**.
The courts	Historically vital as law-makers because we had judges before we had a Parliament, the courts continue to be integral to the constitutional framework of the ELS under the **Rule of Law** and the **Separation of Powers doctrine**.

The words in bold in the explanations above are important key terms which you need to understand. They are defined below:

Parliamentary sovereignty	Parliament is able to pass laws on any subject; these laws can regulate the activities of anyone, anywhere; Parliament cannot bind its successors as to the content of subsequent legislation; and laws passed by Parliament cannot be declared void by the courts.
The Rule of Law	Individuals' liberties can be ensured only by regulating behaviour **by** the law (not arbitrarily), punishing only **according** to the law and making all citizens **subject** to the law.
The Separation of Powers doctrine	Abuse of state power can be prevented only by sharing the power of the state among the Executive (the government), the Legislature (Parliament) and the Judiciary (the courts). In this way, checks and balances are in place to reduce the risk of abuse.

The key law-makers from outside the ELS but which affect the citizens governed by English law are:

The EU	The UK's membership of the EU dictates an obligation to incorporate into UK law the laws of the institutions established by the EU treaties (see section 1.7 below). Despite the result of the June 2016 referendum on membership of the EU, where a majority of voters chose to leave the Union, the UK will remain a member of the EU until it formally leaves the EU. This process will take at least two years. Until this process is completed, EU law will remain a part of UK law.
The Council of Europe	As you will see at section 1.8, the ECHR is the work of the Council of Europe (not the EU) and is fundamental to the operation of UK law – whether made by Parliaments or the courts – because of the Human Rights Act 1998 (HRA 1998).

There are some other sources of law which are considered later in this chapter (for example, law reform agencies and academics).

1.3 The courts

There is no legislative or express democratic authority for the courts to be law-makers but, nevertheless, it is clear that judges do make the law (see section 2.5 for more information). How do the judges make the law? In two key ways:

- developing the common law;
- interpreting Acts of Parliament.

We will consider each of these roles below. First, you need to understand that there is a court hierarchy. The structure you will see in Figure 1.1 does not merely indicate which courts hear which cases (the basic jurisdiction of each court is shown, but note that this is not detailed and you must refer to Chapters 4, 5 and 6 for more detail), but also that because there is a clear hierarchy, courts at the top of the diagram have more seniority and authority than the courts below. This is one of the reasons the courts at the top of the hierarchy hear appeals. Appeals are almost always on points of **law**, so this is where the law made by the judges stems from.

1.3.1 The Supreme Court of the UK

Until 2009, when lawyers referred to 'the House of Lords', they meant *either*:

- the House of Lords in its legislative capacity, as part of Parliament; *or* the House of Lords as the most superior of the courts in England and Wales (and, for civil cases, Scotland too) which was its judicial or appellate capacity. The court was housed in the Houses of Parliament building, and the Law Lords could, in theory, also sit in the legislative chamber of the House of Lords and enter into the debates (something they rarely did in practice).

In July 2009, the House of Lords *as a court* ceased to exist and was replaced in October 2009 by a Supreme Court of the UK. You will find more information on the Supreme Court in Chapters 6 (Appeals) and 11 (The judiciary).

PRIVY COUNCIL

Devolution issues (esp. Wales and Scotland).

Appeals from the Commonwealth on civil and criminal law.

THE SUPREME COURT OF THE UK (ex HOUSE OF LORDS)

Appeals on civil and criminal law from English courts and Northern Ireland. Appeals on civil law from Scotland.

COURT OF JUSTICE OF THE EUROPEAN UNION

References from any court on a question of EU law and disputes between member states and institutions of the EU.

COURT OF APPEAL

CRIMINAL DIVISION	CIVIL DIVISION
Appeals in criminal cases from the Crown Court.	Appeals in civil cases from the High and County Courts.

THE HIGH COURT

ADMINISTRATIVE COURT (ex QUEEN'S BENCH DIVISIONAL COURT)	FAMILY DIVISIONAL COURT	CHANCERY DIVISIONAL COURT
Judicial review and appeals in some criminal cases.	Appeals in family matters from the County Courts.	Appeals in land and tax cases from the County Courts.
QUEEN'S BENCH DIVISION	FAMILY DIVISION	CHANCERY DIVISION
Hearings in civil cases according to value of claim.	Hearings in family and child law cases.	Hearings in land, trusts and tax cases.

CROWN COURT

Criminal trials on indictment and appeals in criminal cases from the Magistrates' Court.

MAGISTRATES' COURT

Criminal trials.

Family cases.

Non-payments of bills.

COUNTY COURT

Hearings in civil cases according to value of claim and family matters.

Figure 1.1 The court hierarchy

1.4 The common law

As stated above, one of the ways in which the judges make the law is by developing the common law. However, the phrase 'common law' is not a particularly easy one to get to grips with because it can have up to five different meanings, according to the context in which it is used.

	Meaning	Example
1.	The term 'common law' can be taken to refer to the system of law which is common to the whole country.	Murder is an offence under the common law of England; however, walking on the grass in a local park may be an offence under a local bylaw, but is not part of the common law of England.
2.	The term may also be used to distinguish that law which is not equity (see further below).	Damages (a monetary award; compensation) are common law remedies, whereas the injunction is an equitable remedy.
3.	It might be used to mean case law: that is law developed by judges through cases. This is the context in which the term was used at section 1.3 above.	The common law principle that a manufacturer is liable in negligence to the ultimate consumer of its products derives from the case of *Donoghue v Stevenson* [1932] AC 562.
4.	It could be used to indicate law which has not been made by Parliament (the law made by Parliament is called a statute or legislation).	Murder is a common law offence, but the defences of diminished responsibility and provocation are statutory under ss2 and 3 Homicide Act 1957.
5.	The term may also be used to describe those legal systems that developed from the English system. In this final sense, a common law system is distinguished from a civil law system. Civil law developed from the Romano-Germanic legal system and is the dominant legal system in continental Europe including the EU itself.	France does not have a common law system because it developed from the Roman tradition with a civil law system. On the other hand, England, Australia and New Zealand are common law jurisdictions.

Figure 1.2 Uses of the term 'common law'

An understanding of the historical development of the common law of England will assist you in using the term correctly; but to understand this, you also need to have a grasp of the development of equity.

1.4.1 Problems of the common law

The story starts before William the Conqueror conquered England in 1066. Before this date, there was no national legal system. Local laws were enforced by local lords or sheriffs. When William took the throne in 1066, he was a shrewd leader and he recognised that he would have to establish a system of central or national government and, with that, a centralised system of justice over which he would have control. Only in this way would he attain real power and control over his new subjects.

William travelled throughout the land, listening to people's grievances. He and his most powerful advisers would judge the merits of the complaints and deliver judgments.

This travelling court system became known as the *Curia Regis* (King's Court) and it is from this court that we see the development of the common law. Subsequent kings appointed judges to the *Curia Regis* and over time a national and uniform system of laws was put in place. In this way many local customary laws were replaced by new national laws. As these national laws would apply to everyone, they would be common to all. These laws therefore became known as the common law. However, there were a number of problems with the operation of the common law:

....

stare decisis
Stand by what is decided; it means that judges are bound by previous decisions. See Chapter 2 for more detail
....

- First, the common law operated on the basis of ***stare decisis***; that means binding precedent. One of the main criticisms of this doctrine is that a court is bound to follow a previous decision even if the judge disagrees with that previous decision. Mechanisms do exist in the modern ELS for a judge to avoid this process today, but such mechanisms did not exist, or were rarely used, in the more antiquated system. This meant that the common law did not develop and parties could not persuade a judge to change the law, even when it was obviously in need of change.

- Second, cases in the common law courts were started by means of a writ. A writ is a document used by a party to commence a legal action. Documents are still used today, but in a different form (for example, in order to start a civil action, the claimant must issue a 'claim form'). Under the old common law system, the bureaucracy of the rules dictated that if the wrong writ had been chosen or a mistake had been made on the writ, that writ was void and could not be amended as happens today. Instead the plaintiff (the old term for 'claimant') had to go to the expense and trouble of starting all over again. Additionally, the common law rules required that certain civil actions (this was in the days before a formal legal system for the resolution of criminal cases existed) had to involve certain types of conduct. For example, an action for trespass had to involve an allegation that violence had been used against the plaintiff. Therefore, in theory, if no violence had been used, the action could not succeed. In practice, some common law judges were prepared to imply that violence had occurred when they knew very well that none had.

- Third, the only remedy available at common law was damages. This is a monetary award (compensation). In many cases, for example a breach of contract, this remedy was perfectly adequate, but if we continue with the trespass example above, the successful plaintiff would not have found money to be an adequate remedy – he wanted the trespasser to stop (but the order we now call an injunction did not exist).

1.4.2 Development of equity

Many people felt let down by the common law system because it was unable to remedy these defects for itself so, as had been the practice before the *Curia Regis*, they petitioned the king directly for a remedy. Initially, kings would consider these petitions themselves but at some time during the fifteenth century this work was handed over to the Lord High Chancellor, known subsequently just as the Lord Chancellor. The number of petitions rose dramatically, so the Lord Chancellor established a court to hear the petitions. This court was called the Court of Chancery. The rules which the Lord Chancellor adopted in this court were not the rules from the common law courts. Actions were started by a petition rather than a writ, and the Lord Chancellor was not bound by precedent. Instead, rules were established to ensure that justice was obtained in those cases where the parties were able to show that the common law courts were not able or prepared to provide a suitable remedy. These rules became known as the **rules of equity**, 'equity' meaning even-handedness and fairness. It was never intended that the principles of equity would replace the common law rules, simply that they would fill the gaps in it and make up for its defects.

Maxims of equity

One of the ways in which equity was able to plug the gaps of the common law was by using guidelines called **maxims of equity**. One of the better-known maxims is 'He who comes to equity must come with clean hands.' This means that equity will not assist a party who has acted in bad conscience.

CASE EXAMPLE

D & C Builders v Rees [1966] 2 QB 617, CA

The plaintiff company sued Mr and Mrs Rees for failure to pay a bill in full for building work done to their home. The plaintiffs had sent three bills and the defendants had paid only one-third 'on account'. The defendants then made complaints about the quality of the work and, knowing that the plaintiff company was in severe financial difficulty, offered to pay a further third, but 'in full settlement'. The plaintiff company agreed, only because without the money the company would have gone bankrupt. The company later sued the defendants for the outstanding amount.

Lord Denning MR (denoting that he was, at the time of the judgment, the Master of the Rolls) held at the Court of Appeal:

JUDGMENT

'The creditor [the plaintiff] is only barred from his legal rights when it would be *inequitable* for him to insist upon them. Where there has been a *true accord*, under which the creditor voluntarily agrees to accept a lesser sum in satisfaction, and the debtor *acts upon* that accord by paying the lesser sum and the creditor accepts it, then it is inequitable for the creditor afterwards to insist on the balance. But he is not bound unless there has been truly an accord between them.

... In the present case, on the facts as found by the judge, it seems to me that there was no true accord. The debtor's wife held the creditor to ransom. The creditor was in need of money to meet his own commitments, and she knew it. When the creditor asked for payment of the £480 due to him, she said to him in effect: "We cannot pay you the £480. But we will pay you £300 if you will accept it in settlement. If you do not accept it on those terms, you will get nothing. £300 is better than nothing." She had no right to say any such thing ... There is also no equity in the defendant to warrant any departure from the due course of law. No person can insist on a settlement procured by intimidation.'

As you can see, Lord Denning was scathing of the conduct of Mr and Mrs Rees. The other Lord Justice, Danckwerts LJ, found that the Reeses 'really behaved very badly'. A person who behaves 'very badly' is unlikely to benefit from equity's protection, as the Reeses found to their cost. As equity would not intervene on behalf of the couple to protect them from having to pay the full amount, the common law rules prevailed. One of these rules is that part-payment of a debt does not satisfy (fulfil) the debt. They had to pay up.

The 'clean hands' maxim is one of many maxims of equity. Others include:

- 'equity is equality' (unless there is clear evidence one way or another, property should be divided in equal shares);
- 'equity looks to the intention and not the form' (equity looks at what the parties meant to do, not necessarily what they did do);

- 'equity acts *in personam*' (equitable remedies take effect against the person, not their property, so in the days of the development of equity, a defendant could go to prison for failure to honour an equitable remedy made against him);
- 'equity will not suffer a wrong without a remedy' (if equity considers that a person has a good claim, equity will ensure that that person has the right to bring a legal action).

The trust

What is a trust? The distinction between law (i.e. the common law) and equity is most apparent if you consider that **different** people can own the **same** piece of property in **different** ways, at the same time. This is called a trust and is recognised only in equity.

Example

Sidney (S, the settlor) is writing his will. He has 10,000 shares in BT and he wants to leave these shares to Betty, his nine-year-old granddaughter. In his will (and in accordance with the common law rules), S appoints Trevor (T) to be the trustee of the will. When S dies, T, as trustee, is the **legal** owner of the shares. He, and only he, can exercise the legal rights over the shares. However, B, as beneficiary of the will, also has rights in the shares; she is entitled to the dividends on the shares because she is the **equitable** owner of them, but she cannot sell them because T is the legal owner. Despite T's legal ownership, B has the benefit of the equitable interests in the property. It may be that when B attains the age of 18 (or at some other specified age or on some specified event, such as marriage), B will become the legal owner of the shares and T's rights will be extinguished.

Equitable remedies

Equity created not only new rights, such as the trust above, but also new remedies. As stated above, the only common law remedy was damages. Equity recognised the limits of the usefulness of money as an award and developed, among others, the following additional remedies:

Injunction	This is an order of the court compelling or restraining the performance of some act.
Specific performance	This is an order compelling a party to perform his part of an agreement that he had promised to fulfil.
Rescission	This is an order restoring parties to a contract to their precontractual positions, releasing them entirely from their contractual obligations.

Figure 1.3 Equitable remedies

Conflict with the common law

The common law judges came to view the Court of Chancery as a rival to their authority. This rivalry came to a head in the *Earl of Oxford's Case* [1616] 1 Rep Ch 1 where the common law judges refused to recognise the interest of a beneficial owner of a trust; yet the Chancery judges threatened to imprison the trustees (the legal owners) unless they recognised that same interest. James I was required to intervene and he settled the situation: where the common law and equity conflict, equity was to prevail. Had James I not decided the matter in this way, the purpose of equity would have been fundamentally undermined.

Having a dual system of courts administering different remedies did cause other problems, however, and by the passing of the Judicature Acts of 1873–75, the court system was reformed. The result was that the administration of the common law courts and the Court of Chancery was merged, to create a unified system of courts and procedures. Thus, all courts in the modern legal system can use both common law and equitable principles and give either type of remedy. In the event of a conflict, s25 of the Judicature Act 1873 provided that equity should prevail and s49(1) of the Senior Courts Act 1981 is the modern embodiment of that rule. Common law rules and equitable 'rules' have not merged into one source of law, however. For example, common law rules have a strong influence in contract, tort and criminal law, and common law remedies such as monetary damages are frequently used in the first two mentioned areas. By contrast, the Chancery Division of the High Court (the modern Court of Chancery) deals with matters of company law, partnership, conveyancing (the legal transfer of property involved in the buying and selling of land and buildings), wills and probates (administration of the property of persons who have died) and patent and copyright law where the rules of equity are used frequently. Another important aspect of Chancery work is the administration of trusts.

ACTIVITY

Self-test questions

1. The first national court system was evolved by the Judicature Acts 1873–75. True/False
2. The main defects in the common law system of the *Curia Regis* were

   (a) rigidity,
   (b) the writ system and
   (c) the limited remedies available. True/False

3. Equity will not intervene to protect a defendant unless he has 'clean hands'. True/False
4. A trust is an invention of the common law rather than of equity. True/False
5. If the common law and equity conflict, the common law prevails. True/False

1.5 Parliament

1.5.1 Legislation

You should be aware that lawyers often use the terms 'Act', 'statute' and 'legislation' interchangeably. A statute is a document containing the laws made by Parliament. Parliament consists of the Queen, the House of Lords and the House of Commons. Parliament is the originator of all legislation. All Acts of Parliament (note that we use an upper-case 'A' for Act of Parliament; we never use a lower-case 'a' when we mean legislation) consist of formally enacted rules dealing with a particular subject matter and are broken down into sections for ease of reference (for example, s2 of the Homicide Act 1957). An Act of Parliament must begin life in draft form as a Bill, but a Bill may begin life as consultation paper, sometimes called a Green Paper; or a White Paper which is a document containing the government's proposals for legislative changes. A Bill must be debated by both Houses of Parliament and must undergo set procedures, until it is finally given the Royal Assent by the monarch, at which stage it becomes an Act (it is **enacted**) and enters into force on the day the Bill receives the Royal Assent, unless the Act provides for other dates.

1.5.2 The enactment process

■ *First Reading*: this not a reading of the full Bill. Its purpose is to point out to MPs the existence of the Bill so that they can read it. The Speaker of the House (Commons or Lords) reads out the short title and sets the date for the Second Reading.

- *Second Reading*: here there is a debate dealing with the general principles of the Bill. A vote follows; and this is probably the most important vote in the enactment process because it is likely that if the Bill succeeds, it will later become law.
- *Committee Stage*: this consists of a Standing Committee (or, for Money or constitutionally significant Bills (see below), the whole of the House) reviewing the detailed wording, clause by clause, of the Bill so that the exact wording conforms with the issues debated at the Second Reading.
- *Report Stage*: any amendments made at Committee Stage are reported back to the House and each amendment is voted on.
- *Third Reading*: this may consist of a further debate on the wording of the Bill, but the general principles are not open to a further discussion as these will have been approved on the Second Reading. A second vote is then taken on the Bill.

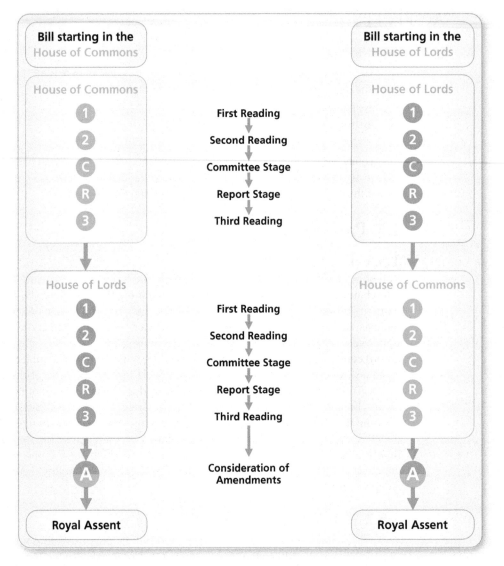

Figure 1.4 Passage of a Bill (source: www.parliament.uk/about/how/laws/passage_bill/index.htm)

Bills may start life in either House of Parliament. Bills dealing with financial matters only (called Money Bills) must start in the House of Commons. The House of Lords then debates the Bill, but after one month the Bill may be presented for Royal Assent without the Lords' approval. All other Bills must be passed to the other House for approval.

The Parliament Acts 1911–49 provide that certain Bills may receive Royal Assent without the Lords having passed the Bill. In addition to Money Bills (above), all Bills may be presented for Royal Assent where

1. the Bill has been passed by the House of Commons in two consecutive sessions and the House of Lords has failed to pass it in each session;

2. one year has passed between the Second Reading in the first session and the Third Reading of the second session in the House of Commons;

3. the Bill was sent to the House of Lords at least one month before the end of each session; and

4. the Speaker of the House of Commons issues a certificate to state that the above requirements have been complied with.

judicial review
The process where certain courts can review and annul the acts or decisions of certain bodies, including the legislature and executive

The procedure has been used on very few occasions, including the Welsh Church Act 1914, the Parliament Act 1949, the War Crimes Act 1991, the Sexual Offences (Amendment) Act 2000 and the Hunting Act 2004. After the latest Act, a legal challenge (**judicial review**) was brought by the Countryside Alliance against the Parliament Act 1949 on the basis that any use of the 1911 Act to force legislation through without the Lords' approval would be void because the 1949 Act itself did not receive the Lords' approval. The argument failed at the High Court, the Court of Appeal and the House of Lords.

Royal Assent is the formal process whereby the Queen, in theory, approves the Bill, but in reality it is a formal process consisting of a reading of the title of the Act.

Statutes are probably the single most important source of law in the modern ELS and this is because of the principle called parliamentary sovereignty explained above. A V Dicey explained:

QUOTATION

"In theory Parliament has total power. It is sovereign.'
A V Dicey, The Law of the Constitution (Macmillan, 1885)

So what are the pros and cons of the legislative process and of legislation being the principal sources of law?

ACTIVITY

Self-test questions

1. Explain (in words) the enactment process of nonMoney Bills which start life in the House of Commons.

2. To what extent does the House of Lords have the power to (a) deny and/or (b) delay legislation?

Positive	Negative
All Bills have to pass through both the House of Commons and the House of Lords. Notwithstanding efforts to reform this chamber's composition, to make it a more accountable institution – House of Lords Act 1999 – including public consultations, a Royal Commission and a White Paper, none has yet succeeded.	It was as a result of the civil war in the seventeenth century that Parliament gained the sole right to make law, but the result of this is that most new laws are a result of political persuasion and policy. One of the consequences of this is that where a political party has a majority, it can implement laws without the consent of democratically elected opposition.
Statute-made law upholds the doctrine of the Separation of Powers (judge-made law is made and enforced by the judiciary; statutory law is made by one body but enforced by another, thus providing checks and balances). Statute law can be known in advance (whereas case law is decided on an ad hoc basis). The Legislature is free to make law on any subject it thinks fit; the judiciary is limited to dealing with the facts of the case before it.	There is limited scope for MPs who are not part of the Cabinet (private members) to have legislation passed unless it receives the blessing of the whole government. Statutory law can be very ambiguous because of problems in drafting, resulting in the situation in which statutory law is inaccessible to all but lawyers. Approximately 75 per cent of all cases heard by the highest courts a year deal only with a question of statutory interpretation. Normal citizens are not fully involved in the enactment process – but nevertheless are subject to the laws of the country. It is very difficult to find out which parts/ sections have been brought into force.
Statutory laws can be passed very quickly –	but **just** law is more important than **quick** law.

Figure 1.5 Advantages and disadvantages of legislation and the legislative process

1.6 Delegated legislation

If the authority or power to do something is 'delegated', it is given or passed on to someone else. Only Parliament has the power or authority to make the law (pass legislation) in England and Wales, but this power may be given by Parliament to someone else (i.e. delegated legislation, also called secondary legislation). The power to make delegated law must be given under a statute (called the parent or enabling Act). Each type of delegated legislation will have a different parent Act and it is the parent Act that lays down the requirement and scope of the delegated legislation.

The three ways to make delegated legislation are indicated in Figure 1.6.

1.6.1 Statutory instruments

The process involves Parliament passing a very broadly drafted statute (called a parent or enabling Act) which delegates the law-making power upon a government department or minister. The delegated legislation is called a statutory instrument (SI) because it carries out (is **instrumental** in giving effect to) the requirements of the statute. The rules and regulations passed under the enabling Act are in no way inferior to primary legislation (the Act itself).

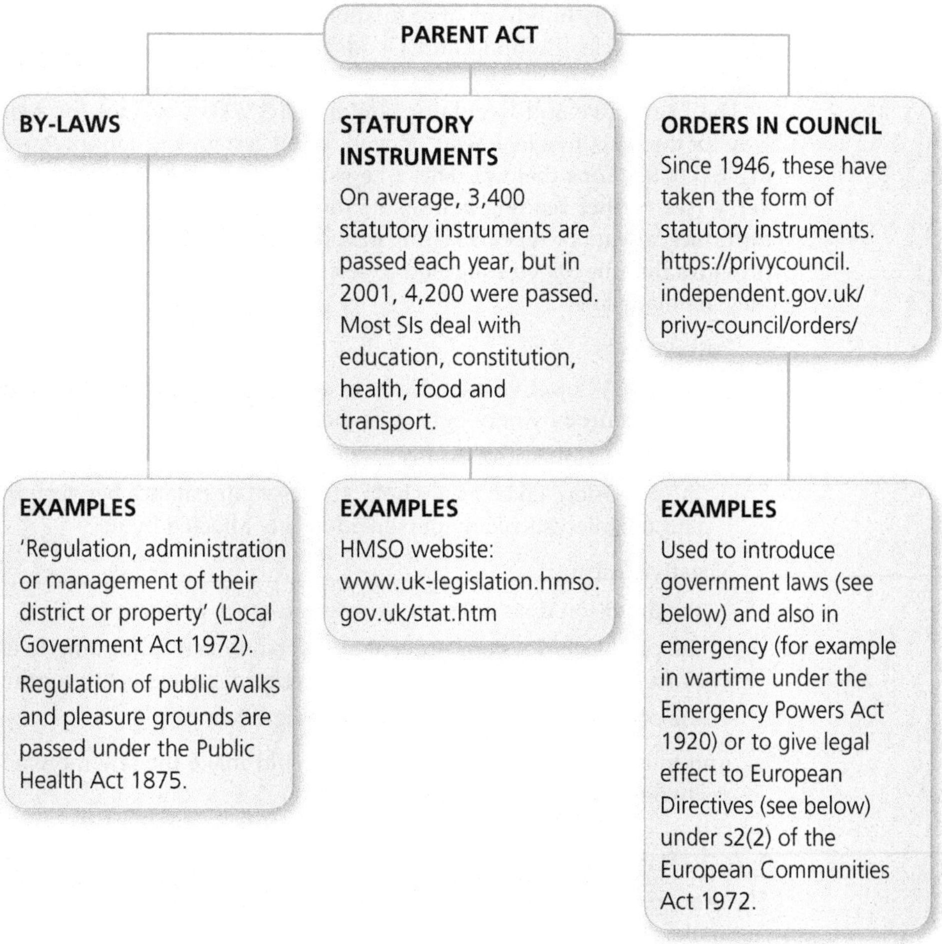

Figure 1.6 The types of delegated legislation

For example, the Road Traffic Act 1988, s41 provides:

SECTION

'41. – Regulation of construction, weight, equipment and use of vehicles.

(1) The Secretary of State may make regulations generally as to the use of motor vehicles and trailers on roads, their construction and equipment and the conditions under which they may be so used.

Subsections (2) to (4) below do not affect the generality of this subsection.

(2) In particular, the regulations may make provision with respect to any of the following matters –
   (a) the width, height and length of motor vehicles and trailers and the load carried by them, the diameter of wheels, and the width, nature and condition of tyres, of motor vehicles and trailers,
   (b) the emission or consumption of smoke, fumes or vapour and the emission of sparks, ashes and grit,
   (c) noise ...'

There are literally hundreds of regulations made under this parent Act, one of which is the Road Vehicles Lighting and Goods Vehicles (Plating and Testing) (Amendment) Regulations 2009/3220.

The Legislative and Regulatory Reform Act 2006 provides for a simpler and faster way for the executive to amend or even repeal certain legislation, as well as implementing EU obligations (below). These Legislative Reform Orders are not without controversy (see further reading below), as they give the executive considerable powers to introduce, amend or repeal existing primary and secondary legislation, but s3 of the Act provides that the SIs be subjected to tests which are both positive and negative before they are made law.

- Positive tests:
  - the policy objective intended to be secured by the provision could not be satisfactorily secured by non-legislative means;
  - the effect of the provision is proportionate to the policy objective;
  - the provision, taken as a whole, strikes a fair balance between the public interest and the interests of any person adversely affected by it.
- Negative tests:
  - the provision does not remove any necessary protection;
  - the provision does not prevent any person from continuing to exercise any right or freedom which that person might reasonably expect to continue to exercise;
  - the provision is not of constitutional significance.
- And in all cases, the provision made would make the law more accessible or more easily understood.

1.6.2 By-laws

These are passed by local authorities, or, for example, the British Rail Board, to regulate certain local activities.

1.6.3 Orders of the Legislative Committee of the Privy Council

The Privy Council was originally established to advise the Crown (the monarch) on the administration of government. Its functions are now more concerned with the administration and supervision of the Commonwealth. In addition, it is used to pass domestic delegated legislation. For example, when a change in the terminology under the Civil Partnerships Act 2004 was needed in 2012, this was effected by Orders in Council, including:

SECTION

'2012 No. 3063
CIVIL PARTNERSHIP
The Civil Partnership (Registration Abroad and Certificates) (Amendment) Order 2012

Made *12th December 2012*

Laid before Parliament   *19th December 2012*

Coming into force   *9th January 2013*

At the Court at Buckingham Palace, the 12th day of December 2012

Present,

The Queen's Most Excellent Majesty in Council

Her Majesty, in exercise of the powers conferred on Her by sections 210, 240, 241 and 244 of the Civil Partnership Act 2004, is pleased, by and with the advice of Her Privy Council, to order as follows:

1. This Order may be cited as the Civil Partnership (Registration Abroad and Certificates) (Amendment) Order 2012 and shall come into force on 9th January 2013.

2. The Civil Partnership (Registration Abroad and Certificates) Order 2005 is amended as follows.

3. In Article 2 –

    (a) Delete the definition of "civil partnership officer"; and

    (b) After the definition of "overseas relationship", insert –"
    'registration officer' has the same meaning as in section 210(6) of the Act".

4. Substitute the term "registration officer" for the term "civil partnership officer" wherever it appears –

    (a) in the Order; and

    (b) in the form in the Schedule to the Order.

Richard Tilbrook
Clerk of the Privy Council'

1.6.4 Parliamentary control of secondary legislation

Just as Parliament gives the power to make delegated legislation, it can take the power away. However, rather than use this extreme measure, Parliament will often provide in the parent Act that the delegated legislation made under it has to be laid before Parliament for approval. This enables MPs to know what a minister is proposing and therefore he can be held accountable. The negative resolution procedure requires the delegated legislation to be laid before Parliament for 40 days and, if it is not voted against in that time, it becomes law. The positive resolution procedure requires the delegated legislation to be voted for in order for it to become effective. Following the correct procedure is vital, as the Home Office discovered, to its embarrassment, when it announced that the new Codes of Practice under the Police and Criminal Evidence Act 1984 would be coming into force on 1 May 2004 under the negative resolution procedure. In fact, the Codes were subject to the positive resolution procedure and had to be delayed until 1 August 2004. The precise wording is reproduced in bold below:

SECTION

'2004 No. 1887
POLICE, ENGLAND AND WALES
The Police and Criminal Evidence Act 1984 (Codes of Practice) Order 2004
Made 16th July 2004

Coming into force   1st August 2004

Whereas the Secretary of State:

(1) has, in pursuance of sections 60(1)(a), 60A(1)(a) and 66(1)(a) to (d) of the Police and Criminal Evidence Act 1984[1] ("the Act"), issued codes of practice in connection with the:

    (a) exercise by police officers of statutory powers of stop and search;

(b) searching of premises by police officers and the seizure of property found by police officers on persons or premises;

(c) detention, treatment and questioning of persons by police officers;

...

(4) has, in accordance with section 67(7B) of the Act, laid each revised code of practice before Parliament;

And whereas a draft of this Order has been laid before Parliament and has been approved by each House of Parliament'

There are special rules governing the coming into force of the Legislative Reform Orders (above). The minister must consult widely with those affected by the proposals, lay a draft order and explanatory document before Parliament, allow time for parliamentary consideration and obtain Parliament's sanction for making the order. The draft order must also advise whether the order should be subject to the negative or positive resolution procedure (above), or should be subject to a new type of order called a super-affirmative procedure, which requires active consultation across the Houses of Parliament committees within 60 days. Only once the required steps have been successfully completed may the order become law.

There is also a Joint Committee (i.e. one consisting of members of both Houses of Parliament) on Statutory Instruments, but this committee is a technical committee rather than one concerned with the merit of the instruments. Also, it has no formal power and no legal effect; its reports can safely be ignored. The Joint Committee reports to both Houses on the regulations to ensure that the correct procedures are being followed.

There are two Standing (i.e. permanent) Committees on Statutory Instruments. These committees allow for parliamentary discussion to take place and thus help to relieve the pressure on the House of Commons which often does not have enough time to consider all SIs, but the committees do not have the power to change the wording of the SIs.

There is a Commons Select Committee on European Secondary Legislation and a Lords Select Committee on the European Communities. These two committees bring to the attention of Parliament the more important pieces of European legislation. These Select Committees will continue to operate until the UK leaves the EU.

The Delegated Powers Select Committee scrutinises those Bills that are intended to become parent Acts for inappropriate grant of power or legislation with inappropriate delegation (a Lords-only committee).

1.6.5 Judicial control of secondary legislation

The judiciary cannot generally review primary legislation, but can review delegated legislation. The process is called judicial review.

This review can take place only after the delegated legislation has come into force. The court may declare it void for being *ultra vires* (beyond the powers of the person or body who made it). There are two types of *ultra vires*:

- **procedural *ultra vires***: this is where the parent Act lays down procedural rules which must be followed by the subordinate authority – if these rules are not followed, the court can find the delegated legislation *ultra vires* and void;

- **substantive *ultra vires***: where the delegated legislation goes beyond what Parliament intended then the court can declare it void on substantive grounds.

CASE EXAMPLE

R v Secretary of State for Education and Employment, ex p National Union of Teachers, The Times, 8 August 2000

The National Union of Teachers sought judicial review of the Education (School Teachers' Pay and Conditions) (No 2) Order 2000 which proposed changes to the contracts of employment of school teachers and teachers' eligibility for higher rates of pay by introducing a system of performance-related pay. The NUT argued that the Secretary of State had failed to use the necessary statutory procedure for altering teachers' pay and conditions as detailed in s2 of the School Teachers' Pay and Conditions Act 1991 and also that he had used a consultation process that was unfair.

The High Court allowed the application and quashed the SI. The court held that the Secretary of State had bypassed the independent review that was required when a significant and controversial change was to be made to teachers' pay and conditions of service. The court also held that the four-day consultation period was wholly inadequate because the Order introduced a change that was outside the scope of any previous consultations.

Advantages	Disadvantages
Expertise – MPs have expertise in party politics. They may also have interests in broader areas of social policy, but are unlikely, as a body, to have the requisite expertise to enact legislation in very specialised or technical a reas of the law or more local requirements (by-laws). Through a consultation process, those with the necessary expertise can be relied on to contribute to the effective regulation of the law in the form of delegated legislation.	*Democratic accountability* – The real source of law in this regard is civil servants and experts, with a government minister providing supervision only. The law-makers are thus not democratically elected and it is difficult to hold them to account.
Time – It is far quicker to introduce, amend and repeal laws that are in urgent need of change by way of delegated legislation than by following the full enactment procedure required by an Act of Parliament outlined above. The use of delegated legislation also saves parliamentary time so that Parliament can focus its resources on the general principles of the law rather than the minutiae.	*Sub-delegation* – The parent Act delegates the law-making power on to a government minister or a local authority or the Privy Council; but in the case of the former, it is not the named individual who will make the law but he will be able to pass the authority to someone else. They may in turn sub-delegate the task to another (an expert, for example). The question arises of how far from the authority and sovereignty of Parliament the law-making stretches.
Flexible – Linked to the point above, the speed allows changes to the law to be made quickly, as and when the need arises.	*Publishing* – The process for bringing delegated legislation into force is subject to cursory glance only by Parliament, to save parliamentary time. If MPs are unlikely to keep *continually* abreast of changes in the law by delegated legislation, how are normal individuals supposed to discover and abide by secondary laws? As you might imagine, from the sheer bulk of delegated legislation, few publications contain reference to all of them introduced in any year. (N.B. The *New Law Journal* contains a regular list of SIs but by title only.)

Figure 1.7 Advantages and disadvantages of secondary legislation

The sources of English law

Parliament		Case	
Legislation	Delegated legislation	Common law	Equity
Parliament is the principal law-maker of England and Wales. Laws passed by Parliament are called statutes, Acts of Parliament or legislation. Parliament is supreme.	Where Parliament passes the power to make law to another body, the law made under that power is called delegated legislation. There are three types: SIs, by-laws and Orders in Council. There are benefits to allowing someone other than Parliament to pass law, but it is also said that there is too much delegated legislation and the controls that exist are inadequate.	The common law has developed over the centuries through judges' decisions. England has a common law system and the key feature of common law systems is binding precedent (*stare decisis*). This means that some decisions of some English courts are binding on some future cases of the same courts and inferior courts.	Equity developed to fill in the gaps of the common law and provide effective remedies where the common law did not. Where common law and equity conflict, equity prevails.

1.7 The European Union

1.7.1 A brief history of the European Union

Following the effective destruction of the European economy caused by the Second World War, many of the Allied countries made legal moves towards increased co-operation in the fields of trade and energy. In 1951, the Treaty of Paris established the European Coal and Steel Community and, in 1957, two Treaties of Rome established Euratom (the European Atomic Agency) and, most importantly for the student of law, the European Economic Community. It is this latter body which has affected English law so much in the last three decades. In 1986, the Single European Act established a single market across the member states and in 1993 the European Economic Community became the European Community (EC) by means of the Maastricht Treaty (the Treaty on European Union). This Treaty also created a new body – the European Union. The EU was a far larger body than the EC. The EU included the EC and it dealt with common foreign and security policies as well as co-operation between states on criminal matters. For our purposes, all of the law emanating from the EC and the EU shall be referred to as 'EU law' because under the Lisbon Treaty, the EC ceased to exist. The Lisbon Treaty 2009 also restructured the EU. There are now two treaties setting out its rules. These are:

▪ Treaty on European Union (TEU);

▪ Treaty on the Functioning of the European Union (TFEU).

Both the Maastricht Treaty and the Lisbon Treaty in turn renumbered the articles of the original Treaty of Rome, so you may see an article referred to by three numbers. For example, Article 267 was previously 234 and before that it was 177. You should use only the most up-to-date number, but when you study EU law and read older cases, it will help you to understand that Article 267 today was Article 234 after the Maastricht Treaty and Article 177 under the original Treaty of Rome.

Country	Year joined the EU	Country	Year joined the EU
Austria	1995	Italy	1958
Belgium	1958	Latvia	2004
Bulgaria	2007	Lithuania	2004
Croatia	2013	Luxembourg	1958
Cyprus	2004	Malta	2004
Czech Republic	2004	Netherlands	1958
Denmark	1973	Poland	2004
Estonia	2004	Portugal	1986
Finland	1995	Romania	2007
France	1958	Slovakia	2004
Germany	1958	Slovenia	2004
Greece	1981	Spain	1986
Hungary	2004	Sweden	1995
Ireland	1973	UK	1973

Figure 1.8 The member states of the EU

1.7.2 UK membership of the EU

In June 2016, there was a referendum on the UK's continuing membership of the EU. This referendum was held to fulfil a pledge made by the then-Prime Minister, David Cameron, to hold such a referendum if the Conservative Party won the 2015 General Election, which they did. In this referendum, by a majority of 52 per cent to 48 per cent, the electorate voted for the UK to leave the EU. However, this referendum was not binding. What this means is that the UK did not automatically leave the EU following the vote. Instead, the referendum was advisory, meaning that the UK government needed to take further legislative steps in order to leave the Union. Following the vote, David Cameron resigned as Prime Minister and was replaced by Theresa May. Prime Minister May promised to uphold the will of the majority and ensure the UK leaves the EU.

However, this process is not straightforward. In order for the UK to leave the EU, a special legal procedure needs to be invoked under Article 50 of the TEU. Once invoked, this will allow the UK a period of two years to negotiate its exit from the EU. Only after this process is complete will the UK no longer be a member of the EU. Until this process is complete, the UK will remain a full member of the EU. In October 2016, Prime Minister May announced that the UK would invoke Article 50 TEU by the end of March 2017. This would mean that the UK would leave the EU by March 2019. Despite this, EU law still remains, for the time being, an important part of the ELS.

International legal obligations such as those contained in treaties are generally intended to regulate the relationships between states (countries) and they do not affect the individuals living in those states. Another way of saying this is that treaties, on the whole, do not affect domestic law; but the law of the EU is different because these laws have been transferred into UK domestic law by a statute – the European Communities Act 1972. This statute will remain in force until the UK formally leaves the EU, so courts are bound to apply it until this point. In October 2016, Prime Minister May announced plans for a 'great repeal Bill'. This Bill would repeal the European Communities Act 1972, but would also enshrine all existing EU law into UK law. This move would allow Parliament in the future to decide which EU laws they wish to retain and which they wish to repeal. Even if passed, this repeal Bill will not come into force until the UK leaves the EU, so the 1972 Act will still have force until this point.

Section 2 of the 1972 Act provides:

SECTION

's 2 (1) All such rights, powers, liabilities, obligations and restrictions … created or arising by or under the Treaties … as in accordance with the Treaties are without further enactment to be given legal effect … in the United Kingdom

(2) … Her Majesty may by Order in Council, and any designated Minister or department may by order, rules, regulations or scheme, make provision … for the purpose of implementing any Community obligation of the United Kingdom.'

'Without further enactment'

The effect of s2(1) of the 1972 Act is that there is a mandatory incorporation of EU law into UK law. The UK **must** give effect to any laws passed by the EU.

CASE EXAMPLE

Marshall v Southampton Health Authority [1986] 2 All ER 584, ECJ

Ms Marshall was told that she had to retire at the age of 62 from her job with the National Health Service. The retirement age for men at this time was 65; but 60 for women. National law (the Sex Discrimination Act 1975) excluded matters related to retirement from its provisions, but EU law (the Equal Treatment Directive 1976) did not. Ms Marshall took her case to the Court of Justice of the European Union (more commonly referred to as the CJEU). The CJEU held that Ms Marshall was entitled to succeed, and could use the provisions of the 1976 Directive against her employers because the UK had not implemented the Directive properly.

A more politically controversial case arose in *R v Secretary of State for Transport, ex p Factortame (No 2)* [1991] 1 All ER 70, HL/ECJ and *R v Secretary of State for Transport, ex p Factortame (No 3)* [1991] 3 All ER 769, ECJ.

CASE EXAMPLE

R v Secretary of State for Transport, ex p Factortame (No 2) [1991] 1 All ER 70, HL/ECJ and *R v Secretary of State for Transport, ex p Factortame (No 3)* [1991] 3 All ER 769, ECJ

The Merchant Shipping Act 1988 provided that fishing licences should be granted only to boats whose owners and crews were predominantly British. Some Spanish fishermen, who could not be granted fishing licences as a result of these provisions, claimed that the 1988 Act was contrary to EU law. They sought an injunction preventing the Secretary of State from enforcing the 1988 Act pending a full trial of the issue. The Divisional Court referred the question to the CJEU, but issued the injunction in the meantime. The Court of Appeal and the House of Lords held that no national court had the power to suspend the operation of an Act of Parliament, but the CJEU disagreed, holding that the Divisional Court had correctly decided that a rule of national (domestic) law which conflicts with EU law should be set aside. The CJEU also said the 1988 Act breached Article 43 (ex 52) of the EU Treaty, which guaranteed citizens of any member state the freedom to establish their businesses anywhere in the Community, and the UK government was obliged to amend the legislation accordingly.

1.7.3 The role of the Court of Justice of the European Union

Article 267 (previously 234, and before that, 177) of the TFEU provides:

ARTICLE

'Article 267
The Court of Justice of the European Union shall have jurisdiction to give preliminary rulings concerning:

(a) the interpretation of the Treaties;
(b) the validity and interpretation of acts of the institutions, bodies, offices or agencies of the Union;'

Where such a question is raised before any court or tribunal of a member state, that court or tribunal may, if it considers that a decision on the question is necessary to enable it to give judgment, request the Court to give a ruling thereon.

Where any such question is raised in a case pending before a court or tribunal of a member state against whose decisions there is no judicial remedy under national law, that court or tribunal shall bring the matter before the Court.

If such a question is raised in a case pending before a court or tribunal of a member state with regard to a person in custody, the CJEU shall act with the minimum of delay.

The effect of Article 267 is that the CJEU, which sits in Luxembourg, has the final say on the interpretation of EU law. The courts in the member states may (or sometimes must) make a reference under Article 267.

An example of a case which was referred to the CJEU under Article 267 is given below.

CASE EXAMPLE

Webb v EMO Air Cargo [1994] 4 All ER 115

Mrs Webb applied for a job as a clerk with EMO. The job was initially just to cover the maternity leave of an existing employee, but would then become permanent. Two weeks after starting work, Mrs Webb discovered that she was pregnant and would also have to take maternity leave. EMO decided to dismiss her. She challenged her dismissal on the ground of sexual discrimination contrary to the Sex Discrimination Act 1975, but that Act did not directly deal with this type of situation. The case reached the House of Lords which made a reference to the CJEU under Article 177 (now 267). The CJEU held that she had been discriminated against on the ground of sex: pregnancy could not be likened to other illnesses (such as those suffered by men), and since Mrs Webb had been employed on a permanent basis she would not be absent for the whole of the intended employment period.

1.7.4 Effect on parliamentary sovereignty

You may have noticed that in the three cases concerning EU law above (*Marshall v Southampton Health Authority, R v Secretary of State for Transport, ex p Factortame* and *Webb v EMO Air Cargo*), the decision went against the UK. You may also recall that it was stated above that one of the constitutional doctrines of the UK is parliamentary sovereignty.

How can parliamentary sovereignty be claimed if there is another authority which can declare Parliament's legislation to be in conflict with another type of law? There is little doubt that the sovereignty has been eroded. The following case illustrates this.

CASE EXAMPLE

Costa v ENEL [1964] CMLR 425, ECJ

Costa was a shareholder in an Italian electricity company and he was financially adversely affected by the nationalisation of the Italian electricity industry. He claimed that the nationalisation had been unlawful because (among other things) EU law had not been complied with. The Italian court ruled that domestic law made in contravention of a treaty was still valid. The CJEU disagreed, saying that, unlike other international treaties, the treaty establishing the EU had created its own order which was integrated with the national orders of the member states as soon as the treaty came into force, and as such was binding upon them.

JUDGMENT

'The transfer by the states from their domestic legal system to the Community legal system of the rights and obligations arising under the Treaty carries with it a permanent limitation of their sovereign rights, against which a subsequent unilateral act incompatible with the concept of the Community cannot prevail.'

The UK Parliament specifically recognises the supremacy of EU law in s2(4) of the European Communities Act 1972; note the words in italics below:

SECTION

's 2(4) ... any such provision (of any such extent) as might be made by Act of Parliament, and any enactment passed or to be passed, other than one contained in this part of this Act, shall be construed and have effect subject to the foregoing provisions of this section'.

As regards domestic law, Parliament continues to be supreme. As regards EU law, the situation is rather more complicated. Pro-sovereignty advocates have long argued that Parliament has merely lent sovereignty to the EU and can easily reclaim it by repealing the European Communities Act 1972 and taking the UK out of the EU. The current government is committed to withdrawing the UK from the EU, and in October 2016 announced plans to repeal the European Communities Act 1972. Alongside this, this repeal Bill would incorporate all current EU laws into UK law, with future Parliaments deciding which laws to keep and which to repeal. It is safe to say that the final details of the UK's exit from the EU cannot yet be known, and we have little details of how EU law will continue to impact on the ELS in the future.

ACTIVITY

Self-test questions

1. There are 15 member states of the EU.   True/False
2. The Treaty of Maastricht established the European Economic Community.   True/False
3. The Treaty of Rome renumbered the articles of the Treaty of Maastricht.   True/False
4. Section 2 of the European Communities Act 1972 provides that if UK and EU law conflict, UK law prevails.   True/False
5. Article 345 of the Treaty of Rome governs the procedure for making a reference to the CJEU.   True/False
6. Following the vote in the June 2016 referendum, the UK has automatically left the EU and EU law no longer applies to the UK.   True/False

1.8 European Convention on Human Rights

It is easy to confuse the EU (formerly the EEC) with the Council of Europe, but the two things are completely different and it is the Council of Europe that introduced and now governs the ECHR. It is perhaps easy to understand why the two entities are confused: they are both 'European' institutions and they were both created as a result of reaction to the Second World War, but the ECHR shows states' commitment to basic human rights and fundamental freedoms rather than political or economic integration with each other (the EU).

The European Convention on Human Rights and Fundamental Freedoms, to give it its full title, was ratified (signed) by the member states of the Council of Europe in 1953; then in 1966, the UK granted individuals in the UK a right of 'individual petition'. This meant that if an infringement of the rights on the Convention was alleged, the wronged person could sue the UK for the breach at the European Court of Human Rights (ECtHR) in Strasbourg. Individuals could not, however, sue in the UK courts for infringement because the domestic courts did not have the jurisdiction to hear such cases.

1.8.1 The Human Rights Act 1998

Domestic courts do now have jurisdiction. This is one of the effects of the HRA 1998. This highly significant Act did not (contrary to what you might read elsewhere) intend to incorporate the ECHR directly into English law (unlike the European Communities Act 1972 and the EU) because the HRA 1998 does not state that the articles in the ECHR are the law of the land (again, unlike the 1972 Act and the EU). Rather, the HRA 1998 allows Parliament to retain rather more sovereignty than the 1972 Act does, as the HRA 1998 provides that all legislation should be read and given effect in a way which is compatible with the Convention and that the common law should also be developed in a compatible manner. How does the HRA 1998 achieve this? Through the two key sections: 2 and 3.

SECTION

's 2 Interpretation of Convention rights
(1) A court or tribunal determining a question which has arisen in connection with a Convention right must take into account any
    (a) judgment, decision, declaration or advisory opinion of the European Court of Human Rights,
    (b) opinion of the Commission ...

    (c) decision of the Commission ...
    (d) decision of the Committee of Ministers ... whenever made or given, so far as, in the opinion of the court or tribunal, it is relevant to the proceedings in which that question has arisen.

s 3 Interpretation of legislation

(1) So far as it is possible to do so, primary legislation and subordinate legislation must be read and given effect in a way which is compatible with the Convention rights.
(2) This section
    (a) applies to primary legislation and subordinate legislation whenever enacted;
    (b) does not affect the validity, continuing operation or enforcement of any incompatible primary legislation; and
    (c) does not affect the validity, continuing operation or enforcement of any incompatible subordinate legislation if (disregarding any possibility of revocation) primary legislation prevents removal of the incompatibility.'

So what are the ECHR rights with which English law should be compatible? These can be found (obviously) in the Convention itself; but for ease of reference, they are reproduced in Schedule 1 to the 1998 Act and are summarised in Figure 1.9.

Say that a defendant who has been convicted of a criminal offence wishes to appeal against his conviction, alleging breach of his fair trial rights under Article 6. The role of the English appeal court in that case is to consider the relevant domestic law, together with the ECtHR's cases and the articles themselves, to interpret the domestic law to be compatible with the latter two. However, if the court cannot interpret the domestic legislation so that it is compatible with the ECHR obligations, it must make a declaration of incompatibility under s4 HRA 1998. If it does so, this does not affect the validity, continuing operation or enforcement of the Act in respect of which it is given.

CASE EXAMPLE

R v A [2001] UKHL 25

A complainant had alleged that the defendant (D) had raped her. D's defence was that sexual intercourse had taken place, but with the complainant's consent, or, if she had not in fact consented, that he believed she had consented. Defence counsel had applied to the trial judge for leave (permission) to cross-examine the claimant about the alleged previous sexual activity of the claimant and D.

Section 41 of the Youth Justice and Criminal Evidence Act 1999 prohibits the giving of evidence and cross-examination about any sexual behaviour of the complainant except with leave of the court, which can be given only in certain limited circumstances (ss41(3) and (5)). This prohibition is designed to prevent the jury from drawing incorrect assumptions that either:

1. a woman who has had sex with a number of partners is more likely to consent to sex than a woman with no sexual experience; or that
2. a woman who has had a sexual relationship with the defendant on previous occasions is more likely to have consented on this occasion.

Their Lordships refer to these incorrect assumptions as the 'two myths'. However, a defendant in the latter situation above may wish to adduce evidence of the previous sexual relationship to show that the complainant did consent on this occasion, but s41 seems to prohibit this. At the same time, however, that same defendant has certain minimum rights guaranteed under Articles 6(1) and (3)(d) of the ECHR.

Article	Title	Further information (summary only – refer to Sch 1 HRA 1998 for the full article)
Art 2	Right to life	Everyone's right to life shall be protected by law. No one shall be deprived of his life intentionally save in the execution of a sentence of a court following his conviction of a crime for which this penalty is provided by law.
Art 3	Prohibition of torture	No one shall be subjected to torture or to inhuman or degrading treatment or punishment.
Art 4	Prohibition of slavery and forced labour	No one shall be held in slavery or servitude. No one shall be required to perform forced or compulsory labour.
Art 5	Right to liberty and security	Everyone has the right to liberty and security of person. Everyone who is arrested shall be informed promptly, in a language which he understands, of the reasons for his arrest and of any charge against him.
Art 6	Right to a fair trial	In the determination of his civil rights and obligations or of any criminal charge against him, everyone is entitled to a fair and public hearing within a reasonable time by an independent and impartial tribunal established by law. Everyone charged with a criminal offence shall be presumed innocent until proved guilty according to law.
Art 7	No punishment without law	No one shall be held guilty of any criminal offence on account of any act or omission which did not constitute a criminal offence under national or international law at the time when it was committed.
Art 8	Right to respect for private and family life	Everyone has the right to respect for his private and family life, his home and his correspondence.
Art 9	Freedom of thought, conscience and religion	Everyone has the right to freedom of thought, conscience and religion. This right includes freedom to change his religion or belief and freedom, either alone or in community with others, and, in public or private, to manifest his religion or belief, in worship, teaching, practice and observance.
Art 10	Freedom of expression	Everyone has the right to freedom of expression. This right shall include freedom to hold opinions and to receive and impart information and ideas without interference by public authority and regardless of frontiers.
Art 11	Freedom of assembly and association	Everyone has the right to freedom of peaceful assembly and to freedom of association with others, including the right to form and to join trade unions for the protection of his interests.
Art 12	Right to marry	Men and women of marriageable age have the right to marry and to found a family, according to the national laws governing the exercise of this right.
Art 14	Prohibition of discrimination	The enjoyment of the rights and freedoms set forth in this Convention shall be secured without discrimination on any ground such as sex, race, colour, language, religion, political or other opinion, national or social origin, association with a national minority, property, birth or other status.

Figure 1.9 The ECHR: key provisions

ARTICLE

'Art 6
1. In the determination of his civil rights and obligations or of any criminal charge against him, everyone is entitled to a fair and public hearing ...
3. Everyone charged with a criminal offence has the following minimum rights ... d. to examine or have examined witnesses against him.'

The House of Lords had to decide in the appeal whether s41 of the Youth Justice and Criminal Evidence Act 1999 could be given effect, in accordance with s3 of the HRA 1998, in such a way that was compatible with the defendant's rights to a fair trial and to present a full and complete defence under Article 6, and, if it could not, whether the House should make a declaration of incompatibility between the 1999 Act and the ECHR.

Lord Steyn adopted a very wide reading of s3 of the 1998 Act. He read into s41 of the 1999 Act an implied provision of compatibility with Article 6 so as to avoid a declaration of incompatibility. He did this by giving the trial judge discretion to allow such questioning where it was relevant to a fact that was in issue in the trial and where such questioning was needed to allow the defendant to have a fair trial under Article 6.

It would be incorrect to leave you with the impression that the HRA 1998 has not affected legislation at all; there has been a loss of parliamentary sovereignty, but only a slight one. Parliament must declare all proposed legislation to be compatible with the ECHR articles during the Reading of the Bill.

SECTION

's 19(1) A Minister of the Crown in charge of a Bill in either House of Parliament must, before Second Reading of the Bill

(a) make a statement to the effect that in his view the provisions of the Bill are compatible with the Convention rights ("a statement of compatibility"); or
(b) make a statement to the effect that although he is unable to make a statement of compatibility the government nevertheless wishes the House to proceed with the Bill.

(2) The statement must be in writing and be published in such manner as the Minister making it considers appropriate.'

ACTIVITY

Self-test questions

1. Briefly explain the difference between the Council of Europe and the EU.
2. In your own words, explain the effect of ss3 and 4 of the HRA 1998.
3. State three of the rights under the ECHR Articles.

The sources of English law from outside the UK

The EU	The Council of Europe
• The UK joined the EU (then called the EEC) in 1973. • EU law is supreme over UK law under the European Communities Act 1972. • English courts can refer questions concerning EU law to the CJEU under Art 234 of the Treaty of Rome. • Even though the UK electorate voted to leave the EU in June 2016, the status of EU law will not change until the UK leaves the Union.	• The Council of Europe is responsible for the ECHR and the ECtHR. • English law is now subject to the articles in the ECHR because of the HRA 1998.

1.9 Law reform

A modern legal system needs to be flexible and adaptable to avoid stagnation of the law. So where does the impetus for changes to the law arise?

1.9.1 Judges

How do judges reform the law? This is done through the system of precedent, which is explained in detail in Chapter 2.

Note that there are democracy and accountability issues that deserve your attention. Judges are not elected; yet they clearly do make law. Judges are notoriously difficult to remove from office, so they lack public accountability. Unlike MPs, we cannot vote judges out if we do not like their decisions. Nevertheless, as certain areas of the law have never received legislative attention, or have not for a century or more, there is realistically no alternative but to allow the judges to make the law. For example, murder, arguably the most serious crime, is a common law offence. Without judicial law-making, developments in the interpretation of the elements of the offence would not have occurred. By way of further example, assaults are governed by the antiquated Offences Against the Person Act 1861. You may be familiar with some of the terms used in the 1861 Act ('actual bodily harm' and 'grievous bodily harm'). If not for the judges in the leading case of *R v Ireland and Burstow* [1997] 3 WLR 534, psychological illness suffered by victims of the defendant's harassment and intimidation would not have amounted to **bodily** harm. The House of Lords felt that the old Act had to be reinterpreted for modern times.

However, waiting for the law to be reformed by case law alone is a long process. It could be many years before a case that might reform the law reaches the Supreme Court (this is the only court that has the power to overrule previous law unless a question of human rights under the ECHR arises). Case law is also limited to the facts of the case from which it arises. Legislation, on the other hand, has a wider reach and there can be statutory provisions on every and all aspects of behaviour. That is why, when pressure groups advocate a change to the law, they pressurise Parliament to introduce comprehensive legislation. It is little use petitioning a judge hearing an intellectual property law case to change the law relating to euthanasia. Not only would he not listen; he would not have the power to do so even if he agreed with your proposal.

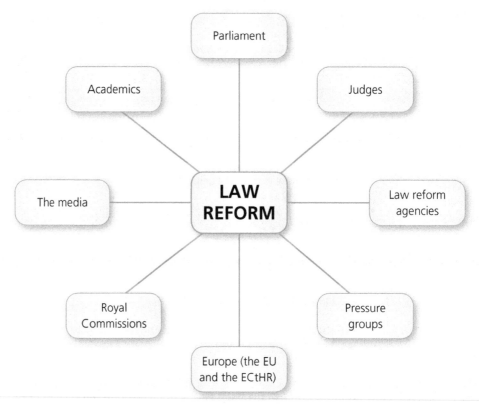

Figure 1.10 The sources of law reform

1.9.2 Parliament

Why do people stand for election to Parliament? Probably because they want the power and ability to change things. What other way is there to change the lives of the citizens of a country than to change the laws of that country? There is surely none better. So, when a new Parliament is elected, a new raft of legislative reforms is introduced. Each year, the current government outlines its legislative intent in the Queen's Speech.

1.9.3 The law reform agencies

It is tempting to think that because law reform agencies exist, then reform of the law is a foregone conclusion. Tempting; but wrong. The politics of law reform must not be forgotten; unless there is political will and time to enact the proposals made by the law reform agencies, the proposals will gather dust on parliamentary shelves.

Law Reform Committee (established 1952)

This part-time body consists of legal practitioners (solicitors and barristers) as well as legal academics. Its remit is to consider such reforms in the civil law as are referred to it by the Lord Chancellor. Its successes include the Occupiers' Liability Act 1957 and the Latent Damage Act 1986.

Criminal Law Revision Committee (established 1959)

This is also a part-time committee, but obviously with a criminal law remit. This committee has not been officially disbanded, but has not sat since 1986. It introduced the

Theft Act 1968. In 1996, Lord Scarman, in an open letter to *The Times*, criticised the government's failure to use the Committee, made up of academics and practical experts as it was, in the introduction of new law.

Law Commissions Act 1965

The 1965 White Paper 'Proposals for English and Scottish Law Commissions', Cmnd 2573 (1965) proposed setting up a full-time body:

QUOTATION

'One of the hallmarks of an advanced society is that its laws should not only be just but also that they be kept up to date and be readily accessible to all who are affected by them.'

The Act set up two Law Commissions: one for England and Wales (jointly) and one for Scotland.

Section 3 of the Law Commissions Act 1965 provides:

SECTION

's 3 It shall be the duty of ... the Commissions ... to keep under review all the law ... with a view to its systematic development and reform, including in particular the codification of such law, the elimination of anomalies, the repeal of obsolete and unnecessary enactments, the reduction of the number of separate enactments and generally the simplification and modernisation of the law.'

The Law Commission for England and Wales consists of five members, namely the chairman (a Court of Appeal Judge, currently Sir David Bean) and four others who must be judges, barristers, solicitors or teachers of law. The Commissioners are appointed initially for five years but may be asked to stay for longer. They are assisted by a staff of 20 lawyers, including four draftsmen from the Office of Parliamentary Counsel, plus 15 research assistants and administrative staff and consultants who are used on an ad hoc basis. The Commission is financed by the Ministry of Justice. The aims of the Commission are to:

- simplify the law;
- codify the law;
- eliminate anomalies;
- reduce the number of separate Acts on a particular matter; and
- repeal obsolete Acts.

The law reform teams at the Commission currently cover:

- Criminal Law and Evidence;
- Public Law;
- Property and Trust Law; and
- Commercial Law and Common Law.

Approximately two-thirds of Law Commission proposals for legislation are (eventually) enacted.

1.9.4 Royal Commissions

Royal Commissions are ad hoc (not permanent; set up for one task and then disbanded) advisory committees established by the government – though formally appointed by the Crown (hence 'Royal') to investigate a matter of public concern and make recommendations on any actions to be taken in connection with it, including changes in the law. A government is not, however, bound to accept the advice of any Royal Commission. Interestingly, and perhaps because of this, no Royal Commissions were set up during the 11 years of the Thatcher administration (1979–90). The practice was revived by her successor, John Major (1990–97), who appointed, in 1991, the Royal Commission on Criminal Justice, chaired by Lord Runciman, which reported in 1993. Royal Commission reports are often referred to by the name of the Chairman; so we refer to this report as the Runciman Report. Over the past couple of decades, judges have been asked to chair Royal Commissions. Examples include:

- the Taylor Report (to inquire into the Hillsborough football stadium disaster) in 1990;
- the Woolf Report (into the procedures and processes of the civil courts) in 1996; and
- the Auld Report (to review the criminal courts in England and Wales) in 2001.

1.9.5 Academics

Legal academics can be very persuasive in arguing for changes to the law. You will be referred throughout the course of your studies to leading academic texts and journals; and you may well come to recognise the names of the leading academic commentators. What you may well then see is the same names arising in cases where the judges discuss the criticisms and recommendations of the authors of the texts and articles. It used to be that an academic had to be deceased in order to be regarded as an authority (that way, he could not change his mind), but nowadays it is recognised that certain academics' views have authoritative weight, irrespective of their living status.

There are far too many examples of authoritative authors to provide a comprehensive list, but, for example, in the field of the criminal law, keep an eye out for commentary by the late Glanville Williams and the late J C Smith; and Ian Dennis, Andrew Ashworth and Di Birch (all still alive and kicking).

1.9.6 Pressure groups

Pressure groups with widely differing aims also contribute to law reform. Examples include:

- Greenpeace;
- the NSPCC;
- the National Consumer Council (promoting consumers' interests);
- the Howard League for Penal Reform (campaigns for prisoners);
- the Legal Action Group (campaigns to improve legal services for disadvantaged members of society);
- trade unions.

Pressure groups rely (on the whole) on lawful means to raise the profile of their cause, such as petitions and peaceful protests, leaflets and poster campaigns.

1.9.7 Media pressure

The influence of the media must not be forgotten. The increase in law-based TV programmes such as *Rough Justice* and *Panorama* raise the profile of errors or gaps in the law.

Media influence on the public, and therefore also politicians, may have resulted in the recent changes to the law of 'double jeopardy' (that a defendant may now be tried twice for an offence, even where acquitted on the first trial) after the murder of Stephen Lawrence in 1993 and the Macpherson Report in 1999. The new law is found in the Criminal Justice Act 2003.

1.9.8 Europe

As a reminder:

- the UK's membership of the EU and
- the enactment of the HRA 1998

are influences of Europe on the UK, and each has contributed significantly to reform of the law.

ACTIVITY

Essay writing

'Law reform should be a matter for the Law Commission and Parliament, but in fact it is the judiciary and legal academics who provide the major source of law reform in England and Wales.' Discuss.

SAMPLE ESSAY QUESTION

Delegated legislation is not a democratic method of lawmaking, but it is a necessary one. Discuss.

> Explain what delegated legislation is, i.e. where secondary rules and regulations are made under the authority of an enabling Act. Consists of SIs, by-laws and Orders in Council.

> Expand on each type of delegated legislation by giving an example of each; include key facts such as the volume of SIs each year (to show they are necessary).

> Tackle the issue of delegated legislation not being democratic in two ways:
> 1. By comparing their 'enactment' process (as specified in the enabling Act) with that of Acts of Parliament (both Houses of Parliaments; readings, committee stages etc.).
> 2. How much control there is of delegated legislation. See pages 15–17.

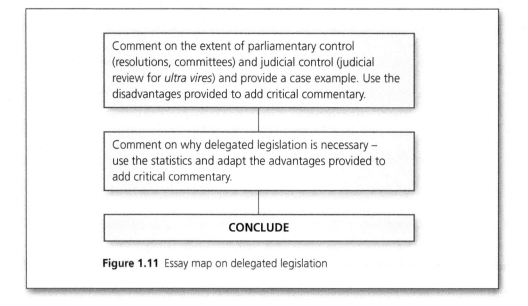

Figure 1.11 Essay map on delegated legislation

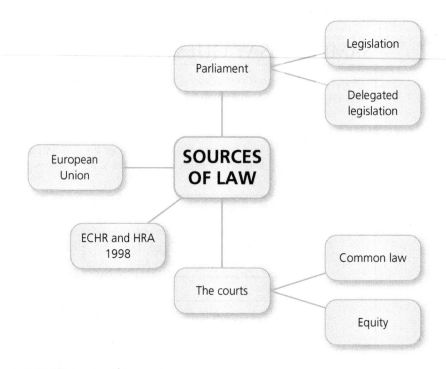

Figure 1.12 The sources of law

SUMMARY

- The main sources of English law are Parliament and the judges.
- The main sources of law from outside the UK are the EU and the Council of Europe.
- Judges in the ELS develop the law by deciding common law cases and by interpreting or construing legislation.
- The House of Lords was the senior court of England and Wales (in its appellate capacity) but was replaced in October 2009 with a Supreme Court of the UK.
- Judge-made law includes common law and equity.
- Parliament is supreme.
- Parliament enacts legislation (Acts of Parliament).
- Acts start as Bills and must go through both Houses of Parliament and receive Royal Assent before being enacted. There are some exceptions to this (e.g. the Parliament Acts).
- Some Acts are enabling, under which delegated legislation may be made.
- There are three types of delegated legislation: SIs, by-laws and Orders in Council.
- The UK is bound by EU law because of the provisions of the European Communities Act 1972; this has had an effect on parliamentary sovereignty.
- EU law will continue to apply until the UK leaves the EU.
- The HRA 1998 provides that all English courts should take account of ECtHR cases, and all English legislation should be construed to comply, so far as it is possible to do so, with the ECHR articles.
- The impetus for reforming the law comes from a variety of sources, including public opinion and the media, but, most importantly, the Law Commission.

33

Further reading

Articles

Davis, P, 'The significance of parliamentary procedures in control of the Executive: a case study: the passage of Part 1 of the Legislative and Regulatory Reform Act 2006' [2007] *PL* 677.

Masterman, R, 'A Supreme Court for the United Kingdom: two steps forward, but one step back on judicial independence' [2004] *PL* 48–58.

Punder, H, 'Democratic legitimation of delegated legislation: a comparative view on the American, British and German law' [2009] *ICLQ* 353–378.

Rogers, N, 'Supremacy and proportionality: the missing element in the UK's implementation of free movement law' [2007] *JIANL* 181–185.

Wilson, S, 'Reforming the Law (Commission): a crisis of identity' [2013] *PL* 20.

Internet links

Acts of Parliament at: www.legislation.gov.uk/ukpga
Bills before Parliament at: http://services.parliament.uk/bills/
Council of Europe at: http://hub.coe.int/
Court of Justice of the European Union at: http://curia.europa.eu/jcms/jcms/j_6/
European Court of Human Rights at: www.echr.coe.int/echr/
European Union at: http://europa.eu

Law Commission at: http://lawcommission.justice.gov.uk/
Parliament Acts at: www.parliament.uk/about/how/laws/parliamentacts/
Parliament home page at: www.parliament.uk
Supreme Court at: www.supremecourt.uk
Supreme Court judgments at: www.youtube.com/user/UKSupremeCourt?feature=watch
UK Parliament's EU law webpage at: www.parliament.uk/business/news/crime-civil-law-justice-and-rights/international-law/eu-law-and-treaties/

2

The doctrine of judicial precedent

AIMS AND OBJECTIVES

After reading this chapter you should be able to:

- Define the doctrine of *stare decisis*
- Identify and distinguish *ratio decidendi* and *obiter dicta*
- Explain the difference between binding and persuasive precedents, and provide examples of each
- Apply the doctrine of precedent to each court in the hierarchy, appreciating the self-binding nature of most previous decisions and the exception(s) to the self-binding rules
- Illustrate the operation of the doctrine within each court by case example(s)
- Explain the impact of the Human Rights Act 1998 within this topic
- Identify how to avoid a precedent

Imagine that you have developed a mysterious illness and that you visit your doctor. He has never encountered this illness before, but remembers that a partner in the practice described something similar a while ago. Your doctor consults the other partner to find out what was prescribed.

Next, imagine that you are a solicitor in private practice. A wealthy client has asked you to draw up his will which is to contain an extremely complex trust. You have not drafted such a clause before, but you know that one of your partners has previously prepared this sort of will. You go in search of the file containing the clauses you need.

What is happening in both of the above cases is that the professional who is faced with an unfamiliar problem seeks a **precedent** to help him in arriving at the best solution to that problem. Using previous decisions to help resolve a current problem is a technique employed in all walks of life, but particularly in the courts of most legal systems.

In the ELS this is referred to as the principle of *stare decisis* (which means 'stand by cases already decided') or the doctrine of **precedent**, and these two terms are interchangeable. It is a concept which has a vital part to play in the day-to-day decision making which takes place in our courts. Note at the outset that there is a difference between *stare decisis*, which describes the doctrine of precedent, and *res judicata*. This latter term means that a court's decision binds the **parties** to the case. The term is Latin for 'the matter has been settled' and is a principle that when a court has decided a case between the parties, after all the appeals if any are brought, the case is not to be reopened by those parties or their successors. *Stare decisis*, which is the focus of this chapter, is the doctrine of following the legal reasoning from one case in a later case when the same points of law arise again.

In this chapter, the operation of the doctrine of precedent (*stare decisis*) in the courts of the ELS will be examined. This chapter will develop your understanding of the way in which the courts and the judges work, and enable you to make some evaluation of the importance of decisions made in different courts.

2.1 What is the doctrine of precedent?

The doctrine simply means that a judge who is hearing a particular type of court case does not have to make a decision using simply his own knowledge of the relevant legal rules, but that similar previous decisions can be consulted to guide and justify the conclusion reached in the instant case. In fact, where a judge in a lower court is aware of a legal principle set by a higher court in a similar case, then this previous decision **must** be followed. It is this element of **binding** precedent which is distinctive within the English system.

So, for example, imagine that Parliament has created a new statute which regulates the activities of accountants. A dispute arises concerning the interpretation of one of the sections of the Act, and a court case ensues. The case reaches the Court of Appeal, which makes a decision about the definition of an 'accountant'. In all future cases in which the definition of an 'accountant' is in issue, lower courts must follow this binding precedent, and apply the decision from the previous case in these situations.

Clearly, if this system is to operate effectively, then it is essential that there is an efficient and reliable system of reporting court cases. This is achieved in three ways. First, all superior courts publish decided cases on the internet. The second way is through the work of the Incorporated Council of Law Reporting for England and Wales, which produces the authoritative version of case reports (known as The Law Reports) and, third, through the publication of alternative series of reports by private publishers such as Butterworths. For example, see:

- www.supremecourt.uk/decided-cases/index.html
- http://iclr.co.uk/
- www.lexisnexis.co.uk/
- www.westlaw.co.uk/
- www.bailii.org.

(For more information on law reporting, the different types of law reports, how to cite cases and how to use reported and unreported cases, refer to another text in this series: *Unlocking Legal Learning*, by J Boylan-Kemp and C Turner (4th edn, Routledge, 2017).)

Because of the vast number of cases decided every year, not every case from every court is published in this way, but the system does provide access to nearly all decisions of the superior courts which concern appeals on points of law. By consulting both the official and the privately published law reports, lawyers and judges are able to obtain valuable information about the way in which cases involving particular facts and legal principles have been decided on previous occasions. Because these precedents are regarded as binding, solicitors and barristers are thus able to give more accurate advice to their clients, and the judges are able to follow the reasoning of previous courts.

2.2 How does the doctrine of precedent operate?

2.2.1 The court hierarchy

The hierarchy of the courts is an important factor in the operation of the doctrine in practice. In Figure 2.1 you will find a basic outline of the court hierarchy, with a summary of the types of cases heard in each court. You should refer to Chapters 4, 5 and 6 for more information on the jurisdiction of each court.

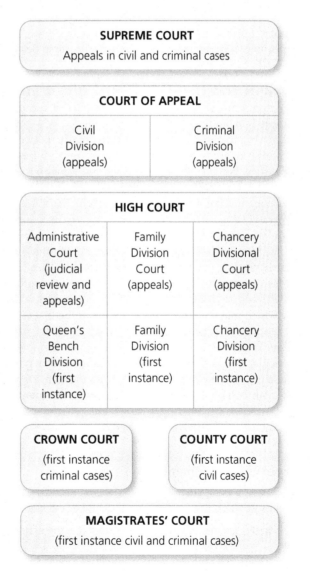

Figure 2.1 Precedent and the court hierarchy

A summary of how the doctrine of precedent operates within the hierarchy was made by the authors Twining and Miers in their book *How to Do Things with Rules* (Weidenfeld & Nicolson, 1991) and it is worth learning these few simple principles which apply whenever a court wishes to know whether or not to follow the decision of a previous case:

1. If the precedent is a decision of a court **superior** to it in the hierarchy then it **must** follow that precedent in the present case (i.e. it is bound by the precedent).

2. If the precedent is one of the court's **own** previous decisions, then, subject to certain exceptions, it **must** follow the precedent.

3. If the precedent is a decision of a court inferior to it in the hierarchy, then it is **not bound** to follow the precedent, but **may** do so if it chooses.

These statements provide a useful outline of the rules and are therefore worth memorising, but, like all summaries, they do not tell the whole story, and in practice the situation is rather more complicated. In order to obtain the full picture, it is necessary to examine the position of each individual court in turn, and so details about the way in which precedent is applied in the different courts can be found below. Before that, however, it is important to appreciate a few of the technical aspects of the doctrine.

2.2.2 *Ratio decidendi* **and** *obiter dicta*

It is important to be aware of which part of the decision of a previous case is to be regarded as binding. The decision itself, i.e. who wins and who loses, is only really of interest to the parties in the case. What really matters, from the point of view of lawyers who wish to apply the doctrine of precedent, is the principle which can be drawn from the case by combining the relevant legal principles with the material facts on which the decision is based. This principle is known as the *ratio decidendi* (literally, the reason for deciding) and it is this part of the case which is absorbed into the general law, and which forms the basis of future legal reasoning. In discussion, lawyers generally abbreviate the term '*ratio decidendi*' to 'the *ratio*'.

The *ratio decidendi* is often contrasted with other parts of the judgment which are said to be *obiter dicta* (that is, sayings by the way). These are remarks made by a judge which are less central to the decision, for example hypothetical examples, statements of law which support dissenting judgments and remarks concerned with broader principles of law which may not be directly in issue in the instant case.

The *ratio decidendi* is therefore that part of a previously decided case which later judges regard as binding on them, because it embodies the legal rule which justifies a particular decision. But how is it identified in any particular case? Discerning the *ratio* of a case requires a close analysis of the judgment or judgments in the case, and is made more difficult by the fact that the judges do not identify it for the benefit of later readers.

ACTIVITY

Looking at judgments

Below, you will find an extract from the famous case of *Carlill v Carbolic Smoke Ball Co* [1892] All ER Rep 127. Read the extract and answer the following questions:

1. Briefly summarise the most important (i.e. the material) facts of the case.
2. Summarise the company's defence.
3. What is the *ratio decidendi* of *Carlill v Carbolic Smoke Ball Co* [1892] All ER Rep 127?
4. Give an example of *obiter dicta*.

Case example

Carlill v Carbolic Smoke Ball Co [1892] All ER Rep 127

On 13 November 1891 the following advertisement was published by the defendants in the *Pall Mall Gazette*:

> £100 reward will be paid by the Carbolic Smoke Ball Co. to any person who contracts the increasing epidemic influenza, colds, or any diseases caused by taking cold, after having used the ball three times daily for two weeks according to the printed directions supplied with each ball. £1,000 is deposited with the Alliance Bank, Regent Street, showing our sincerity in the matter.

The plaintiff (this term is now claimant) bought a smoke ball and used it three times every day, according to the instructions, for several weeks, but then had an attack of influenza. She wrote to the defendants, telling them what had occurred, and asking for the £100 promised by them in the advertisement. The defendants refused to pay and she sued for the money. At the trial, the defendants denied that there was any contract between them and the plaintiff; and, alternatively, that if there was any, it was void. Judgment was nevertheless given for the plaintiff and the defendants appealed.

Bowen LJ:

Judgment

'We were asked by counsel for the defendants to say that this document was a contract too vague to be enforced. The first observation that arises is that the document is not a contract at all. It is an offer made to the public. The terms of the offer, counsel says, are too vague to be treated as a definite offer, the acceptance of which would constitute a binding contract. He relies on his construction of the document, in accordance with which he says there is no limit of time fixed for catching influenza, and that it cannot seriously be meant to promise to pay money to a person who catches influenza at any time after the inhaling of the smoke ball. He says also that, if you look at this document you will find great vagueness in the limitation of the persons with whom the contract was intended to be made – that it does not follow that they do not include persons who may have used the smoke ball before the advertisement was issued, and that at all events, it is a contract with the world in general. He further says, that it is an unreasonable thing to suppose it to be a contract, because nobody in their senses would contract themselves out of the opportunity of checking the experiment which was going to be made at their own expense, and there is no such provision here made for the checking. He says that all that shows that this is rather in the nature of a puff or a proclamation than a promise or an offer intended to mature into a contract when accepted.

Counsel says that the terms are incapable of being consolidated into a contract. But he seems to think that the strength of the position he desires to adopt is rather that the vagueness of the document shows that no contract at all was intended. It seems to me that in order to arrive at this contract we must read it in its plain meaning as the public would understand it. It was intended to be issued to the public and to be read by the public. How would an ordinary person reading this document construe it upon the points which the defendant's counsel has brought to our attention? It was intended unquestionably to have some effect, and I think the effect which it was intended to have was, that by means of the use of the carbolic smoke ball, the sale of the carbolic smoke ball should be increased. It was designed to make people buy the ball. But it was also designed to make them use it, because the suggestions and allegations which it contains are directed immediately to the use of the smoke ball as distinct from the purchase of it. It did not follow that the smoke ball was to be purchased from the defendants directly or even from agents of theirs directly. The intention was that the circulation of the smoke ball should be promoted, and that the usage of it should be increased...

I think that the expression is equivalent to this, that £100 will be paid to any person who shall contract influenza after having used the carbolic smoke ball three times daily for two weeks. It seems to me that that would be the way in which the public would read it. A plain person who read this advertisement would read it in this plain way, that if anybody after the advertisement was published used three times daily for two weeks the carbolic smoke ball and then caught cold he would be entitled to the reward.

Counsel says: "Within what time is this protection to endure? Is it to go on forever or what is to be the limit of time?" ... I think it means during the use. It seems to me that the language of the advertisement lends itself to that construction.

Was the £100 reward intended to be paid? It not only says the reward will be paid, but it says: "We have lodged £1,000 to meet it." Therefore, it cannot be said that it was intended to be a mere puff. I think it was intended to be understood by the public as an offer which was to be acted upon ... The answer to that seems to me to be that, if a person chooses to make these extravagant promises, he probably does so because it pays him to make them, and if he has made them the extravagance of the promises is no reason in law why he should not be bound by them.

It is said it is made to all the world, i.e., to anybody. It is not a contract made with all the world. There is the fallacy of that argument. It is an offer made to all the world, and why should not an offer be made to all the world which is to ripen into a contract with anybody who comes forward and performs the conditions? It is an offer to become liable to anyone, who before it is retracted performs the conditions. Although the offer is made to all the world the contract is made with that limited portion of the public who come forward and perform the conditions on the faith of the advertisement...

Then it was said that there was no notification of the acceptance of the offer. One cannot doubt that as an ordinary rule of law an acceptance of an offer made ought to be notified to the person who makes the offer, in order that the two minds may come together. Unless you do that, the two minds may be apart, and there is not that consensus which is necessary according to the English law to constitute a contract. But the mode of notifying acceptance is for the benefit of the person who makes the offer as well as for the opposite party, and so the person who makes the offer may dispense with notice to himself if he thinks it desirable to do so ... And if the person making the offer expressly or impliedly intimates in his offer that it will be sufficient to act on the proposal without communicating acceptance of it to himself, and the offer is one which in its character dispenses with notification of the acceptance, then according to the intimation of the very person proposing the contract, performance of the condition is a sufficient acceptance without notification ... in the advertisement cases it seems to me to follow as an inference to be drawn from the transaction itself that a person is not to notify his acceptance of the offer before he performs the conditions, but that, if he performs the conditions at once, notification is dispensed with. It seems to me, also, that no other view could be taken from the point of view of common sense. If I advertise to the world that my dog is lost and that anybody who brings him to a particular place will be paid some money, are all the police or other persons whose business is to find lost dogs to be expected to sit down and write me a note saying that they have accepted my proposal? Of course they look for the dog, and as soon as they find the dog, they have performed the condition. The very essence of the transaction is that the dog should be found. It is not necessary under such circumstances, it seems to me, that in order to make the contract binding, there should be any notification of acceptance. It follows from the nature of the thing that the performance of the condition is sufficient acceptance without the notification of it. A person who makes an offer in an advertisement of that kind makes an offer which must be read by the light of that common sense reflection. In his offer he impliedly indicates that he does not require notification of the acceptance of the offer...

In the present case the promise was put forward, I think, with the intention that it should be acted upon, and it was acted upon. It seems to me that there was ample consideration for the promise, and that, therefore, the plaintiff is entitled to recover the reward.'

The *ratio decidendi* of *Carlill v Carbolic Smoke Ball Co* (1892) is that a contract cannot be made with the whole world, but an offer can be made to the world at large. This advert was such an offer. It was accepted by any person who (like Mrs Carlill) bought the product and used it in the prescribed manner. The offer was accepted by conduct. The plaintiff had not been asked to inform the company of her acceptance. It is worth noting at this stage that this 'rule of law' did not in fact exist until Mrs Carlill brought the case – precedents can be made too. This is called an 'original precedent' or a case of 'first impression'. There are plenty of examples of *obiter dicta*, but one of the better known is where Bowen LJ said:

JUDGMENT

'If I advertise to the world that my dog is lost and that anybody who brings him to a particular place will be paid some money, are all the police or other persons whose business is to find lost dogs to be expected to sit down and write me a note saying that they have accepted my proposal? Of course they look for the dog, and as soon as they find the dog, they have performed the condition.'

It is later judges who decide the *ratio* of an earlier case. In *Scruttons v Midlands Silicones* [1962] AC 446, the House of Lords endeavoured to clarify the reasoning used in its own previous decision of *Elder Dempster v Paterson Zochonis* [1924] AC 522. Lord Reid, in *Scruttons v Midlands Silicones* (1962), stated that a later court is entitled to question or limit a previous *ratio decidendi* of an earlier court:

1. where it is obscure; and
2. where it is out of line with other authorities (as in that case); and also
3. where it is much wider than was necessary for the decision.

Academic writers such as Professor A Goodhart have attempted to formulate methods of finding the *ratio*. Goodhart's theory is that the *ratio* can be found by taking account of the facts treated by the judge as material, and the judge's decision as based on them. But it should be noted that this is only a theory and that finding the *ratio* tends to be an intuitive process. It is more of an art than a science. Some help may be derived from the headnote in some of the reported cases. The headnote is the summary of the facts and the decision in each case, inserted by the editor of the reports, but it is unwise to rely on these as a method of finding the *ratio*. There is, unfortunately, no substitute for reading carefully through all the judgments of the case under discussion. In fact, this can reveal that a case may have more than one *ratio*, either because a judge has identified several reasons for a decision, providing several *rationes decidendi*, or because several members of the appeal court(s) have given separate judgments with slightly different *rationes*.

2.2.3 Persuasive precedent

It is easy to focus on the binding nature and the binding element (*ratio decidendi*) of the system of precedent to the exclusion of all other factors. However, the final element to be examined before we look at how each court operates in the system is that of persuasive precedent. If something is persuasive it is 'influencing', 'inducing' or 'urging' you to go along with it or agree with it. A persuasive precedent is exactly that. Examples of persuasive precedent include:

- all *obiter dicta*;
- a dissenting judgment (that is, where there is more than one judge, where one disagrees with the majority decision);

- a minority judgment (that is, where there is more than one judge, where one agrees with the majority decision but does so for a different reason);
- the *ratio* of a decision of a lower court in the hierarchy;
- the *ratio* of a decision of a court abroad or the Privy Council (see below);
- writings of authors of repute, also known as books of authority;
- reports of law reform bodies, such as the Law Commission;
- custom.

You should now have a reasonable grasp of the following technical expressions:

- *stare decisis;*
- *ratio decidendi;*
- *obiter dicta;*
- persuasive precedent.

ACTIVITY

Self-test questions

1. What is the doctrine of binding precedent?
2. What does the term '*ratio decidendi*' mean?
3. Suggest how the *ratio decidendi* of a case can be found.
4. What does the term '*obiter dicta*' mean?
5. How does a persuasive precedent differ from a binding precedent?

KEY FACTS

The basic operation of precedent

Stare decisis	Previous decisions of higher and the same level courts are normally binding on judges hearing later cases with similar facts.
Previous decisions of superior courts	Binding (unless can be distinguished, see below).
Previous decisions of the same court	Normally binding.
Decisions of inferior courts	Not binding, but persuasive.
Ratio decidendi	That part of the decision which is binding.
Obiter dicta	Comments made outside the judgment; these are not binding but persuasive.

2.3 The doctrine as applied in individual courts

2.3.1 The Supreme Court

Until October 2009, the highest court in the English court hierarchy was the House of Lords. In October 2009, the House of Lords in its court (judicial) capacity was replaced with the Supreme Court of the United Kingdom. Decisions of the House of Lords do, however, still bind all inferior courts (unless and until they are overruled or reversed by, for example, a

Supreme Court judgment, or a decision of the ECtHR, see section 2.4 below), and as we will see, decisions of the House of Lords are normally binding on the Supreme Court.

In fact, until 1966, the House of Lords regarded itself as bound by its own previous decisions, according to the law as stated in *London Tramways Co Ltd v London County Council* [1898] AC 375. This was because it was felt that there had to be an end to litigation, i.e. it had to be possible for people to see that once a case had been to the House of Lords, then there would be no further debate on that legal point. The question of law would be conclusive and, if wrong, could be set right only by an Act of Parliament. However, this approach proved to be unduly restrictive, in that it effectively prohibited any development in the law. Therefore in 1966, Lord Gardiner LC, on behalf of himself and the other Law Lords, issued a Practice Statement:

JUGDMENT

Practice Statement [1966] 3 All ER 77

'Their Lordships regard the use of precedent as an indispensable foundation upon which to decide what is the law and its application to individual cases. It provides at least some degree of certainty upon which individuals can rely in the conduct of their affairs, as well as a basis for orderly development of legal rules.

Their Lordships nevertheless recognise that too rigid adherence to precedent may lead to injustice in a particular case and also unduly restrict the proper development of the law. They propose therefore to modify their present practice and, while treating former decisions of this House as normally binding, to depart from a previous decision when it appears right to do so.

In this connexion they will bear in mind the danger of disturbing retrospectively the basis on which contracts, settlements of property and fiscal arrangements have been entered into and also the especial need for certainty as to the criminal law.

This announcement is not intended to affect the use of precedent elsewhere than in this House.'

An explanatory note was also published with the Practice Statement (which is also sometimes referred to as the Practice Direction) which provides further information on the anticipated operation of the House of Lords:

QUOTATION

'Explanatory note for press:

Since the House of Lords decided the English case of *London Street Tramways* [*sic*] *v London County Council* in 1898, the House have considered themselves bound to follow their own decisions, except where a decision has been given *per incuriam* in disregard of a statutory provision or another decision binding on them.

The statement made is one of great importance, although it should not be supposed that there will frequently be cases in which the House thinks it right not to follow their own precedent. An example of a case in which the House might think it right to depart from a precedent is where they consider that the earlier decision was influenced by the existence of conditions which no longer prevail, and that in modern conditions the law ought to be different.

One consequence of this change is of major importance. The relaxation of the rule of judicial precedent will enable the House of Lords to pay greater attention to judicial decisions reached in the superior courts of the Commonwealth, where they differ from earlier decisions of the House of Lords. That could be of great help in the development of our own law. The superior courts of many other countries are not rigidly bound by their own decisions and the change in the practice of the House of Lords will bring us more into line with them.'

The key words in the Practice Direction are 'when it appears right to do so'. The House was very conscious of the need for caution in the exercise of its new power. This was felt to be especially important in cases where contracts, dealings with property and financial arrangements had been made in reliance on previous House of Lords' decisions. The Law Lords also wished to avoid any reduction in the degree of certainty required in the sphere of criminal law where changes could cause an injustice. However, the House also recognised that there would be circumstances where modern conditions would require a change in the law, and that decisions which had been made in the past in response to factors which had since ceased to operate could now be overruled by the use of the Practice Statement.

The use of the Practice Statement by the House of Lords

In practice, the Law Lords did indeed exercise caution in their use of this power, and, following the publication of the Practice Statement in 1966, two years passed before the House of Lords departed from one of its own previous decisions. The first case in which the authority of the Statement was invoked was that of *Conway v Rimmer* [1968] AC 910, HL in which the case of *Duncan v Cammell Laird & Co* [1942] AC 624, HL was overruled. Each of these cases concerned the extent to which the Crown could claim the right not to disclose information during a court case. The earlier case of *Duncan v Cammell Laird & Co* (1942) had been decided during the Second World War, and this had enabled the government to claim 'public interest immunity', and thus avoid the need to comply with an order of the court requiring disclosure of certain documents. The different circumstances under which the case of *Conway v Rimmer* (1968) arose meant that the House of Lords removed this immunity from the government. This case was therefore a good example of the way in which the Practice Statement could be used to adapt the law to changes in society.

However, this decision did not mean that a judicial 'free-for-all' would ensue and, in the intervening years, the House of Lords continued to use its power in a relatively small number of cases. For example, in *Herrington v British Railways Board* [1972] 1 All ER 749, a rule which had been propounded in the earlier House of Lords case of *Addie & Sons v Dumbreck* [1929] AC 358, HL was relaxed as a result of the Practice Statement. In *Addie & Sons v Dumbreck* (1929), the House had ruled that an occupier of property owed only a minimal duty of care to a trespasser, even where that trespasser happened to be a child. However, changes in society's opinion as to the appropriate duty owed in these circumstances led the Law Lords to formulate a duty on the part of an occupier to act humanely towards trespassers.

In *Murphy v Brentwood Borough Council* [1991] 1 AC 398, the House of Lords held, overruling the previous case of *Anns v Merton Borough Council* [1978] AC 728, that a local authority is not liable in tort for negligent inspection of building foundations, where the resulting defects are discovered before physical injury occurs. This was because the loss suffered is purely economic and, under the rule in *Anns v Merton Borough Council* (1978), a far too broad approach had been taken that had drawn the law wider than in any other areas of liability for 'pure economic loss' rather than for, say, physical damage to person. In *Miliangos v George Frank (Textiles) Ltd* [1975] 1 All ER 1076, new developments in rules relating to the exchange rates for foreign currencies, and in particular the less favourable position of sterling, led the House of Lords to change its own earlier ruling in the case of *Re United Railways of Havana & Regla Warehouses Ltd* [1960] 2 All ER 332, that damages awarded by an English court could only be awarded in sterling. As a result of the case of *Miliangos v George Frank (Textiles) Ltd* (1975), damages may be awarded by a court in England based on the currency specified in the contract which gave rise to the dispute.

Cases such as these, in which the Practice Statement was used to positive effect, indicate that the House expected to see that broad issues of justice and public policy were involved before altering a previous decision, and would not usually overturn a previous ruling simply because it was felt that the earlier decision was wrong. A good example of this line of reasoning can be seen in the case of *Jones v Secretary of State for Social Services* [1972] 1 All ER 145. This case concerned the interpretation of a statute, on which the House of Lords had previously given a ruling in the case of *Re Dowling* [1967] 1 AC 725. Despite the fact that four of the seven Law Lords who heard the *Jones* (1972) case felt that *Re Dowling* (1967) was wrongly decided, the House declined to depart from its earlier decision. Some of the reasons offered as justification for this decision were that no broad issues of justice or public policy or legal principle were involved; the case involved the interpretation of a statute and therefore any harmful consequences of the interpretation could be cured by further statutory provisions; and the need for finality in litigation.

The case of *R v Shivpuri* [1986] 2 All ER 334 proved to be an exception to the principles set out in the *Jones v Secretary of State for Social Services* (1972) case above. Here, the Lords took the unusual step of overruling a previous decision of their own which had been made only one year before. The case of *Anderton v Ryan* [1985] 2 All ER 355 was felt to have been wrongly decided, and to contain an error which distorted the law. The Law Lords felt that this situation needed to be remedied as quickly as possible by overruling the previous decision, despite the fact that this was a case which affected the criminal law and the interpretation of a statute, both factors which were thought to militate against the use of the Practice Statement. As Lord Bridge explained:

JUDGMENT

'The Practice Statement is an effective abandonment of our pretention to infallibility. If a serious error embodied in a decision of this House has distorted the law, the sooner it is corrected the better.'

However, the Lords emphasised that this was an exceptional case, and that use of the Practice Statement generally would remain a rare occurrence. But, within a year, the House of Lords in *R v Howe* [1987] AC 417 overruled its own previous decision in *DPP for Northern Ireland v Lynch* [1975] 2 WLR 641. In *Howe* (1987) the House held that the defence of duress is not available to a charge of murder, even though previously it had said that it could be.

It became clear that even though a case had been followed for a number of years, the House of Lords could and would overrule it 'when it appears right to do so'. The case of *MPC v Caldwell* [1982] AC 341 involved a charge of criminal damage. This offence is committed where a person destroys or damages property belonging to another, where the person intends to destroy or damage the property or is reckless about doing so. In the case of *Cunningham* [1957] 2 QB 396, the Court of Criminal Appeal had decided that a person acted 'recklessly' where they were aware of a risk and took the risk anyway. This is sometimes referred to as conscious or advertent risk-taking.

CASE EXAMPLE

MPC v Caldwell [1982] AC 341

The defendant, Caldwell, was a chef. He had an argument with the owner of the hotel where he worked, and in a drunken and angry state he set fire to the kitchens. He was charged with arson which is a form of criminal damage.

He could have been convicted using the *Cunningham* (1957) definition above, because drunkenness is no defence in these circumstances, but, nevertheless, the House of Lords decided to widen the *Cunningham* (1957) definition of 'reckless' to include not just thinking about a risk and taking it anyway, but failing to think about an obvious risk.

Later cases then had to answer the question: 'If the defendant could be convicted because he didn't think about an **obvious** risk, to whom must the risk be obvious?' What if the defendant was blind, or very young, or suffering from a learning difficulty, and the risk was not obvious to him?

The Queen's Bench Divisional Court in *Elliott v C* [1983] 1 WLR 939 held that the answer to the question was 'Obvious to the reasonable person; that is, a sober and reasonable adult.'

CASE EXAMPLE

Elliott v C [1983] 1 WLR 939

C was a 14-year-old schoolgirl. She had learning difficulties and was in a remedial class at school. One evening she stayed out all night and at 5 a.m. she entered a garden shed, found white spirit there and poured it on to the carpet on the floor of the shed and threw two lit matches on to the spirit. The second match ignited; a fire immediately flared up out of control and she left the shed, which was destroyed. When interviewed later that day by the police she said she did not know why she had set fire to the shed but 'just felt like it'. She was charged with criminal damage (arson).

The magistrates found that the girl had given no thought at the time she started the fire to the possibility of there being a risk that this would happen, having regard to her age and understanding, and lack of experience of dealing with inflammable spirit and that she must have been exhausted at the time. However, the Divisional Court held that the risk of damage must have been obvious to a reasonably prudent man, even though on the facts of the particular case, the accused did not in fact, for some reason, appreciate the risk.

This case is generally considered to be harsh, if not completely wrong. However, despite a number of challenges, the case of *Caldwell* (1982) remained good law for 21 years until *R v G* [2003] UKHL 50. Lord Bingham, with unanimous support, felt that conviction of a serious crime should depend on proof that the offender had a culpable or blameworthy state of mind. If the defendant genuinely did not perceive that risk, he may 'fairly be accused of stupidity or a lack of imagination', but that was insufficient for culpability. The need for the House to rectify this situation was 'compelling' and a matter of legal principle. The House used the 1966 Statement to overrule *Caldwell* (1982).

Finally, the House of Lords, in *Horton v Sadler* [2006] UKHL 27, used the 1966 Statement to overrule a 27-year-old precedent, *Walkley v Precision Forgings* [1979] 2 All ER 548. Both cases concerned the rule preventing a party from bringing a second action for personal injury after the limitation period had expired. Lord Bingham explained that the House would depart from the previous case because it had unfairly deprived claimants of a right Parliament had intended for them to have; it had caused 'hair-splitting' decisions at the Court of Appeal; and it had clearly subverted the intention of Parliament. He also considered that the decision to overrule had no impact on contract law, settlements of property or criminal law, where the 1966 Statement itself had identified that special care had to be taken.

In the Practice Statement, the House of Lords emphasised that the practice of overruling previous decisions of the same court was not intended to affect the use of precedent in any other court. However, you will soon discover that Lord Denning, a former well-known Master of the Rolls, would have liked to extend the powers of the Court of Appeal in this direction, but was restrained by the House of Lords.

The use of the Practice Statement by the Supreme Court

In *Austin v Southwark London Borough Council* [2011] 1 AC 355, Lord Hope explained (at [24] and [25]), that the Supreme Court had not thought it necessary to reissue the 1966 Practice Statement in its own name, because it has the same effect at the Supreme Court as it had at the House of Lords. So, the Supreme Court is bound by its own or a House of Lords' decision; it is ordinarily bound but may depart when it appears right to do so. Most recently, the Supreme Court invoked the Practice Statement in *Knauer v Ministry of Justice* [2016] UKSC 9, when it overruled two previous House of Lords cases that related to the date from which damages in Tort law are calculated.

1966 PRACTICE DIRECTION

'Indispensable foundation to decide what is the law ... while treating former decisions of this house as normally binding, to depart from a previous decision when it appears right to do so.'

A cautionary approach – first used in *Conway v Rimmer* (1968).

Not used merely because earlier decision felt to be wrong – *Jones v Secretary of State for Social Services* (1972).

Used where there is a change in society's or public opinion, e.g. *BRB v Herrington* (1972).

Used to bring key areas of law into alignment, e.g. *Murphy v Brentwood BC* (1991).

Used to reflect changes in business and technology, e.g. *Miliangos v George Frank* (1975).

Despite 'the especial need for certainty in the criminal law', the Practice Statement has been used in:

- *R v Shivpuri* (1986);
- *R v Howe* (1987);
- *R v G* (2003).

Figure 2.2 Precedent and the House of Lords/Supreme Court

2.3.2 The Court of Appeal (Civil Division)

There are three main rules which apply to the Court of Appeal:

1. The Court of Appeal is bound by decisions of the House of Lords (and now Supreme Court) whether it agrees with them or not.

2. The decisions of the Court of Appeal itself are binding on the inferior courts in the hierarchy.

3. The Court of Appeal is normally bound by its own previous decisions. This is known as the 'self-binding rule', and means that unless one of the established exceptions to this rule applies, then the Court of Appeal will follow its own previous precedents.

The classic statement of the exceptions to the self-binding rule can be found in the case of *Young v Bristol Aeroplane Co Ltd* [1944] 2 All ER 293. Here, Lord Greene MR identified three situations in which it would be possible for the Court of Appeal to depart from its own previous decisions:

1. Where previous decisions of the Court conflict with each other. In these circumstances the Court can decide which decision to follow and which to ignore (in

practice, the Court of Appeal invariably follows the later of two conflicting decisions, but need not do so: *Great Peace Shipping v Tsavliris Salvage* [2002] 4 All ER 689).

2. Where a previous decision of the Court conflicts with a subsequent decision of the House of Lords (now Supreme Court of course). Here, the Court of Appeal must follow the superior court's ruling rather than its own, even if it thinks that ruling is wrong.

3. Where a previous decision of the Court appears to have been made *per incuriam*. This literally means 'through lack of care', which sounds as though it should enable later judges to ignore any previous precedent which seems to the later court to be wrong. The true position is not quite so simple, however, as the technical application of the *per incuriam* rule is actually quite narrow.

According to the case of *Morelle v Wakeling* [1955] 1 All ER 708, a decision was regarded as having been made *per incuriam* if the Court of Appeal was in a state of ignorance or forgetfulness with regard to a relevant part of statute law or a binding precedent and, as a result, some part of the decision, or some step in the reasoning, was found to be demonstrably wrong. In the case of *Williams v Fawcett* [1985] 1 All ER 787, however, the Court of Appeal felt that there were special features justifying an extension of this traditionally accepted form of the *per incuriam* rule above. Three of these features seem to be prominent in the judgment. They were:

1. the clarity with which the growth of the error could be detected if the previous decisions were read consecutively;

2. the fact that the cases were concerned with the liberty of the subject; and

3. that the cases were most unlikely to be appealed to the higher court, which meant that there would be no further opportunity to correct the error which had crept into the law.

The rules in *Young v Bristol Aeroplane Co Ltd* (1944) above describe the currently accepted understanding of the doctrine of precedent as it relates to the Court of Appeal (Civil Division) where the ECHR is not concerned. However, you should be aware of the fact that, during the 1970s, the then Master of the Rolls, Lord Denning, challenged this accepted view of the role of the Court of Appeal. In a number of controversial cases he led a campaign, first, to establish that the Court of Appeal was not always strictly bound by House of Lords' decisions, and could even declare them to be wrongly decided using the doctrine of *per incuriam*. Second, he argued that the Court of Appeal should adopt the philosophy of the 1966 House of Lords' Practice Statement, so that the Court of Appeal could choose not to follow its own previous decisions in circumstances where it felt that it was right to do so, without having to bring the case within the exceptions outlined in the case of *Young v Bristol Aeroplane Co Ltd* (1944).

Lord Denning received a great deal of criticism from the House of Lords as a result of expressing these radical views. In the case of *Broome v Cassell & Co Ltd* [1971] 1 All ER 801, he had led the Court of Appeal to reject an earlier House of Lords case concerning the award of exemplary damages (*Rookes v Barnard* [1964] 1 All ER 367) on the ground that it had been decided *per incuriam*. When *Broome v Cassell & Co Ltd* (1971) reached the House of Lords ([1972] AC 1136) Lord Hailsham reminded Lord Denning that it was not open to the Court of Appeal

> to give gratuitous advice to judges of first instance to ignore decisions of the House of Lords in this way … it is necessary for each lower tier, including the Court of Appeal, to accept loyally the decisions of the higher tiers.

Lord Denning's final rebuke came from the House of Lords in *Davis v Johnson* [1978] 1 All ER 1132 where his attack on the self-binding rule of the Court of Appeal was defeated. The matter is now resolved and the Court of Appeal operates (on the whole) on the basis of the rules in *Young v Bristol Aeroplane Co Ltd* (1944). However, the debate between Lord Denning in the Court of Appeal and Lord Diplock in the House of Lords in *Davis v Johnson* (1978) provides us with interesting perspectives on the balance that has to be struck between certainty and justice. The tension between these two conflicting aims is the challenge of a fair but predictable system of administering the law. Extracts from the judgments of each Lord are below.

JUDGMENT

Davis v Johnson [1978] 1 All ER 1132, per Lord Denning in the Court of Appeal

'On principle, it seems to me that, whilst this court should regard itself as normally bound by a previous decision of the court, nevertheless it should be at liberty to depart from it if it is convinced that the previous decision was wrong. What is the argument to the contrary? It is said that, if an error has been made, this court has no option but to continue the error and leave it to be corrected by the House of Lords. The answer is this: the House of Lords may never have an opportunity to correct the error; and thus it may be perpetuated indefinitely, perhaps for ever. That often happened in the old days when there was no legal aid. A poor person had to accept the decision of this Court because he had not the means to take it to the House of Lords ... Even today a person of moderate means may be outside the legal aid scheme, and not be able to take his case higher, especially with the risk of failure attaching to it.'

Lord Denning then went on to explain that one decision, widely considered to have been wrongly decided by the House of Lords (*Carlisle and Cumberland Banking Co v Bragg* [1911] 1 KB 489), was only finally overruled in *Saunders (Executrix of Estate of Gallie) v Anglia Building Society* [1970] 3 All ER 961, which you can see was almost 60 years later. As Lord Denning pointed out, this left the lower courts in a difficult position; a position of the House of Lords' making. Should they have applied law they openly recognised to be wrong (and which the Court of Appeal had stated to be wrong)? Should they have adjourned the case to wait with hope for a decision of the House of Lords? That was hardly possible where the lapse of time is so great. He concluded:

JUDGMENT

'justice is delayed, and often denied, by the lapse of time before the error is corrected'.

Lord Denning further criticised the power of insurance companies or big employers to force a settlement on poorer or weaker parties:

JUDGMENT

'When such a body has obtained a decision of this court [the Court of Appeal] in its favour, it will buy off an appeal to the House of Lords by paying ample compensation to the appellant. By so doing, it will have a legal precedent on its side which it can use with effect in later cases ... By such means an erroneous decision on a point of law can again be perpetuated forever. ... To my mind, this Court should apply similar guidelines to those adopted by the House of Lords in 1966. Whenever it appears to this Court that a previous decision was wrong, we should be at liberty to depart from it if we think it right to do so. Normally, in nearly every case of course, we would adhere to it. But in an exceptional case we are at liberty to depart from it'.

On appeal to the House of Lords, however, Lord Diplock took the opposite view:

JUDGMENT

'I do not find it necessary to trace the origin and development of the doctrine of *stare decisis* before the present structure of the courts was created in 1875. In that structure the Court of Appeal ... has always played, save in a few exceptional matters, an intermediate and not a final appellate role. The application of the doctrine of *stare decisis* to decisions of the Court of Appeal was the subject of close examination by a Court of Appeal composed of six of its eight regular members in *Young v Bristol Aeroplane Co Ltd* [1944] 2 All ER 293 ...

... the rule as it had been laid down in the *Bristol Aeroplane* case had never been questioned ... until, following on the announcement by Lord Gardiner LC in 1966 that the House of Lords would feel free in exceptional cases to depart from a previous decision of its own, Lord Denning MR conducted what may be described, I hope without offence, as a one-man crusade with the object of freeing the Court of Appeal from the shackles which the doctrine of *stare decisis* imposed on its liberty of decision by the application of the rule laid down in the *Bristol Aeroplane* case to its previous decisions; or, for that matter, by any decisions of this House itself of which the Court of Appeal disapproved ...

In an appellate court of last resort a balance must be struck between the need on the one side for the legal certainty resulting from the binding effect of previous decisions and on the other side the avoidance of undue restriction on the proper development of the law.'

Lord Diplock continued that the Court of Appeal was not and is not a court of final appeal. It is merely an intermediate appellate court. He said that the proper development of the law (his second point above) can be achieved by the Court of Appeal granting permission to appeal. However, he pointed out, legal certainty would be at risk if the Court of Appeal was not bound by its own previous decisions. He concluded:

JUDGMENT

'the balance does not lie in the same place as in the case of a court of last resort. That is why Lord Gardiner LC's announcement about the future attitude towards precedent of the House of Lords in its judicial capacity concluded with the words: "This announcement is not intended to affect the use of precedent elsewhere than in this House." '

ACTIVITY

Self-test questions

The Court of Appeal (Civil Division) is in the process of hearing appeals in the following five cases. Explain how the doctrine of precedent will apply in each case. In order to answer these questions, the traditional view of the doctrine of precedent must be adopted, Lord Denning's views having been rejected by the House of Lords.

- Case 1. There is a previous decision of the Court of Appeal (Case A), made in 1880, involving similar facts and legal issues. The Court of Appeal hearing Case 1 thinks that while Case A was correctly decided in 1880, the decision is outdated in today's social climate.
- Case 2. A previous case involving similar facts and legal issues was decided by the Court of Appeal in 1990 (Case B). The House of Lords has also made a ruling in a similar case (Case C) in 1993 but cases B and C conflict.

- Case 3. There are two previous Court of Appeal precedents relevant to the point in issue. Both were decided on the same day, by differently constituted Courts of Appeal, and these two decisions conflict with each other.
- Case 4. Case D was decided by the House of Lords in 1995. In 1996, the Court of Appeal decided Case E which conflicts with Case D, but Case D was not cited to the Court of Appeal in Case E.
- Case 5. Case F was decided by the House of Lords in 1995. In 1996, the Court of Appeal decided Case G which conflicts with Case F. Case F was cited to the Court of Appeal in Case G, but the Court of Appeal in Case G distinguished Case F. The Court of Appeal in Case 5 thinks the Court of Appeal in 1996 (Case G) was wrong to have distinguished Case F.

2.3.3 The Court of Appeal (Criminal Division)

The rules of precedent are in theory identical in the two divisions of the Court of Appeal, i.e. that the Court is bound by decisions of the House of Lords, and by its own previous decisions, subject to the exceptions outlined in the case of *Young v Bristol Aeroplane Co Ltd* (1944). While the rule regarding House of Lords' decisions remains the same, the self-binding rule is applied in a slightly different way in the Criminal Division. Case law indicates that the Court of Appeal (Criminal Division) may depart from its own previous decisions if it is satisfied that the law was misapplied or misunderstood, and that this power to deviate from the self-binding rule exists in addition to the exceptions set out in the *Young v Bristol Aeroplane Co Ltd* (1944) case.

As you will appreciate, the liberty of the individual is at stake in cases which are heard by the Court of Appeal (Criminal Division), and this is felt to be a more important factor than the consistency which is produced by rigid adherence to precedent. The danger of a wrongful conviction outweighs the need to follow the doctrine in its strict form. A slightly different view of precedent is therefore taken in such cases.

In *R v Taylor* [1950] 2 All ER 170, Lord Goddard CJ stated:

JUDGMENT

'This court, however, has to deal with questions involving the liberty of the subject, and if it finds, on reconsideration, that, in the opinion of a full court assembled for that purpose, the law has been either misapplied or misunderstood in a decision which it has previously given, and that, on the strength of that decision, an accused person has been sentenced and imprisoned it is the bounden duty of the court to reconsider the earlier decision with a view to seeing whether that person had been properly convicted.'

In *R v Simpson* [2003] EWCA Crim 1499, Lord Woolf CJ held that the Court of Appeal (Criminal Division) has a residual discretion to decide whether one of its own previous decisions should be treated as binding where there are grounds for saying that the previous case is wrong. He stated that the rules of precedent should be applied, bearing in mind that their objective is to assist the administration of justice and should not be regarded as so rigid that they cannot develop in order to meet the needs of contemporary society. While he endorsed a restrictive and cautious approach, he also recognised that a wrong decision in the Criminal Division could create greater problems than a wrong decision in the Civil Division, especially as, in practice, there is little prospect of obtaining **leave to appeal** to the Supreme Court in a criminal matter. However, in *R v Magro* [2010] EWCA Crim 1575, the Court held that *Simpson* discretion does not apply where the previous decision of a three-judge Court of Appeal is the only decision on a distinct and clearly identified point of law reached after full argument and close analysis of the relevant legislative provisions. That decision remains binding on the Court of Appeal.

University of Ulster LIBRARY

leave to appeal
Permission to
appeal

Therefore the only way such a case can be reconsidered is before the Supreme Court (*if* permission to appeal can be obtained).

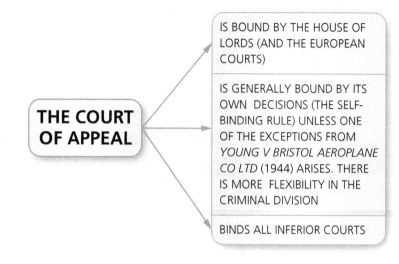

Figure 2.3 Precedent and the Court of Appeal

THE COURT OF APPEAL

IS BOUND BY THE HOUSE OF LORDS (AND THE EUROPEAN COURTS)

IS GENERALLY BOUND BY ITS OWN DECISIONS (THE SELF-BINDING RULE) UNLESS ONE OF THE EXCEPTIONS FROM *YOUNG V BRISTOL AEROPLANE CO LTD* (1944) ARISES. THERE IS MORE FLEXIBILITY IN THE CRIMINAL DIVISION

BINDS ALL INFERIOR COURTS

2.3.4 The Divisional Courts of the High Court

The Divisional Courts of the High Court (including the Administrative Court of the Queen's Bench Division) are bound by decisions of the Supreme Court, previous decisions of the House of Lords and decisions of the Court of Appeal.

Decisions of the Divisional Courts are binding on inferior courts.

The Divisional Courts are normally bound by their own previous decisions, unless one or more of the three exceptions enunciated in the case of *Young v Bristol Aeroplane Co Ltd* (1944) applies. As in the Court of Appeal, there may be a greater degree of flexibility in this rule when the Divisional Court of the Queen's Bench Division (the Administrative Court) considers appeals in criminal cases.

The similarity of the rules concerning precedent in the Court of Appeal and the Divisional Courts of the High Court can be explained in terms of function. The Divisional Courts are not generally courts of first instance: as with the Court of Appeal, they are appellate courts, and in certain circumstances they replace the Court of Appeal as the appropriate forum for appeal. In such cases, the next avenue of appeal is the Supreme Court, which means that the Divisional Courts enjoy a great degree of authority and seniority. It is therefore logical for the same rules of precedent to be adopted here.

2.3.5 The High Court

The High Court is bound by decisions of those courts which are superior to it in the hierarchy.

Decisions of the High Court are binding on courts which are inferior to it in the hierarchy.

The High Court does not regard itself as bound by its own previous decisions, but they are of the strongest persuasive value.

2.3.6 The Crown Court

The Crown Court is bound by decisions of superior courts.

Its decisions are binding on those courts which are inferior to it in the hierarchy.

Decisions of the Crown Court are of persuasive, but not binding, authority for other judges in the Crown Court.

2.3.7 County Courts and Magistrates' Courts

These courts are bound by all superior courts. Their own decisions are not binding on any courts, not even on other courts at the same level in the hierarchy.

2.3.8 The Court of Justice of the European Union

The CJEU does not bind itself, but its decisions will remain binding on the courts in England until the UK leaves the EU.

2.3.9 The Judicial Committee of the Privy Council

The Judicial Committee of the Privy Council (JCPC) hears (among other things) appeals from Commonwealth countries, British Overseas Territories, the Channel Islands and the Isle of Man. The Committee is composed of the Law Lords, ex-Law Lords and superior judges from Canada, Australia and New Zealand by invitation. Like the Supreme Court, the Privy Council is not strictly bound by its own previous decisions. As you can see, the composition of the Committee is impressive and although the Privy Council is not technically a UK court, its decisions are highly persuasive. Given that the Committee is not a UK court, decisions (technically advice) are not binding on English courts, but the exact status of the Privy Council has, until recently, been a matter of debate.

The role of the Privy Council in the development of the law was pushed into the limelight in 2006, however, when it departed from a House of Lords case. All of the cases to be examined below concern the defence of provocation (which has now been replaced). For our purposes, you need to understand that where a defendant was charged with murder, they may have been convicted of the lesser crime of manslaughter where the jury accepted they were provoked. The defence failed, however, if the jury concluded that 'the reasonable man' would not do what the defendant had done. The question which arose in 2006 was whether the reasonable man for the purposes of this defence could share any particular characteristics of the defendant which might have made him more likely to react than a reasonable man.

The first case for our consideration is the House of Lords' decision in *Smith (Morgan)* [2000] 4 All ER 289. The defendant (D) had killed his friend after an argument. There was evidence that D suffered from serious clinical depression which would have 'disinhibited' him and lowered his powers of self-control. Quite simply, he was more provocable than the average person. Lord Hoffmann, giving the leading speech, held that the question for the jury was whether they thought 'the behaviour of the accused had measured up to the standard of self-control which ought reasonably to have been expected of *him*'.

JUDGMENT

'The jury must think that the circumstances were such as to make the loss of self-control sufficiently excusable to reduce the gravity of the offence from murder to manslaughter. This is entirely a question for the jury. In deciding what should count as a sufficient excuse, they have to apply what they consider to be appropriate standards of behaviour.'

This meant that being more provocable *could* be relevant to the question for the jury.

The decision of the House of Lords conflicted with a previous decision of the Privy Council (*Luc Thiet Thuan v R* [1996] 2 All ER 1033). Many academic commentators preferred the earlier decision (s3 of the Homicide Act 1957 refers expressly to the reasonable man, and numerous previous decisions indicated this was in order to provide a level of objectivity in the defence), but *Luc* could not represent the law, because the House of Lords cannot be bound by the Privy Council.

However when *Attorney General for Jersey v Holley* [2005] UKPC 23 went on appeal to the Privy Council, the Council departed from *Smith (Morgan)* (2000). The majority agreed (by six to three):

JUDGMENT

'the provocation … is to be judged by one standard, not a standard which varies from defendant to defendant … their Lordships, respectfully but firmly, consider the majority view expressed in the *Morgan Smith* case is erroneous'.

Approving the minority's view in *Smith (Morgan)* (2000), Lord Nicholls stated:

JUDGMENT

'The standard is a constant, objective standard in all cases. The jury should assess the gravity of the provocation to the defendant … the standard of self-control by which his conduct is to be evaluated for the purpose of the defence of provocation is the external standard of a person having and exercising ordinary powers of self-control.'

The Privy Council was, on the whole, praised for its decisive stance against *Smith (Morgan)* (2000) and in favour of the preferred *Luc* (1996), but as Privy Council's advices (strictly a judgment is an 'advice' to the Crown only) are not binding on courts in England and Wales, the strength of the decision in the court hierarchy was in doubt. Then a five-strong Court of Appeal held in *James* [2006] EWCA Crim 14 that, because in *Holley* (2005) all nine members of the Privy Council were serving Lords of Appeal in Ordinary, six of whom agreed (and those six constituted half of the Law Lords at the time) and all nine agreed that the decision had definitively clarified the law (notwithstanding the dissents on what the law should be), the inferior courts were bound to prefer that Privy Council decision over an earlier conflicting decision of the House of Lords.

In effect, therefore, the Privy Council (*Holley* (2005)) overruled the House of Lords (*Smith (Morgan)* (2000)).

The exact position of the JCPC was clarified by the Supreme Court case of *Willers v Joyce and another (2)* [2016] UKSC 44. In this case, Lord Neuberger, President of the Supreme Court, delivered a judgment in which he reaffirmed that a court should not follow a decision of the Privy Council if it is inconsistent with the decision of a court which is binding on them. However, Lord Neuberger added an important clarification:

JUDGMENT

'There will be appeals to the JCPC where a party wishes to challenge the correctness of an earlier decision of the House of Lords or the Supreme Court, or the Court of Appeal on a point of English law, and where the JCPC decides that the House of Lords or Supreme Court, or, as the case may be, the Court of Appeal, was wrong. It would plainly be unfortunate in practical terms if, in such circumstances, the JCPC could never effectively decide that courts of England and Wales should follow the JCPC decision rather than the earlier decision of the House of Lords or Supreme Court, or of the Court of Appeal.'

The Supreme Court therefore ruled that, if the JCPC is deciding a case from another jurisdiction on a point of law which is the same in English law, the Committee cannot only decide that an earlier decision of the House of Lords, Supreme Court or Court of Appeal was wrong, but also direct all domestic courts to treat the decision of the Committee as representing the law of England and Wales.

2.4 The Human Rights Act 1998

Section 2 of the HRA 1998 provides:

SECTION

'Interpretation of Convention rights

2 (1) A court or tribunal determining a question which has arisen in connection with a Convention right must take into account any –

(a) judgment, decision, declaration or advisory opinion of the European Court of Human Rights,

(b) opinion of the Commission given in a report adopted under Article 31 of the Convention,

(c) decision of the Commission in connection with Article 26 or 27(2) of the Convention, or

(d) decision of the Committee of Ministers taken under Article 46 of the Convention, whenever made or given, so far as, in the opinion of the court or tribunal, it is relevant to the proceedings in which that question has arisen.'

This section has the potential radically to alter the operation of *stare decisis*. The first controversy is what 'take into account' actually means. It actually means neither follow, nor ignore. Other sections of the HRA impose a duty on Parliament to follow decisions of the ECtHR, but no such obligation is placed on English *courts*. This is because it is the state which ensures compliance with the Convention, not the courts. Second, what of the word 'must' in s2(1)? Might that make ECtHR decisions binding? There is no agreement amongst the English judges, see for example *R (Ullah) v Secretary of State for the Home Department* [2004] 2 AC 323, and *Horncastle* [2010] 2 AC 373, two cases which show that even Supreme Court justices disagree on this question. Finally, does the word 'must' permit an inferior English court to avoid (and impliedly overrule) a decision of a superior court where the lower court felt that the higher court's decision was incompatible with a decision of the ECtHR? The answer appears to be 'yes'; the case in question is the Court of Appeal's decision in *Mendoza v Ghaidan* [2004] UKHL 30; [2002] EWCA Civ 1533; [2003] 2 WLR 478.

CASE EXAMPLE

Mendoza v Ghaidan [2004] UKHL 30; [2002] EWCA Civ 1533; [2003] 2 WLR 478

Mr Mendoza had lived with his homosexual partner since 1972 and moved into a flat with him in 1983. The partner had a statutory tenancy on the flat. The relationship between Mr Mendoza and his partner was described as close, monogamous and loving. Essentially, they lived together as spouses, except for the fact that the relationship was a same-sex relationship. After the death of his partner, the landlord granted Mr Mendoza a different type of tenancy (an assured tenancy) which had less protection for the tenant.

The landlord had relied on the House of Lords' decision in *Fitzpatrick v Sterling* [2001] 1 AC 27 where it had been held that a homosexual partner in a long-term relationship was entitled to an assured tenancy as a member of the deceased's family, but could not obtain a statutory tenancy as these were available only to people living with the original tenant as his wife or her husband.

Mr Mendoza argued that his rights had been infringed under Article 8 (interest in home) and Article 14 (the right to exercise all of the Convention rights without discrimination) of the ECHR.

The problem which the Court of Appeal had to face, however, was that on the one hand *Fitzpatrick v Sterling* (2001) was a House of Lords case and the Court of Appeal was bound by decisions of the House of Lords (as it is now bound by the decision of the Supreme Court). On the other hand, it was clear that Mr Mendoza was being discriminated against under ECtHR case law (*Petrovic v Austria* [2001] 33 ECHR 14). While neither s2 of the HRA 1998 nor the operation of *stare decisis* was mentioned by Buxton LJ in the case, he nevertheless found that the decision in *Fitzpatrick v Sterling* (2001) had infringed Article 14 and Mr Mendoza was granted a statutory tenancy. In effect, the Court of Appeal used the power under s2 of the HRA 1998 to overrule a House of Lords case to follow an ECHR case, but without clearly saying that s2 HRA 1998 was being used. In June 2004, the House of Lords itself ([2004] UKHL 30) approved the decision in the Court of Appeal and thus implicitly approved the new operation of the doctrine, allowing the inferior court to overrule the decision of the superior court.

KEY FACTS

Precedent in practice

Court	Is the court bound by a higher court?	Does the court bind any lower courts?	Is the court bound by its own previous decisions?
CJEU	n.a.	Yes, s3 European Communities Act.	The CJEU does not regard itself as bound by its own previous decisions but tends to follow them.
ECtHR	n.a.	Not in a strict *stare decisis* sense, no, but see above.	The ECtHR does not regard itself as bound by its own previous decisions.
Privy Council	Strictly no, but it is rare (but not unknown) for it to depart from a House of Lords' decision.	No, but it is strongly persuasive, and it can direct lower courts to follow its decisions in certain cases.	No.
Supreme Court	Yes, on matters of EU law, it is bound by the decisions of the CJEU.	Yes.	Before 1966, the House of Lords was bound. Since the Practice Statement 1966, the court can depart from its own decisions when it appears right to do so.
Court of Appeal (Civil Division)	Yes.	Yes.	It is normally bound unless the three rules from *Young v Bristol Aeroplane Co Ltd* (1944) are relevant. Note the effect of the HRA 1998 if European Convention rights are involved in the case (*Mendoza v Ghaidan* (2003)).

Court	Is the court bound by a higher court?	Does the court bind any lower courts?	Is the court bound by its own previous decisions?
Court of Appeal (Criminal Division)	Yes.	Yes.	Generally operates in the same way as the Civil Division, but the approach adopted in *R v Taylor* (1950) is also relevant.
Divisional Courts	Yes.	Yes.	Treated as the Court of Appeal because they have appellate jurisdiction.
High Court	Yes.	Yes.	Previous decisions are strongly persuasive. It may overrule its own previous decisions, but this is rare.
Crown Court	Yes.	Yes.	Persuasive only.
County Court	Yes.	n.a.	No.
Magistrates' Court	Yes.	n.a.	No.

ACTIVITY

Essay writing

'The literal translation of *stare decisis* (that all courts stand by all previous decisions) does not reflect the operation of judicial precedent in the twenty-first century.' Discuss the validity of this view.

2.5 The declaratory theory

The declaratory theory of judicial law-making was famously explained by William Blackstone, writing during the eighteenth century:

QUOTATION

'[the judge] being sworn to determine, not according to his private sentiments … not according to his own private judgment, but according to the known laws and customs of the land: not delegated to pronounce a new law, but to maintain and expound the old one'.

Blackstone's Commentaries, p 69

Sir William Holdsworth in his article explained the theory thus:

QUOTATION

'Cases do not make the law, but are only the best evidence of what the law is.'

'Case Law' [1934] 50 LQR 180

This view supposes that judges have no choice to make when deciding the outcome of a case. The law, in this regard, is seen as a web of legal principles that readily supply the answer (there is only one answer) to each problem that arises. Previous cases supply the evidence of the legal principles that have been adopted. This was Ronald Dworkin's view of the declaratory theory. An overruled case is regarded as never having been the law and it is said that the new (i.e. the correct) decision is not only to be applied from now on, but also retrospectively. Retrospectivity essentially means that the law as decided in 2005 will be applied to acts that took place in 1980. This retrospective effect is complicated. For example, consider a commercial contract that was made in 1993 for the supply of goods until 1999, on the basis of the law as it was understood to be in 1993. Consider further what might happen if that law was overruled in 1997. The terms of the 1993 contract have to be interpreted after 1997 in a completely different light and this may affect the nature of the contractual relationship between the parties. The House of Lords has confirmed the retrospective nature of precedent in *Kleinwort Benson v Lincoln City Council* [1998] 4 All ER 513.

David Kairys has argued that judges do have a choice to make in their decision; but not an unfettered (free or unlimited) choice. The outcome of any particular case will be based upon those precedents that the judge believes to be correct, but also on his concept of what is socially and politically correct or justified. JAG Griffith (*The Politics of the Judiciary* (Fontana, 1991)) agrees with Kairys, but also argues that the judge's view of what is socially and politically correct is dictated by the narrow social background of the judiciary (see Chapter 11). He contends that the judges are part of the 'Establishment' and their decisions in cases are pro-Establishment. Lord Reid, in a lecture in 1972, sided more with Kairys than Dworkin. He stated that the declaratory theory was a 'fairytale', that judges do have choices, but 'where there is freedom to go in one direction or another … we should have regard to common sense, legal principle and public policy in that order'. Lord Hobhouse, in *R v Governor of Brockhill Prison, ex p Evans (No 2)* [2001] 2 AC 19 at 48, said:

JUDGMENT

'The common law develops as circumstances change and the balance of legal, social and economic needs changes. New concepts come into play; new statutes influence the non-statutory law. The strength of the common law is its ability to develop and evolve. All this carries with it the inevitable need to recognise that decisions may change. What was previously thought to be the law is open to challenge and review; if the challenge is successful, a new statement of the law will take the place of the old statement.'

While judges do now seem to recognise openly the need for the development of the common law, they also recognise that their job is not to act as legislators. In *C v DPP* [1995] 2 All ER 43, the House of Lords was asked to consider changing the law regarding children's criminal liability. There was a rebuttable common law presumption that 10–14-year-old children were incapable of committing crime. This meant that a child aged 10–14 was presumed to be incapable of committing a crime unless the prosecution could prove otherwise. This would be called rebutting the presumption. The House of Lords refused to overrule the previous law and Lord Lowry (at [51]) laid down guidelines for judicial law-making:

JUDGMENT

'(1) if the solution is doubtful, the judges should beware of imposing their own remedy;
(2) caution should prevail if Parliament has rejected opportunities of clearing up a known difficulty or has legislated while leaving the difficulty untouched;
(3) disputed matters of social policy are less suitable areas for judicial intervention than purely legal problems;
(4) fundamental legal doctrines should not be lightly set aside;
(5) judges should not make a change unless they can achieve finality and certainty.'

On the other hand, without referring to Lord Lowry's speech above, in *Fitzpatrick v Sterling Housing Association* [1999] 4 All ER 705, Lord Slynn said:

JUDGMENT

'It has been suggested that for your Lordships to decide this appeal in favour of the appellant would be to usurp the function of Parliament. It is trite that that is something the courts must not do. When considering social issues in particular judges must not substitute their own views to fill gaps … it would be a court's duty to give effect to it whatever changes in social attitudes a court might think ought to be reflected in the legislation. Similarly, if it were explicit or clear that the word must be given a very wide meaning so as to cover relationships for which a court, conscious of the traditional views of society might disapprove, the court's duty would be to give effect to it. It is, however, for the court in the first place to interpret each phrase in its statutory context. To do so is not to usurp Parliament's function; not to do so would be to abdicate the judicial function. If Parliament takes the view that the result is not what is wanted it will change the legislation.'

Where there is no binding precedent in a particular situation, judges still have to decide the outcome of a case. They cannot refuse to do so, and say it is a matter for Parliament and Parliament alone. It is generally accepted nowadays that judges do make law and the declaratory theory is seen as being unrealistic insofar as it suggests that judges have no choice to make when deciding cases. The system of precedent is certainly not so rigid as to prevent development of the law. For example, the House of Lords created new law in *Shaw v DPP* [1962] AC 220.

CASE EXAMPLE

Shaw v DPP [1962] AC 220

Shaw decided to fill what he perceived to be a gap in the market by publishing a directory of the names and addresses of prostitutes. Even though he had obtained advice from Scotland Yard that such activity would not be unlawful, he was subsequently convicted of the previously unknown offence of conspiracy to corrupt public morals.

Most law students ask how Shaw could have been convicted of an offence that did not appear to have existed at the time he committed the act constituting the offence. Certainly, such an occurrence is both rare and highly controversial. If it were to occur today, there might be a successful appeal on the basis that the conviction breached Article 7 of the ECHR (no one shall be held guilty of any criminal offence on account of any act or omission which did not constitute a criminal offence under national or international law at the time when it was committed). However, the House of Lords insisted that even if the offence had not been prosecuted in that way previously, it did exist. The House referred to the old case of *R v Curl* (1727) 2 Stra 788. In that case the charge against the accused was that of publishing an obscene libel. The Court of King's Bench agreed with the argument submitted by the Attorney General:

JUDGMENT

'What I insist upon is that this is an offence at common law, as it tends to corrupt the morals of the King's subjects, and is against the peace of the King. … I do not insist that every immoral act is indictable, such as telling a lie, or the like; but if it is destructive of morality in general, if it does, or may, affect all the King's subjects, it then is an offence of a public nature.'

In *Shaw v DPP* (1962), Viscount Simonds agreed with this reasoning and at p 268 said:

JUDGMENT

'there is in that court a residual power, where no statute has yet intervened to supersede the common law, to superintend those offences which are prejudicial to the public welfare. Such occasions will be rare, for Parliament has not been slow to legislate when attention has been sufficiently aroused. But gaps remain and will always remain since no one can foresee every way in which the wickedness of man may disrupt the order of society.'

The declaratory theory does still receive some attention: in *Re A (children) (conjoined twins: surgical separation)* [2000] 4 All ER 961, Ward LJ said at 968:

JUDGMENT

'This court is a court of law, not of morals, and our task has been to find, and our duty is then to apply the relevant principles of law to the situation before us – a situation which is quite unique.'

But such attention is not unanimous, as Lord Hoffmann stated in *Arthur J S Hall v Simons* [2000] 3 All ER 673:

JUDGMENT

'I hope that I will not be thought ungrateful if I do not encumber this speech with citations. The question of what the public interest now requires depends upon the strength of the arguments rather than the weight of authority.'

ACTIVITY

Critiquing the law

Quotation

'[I]t is revolting to have no better reason for a rule of law than that so it was laid down in the time of Henry IV.'

O W Holmes, 'The path of the law' [1997] Harv L Rev 991, 1001

In this statement, Oliver Wendell Holmes, who was a famous American judge, is denouncing the rigidity of *stare decisis*. For Holmes, the idea that judges have to follow past decisions just because they were made in the past, and not because they are just or right, is 'revolting'. You may agree with this sentiment. In thinking about this, consider these questions:

1. Do you agree that judges should have to follow decisions under the doctrine of precedent that they disagree with?
2. What would be the consequences for the legal system of judges overruling past decisions that they disagree with?
3. Do you think that judges should have the power in a democracy to make and remake the common law?

2.6 Avoiding precedents

2.6.1 Distinguishing

If a court can find sufficient differences between the material facts of a previous and a current case, then it may depart from the previous decision. It may also be that although a judge is bound by a precedent in a particular case, there are good reasons why the judge may wish not to follow it. In these circumstances it is likely that the judge will try to distinguish the precedent, so as to avoid having to follow the previous decision. This process of distinguishing cases is extremely important in practice, because it enables judges to develop the law, rather than being bound by precedent in every situation.

For example, read the facts and decisions of the two cases below and consider how a judge might distinguish the first (*King v Philips* [1953] 1 QB 429) in the second case (*Boardman v Sanderson* [1964] 1 WLR 1317).

CASE EXAMPLE

King v Philips [1953] 1 QB 429

A taxi driver reversed his taxi into a small boy on a tricycle. The boy and his tricycle luckily suffered only slight damage, but the boy's mother heard him scream and looked out of the upstairs window of their home which was about 70 to 80 yards away. She saw the tricycle under the taxicab but could not see the boy. He eventually ran home, but his mother had suffered nervous shock, a psychiatric injury, for which she claimed damages from the defendant.

The Court of Appeal held that the defendant was not liable to the mother because, on the facts, no 'hypothetical reasonable observer' could have anticipated that any injury, either physical or psychiatric, could have been caused to her by the backing of the taxi without due attention as to where it was going, and, accordingly, the driver owed no duty to the mother.

CASE EXAMPLE

Boardman v Sanderson [1964] 1 WLR 1317

The defendant ran his car wheel on to a young boy's foot. The boy screamed and his father heard the scream. The father ran to the scene, saw what had happened and suffered psychiatric shock. The defendant knew that the father was within earshot and was certain to come if his son screamed.

The Court of Appeal held that the father was entitled to damages for the shock he had suffered.

As you will have seen from the two sets of facts, the defendant in *Boardman v Sanderson* (1964) knew that the father was in the vicinity, which makes the case quite easy to distinguish from *King v Philips* (1953) where neither the taxi driver nor a 'hypothetical reasonable observer' would have foreseen any injury to the boy's mother. Where there is a significant difference between the facts of two cases, the previous case is distinguished in the present case.

A further example taken from the criminal law will also illustrate how cases can be distinguished. Consider how in the cases below, the third case (*R v Kendrick and Hopkins* [1997] 2 Cr App R 524) distinguished the second (*R v Mazo* [1997] 2 Cr App R 518), which had distinguished the first (*DPP v Gomez* [1993] 96 Cr App R 359).

CASE EXAMPLE

DPP v Gomez [1993] 96 Cr App R 359

Gomez worked as an assistant manager in a shop. A third party asked him if he would supply goods from the shop in exchange for two stolen cheques. Gomez went to the shop owner and asked him to authorise the supply of goods for the cheques but he did not inform the owner that the cheques were worthless. The owner agreed and the goods were supplied. Gomez was charged with theft.

For the defendant to be guilty of theft, the prosecution must prove that the defendant dishonestly appropriated property belonging to another, with the intention permanently to deprive the other of it. Gomez was convicted, but appealed against his conviction on the ground that while the contract of sale was voidable, the transfer to the third party was with the consent and express authority of the owner and, therefore, there was no 'appropriation'. The House of Lords rejected this argument, holding that an act which was authorised by the owner of goods may be an appropriation for the purposes of the Theft Act 1968, even though it was done with the owner's consent.

CASE EXAMPLE

R v Mazo [1997] 2 Cr App R 518

Mazo worked as a maid to Lady S. Over a two-year period, she cashed cheques totalling £37,000 made payable to her by Lady S. Mazo was charged with theft in relation to the cashing of the cheques. At her trial the prosecution case was that she had taken advantage of Lady S's mental incapacity. The jury convicted her.

Mazo appealed against her conviction on the ground that the transfers to her were valid gifts and that the trial judge had summed up incorrectly regarding Lady S's mental incapacity to make such gifts. Her appeal was allowed. The Court of Appeal held that while a transaction might be theft for the purposes of the Theft Act 1968 even if it was done with the owner's consent, the recipient of a valid gift could not be the subject of a conviction for theft. The court agreed that the jury had not been directed correctly about Lady S's mental incapacity.

CASE EXAMPLE

R v Kendrick and Hopkins [1997] 2 Cr App R 524

Kendrick and Hopkins ran a small residential home for the elderly where the victim, a lady aged 99 who was virtually blind, went to live in 1991. Kendrick and Hopkins took complete control of the victim's financial affairs, including writing cheques to themselves from her account, which they said were gifts from the victim. The appellants were charged with con-spiracy to steal. The trial judge directed the jury in line with the law as represented by *DPP v Gomez* (1993) above. Kendrick and Hopkins were convicted.

They appealed on the ground that, under *R v Mazo* (1997), the judge should have directed the jury that the recipient of a valid gift could not be the subject of a conviction for theft. Therefore, they argued, the consent of the victim negated theft because the victim's mind had not been established to have been incapacitated. The Court of Appeal dismissed the appeals on the ground that it was not proper to read into the Theft Act 1968 the words 'without the consent of the owner'; and that there was nothing in the summing-up which would have resulted in the jury being confused as to whether the victim lacked the capacity to manage her affairs.

2.6.2 Reversing

Precedent may also be avoided by a superior court in the hierarchy reversing the decision of a court lower down in the hierarchy during the course of the same case. This will occur if, for example, the Court of Appeal has reached a particular decision in a particular case, but then the Supreme Court reaches the opposite conclusion in the ensuing appeal in that case.

2.6.3 Overruling

The Court of Appeal and Supreme Court also have the power to overrule the decision of a lower court, in a later, different, case. For example, the High Court may reach a decision in Case X, and that decision becomes a precedent for the future. Some time later, a similar case, Case Y, is heard by the High Court. Case X is used as a precedent, but the losing party appeals to the Court of Appeal. The Court of Appeal finds the original decision in Case X to have been erroneous (wrong), and overrules it.

The House of Lords overruled a very long-standing law in *R v R (Marital Exemption)* [1992] 1 AC 599.

CASE EXAMPLE

R v R (Marital Exemption) [1992] 1 AC 599

The defendant had married his wife in 1984, but they separated in 1989 and his wife returned to live with her parents. The parties had talked about divorcing. However, one evening, the defendant forced his way into his wife's parents' house and attempted to have sexual intercourse with her, in the course of which attempt he assaulted her. He was charged with attempted rape and assault. He was convicted.

He appealed on the ground that a husband could not be convicted of raping his wife (and therefore he could not be convicted of attempting to do so). The House of Lords recognised that, since the eighteenth century, there had been a rule of law that a wife was deemed to have consented irrevocably to sexual intercourse with her husband. Sir Matthew Hale's text, *History of the Pleas of the Crown*, published in 1736, had stated: 'the husband cannot be guilty of a rape committed by himself upon his lawful wife, for by their mutual matrimonial consent and contract the wife hath given up herself in this kind unto her husband which she cannot retract'.

However, Lord Keith of Kinkel, who gave the leading speech of a unanimous House, went on to hold:

JUDGMENT

'It may be taken that the proposition was generally regarded as an accurate statement of the common law of England [in 1736]. The common law is, however, capable of evolving in the light of changing social, economic and cultural developments. Hale's proposition reflected the state of affairs in these respects at the time it was enunciated. Since then the status of women, and particularly of married women, has changed out of all recognition in various ways which are very familiar and upon which it is unnecessary to go into detail. Apart from property matters and the availability of matrimonial remedies, one of the most important changes is that marriage is in modern times regarded as a partnership of equals, and no longer one in which the wife must be the subservient chattel [property] of the husband. Hale's proposition involves that by marriage a wife gives her irrevocable consent to sexual intercourse with her husband under all circumstances and irrespective of the state of her health or how she happens to be feeling at the time. In modern times any reasonable person must regard that conception as quite unacceptable.'

For the sake of accuracy, it is important to note that a judge distinguishes on the facts, but reverses or overrules a decision or judgment on the law. Also, note that distinguishing does not affect the validity of the precedent of the previous case. It is merely felt not to be relevant law on the given facts. An overruled case is regarded as never having been the law and it is not applied again in later cases. Although this last sentence might strike you as odd – men were not charged or were acquitted of raping their wives according to the law before *R v R* in 1992 – you will recognise the concept from the discussion of the declaratory theory from section 2.5 above.

2.7 Pros and cons of precedent

Finally, it is important to notice some of the arguments in favour of the doctrine of precedent as it is operated in the ELS, and also to be aware of some of the drawbacks; not all lawyers (and not even all judges) agree with a strict application of the principle of *stare decisis*.

It is true that the doctrine of precedent is efficient because it enables judges to avoid having to solve the same legal problem more than once, and thus may save a considerable amount of judicial time and energy. A further advantage is that this system lends some degree of predictability to legal decision-making. This is of great importance to lawyers when attempting to advise their clients as to the likely outcome of litigation. When a particular factual situation or legal principle has featured in a previous court case, the lawyer is able to assess the case before him in the light of the previous decision, and guide the client according to whether the outcome is likely to be in the client's favour or not. Another argument in favour of a strict application of the doctrine is that use of previous precedents satisfies the requirements of justice, i.e. that people be treated alike in like circumstances. Thus, a case heard in the High Court in Manchester, to which a precedent of the Court of Appeal is applicable, will, by the application of that precedent, be dealt with in the same way as a similar case being heard by the High Court in Nottingham. This means that the doctrine can be regarded as being certain and consistent. There are ways, however, for precedents to be avoided, so there is an element of flexibility too. Critics have nevertheless argued that this system is unconstitutional because it allows judges to change the law, rather than for law reform to be for Parliament alone within the separation of powers doctrine (see Chapter 1.2). Alternatively, other critics have pointed out that *stare decisis* can lead to judicial laziness as it may discourage members of the judiciary from taking responsibility for thinking through solutions to legal problems. Certainly, because the doctrine is essentially backward-looking, it may stifle creativity in decision making, and may lead to stagnation in the law. Related to this latter point is the criticism that, unless a case arises which allows a court the opportunity to amend a previous decision by not following the precedent, the law cannot develop and respond to changes in social circumstances. Legal change could therefore become dependent upon those who have the money to be able to afford to pursue litigation.

SUMMARY

....

- The doctrine of *stare decisis* means that in certain circumstances a judge has to (is bound to) follow the legal reason for the decision (the legal rule) from a previous case.
- A judge is bound when the material facts of the previous and present case are the same or too similar to distinguish (avoid) and the previous decision was made in a higher court in the hierarchy or at the same level.

- The part of the previous decision which is binding is the *ratio decidendi*.
- The judges in later cases identify the *ratio decidendi* of the previous case.
- There are other parts of a judgment, but these are not binding. This includes comments made *obiter dicta* (outside the judgment, or by the way). *Obiter dicta* are persuasive.
- Other persuasive precedent includes decisions of inferior courts, dissenting judgments, minority judgments, decisions of courts outside England and Wales and decisions of the Privy Council.
- The rules governing the operation of *stare decisis* are particular to each court in the hierarchy. For example, the House of Lords (now the Supreme Court) usually follows its own previous decisions but does not have to. The Court of Appeal is normally self-binding unless the exceptions in *Young v Bristol Aeroplane Co Ltd* (1944) apply.
- The HRA 1998 has apparently changed the traditional binding effect of higher courts' decisions (and presumably the self-binding rules too) where the previous decision is in conflict with the ECHR and/or a decision of the ECtHR.

SAMPLE ESSAY QUESTION

How, if at all, has the enactment of the HRA 1998 changed the traditional operation of *stare decisis*?

Explain what *stare decisis* means and how the *ratio decidendi* is the 'potentially' binding part of a decision.

Then explain that decisions of superior courts and, usually, the same courts, are normally binding on future decisions.

Explain that the House of Lords was traditionally bound by its own decisions but that the 1966 Practice Direction gave it the power to overrule when it appeared 'right to do so'. The Supreme Court operates the same rule.

Explain the operation of precedent at the Court of Appeal including the exceptions to the self-binding rule (and the flexibility in the Criminal Division).

Briefly recite s2 HRA 1998.

> Explain how, in *Mendoza v Ghaidan* (2004) (see section 2.4), the Court of Appeal chose to ignore a binding decision of the House of Lords to make an ECHR-compliant decision. What this means in practice is that an inferior court may ignore a superior court's binding decision to follow the ECHR, contrary to the 'traditional' operation of *stare decisis*.

CONCLUDE

Figure 2.4 Essay map on precedent

Further reading

Articles

Buck, T, 'Precedent in tribunals and the development of principles' [2006] *CJQ* 458.

Caldarone, RP, 'Precedent in operation: a comparison of the judicial House of Lords and the US Supreme Court' [2004] *PL* 759.

Clayton, R, 'Smoke and mirrors: the HRA and the impact of Strasbourg case law' [2012] *PL* 659.

Entchev, I, 'A response-dependent theory of precedent' [2011] *Law & Phil* 273.

Fernandez, PA and Ponzetto GAM, '*Stare decisis*: rhetoric and substance' [2012] *JLE & O* 313.

Masterman, R, 'Section 2(1) of the Human Rights Act 1998: binding domestic courts to Strasbourg?' [2004] *PL* 725.

Mowbray, A, 'An examination of the European Court of Human Rights' approach to overruling its previous case law' [2009] *HRL Rev* 179.

O'Brien, D, 'The Privy Council overrules itself: again!' [2008] *PL* 28.

Simpson, A, 'The *ratio decidendi* of a case' [1957] *MLR* 413.

Stone, J, 'The *ratio* of the *ratio decidendi*' [1959] *MLR* 597.

Internet links

Fenwick, H, 'What's wrong with s. 2 of the HRA?' at: http://ukconstitutionallaw. org/2012/10/09/helen-fenwick-whats-wrong-with-s-2-of-the-human-rights-act/

Supreme Court of the UK at: www.supremecourt.uk

3

Statutory interpretation

AIMS AND OBJECTIVES

After reading this chapter you should be able to:

- Understand the need for statutory interpretation
- Distinguish between the literal and purpose approach
- Discuss the advantages and disadvantages of each approach
- Identify the literal, golden and mischief rules
- Illustrate the operation of the rules by case example(s)
- Recognise the difficulty of finding Parliament's intention
- Understand the effect of membership of the EU on statutory interpretation in the UK
- Understand the importance of human rights in applying the rules of statutory interpretation

3.1 Introduction

In Chapter 1 we looked at the enactment of statutes by Parliament and also the making of secondary legislation such as SIs. In each year approximately 60 Acts of Parliament are passed and, in addition, about 3,000 SIs become law. With so much legislation each year, it would appear that judges only have to apply the law. In fact, it is said that the role of Parliament is to **make** the law and the role of the judges is to **apply** the law. However, the division between making and applying is not as straightforward as this. Many of the disputes that come before the courts concern the meaning of words in an Act or secondary legislation. In such cases judges may well often have to decide on which of two possible meanings should be used or even whether they should 'fill in the gaps' where an Act does not make it clear whether a certain situation should be covered.

3.1.1 The need for statutory interpretation

There are many reasons why the meaning of legislation may be unclear and the judges, therefore, have to interpret it. The main reasons are:

1. Failure of legislation to cover a specific point

The legislation may have been drafted in great detail, with the draftsman trying to cover every possible contingency. Despite this, situations can arise which were not specifically covered. The question then is whether the courts should interpret the legislation so as to include the situation which is omitted from it, or whether they should limit the legislation to the precise points listed by Parliament. This has led to the biggest dispute in how legislation should be interpreted. What may be termed 'active' judges take the view that they should 'fill in the gaps' while passive judges think that this should be left to Parliament as it is not the role of a judge to make law.

The passive line of reasoning can be seen in the following case:

CASE EXAMPLE

London & North Eastern Railway Co v Berriman [1946] 1 All ER 255

Mr Berriman was a railway worker who was hit and killed by a train while he was doing maintenance work, oiling points on a railway line. A regulation made under the Fatal Accidents Act stated that a look-out should be provided for men working on or near the railway line 'for the purposes of relaying or repairing' it. Mr Berriman was not relaying or repairing the line; he was maintaining it. His widow tried to claim compensation for his death because the railway company had not provided a look-out man while Mr Berriman had to work on the line, but the court ruled that the relevant regulation did not cover maintenance work and so Mrs Berriman's claim failed.

The court looked only at the specific words in the regulations. It was not prepared to look at any broad principle that the purpose of making a regulation that a look-out man should be provided was to protect those working on railway lines. Under this view it could be argued that it did not matter whether oiling points was maintenance rather than repair work. Men doing either were equally in need of protection. The different attitudes towards statutory interpretation are discussed further at section 3.4.

2. A broad term

In order to avoid the problems of having to list all possible contingencies, legislation may use words designed to cover several possibilities. But a word or words with a wide meaning can lead to problems as to what exactly they cover. In the Dangerous Dogs Act 1991 there is a phrase 'any dog of the type known as the pit bull terrier'. This seems a simple phrase but it has led to problems. What is meant by 'type'? Does it mean the same as 'breed'? In *Brock v DPP*, *The Times*, 23 July 1993 this was the key point in dispute. The Queen's Bench Divisional Court decided that 'type' had a wider meaning than 'breed'. It could cover dogs that were not pedigree pit bull terriers, but had a substantial number of the characteristics of such a dog.

3. Ambiguity

Ambiguity occurs where a word or phrase has more than one meaning. It may not be clear which meaning should be used. Section 57 of the Offences Against the Person Act 1861 made it an offence to 'marry' while one's original spouse was still alive (and there had been no divorce). In *R v Allen* [1872] LR 1 CCR 367 it was accepted that the word 'marry' can mean to become legally married to the other person or in a more general way it can mean that the person takes part or 'goes through' a ceremony of marriage. This was important because, if only the first meaning was accepted, the offence of bigamy could never be committed since a person who is still married to another person cannot legally marry anyone else (see section 3.2.2 for further discussion).

4. A drafting error

It is possible that the Parliamentary Counsel who drafted the original Bill may have made an error which has not been noticed by Parliament; this is particularly likely to occur where the Bill is amended several times while going through Parliament.

5. New developments

New technology may mean that an old Act of Parliament does not apparently cover present-day situations. This was seen in the case of *Royal College of Nursing v DHSS* [1981] 1 All ER 545 where medical science and methods of producing an abortion had changed since the passing of the Abortion Act in 1967. This case is discussed more fully at section 3.2.3. It was also seen in *R (Quintavalle) v Secretary of State for Health* [2003] UKHL 13 where scientific advances made it possible to create human embryos by cell nuclear replacement. This had not been foreseen when the Human Fertilisation and Embryology Act 1990 was passed. In such cases the problem for the courts is whether to extend the Act to cover the new development. There is an exercise on this case later in this chapter.

6. Changes in the use of language

The meaning of words can change over the years. Sometimes it is necessary to interpret an Act of Parliament enacted in the 1800s. Language used then can have different meanings from those of today. An example is the case of *Cheeseman v DPP*, *The Times*, 2 November 1990 in which the meaning of the word 'passengers' was important to the case. The Act which had to be considered by the court dated from 1847 and so the court looked at the *Oxford English Dictionary* for that date to check on the meaning. The meaning given to the word then was 'a passer-by or through'. This is completely different from today's meaning of the word as someone who is carried in vehicle, train, plane or ship (see section 3.2.1 for further consideration of this case).

So it can be seen that legislation which appears to be simply expressed can lead to a disputed case in the courts in which the interpretation of words or a phrase is crucial to the outcome of the case. The method that judges use is also critical as the decision of an activist judge may well be different from that of a passive judge in the same case.

The need for statutory interpretation appears to be increasing, with the large number of statutes passed by Parliament in recent years. This is particularly true in the criminal law where it is estimated that over 3,000 new criminal offences have been created in the last ten years. JR Spencer is very critical of the standard of much of recent legislation. In a recent article he points out that with so much legislation being passed, neither the draftsmen nor Parliament have time to scrutinise Bills properly. He also identifies other problems:

QUOTATION

'But excessive speed is not the only problem, because it seems to me that we often make a mess of criminal justice legislation even when we there was time enough to get it right. And it seems to me that, even when not in haste, we bungle, in particular, by passing criminal justice legislation that:

(a) is much too detailed and prescriptive;
(b) fails to take account of the basic rules of substantive criminal law, or criminal procedure, or both;
(c) is obtuse – and makes a meal of doing simple things, apparently for the sake of it.'

JR Spencer, 'The drafting of criminal legislation: need it be so impenetrable?'
[2008] CLJ at 590

3.1.2 Applying the law

Even where the judge is applying the law in a passive manner, there are still many points to be considered. These are known as aids to interpretation. An interesting example of this was seen in *DPP v Bull* [1994] 4 All ER 411 where the words in s1(1) of the Street Offences Act 1959 had to be considered by the courts. This section states:

SECTION

's 1(1) It shall be an offence for a common prostitute to loiter or solicit in a public street or public place for the purposes of prostitution.'

The word which caused difficulty in this section was 'prostitute'. This is a word which most people would say was easily understandable. You probably can give a definition for it, and can look it up in a dictionary. It might also be interesting to ask other people how they would define it. So why was there a problem of interpretation in *DPP v Bull* (1994)?

CASE EXAMPLE

DPP v Bull [1994] 4 All ER 411

Bull was a male prostitute charged with an offence against s1(1) of the Street Offences Act 1959. The case was heard by a stipendiary magistrate at Wells Street Magistrates' Court. The magistrate dismissed the case on the ground that the words 'common prostitute' applied to female prostitutes only. The prosecution appealed by way of case stated and the Queen's Bench Divisional Court had to decide whether the words were meant to apply to women only or could also cover male prostitutes.

The prosecution counsel in the case put forward six reasons why the court should decide that 'prostitute' could apply to both males and females. These points were listed by Lord Justice Mann in his judgment.

JUDGMENT

'The submission for the appellant was that s1(1) of the 1959 Act is unambiguous and is not gender specific. Our attention was drawn to the following six factors which were relied upon:

(i) The phrase in s1(1) "a common prostitute" was linguistically capable of including a male person. The *Oxford English Dictionary* (1989) includes within the possibilities for "prostitute", "a man who undertakes male homosexual acts for payment".

(ii) Lord Taylor has recently said in *R v McFarlane* [1994] 2 All ER 283:

"both the dictionary definitions and the cases show that the crucial feature in defining prostitution is the making of an offer of sexual services for reward".

(iii) Section 1(2) and (3) of the 1959 Act refer respectively to "a person" and "anyone".

(iv) In contrast s2(1) refers specifically to "a woman" …

(v) Since 1967 male prostitution has been in certain circumstances not unlawful and accordingly in the new environment it is open to the court to interpret s1(1) of the 1959 Act as being applicable to prostitutes who are male, "even if this was not the original intention of the provision" …

(vi) Where Parliament intends to deal with gender specific prostitution it uses specifically the words "woman", "girl" or "her".'

However, the court rejected all these arguments and preferred the point put by the defendant's lawyer. This was also explained by Lord Justice Mann:

JUDGMENT

'Mr Fulford's [counsel for Bull] main submission was that the court should avail itself of the report which led to the 1959 Act and of the parliamentary debate upon the Bill for the Act ... Section 1(1) of the Act was as a result of a recommendation in the *Report of the Committee on Homosexual Offences and Prostitution* [the Wolfenden Report Cmnd 247, 1957]. The relevant chapter of the report leaves me in no doubt that the committee was only concerned with the female prostitute. ... It is plain that the "mischief" that the Act was intended to remedy was a mischief created by women.'

So the decision of the court was that 'prostitute' in the Street Offences Act 1959 only applied to female prostitutes. But to reach that decision the court had considered a number of points. This is an example of applying the law. In other cases the judges may actually create law. An example of this is considered next.

3.1.3 Judicial law-making

In *Mendoza v Ghaidan* [2002] EWCA Civ 1533 the Court of Appeal (Civil Division) had to consider the wording of the Rent Act 1977. The relevant part of the Act was paras 2 and 3 of Sch 1 to the Rent Act 1977 as amended which read:

SECTION

's 2(1) The surviving spouse (if any) of the original tenant, if residing in the dwelling-house immediately before the death of the original tenant, shall after the death be the statutory tenant if and so long as he or she occupies the dwelling-house as his or her residence.

(2) For the purposes of this paragraph, a person who was living with the original tenant as his or her wife or husband shall be treated as the spouse of the original tenant.

3(1) Where paragraph 2 above does not apply, but a person who was a member of the original tenant's family was residing with him in the dwelling-house at the time of and for the period of two years immediately before his death then, after his death, that person ... shall be entitled to an assured tenancy of the dwelling-house by succession.'

The point involved in *Mendoza v Ghaidan* (2002) was whether there could be the transfer of a statutory tenancy to a same-sex partner. The wording of paras 2 and 3 appears to make it quite clear that a same-sex partner only qualifies by virtue of being a member of the family under para 3(1) and so is entitled to only an assured tenancy. This was the decision which had been reached by the House of Lords in the earlier case of *Fitzpatrick v Sterling Housing Association* [2001] 1 AC 27. The Court of Appeal reconsidered the law because of the effect of the HRA 1998 and decisions of the ECtHR. They had to decide whether this provision of the Rent Act 1977 infringed Article 14 (which prohibits discrimination) of the ECHR. The Court of Appeal held that the wording did appear to breach the Convention. Giving judgment, Buxton LJ said:

JUDGMENT

'In order to remedy this breach of the Convention the court must, if it can, read the Schedule so that its provisions are rendered compatible with the Convention rights of the survivors of same-sex partnerships. The width of this duty, imposed by section 3 of the HRA 1998, has been emphasised by Lord Steyn in *R v A* [2001] 2 WLR 1546.

That duty can be properly discharged by reading the words "as his or her wife or husband" to mean "as *if they were* his or her wife or husband". That wording achieves what is required in the present case, and does not open the door to lesser relationships (such as, for instance, sisters sharing a house, or long-term lodgers) because those relationships do not enjoy the marriage-like characteristics that for instance Lord Nicholls discerned in *Fitzpatrick*.'

So in *Mendoza v Ghaidan* (2002) the judges were prepared to read words into the Rent Act 1977 to achieve the result they desired. In the case of *Fitzpatrick v Sterling Housing Association* (2001) the House of Lords had not been prepared to do this. The Lords thought that the 1977 Act was clear and that only a husband or a wife was entitled to be a statutory tenant. In fact, it is almost certainly true that Parliament, when passing the Act, did intend that only a husband or wife was entitled to a statutory tenancy. The case also raises an interesting comparison to *DPP v Bull* (1994). In *Mendoza v Ghaidan* (2002) it could be argued that the words 'husband' and 'wife' are gender-specific, unlike the word 'prostitute' considered in *DPP v Bull* (1994) which is gender-neutral. However, the Court of Appeal was prepared to ignore this, as Buxton LJ went on to say:

JUDGMENT

'It is quite true, as Mr Small pointed out, that the words "husband" and "wife" are in their natural meaning gender-specific. They are also, however, in their natural meaning limited to persons who are party to a lawful marriage. Parliament, by paragraph 2(2), removed that last requirement. And Parliament having swallowed the camel of including unmarried partners within the protection given to married couples, it is not for this court to strain at the gnat of including such partners who are of the same sex as each other.'

In fact, the Court of Appeal could have held that the words were limited to their natural gender-specific meanings. It could then have declared that the Rent Act 1977 was incompatible with human rights and so left it to Parliament to amend the Act. This route would have been the passive one. Instead, the Court of Appeal chose to be more active and create law.

3.1.4 Interpretation or construction?

Many old textbooks write about the construction of statutes. Is this the same as interpretation? Well, no. 'Interpretation' really means making out the meaning of the words, while 'construction' is what happens when judges resolve any ambiguities or uncertainties. This means that every time there is a dispute as to what an Act means the court has to interpret it, i.e. decide what the meaning is. However, it is only if that meaning is not clear from the actual words, because, for example, there are uncertainties or ambiguities, that the court will have to construct the statute. 'Construct' in this sense means build up the meaning. This was made very clear in a judgment in *Franklin v Attorney General* [1973] 1 All ER 879 when Lawson J said:

'I approach the answer to the question in two stages. Stage one is this: whether the meaning of the Cyprus Act 1960 in this respect is clear and unambiguous, and if so, what does it mean? At this stage I look at the words of the enactment as a whole, including the Schedule, and I use no further aids, no further extrinsic aids in order to reach a conclusion as to the clear and unambiguous meaning of the words … If I find that the answer on the first stage in my inquiry is that the meaning of the Act in this respect is ambiguous, then I have to go on to the second stage and consider two possible different meanings … Now if I get to this second stage, then in my judgment, and then only, am I entitled to look at extrinsic aids, such as the long title, the headings, the side-notes, other legislation; then only am I entitled to resort to maxims of construction.'

Although 'interpretation' and 'construction' have different meanings, today it is more usual to refer only to 'interpretation' in a wider sense covering both meanings.

3.1.5 Parliamentary definitions

In order to help with the understanding of a statute, Parliament sometimes includes sections defining certain words used in that statute. Such sections are called interpretation sections. In the Theft Act 1968, for example, the definition of 'theft' is given in s1, and then ss2–6 define the key words in that definition.

In some Acts where Parliament wants to make sure that a particular word covers a wider than usual range, this can be made clear in the Act. For example, in the Theft Act 1968 an important element in the offence of burglary is that the defendant has to enter a building or part of a building as a trespasser. The Act does not define 'building' but instead gives an extended meaning to it, to include inhabited places such as houseboats or caravans, which would otherwise not be included in the offence. This is set out in s9(4) of the Theft Act 1968:

SECTION

's 9(4) References … to a building shall apply also to an inhabited vehicle or vessel, and shall apply to any such vehicle or vessel at times when the person having a habitation is not there as well as at times when he is.'

To help the judges with general words, Parliament has also passed the Interpretation Act 1978 which sets down some general rules for interpretation. Among these are the rules that in any Act, unless the contrary appears, 'he' includes 'she', and singular includes plural. This rule does not apply to Acts setting out sexual offences, so the provisions of the Interpretation Act 1978 could not be used in *DPP v Bull* (1994).

3.2 The three 'rules'

As we have seen, despite various parliamentary aids, there may still be problems in deciding exactly what a particular Act refers to or what precisely it covers. Judges have coped with this problem over the centuries by developing the three so-called 'rules' of interpretation. These are:

- the literal rule;
- the golden rule;
- the mischief rule.

These rules take different approaches to interpretation and some judges prefer to use one rule, while other judges prefer another rule. This means that in English law the interpretation of a statute may differ according to which judge is hearing the case. However, once an interpretation has been laid down, it may then form a precedent for future cases under the normal rules of judicial precedent. Since the three rules can result in very different decisions, it is important to understand them. However, they do not have to be used and, in more recent times, judges have tended to use two main approaches instead of the supposed 'rules'. These are:

- the literal approach;
- the purposive approach.

3.2.1 The literal rule

Under this rule courts will give words their plain, ordinary or literal meaning, even if the result is not very sensible. This idea was expressed by Lord Esher in *R v Judge of the City of London Court* [1892] 1 QB 273 when he said:

JUDGMENT

'If the words of an Act are clear then you must follow them even though they lead to a manifest absurdity. The court has nothing to do with the question whether the legislature has committed an absurdity.'

This does not seem to be a very constructive attitude towards applying words in legislation. Parliament would certainly not have intended the effect of any Act to be absurd. However, it does mean that judges are not imposing their ideas of what they think the law should be; they are leaving it to Parliament to make the law. The reason for using the literal rule was explained rather better by Lord Bramwell in *Hill v East and West India Dock Co* [1884] 9 App Cas 448 when he said:

JUDGMENT

'I should like to have a good definition of what is such an absurdity that you are to disregard the plain words of an Act of Parliament. It is to be remembered that what seems absurd to one man does not seem absurd to another. … I think it is infinitely better, although an absurdity or an injustice or other objectionable result may be evolved as the consequences of your construction, to adhere to the words of an Act of Parliament and leave the legislature to set it right than to alter those words according to one's notion of an absurdity.'

The literal rule developed in the early nineteenth century and has been the main rule applied by the courts ever since then. It has been used in many cases, even though the result may in some cases create an absurdity. This is illustrated in the following case:

CASE EXAMPLE

Whiteley v Chappell [1868] 4 LR QB 147

The defendant was charged under a section which made it an offence to impersonate 'any person entitled to vote'. The defendant had pretended to be a person whose name was on the voters' list, but who had died. The court held that the defendant was not guilty since a dead person is not, in the literal meaning of the words, 'entitled to vote'.

Another case in which the use of literal rule made the law as Parliament had intended it virtually unenforceable was *Fisher v Bell* [1960] 3 All ER 731. That case involved the interpretation of s1(1) of the Restriction of Offensive Weapons Act 1959. This section stated:

SECTION

's 1(1)   Any person who manufactures, sells or hires or offers for sale or hire or lends or gives to any other person –

(a) any knife which has a blade which opens automatically by hand pressure applied to a button, spring or other device in or attached to the handle of the knife, sometimes known as a "flick knife" … shall be guilty of an offence.'

In *Fisher v Bell* (1960) the defendant was a shop-keeper who had displayed a flick knife marked with a price in his shop window but had not actually sold any. He was charged under s1(1) of the 1959 Act and the court had to decide whether he was guilty of offering the knife for sale. There is a technical legal meaning in contract law of 'offer'. This has the effect that displaying an article in a shop window is not an offer; it is only an invitation to treat. The Court of Appeal held that under the literal legal meaning of 'offer', the shop-keeper had not made an offer to sell and so was not guilty of the offence. Parliament immediately changed the law to make it clear that displaying a flick knife in a shop window was an offence.

Yet another case which may be considered to have led to an absurd result is *Cheeseman v DPP*, *The Times*, 2 November 1990:

CASE EXAMPLE

Cheeseman v DPP, *The Times*, 2 November 1990

The defendant was charged with wilfully and indecently exposing his person in a street to the annoyance of passengers contrary to s28 of the Town Police Clauses Act 1847. Members of the public had complained of the behaviour of a man in a public lavatory. Police officers were stationed in the lavatory following these complaints in order to catch the offender. They witnessed the defendant masturbating and they arrested him. The defendant's conviction was quashed by the Queen's Bench Divisional Court because the police officers were not 'passengers' within the meaning of s28.

The whole case rested on the meaning of the word 'passengers' and, as already explained at section 3.1, the meaning in 1847 was 'a passer-by or through; a traveller (usually on foot); a wayfarer'. Although the behaviour had occurred in a public lavatory rather than the street, that did not prevent the defendant from being guilty as s81 of the Public Health Amendment Act 1902 had extended the meaning of the word 'street' in s28 of the Town Police Clauses Act 1847 to include any place of public resort under the control of the local authority.

The judges in the Divisional Court pointed out that before the meaning of 'street' was enlarged in 1907 the old dictionary definition of 'passenger' was not hard to apply: it clearly covered anyone using the street for ordinary purposes of passage or travel. The problem was that the dictionary definition could not be so aptly applied to a place of public resort such as a public lavatory. However, the judges thought that on a common-sense reading and when applied in context, 'passenger' had to mean anyone resorting in the ordinary way to a place for one of the purposes for which people would normally resort to it. Applying this to the case, they held that the two police officers were not 'passengers' because they had been stationed in the public lavatory in order to catch the person committing acts which had given rise to earlier complaints. They were not resorting to that place of public resort in the ordinary way but were there for a special purpose.

The literal rule is also criticised because it can lead to what are considered harsh decisions, as in *London & North Eastern Railway Co v Berriman* (1946) (see section 3.1.1) where a railway worker was killed while doing maintenance work on a railway line. His widow tried to claim compensation because no look-out man had been provided. The court took the words 'relaying' and 'repairing' in their literal meaning and said that oiling points was maintaining the line and not relaying or repairing, so that Mrs Berriman's claim failed. With decisions such as those above it is not surprising that Professor Michael Zander has denounced the literal rule as being mechanical and divorced from the realities of the use of language. The Law Commission, which produced a report 'The Interpretation of Statutes' in 1969, also thought that the literal rule creates problems. It wrote:

QUOTATION

'To place undue emphasis on the literal meaning of words of a provision is to assume an unattainable perfection in draftsmanship; it presupposes that the draftsmen can always choose words to describe the situations intended to be covered by the provision which will leave no room for a difference of opinion as to their meaning. Such an approach ignores the limitations of language, which is not infrequently demonstrated even at the level of the House of Lords when Law Lords differ as to the so-called "plain meaning" of words.'

In fact, many words have more than one meaning, as can be seen by looking up words in a dictionary. Since the literal rule cannot always provide clarity, other methods of interpretation have been created by the judges.

3.2.2 The golden rule

This rule is a modification of the literal rule. The golden rule starts by looking at the literal meaning but the court is then allowed to avoid an interpretation which would lead to an absurd result. The first use of the name 'golden rule' is thought to have been in *Mattison v Hart* [1854] 14 CB 357 when Jervis CJ said:

JUDGMENT

'We must, therefore, in this case have recourse to what is called the golden rule of construction, as applied to Acts of Parliament, viz, to give the words used by the legislature their plain meaning unless it is manifest from the general scope and intention of the statute, injustice and absurdity would result.'

Although this says that the plain meaning of the words should be applied (i.e. the literal rule), it does seem to allow quite wide deviation from the literal rule. This is because it can be done where there is 'injustice or absurdity'. The rule was more closely defined in *Grey v Pearson* [1857] 6 HL Cas 61 by Baron Parke when he stated:

JUDGMENT

'The grammatical and ordinary sense of the words is to be adhered to, unless that would lead to some absurdity, to some repugnance or inconsistency with the rest of the instrument, in which case the grammatical and ordinary sense of the words may be modified, so as to avoid the absurdity and inconsistency, but no further.'

Again it is stressed that the literal rule is the starting point but instead of the wide term 'injustice' the use of the golden rule is restricted to where there is absurdity, repugnance or inconsistency with the rest of the Act. In the twentieth century judges had two views on how far the golden rule should be used. The first is very narrow and is shown by Lord Reid's comments in *Jones v DPP* (1962) when he said:

JUDGMENT

'It is a cardinal principle applicable to all kinds of statutes that you may not for any reason attach to a statutory provision a meaning which the words of that provision cannot reasonably bear. If they are capable of more than one meaning, then you can choose between those meanings, but beyond this you cannot go.'

So under the narrow application of the golden rule the court may only choose between the possible meanings of a word or phrase. If there is only one meaning, then that must be taken. However, the golden rule does allow the courts to modify words of a statute when it is necessary to avoid an absurdity or repugnant situation. This happened in *Adler v George* [1964] 2 QB 7 in which there was a prosecution under the Official Secrets Act 1920 for an offence of obstructing HM Forces 'the vicinity of' a prohibited place. The defendants in the case had obstructed HM Forces *in* a prohibited place. The Divisional Court read the Act as being '*in* or in the vicinity of' to avoid the absurdity of being able to convict someone who was near (in the vicinity of) a prohibited place but not being able to convict someone who carried out the obstruction in the place.

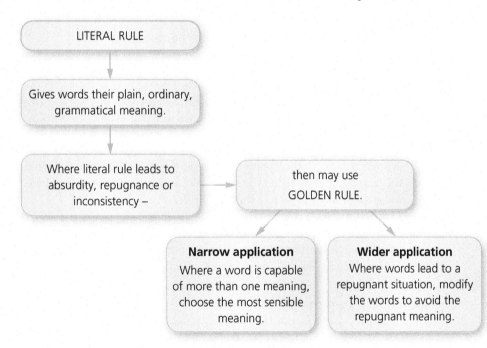

Figure 3.1 The literal and golden rules

A wider application of the golden rule is where the words have only one clear meaning, but that meaning would lead to a repugnant situation. In *Grey v Pearson* (1857) repugnancy was specifically mentioned. This allows the courts more freedom to modify the words of the legislation in order to avoid the problem. A very clear example of this was the case of *Re Sigsworth* [1935] Ch 89:

CASE EXAMPLE

Re Sigsworth [1935] Ch 89

A son had murdered his mother. The mother had not made a will, so normally her estate would have been inherited by her next-of-kin according to the rules set out in the Administration of Justice Act 1925. This meant that the murderer son would have inherited as her 'issue'. There was no ambiguity in the words of the Act, but the court was not prepared to let a murderer benefit from his crime, so it was held that the literal rule should not apply; the golden rule would be used to prevent the repugnant situation of the son inheriting. Effectively, the court was writing into the Act that the 'issue' would not be entitled to inherit where they had killed the deceased.

This use of the golden rule is more in line with the modern purposive approach and decisions such as *R v Registrar General, ex p Smith* [1991] 2 All ER 88 (see section 3.3).

3.2.3 The mischief rule

This rule gives a judge more discretion than the other two rules. The definition of the rule comes from *Heydon's Case* [1584] Co Rep 7a, where it was said that there were four points the court should consider. These, in the original language of that old case, were:

JUDGMENT

'1st What was the Common Law before the making of the Act.

2nd What was the mischief and defect for which the Common Law did not provide.

3rd What remedy the Parliament hath resolved and appointed to cure the disease of the commonwealth.

And, 4th the true reason of the remedy; and then the office of all Judges is always to make such construction as shall suppress the mischief, and advance the remedy.'

So under this rule the court should look to see what the law was before the Act was passed in order to discover what gap or 'mischief' the Act was intended to cover. Then the court should interpret the Act in such a way that the gap is covered. This is clearly a quite different approach to the literal rule.

An example of a case in which the mischief rule was used is *Smith v Hughes* [1960] 2 All ER 859. In this case the court had to interpret s1(1) of the Street Offences Act 1959 which said 'it shall be an offence for a common prostitute to loiter or solicit in a street or public place for the purpose of prostitution'.

CASE EXAMPLE

Smith v Hughes [1960] 2 All ER 859

Six women had been convicted under s1(1) of the Street Offences Act 1959 and in each case they argued on appeal that they were not 'in a street or public place' as required by the Act for them to be guilty. One woman had been on a balcony and the others had been at the windows of ground-floor rooms, with the window either half-open or closed. In each case the women were attracting the attention of men by calling to them or tapping on the window. The court decided that they were guilty.

In this case the court did not use the plain, ordinary grammatical meaning of the words 'in a street or public place'. Instead the judges looked to see what mischief the Act was aimed at. This was explained by Parker LCJ when he said:

JUDGMENT

'For my part I approach the matter by considering what is the mischief aimed at by this Act. Everybody knows that this was an Act to clean up the streets, to enable people to walk along the streets without being molested or solicited by common prostitutes. Viewed in this way it can matter little whether the prostitute is soliciting while in the street or is standing in the doorway or on a balcony, or at a window, or whether the window is shut or open or half open.'

A similar point arose in *Eastbourne Borough Council v Stirling, The Times,* 16 November 2000, where a taxi driver was charged with 'plying for hire in any street' without a licence to do so. His vehicle was parked on a taxi rank on a station forecourt. He was found guilty as, although he was on private land, he was likely to get customers from the street. The court referred to *Smith v Hughes* (1960) and said that it was the same point. A driver would be plying for hire in the street when his vehicle was positioned so that the offer of services was aimed at people in the street.

An interesting point shown by *Smith v Hughes* (1960) is that the same judge may choose to use the literal rule in one case and the mischief rule in another. Parker LCJ, who gave the judgment in *Smith v Hughes* (1960), also gave the judgment in *Fisher v Bell* (1960) where he chose to use the literal rule. This has prompted the comment that judges choose whichever rule gives the result that they wish to achieve in the case.

Another case in which the mischief rule was used is *Royal College of Nursing v DHSS* [1981] 1 All ER 545. However, in this case there was disagreement among the judges in the House of Lords as to the method of interpretation to be used.

CASE EXAMPLE

Royal College of Nursing v DHSS [1981] 1 All ER 545

This case concerned the wording of the Abortion Act 1967, which provided that no criminal offence was committed 'when a pregnancy is terminated by a registered medical practitioner'. When the Act was passed in 1967 the procedure for carrying out an abortion was such that only a doctor (a registered medical practitioner) could do it. However, by 1980, improvements in medical technique meant that pregnancy could be terminated by inducing premature labour with drugs. The first part of the procedure for this was carried out by a doctor, but the second part could be performed by nurses without a doctor present. The Department of Health and Social Security issued a circular giving advice that it was legal for nurses to carry out the second part of the procedure, provided that the termination had been decided upon by a registered medical practitioner, initiated by him and he remained responsible throughout the process for its overall conduct, though he did not have to be present throughout. The Royal College of Nursing sought a declaration that the circular was wrong in law.

At first instance the judge refused the declaration and held that the advice in the circular did not involve the performance of any unlawful act by nurses. The Court of Appeal reversed this decision but on appeal to the House of Lords the majority (three) of the judges reinstated the decision of the judge at first instance. They held that the procedure was lawful under the Abortion Act 1967. However, the other two judges in the House of Lords dissented, holding that the procedure was not lawful. Of the three judges in the majority, Lord Diplock clearly based his judgment on the mischief rule. He said:

Judgment

'The Abortion Act 1967 which it falls to this House to construe is described in its long title as "An Act to amend and clarify the law relating to termination of pregnancy by registered medical practitioners …". Whatever may be the technical imperfections of its draftsmanship, however, its purpose in my view becomes clear if one starts by considering what was the state of the law relating to abortion before the passing of the Act, what was the mischief that required amendment, and in what respect was the existing law unclear … My Lords, the wording and structure of the section are far from elegant, but the policy of the Act, it seems to me, is clear. There are two aspects to it: the first is to broaden the grounds upon which abortions may be lawfully obtained; the second is to ensure that the abortion is carried out with proper skill and in hygienic conditions.'

So Lord Diplock relied on the fact that the mischief Parliament was trying to remedy was the unsatisfactory state of the law before 1967, as a result of which there were a large number of illegal abortions (often called 'back-street abortions') which were carried out in unhygienic conditions. In some cases this led to the death of the woman whose pregnancy was terminated. He also relied on the policy of the 1967 Act (and therefore the policy of Parliament) which was to broaden the grounds for abortion and ensure that they were carried out with proper skill in hospital. Lord Keith of Kinkel also relied on the policy of the Act. He pointed out:

Judgment

' "Termination of pregnancy" is an expression commonly used … to describe in neutral and unemotive terms the bringing about of an abortion. So used, it is capable of covering the whole process designed to lead to that result, and in my view it does so in the present context … This conclusion is the more satisfactory as it appears to me to be fully in accordance with that part of the policy and purpose of the Act which was directed to securing that socially acceptable abortions should be carried out under the safest conditions attainable.'

An interesting point about Lord Keith's judgment is that he was prepared to put a broad literal meaning on the words 'termination of pregnancy', so that he felt that both the literal meaning and the policy view gave the same result in the case. The other judge who held that the drug-induced method of terminating a pregnancy which was carried out by nurses was lawful was Lord Roskill. He came to this conclusion based on the factual situation that the steps taken by a nurse in giving the drugs were lawful:

Judgment

'provided that the entirety of the treatment for the termination of the pregnancy and her participation in it is at all times under the control of the doctor even though the doctor is not present throughout the entirety of the treatment'.

The two dissenting judges took the literal view and said that the words of the Act were clear and that terminations could only be carried out by a registered medical practitioner. Lord Edmund-Davies stated that to read the words 'terminated by a registered medical practitioner' as meaning 'terminated by treatment for the termination of pregnancy in accordance with recognised medical practice' was redrafting the Act 'with a vengeance'.

This case is an example of how even judges in the House of Lords cannot agree on the method of interpretation to be used. At the Court of Appeal it also is another example that judges are inconsistent in their approach to which rule they use. This was shown by the fact that Lord Denning, usually noted for using a more purposive approach and 'filling in the gaps' (see section 3.5), decided that the procedure was unlawful. He based this decision on the literal meaning of the Act, saying:

JUDGMENT

'If the Department of Health want the nurses to terminate a pregnancy, the Minister should go to Parliament and get the statute altered. He should ask them to amend it by adding the words "or by a suitably qualified person in accordance with the written instructions of a registered medical practitioner". I doubt whether Parliament would accept the amendment. It is too controversial. At any rate that is the way to amend the law.'

One of the questions with the mischief rule is what the court can look at to discover the mischief which Parliament was trying to put right. As seen in Lord Diplock's judgment in the *Royal College of Nursing v DHSS* (1981) case, the courts can look at the rest of the Act. Lord Diplock specifically referred to the long title of the Act. It is also allowable to consider outside factors such as the social or other conditions which led to the passing of the Act. The extent to which other outside (extrinsic) aids can be used is considered at section 3.7.

The case of *Royal College of Nursing v DHSS* (1981) also raises the question of whether the mischief rule and the more modern purposive approach are the same. Certainly Lord Diplock appeared to combine the two, but it can also be said that the purposive approach goes beyond looking at the mischief which the Act was passed to cover (see section 3.3 for further discussion of the purposive approach).

ACTIVITY

Applying the law

Read the facts below of the following case: *R v Maginnis* [1987] 1 All ER 907.
The case involved the wording of s5 of the Misuse of Drugs Act 1971 which states:

Section

's 5 …it is an offence for a person to have a controlled drug in his possession, whether lawful or not, with intent to supply it to another'.

The police had found a package of cannabis in Maginnis's car. He told the police that the package was not his but had been left in his car by a friend to be collected by the friend later. The defendant was convicted of the offence and appealed on the ground that his intention to return the drug to its owner could not amount to an intention to 'supply' the drug within the meaning of s5 of the Act.

Consider the word 'supply' and explain how the case could have been decided using:

1. the literal rule;
2. the golden rule;
3. the mischief rule.

3.3 The purposive approach

This goes beyond the mischief rule in that the court is not just looking to see what the gap was in the old law; the judges are deciding what they believe Parliament meant to achieve. The champion of this approach in English law was Lord Denning. His attitude towards statutory interpretation is shown when he said in the case of *Magor and St Mellons v Newport Corporation* [1950] 2 All ER 1226:

JUDGMENT

'We sit here to find out the intention of Parliament and carry it out, and we do this better by filling in the gaps and making sense of the enactment than by opening it up to destructive analysis.'

However his attitude was criticised by judges in the House of Lords when they heard the appeal in the case. Lord Simonds called Lord Denning's approach 'a naked usurpation of the legislative function under the thin disguise of interpretation' and pointed out that 'if a gap is disclosed the remedy lies in an amending Act'. Another judge, Lord Scarman, said:

JUDGMENT

'If Parliament says one thing but means another, it is not, under the historic principles of the common law, for the courts to correct it. The general principle must surely be acceptable in our society. We are to be governed not by Parliament's intentions but by Parliament's enactments.'

This speech shows the problem with the purposive approach. Should the judges refuse to follow the clear words of Parliament? How do they know what Parliament's intentions were? Opponents of the purposive approach say that it is impossible to discover Parliament's intentions; only the words of the statute can show what Parliament wanted. Despite opposition to the approach it is being used more and more often by the courts. An example is *R v Registrar General, ex p Smith* [1991] 2 All ER 88 in which the court had to consider s51 of the Adoption Act 1976 which states:

SECTION

's 51(1) Subject to subsections (4) and (6), the Registrar-General shall on an application made in the prescribed manner by an adopted person a record of whose birth is kept by the Registrar-General and who has attained the age of 18 years supply to that person … such information as is necessary to enable that person to obtain a certified copy of the record of his birth.'

Subsection (4) says that before supplying that information the Registrar General has to inform the applicant about counselling services available. Subsection (6) states that if the adoption was before 1975 the Registrar General cannot give the information unless the applicant has attended an interview with a counsellor.

CASE EXAMPLE

R v Registrar General, ex p Smith [1991] 2 All ER 88

The case involved an application by Charles Smith for information to enable him to obtain his birth certificate. Mr Smith had made his application in the correct manner and was prepared to see a counsellor. On a literal view of the 1976 Act the Registrar General had to supply him with the information, since the Act uses the phrase 'shall … supply'. The problem was that Mr Smith had been convicted of two murders and was detained in Broadmoor as he suffered from recurring bouts of psychotic illness. A psychiatrist thought that it was possible he might be hostile towards his natural mother. This posed a difficulty for the court; should they apply the clear meaning of the words in this situation?

The judges in the Court of Appeal decided that the case called for the purposive approach, saying that, despite the plain language of the Act, Parliament could not have intended to promote serious crime. So, in view of the risk to the applicant's natural mother if he discovered her identity, they ruled that the Registrar General did not have to supply any information.

Another example of the use of the purposive approach is *Jones v Tower Boot Co Ltd* [1997] IRLR 168 in which the Court of Appeal had to interpret s32(1) of the Race Relations Act 1976. This section states:

SECTION

's 32(1) Anything done by a person in the course of employment shall be treated for the purposes of this Act … as done by his employer as well as by him, whether or not it was done with the employer's knowledge or approval.'

CASE EXAMPLE

Jones v Tower Boot Co Ltd [1997] IRLR 168

Raymondo Jones worked for Tower Boot as a machine operative for one month. During this time he was subjected to a number of unpleasant incidents of racial harassment by fellow workers. These included his arm being burnt by a hot screwdriver, being whipped with a piece of welt, having metal bolts thrown at his head. He was also repeatedly called names such as 'chimp', 'monkey' and 'baboon'. It was clear that this was racial harassment by the fellow workers, but the point to be decided was whether the employers were liable for the acts of these employees.

The words 'course of employment' were the critical ones. In the law of tort this phrase has a well-established legal meaning, with the nub of the test being 'whether the unauthorised wrongful act is so connected with that which he was employed to do as to be a mode of doing it'. The employers argued that this literal meaning of 'course of employment' should be used. This would mean that they were not liable for the racial harassment, as burning and whipping another person could not be considered as an improper mode of performing authorised tasks. The Court of Appeal, using the purposive approach, held that the employers were liable for the racial harassment.

Lord Justice Waite considered the principles of statutory interpretation and said:

JUDGMENT

'Two principles are in my view involved. The first is that a statute is to be construed according to its legislative purpose, with due regard to the result which it is the stated or presumed intention of Parliament to achieve and the means provided for achieving it (the "purposive construction"); and the second is that words in a statute are to be given their normal meaning according to the English language unless the context indicates that such words have to be given a special or technical meaning as a term of art (the "linguistic construction").'

Waite LJ also pointed out that the Race Relations Act 1976 and the Sex Discrimination Act 1975 broke new ground in seeking to work upon the minds of men and women and affect their attitude to the social consequences of differences between the sexes or distinction of skin colour. He felt that the general thrust of the Race Relations Act 1976 was to educate, persuade and, where necessary, coerce people into eliminating discrimination. He went on to say:

JUDGMENT

'Since the getting and losing of work, and the daily functioning of the workplace, are prime areas for potential discrimination on grounds of race or sex, it is not surprising that both Acts contain specific provisions to govern the field of employment. Those provisions are themselves wide-ranging ... There is no indication that Parliament intended in any way to limit the general thrust of the legislation.

A purposive construction accordingly requires s32 of the Race Relations Act 1976 to be given a broad interpretation. It would be inconsistent with that requirement to allow the notion of the "course of employment" to be construed in any sense more limited than the natural meaning of those everyday words would allow.'

The use of the purposive approach was particularly important as, if the literal interpretation was taken, it would allow racial harassment on the scale that was suffered by the complainant to 'slip through the net of employer responsibility'. Lord Justice Waite thought that it would be wrong to apply a common law principle which had evolved in another area of the law to deal with vicarious responsibility for a wrongdoing of a wholly different kind. If the literal interpretation was taken it would seriously undermine the Discrimination Acts and 'flout the purpose which they were passed to achieve'.

More recently, in *R (Quintavalle) v Secretary of State* [2003] UKHL 13 the House of Lords used the purposive approach in deciding that organisms created by cell nuclear replacement (CNR) came within the definition of 'embryo' in the Human Fertilisation and Embryology Act 1990. Section 1(1)(a) of this Act states that 'embryo means a live human embryo where fertilisation is complete'. CNR was not possible in 1990 when the Act was passed and the problem is that fertilisation is not used in CNR. Lord Bingham said:

JUDGMENT

'[T]he court's task, within permissible bounds of interpretation is to give effect to Parliament's purpose ... Parliament could not have intended to distinguish between embryos produced by, or without, fertilisation since it was unaware of the latter possibility.'

The House of Lords followed Lord Wilberforce's judgment in *Royal College of Nursing v DHSS* (1981) when he said:

JUDGMENT

'In interpreting an Act of Parliament it is proper, and indeed necessary, to have regard to the state of affairs existing, and known by Parliament to be existing, at the time. It is a fair presumption that Parliament's policy or intention is directed to that state of affairs ... [W]hen a new state of affairs, or a fresh set of facts bearing on the policy, comes into existence, the courts have to consider whether they fall within the Parliamentary intention. They may be held to do so, if they fall within the same genus of facts as do those to which the express policy has been formulated. They may also be held to do so if there can be detected a clear purpose in the legislation which can only be fulfilled if the extension is made.'

In *Inco Europe v First Choice Distribution* [2000] 1 LR 586 the House of Lords pointed out that the courts must be able to correct obvious drafting errors. They held that, in suitable cases, the court can add, omit or substitute words. However, before they do so they must be sure of three matters:

1. the intended purpose of the statute or provision in question;

2. that by inadvertence, the draftsman and Parliament had failed to give effect to that purpose;

3. the substance of the provision that Parliament would have made had the error in the Bill been noticed.

In *R (W a minor) v Leeds Crown Court* [2011] EWHC 2326 (Admin) the Administrative Court looked at the three conditions in *Inco Europe v First Choice Distribution* (2000) and decided that these conditions were not fulfilled. As a result the court could not add words to s29(2) of the Magistrates' Court Act 1980.

CASE EXAMPLE

R (W, a minor) v Leeds Crown Court [2011] EWHC 2326 (Admin)

W was charged with burglary along with an adult. The case was committed to the Crown Court for trial and the adult pleaded guilty. The question arose whether the Crown Court had the power under s29(2) of the Magistrates' Court Act 1980 to remit the case back to a youth court for the defendant to be tried there. The judge at Leeds Crown Court held that there was no power to do so. The Administrative Court confirmed that ruling.

The court pointed out that s29(2) was about the Magistrates' Court. It allows the Magistrates' Court to remit a youth who has been charged with an adult to the Youth Court. Looking at the three matters set out in *Inco Europe v First Choice Distribution* (2000) it was impossible to say that Parliament had intended to include the same power for the Crown Court in the Act.

In explaining the reason for this decision, Sir Anthony May P said:

JUDGMENT

'We would have to find the lacuna in a particular statute and to be sure that Parliament, by sheer oversight, omitted the provision which it is sought to be inserted, and here we are invited to supplement s29(2) of the Magistrates' Court Act 1980, which is about the magistrates' courts and not the plainly obvious place to legislate for a power in the Crown Court. The very subsection has been the subject of an amendment twice in recent years and there is much related legislation where Parliament has considered matters of general relevance ... I am ... not sufficiently confident that I can perceive a lacuna in s29 of the Act.'

This case shows that even the purposive approach has limitations. If the Magistrates' Court has the power to remit youths to the Youth Court rather than be tried in the adult court, it would seem obvious that the Crown Court should also be able to do so. However, the fact that the 1980 Act was only concerned with magistrates' powers, together with the fact that s29 had been amended twice by Parliament, made it impossible for the Administrative Court to find that (as set out in point two of *Inco Europe v First Choice Distribution*) 'by inadvertence, the draftsman and Parliament had failed to give effect to that purpose'.

3.3.1 European influence

The purposive approach is the one preferred by most European countries when interpreting their own legislation. It is also the approach which has been adopted by the CJEU in interpreting EU law. In fact, the Treaty of Rome sets out general principles but without explicit details. Lord Denning said of the Treaty in *Bulmer (HP) Ltd v J Bollinger SA* [1974] 2 All ER 1226:

JUDGMENT

'It lays down general principles. It expresses its aims and purposes. All in sentences of moderate length and commendable style. But it lacks precision. It uses words and phrases without defining what they mean. An English lawyer would look for an interpretation clause, but he would look in vain. There is none. All the way through the Treaty there are gaps and lacunae. These have to be filled in by the judges.'

Since the UK became a member of the EU in 1973 the influence of the European preference for the purposive approach has affected the English courts in two ways. These influences will remain at least until the UK leaves the Union. First, they have had to accept that, at least for law which has been passed as a result of having to conform to a European law, the purposive approach is the correct one to use. This was laid down by the CJEU in *von Colson v Land Nordrhein-Westfalen* (Case 14/83) [1984] ECR 1891; [1986] 2 CMLR 430 when it held:

JUDGMENT

'in applying the national law and in particular the provisions of a national law specifically introduced in order to implement [the Directive], national courts are required to interpret their national law in the light of the wording and the purpose of the Directive'.

This use of the purposive approach to interpret national legislation in the light of an EU directive can be seen in *Pickstone v Freemans plc* [1988] 2 All ER 803. This case involved the interpretation of the Equal Pay Act 1970 which had been amended by adding a new subsection (s(1)(2)(c)), in order to implement the Equal Pay Directive (75/117/EEC). The passing of the Equal Pay Act was a key condition which needed to be met in order for the UK to join the EU. This subsection allowed a claim for equal pay based on the fact that the applicant was doing 'work of equal value' to someone of the opposite sex, even though they were not doing the same job. However, the subsection also stated that if there was someone of the opposite sex doing 'like work' to the applicant, then no claim could be brought under s(1)(2)(c).

CASE EXAMPLE

Pickstone v Freemans plc [1988] 2 All ER 803

Women warehouse operatives were paid the same as male warehouse operatives. However, Ms Pickstone claimed that their work was of equal value to that done by a male warehouse checker, who was paid £4.22 more a week than they were. Their employers argued that as the women were employed on 'like work' to male warehouse operatives then they could not bring a claim under s(1)(2)(c) of the 1970 Act for work of equal value. This was the literal interpretation of the 1970 Act. The House of Lords decided that the literal approach would have left the UK in breach of its treaty obligations to give effect to EU Directives. So it used the purposive approach and held that Ms Pickstone was entitled to claim on the basis of work of equal value even though there was a male employee doing the same work as her.

The second way in which the European use of the purposive approach has influenced statutory interpretation in the English courts is that as judges have to use the purposive approach for EU law, they are becoming more accustomed to it and, therefore, more likely to apply it to English law. It is yet to be seen whether, when the UK leaves the EU, judges will continue to use the 'European' derived purposive approach for interpreting English law.

3.4 Literal approach versus purposive approach

This conflict between the literal approach and the purposive approach is one of the major issues in statutory interpretation. There is still no consensus on which approach should be used. Should judges examine each word and take the words literally or should it be accepted that an Act of Parliament cannot cover every situation and that meanings of words cannot always be exact?

The case of *Cheeseman v DPP* (1990) (see section 3.2.1) illustrates this. In that case the court took the words literally. However, it can be argued that the purposive approach should have been used as the defendant was 'wilfully and indecently exposing his person in a street' and that he was caught doing that. Is it important whether the police officers were 'passengers'? After all they had been sent there because of previous complaints about this type of behaviour. Also, the defendant presumably thought they were ordinary members of the public. It can be argued that the whole purpose of the Act was to prevent this type of behaviour.

In 1969 the Law Commission recommended in its report, 'The Interpretation of Statutes', Law Com No 21, 1969, that legislation should be passed to harmonise the methods of interpretation used by the judges. They put forward draft clauses for this purpose. The most important one stated:

CLAUSE

'cl (b) The principles of interpretation would include:

(i) the preference of a construction which would promote the general legislative purpose over one which would not;

(ii) the preference of a construction which is consistent with the international obligations of the United Kingdom over one which is not.'

Parliament did not act on this recommendation and there is still no legislation which sets out which method of interpretation should be preferred. However, judges are using the purposive approach more readily. In *Notham v London Borough of Barnet* [1978] 1 All ER 1243 Lord Denning quoted from the Law Commission report when he said:

JUDGMENT

'The literal method is now completely out of date … In all cases now in the interpretation of statutes we adopt such a construction as will "promote the general legislative purpose" underlying the provision … Whenever the strict interpretation of a statute gives rise to an absurd and unjust situation, the judges can and should use their good sense to remedy it – by reading words in, if necessary – so as to do what Parliament would have done had they had the situation in mind.'

The use of the purposive approach has been strengthened by the decision in *Pepper (Inspector of Taxes) v Hart* [1993] 1 All ER 42. In this case the House of Lords accepted that it was permissible to look at the records of parliamentary debate in *Hansard* in order to discover Parliament's intention when enacting the relevant legislation (see section 3.7.2 for further discussion on this). In *Pepper v Hart* (1993) Lord Griffiths stated:

JUDGMENT

'The days have long passed when the courts adopted a strict constructionist view of interpretation which required them to adopt the literal meaning of the language. The courts now adopt a purposive approach which seeks to give effect to the true purpose of legislation and are prepared to look at much extraneous material that bears on the background against which the legislation was enacted.'

Yet, despite claims that the purposive approach is now the preferred method, there are still cases in which the courts use the literal approach. An example is the following case:

CASE EXAMPLE

Cutter v Eagle Star Insurance Co Ltd [1998] 4 All ER 417

The claimant was sitting in the front passenger seat of his friend's car, parked in a multi-storey car park. Inflammable gas leaked inside the car from a can of lighter fuel, so that when the driver returned to the car and lit a cigarette, the gas was ignited and the claimant was injured. The claimant sued the driver for negligence and won the case. However, the driver had no money and could not pay the damages. So the claimant tried to claim the money from the driver's insurance company, Eagle Star. The driver's insurance policy provided cover against any liability for death or bodily injury to any person arising out of the use of his car on a 'road'. The Road Traffic Act 1988 defines 'road' as 'any highway and any other road to which the public has access'.

The House of Lords accepted that the true purpose of the Road Traffic Act 1988 was to protect the public from dangers arising from the use of motor vehicles. However, it applied the literal meaning of 'road' and held that the insurance policy did not cover an event occurring in a car park.

Lord Clyde said:

JUDGMENT

'It may be perfectly proper to adopt even a strained construction to enable the object and purpose of legislation to be fulfilled. But it cannot be taken to the length of applying unnatural meanings to familiar words … This must be particularly so where the language has no evident ambiguity or uncertainty about it … Against the employment of a broad approach to express the purpose of the Act must be put the undesirability of adopting anything beyond a strict construction of provisions which have penal consequences.'

So, the rejection of the purposive approach was based on three main points. First, that 'unnatural meanings' should not be applied to ordinary words. Next, that the purposive approach should not be used where the words in the Act are not ambiguous or uncertain. Finally, that where the legislation created a criminal offence, it was undesirable to use a broad approach.

KEY FACTS

Approaches and 'rules' of statutory interpretation

Rule/approach	Comment	Cases
The literal rule	Uses plain ordinary, grammatical meaning of words Avoids judicial law-making *but* Assumes 'unattainable perfection in draftsmanship' May lead to absurd decision May lead to injustice	*Whiteley v Chappell* (1868) *Fisher v Bell* (1960) *London & NE Railway Co v Berriman* (1946)
The golden rule	Starts from the literal approach but avoids absurdity or repugnance or inconsistency Court can modify words or write in words BUT what is an absurdity? Limited in scope	*Re Sigsworth* (1935) *Adler v George* (1964)
The mischief rule	Looks at the gap in the previous law and interprets the words so as to 'advance the remedy' The Law Commission favoured this rule Nearest to the purposive approach	*Smith v Hughes* (1960) *Eastbourne BC v Stirling* (2000) *Royal College of Nursing v DHSS* (1981)
The literal approach	Takes the literal meaning of words (see literal rule above)	
The purposive approach	Looks for the intention of Parliament *but* allows for judicial law-making	*R v Registrar General, ex p Smith* (1991) *Jones v Tower Boot Co* (1997) *R (Quintavalle) v Secretary of State* (2003)

ACTIVITY

Looking at judgments

Read the extract from the judgment below and answer the following questions. References to the relevant paragraphs of the judgment are given for some of the questions.

1. What was the purpose of the Human Fertilisation and Embryology Act 1990? Whereabouts in an Act is the purpose normally expressed?
2. Explain in your own words what Lord Bingham says about parliamentary draftsmen (para 7).
3. When, according to Lord Bingham, is it likely that cases on statutory interpretation will reach the appellate courts?
4. Why does Lord Bingham reject the use of a purely literal interpretation (para 8)?
5. Explain what Lord Bingham means when he says there is a rule that a statute is always speaking (para 9).
6. In your own words, briefly explain the background to the Act.
7. Why did the court need to consider the words 'where fertilisation is complete'?
8. What view did Lord Bingham take of the words 'where fertilisation is complete' (para 14)?

Case example

R v Secretary of State for Health (Respondent), ex parte Quintavalle (on behalf of Pro-Life Alliance) (Appellant) [2003] UKHL 13

Judgment

'1. The issues in this appeal are whether live human embryos created by cell nuclear replacement (CNR) fall outside the regulatory scope of the Human Fertilisation and Embryology Act 1990 and whether licensing of such embryos is prohibited by section 3(3)(d) of that Act. Crane J at first instance held such creation fell outside the scope of the Act and was not prohibited by section 3(3)(d): [2001] 4 All ER 1013: [2001] EWHC Admin 918. The Court of Appeal (Lord Phillips of Worth Matravers MR, Thorpe and Buxton LJJ) agreed with the judge on the second point but reversed his ruling on the first [2002] QB 628; [2002] EWCA Civ 29. Both points were argued before the House.

2. This case is not concerned with embryos created in the ordinary way as a result of sexual intercourse. Nor is it directly concerned with the creation of live human embryos in vitro where the female egg is fertilised by the introduction of male sperm outside the body. CNR, a very recent scientific technique, involves neither of these things. In the Court of Appeal and in the House the parties were content to adopt the clear and succinct explanation given by the judge [Crane J] of what CNR means:

Quotation

"In the ovary the egg is a diploid germ (or reproductive) cell. It is described as 'diploid' because its nucleus contains a full set of 46 chromosomes. By the process of meiotic division the nucleus divides into two parts. Only one of these, a pronucleus containing only 23 chromosomes (described as the 'haploid'), plays any further part in the process. Fertilisation begins when the male germ cell, the sperm, whose pronucleus contains 23 chromosomes, meets the haploid female germ cell and is a continuous process taking up to 24 hours. As part of the process the male and female pronuclei fuse to form one nucleus with a full complement of 46 chromosomes, a process known as syngamy. The one-cell structure that exists following syngamy is the zygote. After several hours the cell divides to create a two-cell zygote. At this stage it is generally referred to as an embryo. At about 15 days after fertilisation a heaping up of cells occurs which is described as the 'primitive streak'. ... Fertilisation may of course take place in the normal way or *in vitro*. ... CNR is a process by which the nucleus, which is diploid, from one cell is transplanted into an unfertilised egg, from which ... the nucleus has been removed. The [replacement] nucleus is derived from either an embryonic or a foetal or an adult cell. The cell is then treated to encourage it to grow and divide, forming first a two-cell structure and then developing in a similar way to an ordinary embryo. ... CNR is a form of cloning. Clones are organisms that are genetically identical to each other. When CNR is used, if the embryo develops into a live individual, that individual is genetically identical to the nucleus transplanted into the egg. There are other methods of cloning ... CNR of the kind under consideration does not ... involve fertilisation".

The Act

3. The 1990 Act was passed "to make provision in connection with human embryos and any subsequent development of such embryos; to prohibit certain practices in connection with embryos and gametes; to establish Human Fertilisation and Embryology Authority", and for other purposes. The sections at the heart of this appeal are sections 1 and 3, which I should quote in full:

Section

"1(1)   In this Act, except where otherwise stated –

    (a) embryo means a live human embryo where fertilisation is complete, and

    (b) references to an embryo include an egg in the process of fertilisation, and, for this purpose, fertilisation is not complete until the appearance of a two cell zygote.

(2)   The Act, so far as it governs bringing about the creation of an embryo, applies only to bringing about the creation of an embryo outside the human body; and in this Act –

    (a) references to embryos the creation of which was brought about *in vitro* (in their application to those where fertilisation is complete) are to those where fertilisation began outside the human body whether or not it was completed there, and creation was brought about *in vitro*.

(3)   This Act so far as it governs the keeping of use of an embryo, applies only to keeping or use of an embryo outside the human body.

(4)   References in this Act to gametes, eggs or sperm, except where otherwise stated, are to live human gametes, eggs or sperm but references below in this Act to gametes or eggs do not include eggs in the process of fertilisation.

    ...

3(1) No person shall –

    (a) bring about the creation of an embryo, or

    (b) keep or use an embryo, except in pursuance of a licence.

(2)   No person shall place in a woman –

    (a) a live embryo other than a human embryo, or

    (b) any live gametes other than human gametes.

(3)   A licence cannot authorise –

    (a) keeping or using an embryo after the appearance of the primitive streak,

    (b) placing an embryo in any animal,

    (c) keeping or using an embryo in any circumstances in which regulation prohibits its keeping or its use, or

    (d) replacing a nucleus of a cell of an embryo with a nucleus taken from a cell of any person, embryo or subsequent development of an embryo.

(4)   For the purpose of subsection (3)(a) above, the primitive streak is to be taken to have appeared in an embryo not later than the end of the period of 14 days beginning with the day when the gametes are mixed, not counting any time during which the embryo is stored."

    ...

7. Such is the skill of parliamentary draftsmen that most statutory enactments are expressed in language which is clear and unambiguous and gives rise to no serious controversy. But these are not the provisions which reach the courts, or at any rate the appellate courts. Where parties expend substantial resources arguing about the effects of a statutory provision it is usually because the provision is, or is said to be, capable of bearing two or more different meanings, or to be of doubtful application to the particular case which has now arisen, perhaps because the statutory language is said to be inapt to apply to it, sometimes because the situation which had arisen is one which the draftsman could not have foreseen and for which he has accordingly made no express provision.

8. The basic task of the court is to ascertain and give effect to the true meaning of what Parliament has said in the enactment to be construed. But that is not to say that attention should be confined and a literal interpretation given to the particular provisions which give rise to difficulty. Such an approach not only encourages immense prolixity [long-windedness] in drafting, since the draftsman will feel obliged to provide expressly for every contingency which may possibly arise. It may also (under the banner of loyalty to the will of Parliament) lead to the frustration of that will, because undue concentration on the minutiae of the enactment may lead the court to neglect the purpose which Parliament intended to achieve when it enacted the statute. Every statute other than a purely consolidating statute is, after all, enacted to make some change, or address some problem, or remove some blemish, or effect some improvement in the national life. The court's task, within the permissible bounds of interpretation, is to give effect to Parliament's purpose. So the controversial provisions should be read in the context of the statute as a whole, and the statute as a whole should be read in the historical context of the situation which led to its enactment.

9. There is, I think, no inconsistency between the rule that statutory language retains the meaning it had when Parliament used it and the rule that a statute is always speaking. If Parliament had, however long ago, passed an Act applicable to dogs, it could not properly be interpreted to apply to cats; but it could properly be held to apply to animals which were not regarded as dogs when the Act was passed but are so regarded now. The meaning of "cruel and unusual punishments" has not changed over the years since 1689, but many punishments which were not then thought to fall within that category would now be held to do so. The courts have frequently had to grapple with the question of whether a modern invention or activity falls within old statutory language ... A revealing example is found in *Grant v Southwestern and County Properties Ltd* [1975] Ch 185, where Walton J had to decide whether a tape recording fell within the expression "document" in the Rules of the Supreme Court. Pointing out that the furnishing of information had been treated as one of the main functions of a document, the judge concluded that the tape recording was a document.

...

The background to the Act

11. The birth of the first child resulting from *in vitro* fertilisation in July 1978 prompted much ethical and scientific debate which in turn led to the appointment in July 1982 of a Committee of Inquiry under the chairmanship of Dame Mary Warnock DBE to

Quotation

"consider recent and potential developments in medicine and science related to human fertilisation and embryology; to consider what policies and safeguards should be applied, including consideration of the social, ethical and legal implications of these developments; and to make recommendations".

The Committee reported in July 1984 (Cmnd 9314). A White Paper was published in November 1987 (Cm 259) when the Department of Health and Social Security recognised (paragraph 6) "the particular difficulties of framing legislation on these sensitive issues against a background of fast-moving medical and scientific development".

12. There is no doubting the sensitivity of the issues. There were those who considered the creation of embryos, and thus of life, *in vitro* to be either sacrilegious or ethically repugnant and wished to ban such activities altogether. There were others who considered that these new techniques, by offering means of enabling the infertile to have children

and increasing knowledge of congenital disease, had the potential to improve the human condition, and this view also did not lack religious and moral argument to support it. Nor can one doubt the difficulty of legislation against a background of fast-moving medical science and scientific development. It is not often that Parliament has to frame legislation apt to apply to developments at the advanced cutting edge of science.

13. The solution recommended and embodied in the 1990 Act was not to ban all creation and subsequent use of live human embryos produced *in vitro* but instead, and subject to certain express prohibitions of which some have been noted above, to permit such creation and use subject to specified conditions, restrictions and time limits and subject to … regimes of control. The merits of this solution are not for the House in its judicial capacity. It is, however, plain that while Parliament outlawed certain grotesque possibilities (such as placing a live animal embryo in a woman or a live human embryo in an animal), it otherwise opted for a strict regime of control. No activity within this field was left unregulated. There was to be no free for all.

Section 1(1)(a)

14. It is against this background that one comes to interpret section 1(1)(a) … [T]he Act is dealing with live human embryos "where fertilisation is complete" … But the Act is directed only to the creation of embryos *in vitro*, outside the human body (section 1(2)). Can Parliament have been intending to distinguish between live human embryos produced by fertilisation of a female egg and live human embryos produced without such fertilisation? The answer must certainly be negative, since Parliament was unaware that the latter alternative was physically possible. This suggests that the four words [where fertilisation is complete] were not intended to form an integral part of the definition of embryo but were directed to the time at which it should be treated as such … The somewhat marginal importance of the four words is in my opinion indicated by the fact that section 1(1)(b) appears to contradict them. The crucial point … is that this was an Act passed for protection of live human embryos created outside the human body. The essential thrust of section 1(1)(a) was directed to such embryos, not to the manner of their creation, which Parliament (entirely understandably on the then current state of scientific knowledge) took for granted.'

Lord Bingham of Cornhill

Applying the rules of interpretation

In the judgment above, Lord Bingham went on to refer to the judgment of Lord Wilberforce in *Royal College of Nursing v DHSS* [1981] 1 All ER 545. Part of this was given at section 3.3 but the whole part quoted by Lord Bingham is now given here.

Judgment

'In interpreting an Act of Parliament it is proper, and indeed necessary, to have regard to the state of affairs existing, and known by Parliament to be existing, at the time. It is a fair presumption that Parliament's policy or intention is directed to that state of affairs. Leaving aside cases of omission by inadvertence, this not being such a case, when a new state of affairs, or a fresh set of facts bearing on the policy, comes into existence, the courts have to consider whether they fall within the Parliamentary intention. They may be held to do so, if they fall within the same genus of facts as do those to which the express policy has been formulated. They may also be held to do so if there can be detected a clear purpose in the legislation which can only be fulfilled if the extension is made. How liberally these principles may be applied must depend upon the nature of the enactment, and the strictness or otherwise of the words in which it has been expressed. The courts should be less willing to extend expressed meaning if it is clear that the Act in question was designed to be restrictive or circumscribed in its operation rather than liberal or permissive. They will be much less willing to do so where the subject matter is different in kind or dimension from that for which the legislation was passed. In any event there is one course which the courts cannot take, under the law of this country; they cannot fill gaps; they cannot by asking the question "What would Parliament have done in the current case – not being one in contemplation – if the facts had been before it?" attempt themselves to supply the answer, if the answer is not to be found in the terms of the Act itself.'

Lord Wilberforce

Lord Bingham then went on to apply the guidance given in Lord Wilberforce's judgment. Lord Bingham considered three points:

1. Does the genus of live human embryos by CNR fall within the same genus of facts as those to which the expressed policy of Parliament has been formulated?
2. Is the operation of the Human Fertilisation and Embryology Act 1990 to be regarded as liberal and permissive in its operation or is it restrictive and circumscribed?
3. Is an embryo created by CNR different in kind or dimension from that for which the Act was passed?

Look back at the facts in *R v Secretary of State for Health (Respondent), ex parte Quintavalle* (2003), apply the guidance of Lord Wilberforce yourself and answer the three points above.

Having done this, compare your answers with those of Lord Bingham which can be found in the online report for the case at para 15.

House of Lords decisions can be found at www.parliament.uk. Search for judgments.

3.5 Rules of language

Even the literal rule does not take words in complete isolation. It is common sense that the other words in the Act must be looked at to see if they affect the word or phrase which is in dispute. In looking at the other words in the Act, the courts have developed a number of minor rules which can help to make the meaning of words and phrases clear where a particular sentence construction has been used. There are three main rules of language. They are:

- the *ejusdem generis* rule;
- *expressio unius est exclusio alterius* (the mention of one thing excludes others);
- *noscitur a sociis* (a word is known by the company it keeps).

3.5.1 The *ejusdem generis* rule

This states that where there is a list of words which is followed by general words, then the general words are limited to the same kind of items as the specific words. This is easier to understand by looking at cases.

CASE EXAMPLE

Hobbs v CG Robertson Ltd [1970] 2 All ER 347

A workman had injured his eye when brickwork which he was removing splintered. He claimed compensation under the Construction (General Provision) Regulation 1961. These regulations made it a duty for employers to provide goggles for workmen when 'breaking, cutting, dressing or carving of stone, concrete, slag or similar material'. The court held that brick did not come within the term 'a similar material'. Brick was not *ejusdem generis* with stone, concrete, slag. The reason was that all the other materials were hard, so that bits would fly off them when struck with a tool, whereas brick was a soft material. This ruling meant that the workman's claim for compensation failed.

Another case illustrating the use of the *ejusdem generis* rule is *Wood v Commissioner of Police of the Metropolis* [1986] 2 All ER 570. The Divisional Court held that in s4 of the Vagrancy Act 1824 the words 'any gun, pistol, hanger, cutlass, bludgeon, or other offensive weapon' did not include a piece of glass. The general words 'other offensive weapon' had to be interpreted in the light of the list of items and all these were items made or adapted for the purpose of causing injury. A piece of glass had not been made for that purpose.

There must be at least two specific words in a list before the general word or phrase for this rule to operate. In *Allen v Emmerson* [1944] KB 362 the Divisional Court had to interpret the phrase 'theatres and other places of amusement' and decide if it applied to a funfair. As there was only one specific word 'theatres', it was decided that a funfair did come under the general term 'other places of amusement' even though it was not of the same kind as theatres.

3.5.2 *Expressio unius est exclusio alterius* (the express mention of one thing excludes others)

Where there is a list of words which is not followed by general words, then the Act applies only to the items in the list. In *Tempest v Kilner* [1846] 3 CB 249 the court had to consider whether the Statute of Frauds 1677, which required a contract for the sale of 'goods, wares and merchandise' of more than £10 to be evidenced in writing, applied to a contract for the sale of stocks and shares. The list 'goods, wares and merchandise' was not followed by any general words, so the court held that only contracts for those three types of things were affected by the statute; because stocks and shares were not mentioned, they were not caught by the statute.

3.5.3 *Noscitur a sociis* (a word is known by the company it keeps)

This means that the words must be looked at in context and interpreted accordingly. It involves looking at other words in the same section or at other sections in the Act. Words in the same section were important in *Inland Revenue Commissioners v Frere* [1965] AC 402, where the section set out rules for 'interest, annuities or other annual interest'. The first use of the word 'interest' on its own could have meant any interest paid, whether daily, monthly or annually. Because of the words 'other annual interest' in the section, the court decided that 'interest' only meant annual interest.

Other sections of an Act were considered by the House of Lords in *Bromley London Borough Council v Greater London Council* [1982] 1 All ER 129. The issue in this case was whether the GLC could operate a cheap fare scheme on its transport systems, where the amounts being charged meant that the transport system would run at a loss. The decision in the case revolved around the meaning of the word 'economy' in the Transport (London) Act 1969. The House of Lords looked at the whole Act and, in particular, at another section which imposed a duty to make up any deficit as far as possible. As a result, it decided that 'economy' meant running on business lines and ruled that the cheap fares policy was not legal since it involved deliberately running the transport system at a loss and this was not running it on business lines.

Another case in which the wording of other sections of the Act was important is the following:

CASE EXAMPLE

Harrow London Borough Council v Shah and Shah [1999] 3 All ER 302

The defendants owned a newsagent's business where lottery tickets were sold. They had told their staff not to sell tickets to anyone under 16 years old. They also told their staff that if there was any doubt about a customer's age, the staff should ask for proof of age, and if still in doubt should refer the matter to the defendants. One of their staff sold a lottery ticket to a 13-year-old boy without asking for proof of age. The salesman mistakenly believed the boy was over 16 years old. The first defendant was in a back room of the premises at the time: the other was not on the premises. Both defendants were charged with selling a lottery ticket to a person under 16, contrary to s13(1)(c) of the National Lottery Act 1993.

The wording in s13(1)(c) provides that 'Any other person who was a party to the contravention shall be guilty of an offence'. It does not have any provision for a due diligence defence (i.e. that the defendant has taken all possible care to prevent the offence occurring). The Divisional Court compared s13(1)(c) with s13(1)(a) which does contain a 'due diligence' defence. Because of this the court held that a defendant could be guilty under s13(1)(c) even though he had taken all reasonable care to prevent the offence from occurring.

3.6 Presumptions

The courts will also make certain presumptions or assumptions about the law, but these are only a starting point. If the statute clearly states the opposite then the presumption will not apply and it is said that the presumption is rebutted. The most important presumptions are:

1. A presumption against a change in the common law

In other words, it is assumed that the common law will apply unless Parliament has made it plain in the Act that the common law has been altered. An example of this occurred in *Leach v R* [1912] AC 305, where the question was whether a wife could be made to give evidence against her husband under the Criminal Evidence Act 1898. Since the 1898 Act did not expressly say that this should happen it was held that the common law rule that a wife could not be compelled to give evidence still applied. If there had been explicit words saying that a wife was compellable then the old common law would not apply. This is now the position under s80 of the Police and Criminal Evidence Act 1984, which expressly states that in a crime of violence one spouse can be made to give evidence against the other spouse.

2. A presumption that mens rea is required in criminal cases

The basic common law rule is that no one can be convicted of a crime unless it is shown that they had the required intention to commit it. In *Sweet v Parsley* [1970] AC 132 the defendant was charged with being concerned with the management of premises which were used for the purposes of smoking cannabis. The facts were that the defendant was the owner of premises which she had leased out and the tenants had smoked cannabis there without her knowledge. She was clearly 'concerned in the management' of the premises and cannabis had been smoked there, but because she had no knowledge of the events she had no *mens rea*. The key issue was whether *mens rea* was required; the Misuse of Drugs Act 1971 did not say there was any need for knowledge of the events. The House of Lords held that the defendant was not guilty as the presumption that *mens rea* was required had not been rebutted.

In *B (a minor) v DPP* [2000] 1 All ER 833 the House of Lords again stressed the presumption that *mens rea* was required in criminal offences when Lord Nicholls said:

JUDGMENT

'The common law presumes that, unless Parliament indicated otherwise, the appropriate mental element is an unexpressed ingredient of every statutory offence.'

3. A presumption that the Crown is not bound by any statute unless the statute says so expressly or by necessary implication

'The Crown' in this presumption means the state. This is an important presumption since the Crown occupies a great deal of land, for example all bases for the armed forces. The Occupiers' Liability Act expressly applies to the Crown: if it did not then the Crown would be exempt from liability for any breach in respect of the duties of an occupier. The Crown is also the employer of a large number of people. Acts in respect of employment, such as the Equal Pay Act 1970, the Health and Safety at Work etc Act 1974 and discrimination law all state that the Crown is expressly bound.

Where a statute does not expressly state that the Crown is bound, then the Crown may not be bound even where a statute has been passed for the benefit of the public.

CASE EXAMPLE

Lord Advocate v Dumbarton District Council [1990] 1 All ER 1

It was decided to build an improved security fence for a submarine base. In order to do this, part of a public road had to be closed during the construction. Normally, planning permission from the local Council is needed before a road can be closed. It was held that this did not apply to the Crown, so the Crown did not need planning permission.

4. A presumption that legislation does not apply retrospectively

This means that no Act of Parliament will apply to past happenings; each Act will normally only apply from the date it comes into effect. However, since this is only a presumption, Parliament can enact legislation with a retrospective effect if it expressly states this in the Act. There are very few Acts where Parliament has stated that there is retrospective effect. Examples are the War Damage Act 1965 and the War Crimes Act 1991.

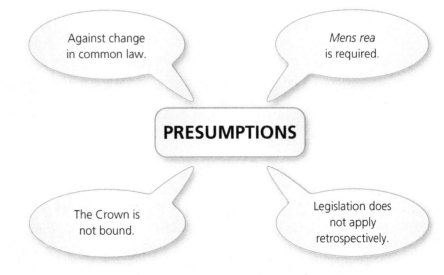

Figure 3.2 Presumptions in statutory interpretation

However, there are some Acts where it has been held that it is a necessary implication that the Act is retrospective in effect. An example of this was seen in the case of *R v Field* [2003] 1 WLR 882. The Court of Appeal had to decide whether s28 of the Criminal Justice and Court Services Act 2000 (which allowed the court to make an order disqualifying a person who had been convicted of certain offences against a child from working with children) applied in respect of offences committed before the Act came into force. They held that it did as the purpose of the Act (the protection of children) would be seriously undermined if a disqualification order could only be made in respect of offences committed after the Act came into force.

3.7 Intrinsic and extrinsic aids

There are certain ways in which the courts can try to discover the intention of Parliament and certain matters which they can look at in order to help with the interpretation of a statute.

3.7.1 Intrinsic aids

These are matters within the statute itself that may help to make its meaning clearer. The court can consider the long title, the short title and the preamble, if any. Older statutes usually have a preamble which sets out Parliament's purpose in enacting that statute. Modern statutes either do not have a preamble or contain a very brief one. For example, the Theft Act 1968 states that it is an Act to modernise the law of theft. The long title may also explain briefly Parliament's intentions. An unusual approach was taken in the Arbitration Act 1996 where a statement of the principles of the Act is set out in s2. This is a new development in statutory drafting and one that could both encourage and help the use of the purposive approach.

The other useful internal aids are any headings before a group of sections, and any Schedules attached to the Act. There are often also marginal notes explaining different sections but these are not generally regarded as giving Parliament's intention as they will have been inserted after the parliamentary debates and are only helpful comments put in by the printer.

3.7.2 Extrinsic aids

These are matters which are outside the Act and it has always been accepted that some external sources can help explain the meaning of an Act. These undisputed sources are:

- previous Acts of Parliament on the same topic;
- the historical setting;
- earlier case law;
- dictionaries of the time.

So far as other extrinsic aids are concerned, attitudes have changed. Originally the courts had very strict rules that other extrinsic aids should not be considered; however, for the following three aids the courts' attitude has changed. These three main extrinsic aids are:

1. *Hansard* – the official report of what was said in Parliament when the Act was debated.
2. Reports of law reform bodies such as the Law Commission which led to the passing of the Act.

3. International Conventions, Regulations or Directives which have been implemented by English legislation.

All of these are considered separately in the next three sections.

3.7.3 The use of *Hansard*

Until 1992 there was a firm rule that the courts could not look at what was said in the debates in Parliament. Some years earlier, Lord Denning had tried to attack this ban on *Hansard* in *Davis v Johnson* [1978] 1 All ER 1132, which involved the interpretation of the Domestic Violence and Matrimonial Proceedings Act 1976. He admitted that he had indeed read *Hansard* before making his decision, saying:

JUDGMENT

'Some may say – and indeed have said – that judges should not pay any attention to what is said in Parliament. They should grope about in the dark for the meaning of an Act without switching on the light. I do not accede to this view.'

This was in the Court of Appeal and when the case was appealed to the House of Lords, it disapproved of Lord Denning's view. Lord Scarman explained the Lords' reasons by saying:

JUDGMENT

'Such material is an unreliable guide to the meaning of what is enacted. It promotes confusion, not clarity. The cut and thrust of debate and the pressures of executive responsibility … are not always conducive to a clear and unbiased explanation of the meaning of statutory language.'

However, in *Pepper (Inspector of Taxes) v Hart* (1993) the House of Lords relaxed the rule and accepted that *Hansard* could be used in a limited way. This case was unusual in that seven judges heard the appeal, rather than the normal panel of five. Those seven judges included the then Lord Chancellor, Lord Mackay, who was the only judge to disagree with the use of *Hansard*. The majority ruled that *Hansard* could be consulted.

CASE EXAMPLE

Pepper (Inspector of Taxes) v Hart [1993] 1 All ER 42

Malvern College, an independent school for boys, allowed sons of teachers to be educated at the college for one-fifth of the fees charged to other people. This concession was a taxable benefit and the teachers had to pay tax on it. The question was exactly how the calculation of the amount to be taxed should be done. Under the applicable Finance Act this had to be done on the 'cash equivalent' of the benefit. Section 63 of the Finance Act defined 'cash equivalent' as 'an amount equal to the cost of the benefit' and further defined the 'cost of the benefit' as 'the amount of any expense incurred in or in connection with its provision'. This was ambiguous as it could mean either:

1. the marginal (or additional) cost to the employer of providing it to the employee (this on the facts was nil); or

2. the average cost of providing it to both the employee and the public (this would involve the teachers having to pay a considerable amount of tax).

The tax inspector took the view that (2) was the correct interpretation but the teachers challenged this.

The case went on appeal to the House of Lords where it was submitted that it should be possible to look at *Hansard* to see what had been said about this point when Parliament was considering the Finance Act. One of the arguments against looking at *Hansard* was that this would infringe s1, Article 9 of the Bill of Rights 1688. This, in its original spelling, states:

Section
's1 of Article 9 That the freedome of speech and debates or proceedings in Parlyament ought not to be impeached or questioned in any court or place out of Parlyament.'

All seven judges in the House of Lords stated that there was no infringement of s1, Article 9 of the Bill of Rights 1688. The courts would be looking at *Hansard* in order to try to implement what was said there. They would not be 'questioning' the debates. Lord Browne-Wilkinson in his judgment summarised the other reasons which had been put forward against the use of *Hansard*. He identified the following points:

- the prohibition on using *Hansard* preserved the 'constitutional proprieties' under which Parliament creates the law and the judges merely apply it;
- the prohibition avoided the practical difficulty of an expensive researching of parliamentary materials;
- *Hansard* does not provide the citizen with an accessible and defined text regulating his legal rights; and
- in many cases it is unlikely that *Hansard* will provide any helpful guidance.

The majority of the Law Lords rejected all these arguments. However, Lord Mackay thought that the expense of researching *Hansard* was a good reason for ruling against its use, particularly as in many cases there would be no useful material in *Hansard*. But the other six Law Lords ruled that *Hansard* could be referred to. However, they put limitations on its use, as set out by Lord Browne-Wilkinson in his judgment:

JUDGMENT

'The exclusionary rule should be relaxed so as to permit reference to parliamentary materials where; (a) legislation is ambiguous or obscure, or leads to an absurdity; (b) the material relied on consists of one or more statements by a minister or other promoter of the Bill together if necessary with such other parliamentary material as is necessary to understand such statements and their effect; (c) the statements relied on are clear. Further than this I would not at present go.'

So *Hansard* may be considered, but only where the words of the Act are ambiguous or obscure or lead to an absurdity. Even then, *Hansard* should only be used if there was a clear statement by the minister introducing the legislation, which would resolve the ambiguity or absurdity. In fact, in *DPP v Bull* (1994) (see section 3.1.2) the court said that it had not looked at *Hansard* because the legislation was not 'ambiguous, obscure nor productive of absurdity'.

The only time that a wider use of *Hansard* is permitted is where the court is considering an Act that introduced an international Convention or European Directive into

English law. This was pointed out by the Queen's Bench Divisional Court in *Three Rivers District Council v Bank of England (No 2)* [1996] 2 All ER 363. In such a situation it is important to interpret the statute purposively and consistently with any European materials and the court can look at ministerial statements, even if the statute does not appear to be ambiguous or obscure.

Since 1993, *Hansard* has been referred to in a number of cases. Lord Mackay's predictions on cost have been confirmed by some solicitors, with one estimating that it had added 25 per cent to the bill. On other occasions it is clear that *Hansard* has not been helpful or that the court would have reached the same conclusion in any event. Pre-*Pepper v Hart* (1993), Vera Sachs did a study of 34 cases and found that reference to *Hansard* would not have helped in these cases. She pointed out:

QUOTATION

'In every case studied the disputed clause was either undebated or received obscure and confusing replies from the Minister.'

V Sachs, 'Towards discovering parliamentary intent', [1982] Stat LR 143

Professor Michael Zander conducted a study of House of Lords' decisions which had been made after November 1992 (when *Pepper v Hart* (1993) allowed reference to *Hansard*). He found that there were virtually no cases in which the court's decision had been influenced by reading *Hansard*. He found that virtually all cases fell into one of three categories:

1. there was no ambiguity or other reason for consulting *Hansard*; or
2. *Hansard* was consulted but it was of no assistance; or
3. the comments by the minister confirmed the view that the court had already taken of the matter.

Professor Zander wrote:

QUOTATION

'Thus even in cases where the court agrees to look at *Pepper v Hart* material, it appears to be exceedingly rare that the material affects the outcome. When considering the balance of advantage flowing from the decision one also has to put into the scale not only the considerable number of cases where the court refuses even to look at the material, but the presumably much greater number of cases where Hansard has been scoured by the lawyers in vain ... In short, it seems that the Lord Chancellor, Lord Mackay, who, as has been seen, dissented in *Pepper v Hart* mainly out of concern that the costs of the reform would outweigh the likely benefits, was probably right.'

M Zander, The Law-Making Process (5th edn, Butterworths, 1999), p 155

In *Wilson v First County Trust (No 2)* [2003] UKHL 40 the Speaker of the House of Commons and the Clerk of the Parliament were joined in the case to make representations on the use of *Hansard* for the purpose of deciding compatibility of an Act with the ECHR. This was the first time that officers of Parliament had sought to be heard on the use of *Hansard* in the courts. It was submitted by counsel for the Speaker that the courts should not treat speeches made in Parliament, whether by ministers or others, as evidence of the policy consideration which led to legislation taking a particular form. He further argued that there were no circumstances in which it was appropriate for a court to refer to *Hansard* in order to decide whether an enactment was compatible with the European Convention.

The House of Lords rejected these arguments and held that *Hansard* could be consulted even where the question of compatibility with Convention rights was an issue. Lord Nicholls said:

JUDGMENT

'The courts would be failing in the discharge of the new role assigned to them by Parliament if they were to exclude from consideration relevant information whose only source was a Ministerial statement in Parliament or an explanatory note prepared by his department while the Bill was proceeding through Parliament.

By having such material the court would not be questioning proceedings in Parliament or intruding improperly into the legislative process or ascribing to Parliament the views expressed by a Minister. The court would merely be placing itself in a better position to understand the legislation.'

However, the Lords pointed out that the occasions when resort to *Hansard* was necessary would seldom arise. In fact, they held that it was not necessary to refer to *Hansard* in this case.

The fact that *Hansard* is rarely used was pointed out in a recent case, *R v JTB* [2009] UKHL 20, where the House of Lords stated that this was 'one of the rare cases where it is both legitimate and helpful to consider Ministerial statements in Parliament'.

CASE EXAMPLE

R v JTB [2009] UKHL 20

D was charged with offences of causing or inciting a child under 13 to engage in sexual activity contrary to s13(1) of the Sexual Offences Act 2003. When interviewed by the police he admitted the activity but said that he had not thought that what he was doing was wrong. As a preliminary point it was argued by the defence that D was ***doli incapax***. The trial judge ruled that the defence was not available to him. D then pleaded guilty. He appealed against his conviction on the basis that the defence of *doli incapax* should have been available to him.

doli incapax
Incapable of wrong

Before 1998 there was a presumption that any child aged 10 to 14 was *doli incapax*. The prosecution could rebut this presumption by proof that the child did know he was doing wrong. Section 34 of the Crime and Disorder Act 1998 changed the law. It stated:

SECTION

'The rebuttable presumption of criminal law that a child aged 10 or over is incapable of committing an offence is hereby abolished.'

The key question for the Lords in the case was whether this section abolished the defence or whether it merely abolished the presumption, so that it was still available as a defence to a child who could prove that he did not know he was doing wrong. The Lords consulted *Hansard* and considered the parliamentary debates on the Act. They held that these made it clear that Parliament intended to abolish the complete defence, so D's conviction was upheld.

Lord Phillips in his judgment said:

JUDGMENT

'I ... consider that this is one of the rare cases where it is both legitimate and helpful to consider Ministerial statements in Parliament under the principle in *Pepper v Hart* [1993] AC 593. In issue is the meaning of a single short section of the [Crime and Disorder] Act. The meaning of that section is, when read in isolation, ambiguous. The clause that was to become the section was debated at some length in Parliament. An amendment was moved to it on two occasions in the House of Lords. Consideration of the debates discloses Ministerial statements that made the meaning of the clause quite clear.'

3.7.4 Law reform reports

The courts used to hold that reports by law reform bodies should not be considered by the courts. However this rule was relaxed in the *Black-Clawson International Ltd v Papierwerke etc AG* [1975] 1 All ER 810 when it was accepted that such a report should be looked at to discover the 'mischief' or gap in the law which the legislation based on the report was designed to deal with. An example of a case in which the court looked at a report is *DPP v Bull* (1994) (see section 3.1.2). Here, the court considered the Wolfenden Report, 'Report of the Committee on Homosexual Offences and Prostitution', Cmnd 247 (1957). This made it clear that the 'mischief' which had been identified was that of women loitering or soliciting for the purposes of prostitution: the report did not identify any problem caused by male prostitutes. Accordingly the court held that s1(1) of the Street Offences Act 1959 applied only to women prostitutes.

In *Black-Clawson* (1975), although all five judges in the House of Lords agreed that reports could be considered to identify the mischief Parliament had intended to deal with, they were divided on whether they could go further and use the report to find the intention of Parliament. However, by 1993 the Lords appear to have accepted that reports could be used to look for the intention of the legislature. This is shown by Lord Browne-Wilkinson in *Pepper v Hart* (1993) when he said:

JUDGMENT

'Given the purposive approach to construction now adopted by the courts in order to give effect to the true intentions of the legislature, the fine distinction between looking for the mischief and looking for the intention in using words to provide the remedy are technical and inappropriate.'

Although all the Law Lords had agreed in *Black-Clawson* (1975) that reports could be considered to identify the mischief Parliament had intended to deal with, there have been cases since then in which the courts have not consulted the relevant report. For example, in *Anderton v Ryan* [1985] 2 All ER 355 the House of Lords did not consult the Law Commission's report 'Criminal Law: Attempt and Impossibility in Relation to Attempt, Conspiracy and Incitement', Law Com No 102 (1980). As a result, they came to a decision which was severely criticised by both practising and academic lawyers. The Lords themselves accepted that they had made a bad error and they corrected it in the following year in *R v Shivpuri* [1986] 2 All ER 334 when they overruled *Anderton v Ryan* (1985).

Another case in which the relevant report was not considered by the House of Lords was *Metropolitan Police Commissioner v Caldwell* [1981] 1 All ER 961. In this case the House of Lords did not look at the report by the Law Commission ('Report on Offences of Damage to Property', Law Com No 29 (1970)) which led to the passing of the Criminal Damage Act 1971. In this report the Law Commission had pointed out the old-fashioned use of the word 'maliciously' in the old Acts where the word was meant to mean that the defendant either intended to do the damage or knew that he was taking a risk that it would be damaged. The Commission proposed that it should be replaced by the phrase 'intending or being reckless'. This was the wording used in both the draft Bill and the final Act. It was clear that the Law Commission meant 'reckless' to cover situations where the defendant had realised that there was a risk but had gone on to take that risk. This is known as 'sub-jective recklessness'.

However in *Caldwell* (1981), when the word 'reckless' in the Criminal Damage Act 1971 was considered by the House of Lords, it ruled that it covered not only subjective risk-taking but also situations where a reasonable person would have realised the risk but the defendant had not given any thought to the possibility of there being any risk (an objective test). This decision was criticised but it remained in force for over 20 years until the House of Lords reconsidered the matter in *R v G* [2003] UKHL 50 and overruled *Caldwell* (1981), holding that in that case the Law Lords had 'adopted an interpretation of section 1 of the 1971 Act which was beyond the range of feasible meanings'. In *R v G* (2003) the Lords emphasised the meaning that the Law Commission had intended and which Parliament must also have intended. Lord Bingham said:

JUDGMENT

'section 1 as enacted followed, subject to an immaterial addition, the draft proposed by the Law Commission. It cannot be supposed that by "reckless" Parliament meant anything differ-ent from the Law Commission. The Law Commission's meaning was made plain both in its Report (Law Com No 29, 1970) and in Working Paper No 23 which preceded it. These mater-ials (not, it would seem, placed before the House in *R v Caldwell*) reveal a very plain intention to replace the old expression "maliciously" by the more familiar expression "reckless" but to give the latter expression the meaning which *R v Cunningham* [1957] 2 QB 396 had given to the former ... No relevant change in the *mens rea* necessary for the proof of the offence was intended, and in holding otherwise the majority misconstrued section 1 of the Act.'

3.7.5 International conventions

We have already seen that where a national law is passed to give effect to an EU treaty or other law, the courts will look at the original EU law when deciding on interpretation. This is also the position where a national law has been passed in order to give effect to any inter-national treaty or convention. In *Salomon v Commissioners of Customs and Excise* [1967] 2 QB 116 the Court of Appeal looked at an international convention because it thought that English law should be interpreted in such a way as to be consistent with international law.

In *Fothergill v Monarch Airlines Ltd* [1980] 2 All ER 696 the House of Lords decided that the original Convention should be considered as it was possible that in translating and adapting the Convention to our legislative process, the true meaning of the original might have been lost. The House of Lords in that same case went further and also held that an English court could consider any preparatory materials or explanatory notes published with an international convention. The reasoning behind this was that other countries allowed the use of such material, known as *travaux préparatoires*, and it should therefore be allowed in this country in order to get uniformity in the interpretation of international rules.

Explanatory Notes

Since 1998 Explanatory Notes have been produced alongside new Bills. (Remember that before a law becomes an Act of Parliament, it is referred to as a Bill.) These notes are much fuller than any previous explanatory memorandum. They are produced by the govern-ment department responsible for the Bill. The notes usually explain the background to any proposed law, summarise its main provisions and, where a point is complicated, give worked examples. These notes are updated as the Bill progresses through Parliament and, when the Bill becomes an Act of Parliament, a final version of the notes is published.

These notes are a potential new extrinsic aid to statutory interpretation. They could be helpful to courts when they have to interpret a law. However, the notes are not part of the law. This is likely to cause conflict on whether they should be used for statutory interpretation. Judges who use the purposive approach are likely to support their use, but judges who use the literal approach will not use them. This is because explanatory notes are not intended to have legal effect; they are not part of the Act itself and using them introduces the risk of changing the meaning of what is stated in the Act.

However, it appears that the government assumes that the Explanatory Notes will be consulted as an aid to interpretation. For example, the clause that became s6 Fraud Act 2006 on the face of it has no *mens rea*. When this clause was debated in the House the Solicitor-General pointed out that the wording of the clause drew on the wording of the previous law in s25 of the Theft Act 1968 and that this was made clear in the Explanatory Notes which referred to cases decided under the previous law.

Example of the use of extrinsic aids

Several extrinsic aids were considered in *Laroche v Spirit of Adventure (UK) Ltd* [2009] EWCA Civ 12. The claimant had been injured as the result of a sudden landing of a hot air balloon in which he was travelling. The meaning of the word 'aircraft' was important. Was a hot air balloon within the definition of 'aircraft'? If so, then the claim would fail as it had not been made within two years of the accident.

In deciding the case the Court of Appeal first looked at the definition of 'aircraft' in the *Pocket Oxford Dictionary*. This defined 'aircraft' as 'aeroplane(s), airship(s) and balloon(s)'. The court also looked at the Air Navigation Order 2000 (an SI). This supported the view that a hot air balloon should be regarded as an 'aircraft'.

In addition, the court pointed out that the English law had to be interpreted in a similar way to international carriage by air which is ruled by an international convention, the Warsaw Convention.

As a result of considering these three extrinsic aids, the court ruled that a hot air balloon was regarded as an 'aircraft'. This meant that the claim failed as it had not been brought within the two years' time limit.

KEY FACTS

Aids to interpretation

Aid	Comment	Cases
Rules of language 1. *Ejusdem generis*	Looks at phrases and other words in the Act General words which follow a list are limited to the same kind	*Hobbs v CG Robertson* (1970)
2. *Expressio unius est exclusio alterius*	The express mention of one thing excludes others	*Tempest v Kilner* (1846)
3. *Noscitur a sociis*	A word is known by the company it keeps	*IRC v Frere* (1965)
Interpretation Act 1978	Makes general rules so that unless the contrary is stated in an Act: • 'he' includes 'she' • singular includes plural etc.	

Intrinsic aids	Matters within the Act, especially: • short title, long title and preamble • definition sections	
Extrinsic aids	*Hansard* Law reform reports International conventions	*Pepper v Hart* (1993) *Black-Clawson* (1975) *Fothergill v Monarch Airlines Ltd* (1980)

3.8 The effect of the Human Rights Act 1998

Section 3 of the HRA 1998 says that, so far as it is possible to do so, legislation must be read and given effect in a way which is compatible with the rights in the ECHR. This applies to any case where one of the rights is concerned, but it does not apply where there is no involvement of human rights.

A good example of the difference the HRA 1998 has made to interpretation is *R v Offen* [2000] 1 WLR 253. This case considered the meaning of the word 'exceptional' in the Crime (Sentences) Act 1997 where any offender committing a second serious offence had to be given a life sentence unless there were 'exceptional circumstances'. Before the HRA 1998 came into force the Court of Appeal in *R v Kelly* [2000] QB 198 had said that 'exceptional' was an ordinary English adjective, saying:

JUDGMENT

'To be exceptional a circumstance need not be unique or unprecedented or very rare; but it cannot be one that is regularly or routinely or normally encountered.'

This led to a strict approach where offenders were given life sentences even when the earlier crime had been committed a long time ago and the second offence was not that serious of its type. In *Offen* (2000), which was decided after the HRA 1998 came into force in October 2000, the Court of Appeal said that this restricted approach in *Kelly* (2000) could lead to the sentence being arbitrary and disproportionate and a breach of both Articles 3 and 5 of the ECHR. In order to interpret the Crime (Sentences) Act 1997 in a way which was compatible with the Convention, it was necessary to consider whether the offender was a danger to the public. If he was not, then he was an exception to the normal rule in the 1997 Act, and this could be considered exceptional circumstances so that a life sentence need not be given.

Another example of the effect of the HRA 1998 on interpretation is *Mendoza v Ghaidan* [2002] EWCA Civ 1533 (see section 3.1.3). In this case the Court of Appeal ignored a House of Lords' judgment which had been made prior to the implementation of the HRA 1998 and read the words 'as his or her wife or husband' in the Rent Act 1977 to mean 'as if they were his or her wife or husband' in order to interpret the 1977 Act in accordance with the ECHR. In 2004 the House of Lords confirmed the Court of Appeal's decision in this case.

If an Act cannot be read so as to be compatible with the ECHR, then s4(2) of the HRA 1998 states:

SECTION

'4(2) If the court is satisfied that the provision is incompatible with a Convention right, it may make a declaration of that incompatibility.'

In *Poplar Housing Association and Regeneration Community Association Ltd v Donoghue* [2001] 3 WLR 183 Lord Woolf CJ gave guidelines on how to apply ss3 and 4 of the HRA 1998:

JUDGMENT

'(a) if the court uses s3 to interpret a legislative provision in such a way as to make it compatible with the Convention, it should bear in mind that its task is still interpretation and not legislation;

(b) the extent of any modified meaning given under s3 should be limited to what is necessary to achieve compatibility;

(c) if the court can only make a legislative provision compatible under s3 by radically altering its effect, this is an indication that it is engaging in more than interpretation;

(d) if it is not possible under s3 to achieve an interpretation which is compatible with the Convention, the court has a discretion, but not a duty, to make a declaration of incompatibility.'

There is a strong obligation on the court to interpret an Act so as to make it compatible with the Convention. However, if the words are clear, then, as a measure of last resort, the court can make a declaration of incompatibility. This view was expressed by Lord Steyn in *R v A* [2001] UKHL 25 when he said:

JUDGMENT

'Section 3 places a duty on the court to strive to find a possible interpretation compatible with Convention rights. Under ordinary methods of interpretation a court may depart from the language of the statute to avoid absurd consequences: section 3 goes much further. Undoubtedly, a court must always look for a contextual and purposive interpretation: section 3 is more radical in its effect. It is a general principle of the interpretation of legal instruments that the text is the primary source of interpretation: other sources are subordinate to it ... Section 3 qualifies this general principle because it requires a court to find an interpretation compatible with Convention rights if it is possible to do so ... The techniques to be used will not only involve the reading down of express language in a statute but also the implication of provisions. A declaration of incompatibility is a measure of last resort. It must be avoided unless it is plainly impossible to do so. If a *clear* limitation on Convention rights is stated *in terms*, such an impossibility will arise.'

ACTIVITY

Self-test questions

1. Explain how the literal rule operates.
2. Explain how the golden rule modifies the literal rule.
3. How does the mischief rule operate?
4. Give two case examples of the operation of: (a) the literal rule (b) the golden rule (c) the mischief rule.
5. What is the purposive approach?
6. What are the advantages and disadvantages of this approach to statutory interpretation?
7. What is meant by 'intrinsic aids'?
8. What limitations are placed on referring to parliamentary debates in *Hansard*?
9. Explain the advantages and disadvantages of looking at parliamentary debates in *Hansard*.
10. When will a court look at the report of a law reform body as an aid to statutory interpretation?

Section 3 of the (fictional) Control of Dangerous Dogs Act 1986 provides that:

> 'The owner of a dangerous dog shall be liable in damages for injury done to any person, property, or animal by his dog, and it shall not be necessary for the party seeking such damages to show previous dangerousness in the dog, or the owner's knowledge of that previous dangerousness, or that the injury was attributable to neglect on the part of the owner ... The owner is defined as the individual who ordinarily keeps the dog.'

Steve lives in a house with a garden on a residential estate. A stray dog began wandering around the estate one month ago. As the dog was malnourished, Steve began to feed it scraps of food. The dog never showed any signs of being aggressive with Steve.

One morning, the dog bit the postman, Simon, without warning. Simon received a deep cut to his arm and had to receive medical treatment as a result. Simon brought an action under the Control of Dangerous Dogs Act against Steve in the High Court.

During the Parliamentary debates of the Control of Dangerous Dogs Act, the Home Secretary assured the House of Commons that the term 'dangerous' was not to have a technical meaning, but should be given its ordinary meaning, which would include dogs that attacked people without warning.

Professor Smith and Professor Jones, commenting on this legislation in their (fictional) learned academic textbook *Animals and the Law* concluded that s3 was never intended to apply to those who look after injured or neglected dogs.

By taking into account the various interpretation rules and aids, discuss the various arguments which can be used both by Steve and Simon on the correct interpretation of s3 of the Control of Dangerous Dogs Act.

To approach the issues in the question, it is important that you:

- summarise the various rules of statutory interpretation that exist;
- summarise the various internal aids to statutory interpretation that judges use;
- summarise the various external aids to statutory interpretation that judges use.

Consider how each of them relate to the (fictional) s3 of the Control of Dangerous Dogs Act:

- in light of your list of the rules and aids for statutory interpretation, identify the key parts of the (fictional) Act which need to be interpreted here;
- key questions to consider include: 'is the dog "owned" by Steve?'; 'Does Steve "ordinarily keep the dog"?'; 'Is the cut on Simon's arm an "injury"?';
- start to identify the connections between the rules and aids of interpretation to the wording of the Act.

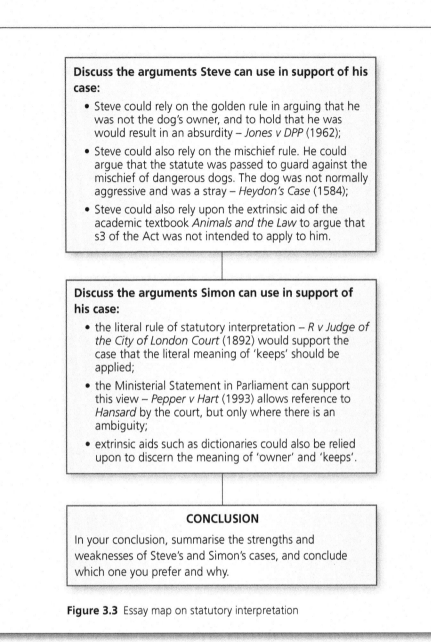

Discuss the arguments Steve can use in support of his case:

- Steve could rely on the golden rule in arguing that he was not the dog's owner, and to hold that he was would result in an absurdity – *Jones v DPP* (1962);
- Steve could also rely on the mischief rule. He could argue that the statute was passed to guard against the mischief of dangerous dogs. The dog was not normally aggressive and was a stray – *Heydon's Case* (1584);
- Steve could also rely upon the extrinsic aid of the academic textbook *Animals and the Law* to argue that s3 of the Act was not intended to apply to him.

Discuss the arguments Simon can use in support of his case:

- the literal rule of statutory interpretation – *R v Judge of the City of London Court* (1892) would support the case that the literal meaning of 'keeps' should be applied;
- the Ministerial Statement in Parliament can support this view – *Pepper v Hart* (1993) allows reference to *Hansard* by the court, but only where there is an ambiguity;
- extrinsic aids such as dictionaries could also be relied upon to discern the meaning of 'owner' and 'keeps'.

CONCLUSION

In your conclusion, summarise the strengths and weaknesses of Steve's and Simon's cases, and conclude which one you prefer and why.

Figure 3.3 Essay map on statutory interpretation

SUMMARY

Interpretation is needed because of such problems as:

- failure of legislation to cover a specific point;
- a broad term;
- ambiguity;
- drafting error;
- new technological developments.

The three 'rules'

- literal rule is the plain ordinary, grammatical meaning of the words;
- golden rule allows modification of words where the literal rule would lead to an absurdity, repugnance or inconsistency;
- mischief rule considers the 'mischief' or gap in the old law and interprets the Act in such a way that the gap is covered.

Purposive approach

- looks for the intention of Parliament.

Rules of language

- the *ejusdem generis* rule;
- *expressio unius est exclusio alterius* (the mention of one thing excludes others);
- *noscitur a sociis* (a word is known by the company it keeps).

Presumptions

- against a change in the common law;
- that *mens rea* is required in criminal cases;
- that the Crown is not bound by any statute unless the statute expressly says so;
- that legislation does not apply retrospectively.

Intrinsic aids

- these are in the legislation;
- they include the long title, the short title and preamble, headings before a group of sections and any Schedules.

Extrinsic aids

- previous Acts of Parliament on the same topic;
- the historical setting;
- earlier case law;
- dictionaries of the time;
- *Hansard* – the official report of what was said in Parliament when the Act was debated;
- reports of law reform bodies such as the Law Commission which led to the passing of the Act;
- international Conventions, Regulations or Directives which have been implemented by English legislation.

The effect of the HRA 1998

- legislation must be read and given effect in a way which is compatible with the rights in the ECHR.

Further reading

Book
Zander, M, *The Law-Making Process* (6th edn, Cambridge University Press, 2004).

Articles
Jenkins, C, 'Helping the reader of Bills and Acts' [1999] *NLJ* 798.

Jenkins, JC, '*Pepper* v. *Hart*: a draftsman's perspective' [1994] *Stat LR* 15, 23, at 25.

Leitch, WA, 'Interpretation and the Interpretation Act 1978' [1980] *Stat LR* 5.

Sales, P and Elkins, R, 'Rights-consistent interpretation and the Human Rights Act 1998' [2011] *LQR* 217.

Spencer, JR, 'The drafting of criminal legislation: need it be so impenetrable?' [2008] *CLJ* 585.

Watson-Brown, A, 'In search of plain English: the Holy Grail or mythical Excalibur of legislative drafting' [2011] *Stat LR* 7.

Williams, G, 'The meaning of literal interpretation' [1981] *NLJ* 1128, at 1149.

4

Civil courts

AIMS AND OBJECTIVES

After reading this chapter you should be able to:

- Understand the differences between civil and criminal cases
- Distinguish between courts of first instance and appellate courts
- Describe the jurisdiction of courts of first instance which hear civil cases
- Understand the problems associated with bringing civil cases in the courts
- Describe reforms made to the system following the Woolf Report
- Understand, in outline, the role of tribunals
- Discuss alternative methods of resolving civil disputes

4.1 Introduction to the courts system

Although the main focus of this chapter is on civil courts, it is necessary to understand some basic points and to put the whole matter into context. The introductory points considered are:

- the differences between civil and criminal cases;
- whether a court is a superior or an inferior court;
- appellate courts and trial courts;
- the differences between courts and tribunals.

4.1.1 Civil and criminal cases

When looking at the court structure, it is important to understand that civil and criminal cases are dealt with differently. This stems from the fact that the purposes of civil and criminal law are different.

Civil law

injunction
A court order to do something or to refrain from doing something

Civil law is concerned with rights and duties between individuals. When there is a breach of a right or a failure of duty then the aim of the civil law is to put the parties into the position they would have been in if there had been no breach or failure. This is not always possible; for example in negligence cases where the claimant has been left paralysed or with other permanent injuries. In such cases the court awards damages (a sum of money) as compensation. Apart from trying to correct past breaches, the courts, in some cases, may be asked to make an order to prevent a future breach of a right. For example, where trespass or harassment is likely to occur in the future, the courts can grant an **injunction** forbidding this.

Civil law has many different branches. The main areas that are likely to lead to court cases are contract law, the law of tort, family law, the law of succession, company law, employment law and land law. However, there are also many other specialist areas, varying from copyright and patents to marine law, on which the courts may be required to adjudicate. This book does not deal with the actual legal rules of any of the areas, only with the system for dealing with disputes.

As civil law involves regulating disputes between private individuals and businesses, it is also called private law. Civil cases are started by the person or business complaining of the breach or failure.

Criminal law

Criminal law sets out what behaviour is forbidden by the state, at risk of punishment. So the purpose of criminal cases is to decide if the defendant is guilty of such behaviour and, if so, to impose a suitable penalty. A person who commits a crime is said to have offended against the state and the state, therefore, has the right to prosecute him. This is so even though there is often an individual victim of a crime as well. For example, if a defendant commits the crime of burglary by breaking into a house and stealing, the state prosecutes the defendant for that burglary, although it is also possible for the victim to bring a private prosecution if the state does not take proceedings. However, if there is a private prosecution, the state still has the right to intervene and take over the matter. Also, at the end of the case, if the defendant is found guilty, the court will punish the defendant for the offence, because he has broken the criminal law set down by the state. The victim will not necessarily be given any compensation, since the case is not viewed as a dispute between the burglar and the householder. However, the criminal courts have the power to order that the offender pays the victim compensation and can make such an order as well as punishing the offender.

Distinctions between criminal cases and civil cases

There are many differences between criminal cases and civil cases. Important ones are:

- the courts in which the trial takes place;
- the way of starting a case and the procedure of the case;
- the standard of proof;
- the outcome of the case.

First, the cases take place in different courts. In general, criminal cases will be tried in either the Magistrates' Court or the Crown Court, while civil cases are heard in the High Court or the County Court.

The person starting the case is given a different name: in criminal cases they are referred to as the prosecutor, while in civil cases they are usually called the claimant. As already stated, the criminal case is taken on behalf of the state, and the main prosecution body is the Crown Prosecution Service (CPS) which is responsible for conducting cases. There are, however, other state agencies which may prosecute certain types of crime, such as the Serious Fraud Office, which prosecutes very complex fraud cases, or the Commissioners of HM Revenue and Customs, who can prosecute for such matters as smuggling and VAT fraud. Local authorities also prosecute cases such as trading standards and public health. Civil cases are started by the person making the claim.

A very important difference is the standard to which the case has to be proved. Criminal cases must be proved 'beyond reasonable doubt'. This is a very high standard of proof, and is necessary since a conviction could result in a defendant serving a long prison sentence. Civil cases have to be proved only 'on the balance of probabilities', a lower standard in which the judge decides who is most likely to be right. This difference in the standard to which a case has to be proved means that even though a defendant in a criminal case has been acquitted, a civil case based on the same facts against that defendant can still be successful. Such situations are not common, but have happened.

The outcome of a civil case is that judgment will be given in favour of one of the parties. If this is the claimant, then the court will then decide on the remedy to which that person is entitled. This will vary with the type of case. It may be a sum of money, an injunction, rescission of a contract or a declaration. In a criminal case, if the defendant is found guilty then the court has to decide on the most suitable penalty. This may be a custodial sentence, a community sentence, a fine or a discharge.

As can be seen, the terminology used in civil and criminal cases is different. A civil case is started by a claimant, whereas there is a prosecutor in criminal cases. In a civil case it is correct to speak of the defendant being sued, but in a criminal case the defendant is charged with or accused of a crime. The outcome of a civil case is that judgment is given for or against the claimant. Alternatively, this can be expressed by saying that the defendant has been found liable or not liable. In a criminal case the verdict is that the defendant is guilty or not guilty. In a civil case the defendant may be ordered to pay damages, whereas in a criminal case the defendant may be fined. The damages are payable to the claimant but the money from a fine in a criminal case goes to the state.

KEY FACTS

The differences between civil and criminal cases

	Civil cases	Criminal cases
Purpose of the case	To enforce rights	To decide if the criminal law has been broken
Person starting case	The individual whose rights have been affected	Usually the state, through the CPS
Legal name for that person	Claimant	Prosecutor
Courts hearing cases	County Court High Court	Magistrates' Court Crown Court
Standard of proof	The balance of probabilities	Beyond reasonable doubt
Person(s) making the decision	Judge Jury for a few cases (mainly defamation)	Magistrates in Magistrates' Court Jury in Crown Court
Decision	Judgment for the claimant (or defendant)	Guilty or not guilty
Powers of the court	Award damages Order an injunction Make a declaration Special remedies for contract law: • specific performance • rescission • rectification	Pass sentence: • prison • community sentence • fine • discharge May also order compensation to be paid to the victim

4.1.2 Superior courts and inferior courts

Another distinction is between superior courts and inferior courts. The Supreme Court, the Court of Appeal, the High Court and the Crown Court are superior courts, while the County Court and the Magistrates' Court are inferior courts. This distinction is important for two reasons. The first is that inferior courts have limited jurisdiction. They hear the less serious cases. Second, inferior courts are subject to the supervisory prerogative jurisdiction of the High Court. This means that the High Court can quash a decision of an inferior court if it was made in breach of the rules of natural justice or where the court did not have power to deal with that particular type of case. On this second point the Crown Court is in an unusual position. It is a superior court but for some matters it is subject to supervision by the High Court. This is set out in the Senior Courts Act 1981:

SECTION

's 29(3) In relation to the jurisdiction of the Crown Court, other than its jurisdiction in matters relating to trial on indictment, the High Court shall have all such jurisdiction to make orders of mandamus, prohibition or certiorari as the High Court possesses in relation to the jurisdiction of an inferior court.'

So, for anything other than matters related to trial on indictment, the High Court has supervisory powers over the Crown Court. This includes decisions on the granting of bail or where the Crown Court is hearing an appeal from the Magistrates' Court.

The powers of the High Court over the Crown Court were considered in *R (Crown Prosecution Service) v Guildford Crown Court* [2007] EWHC 1798 (Admin). In this case the defendant had been convicted of rape. The judge had given him an extended sentence under s227 of the Criminal Justice Act 2003. In fact s227 does not apply to specified serious offences which include rape. Instead, under the Criminal Justice Act 2003, a judge must sentence a dangerous offender who has committed a serious offence to either a sentence of life imprisonment or to an indeterminate period of imprisonment.

It was held that the Queen's Bench Divisional Court did not have any power to quash the unlawful sentence imposed by the Crown Court. This was because passing sentence following a conviction after trial on indictment was clearly a matter relating to a trial on indictment. So under s29(3) of the Senior Courts Act 1981 the High Court had no supervisory jurisdiction over the Crown Court.

In their report, 'The High Court's Jurisdiction in Relation to Criminal Proceedings' (2010) LC 324, the Law Commission pointed out that the phrase 'matters relating to trial on indictment' in s29(3) of the Senior Courts Act 1981 is not that clear. They suggested that there should be no power to review decisions in a trial on indictment from the time that the case goes to the Crown Court for trial to the end of the trial, except where the judge refuses bail. However, the High Court should have power to deal with matters after the end of the trial, for example, where a defendant is acquitted but the Crown Court judge refuses the defendant an order for costs.

4.1.3 Appellate courts and trial courts

The courts in which the initial trial of a case takes place are known as courts of trial or courts of first instance. Courts which hear appeals are called appellate courts. Many courts have both first instance and appellate jurisdiction.

County Courts hear civil cases at first instance but since the Woolf reforms (see section 4.4) they also have appellate jurisdiction. This is because the appeal route for **small claims** cases and **fast-track cases** heard at first instance by a District Judge in the County Court is to a Circuit Judge in the same County Court.

small claims
Usually a claim for up to £10,000

fast-track cases
Usually cases claiming from £10,000.01 to £25,000

Although the High Court is the court of first instance for major civil cases, it also sits as an appeal court. In particular, appeals on fast-track cases heard at first instance by a Circuit Judge in the County Court are heard by a single judge in the High Court. In addition, all the divisions of the High Court have appellate jurisdiction when two or three judges sit as a Divisional Court. The Queen's Bench Divisional is the most important of the Divisional Courts. For more information on appeals, see Chapter 6.

The Court of Appeal and the Supreme Court are only appellate courts. They do not hear any cases at first instance.

4.1.4 Courts and tribunals

The systems of courts and tribunals are distinct. Separate tribunals have been set up to deal with specific rights given by the state to individuals. For example, employment tribunals hear cases where failure to pay wages, unfair dismissal or discrimination against an employee is alleged. Tribunals are considered more fully at section 4.6.

However, there can be confusion because in a general sense a court can be called a tribunal. This is obvious when the dictionary definition of 'tribunal' is considered:

QUOTATION

'a judgment-seat: a court of justice or arbitration: a body appointed to adjudicate in some matter or to enquire into some disputed question'.

It is important to be able to distinguish between a court and a tribunal, as the rules on contempt of court apply only to courts. The actual name given to the tribunal or court is not a totally reliable guide. For example, despite its name, the Employment Appeal Tribunal is a court for the purposes of contempt of court. The problem of how to identify what is a court was considered in *Attorney General v British Broadcasting Corporation* [1980] 3 All ER 161 where the House of Lords held that a local valuation court was not a court even though it had the word 'court' in its title.

Lord Scarman said:

JUDGMENT

'I would identify a court in (or "of") law, ie a court of judicature, as a body established to exercise, either generally or subject to defined limits, the judicial power of the state. In this context judicial power is to be contrasted with legislative and executive (ie administrative) power. If the body under review is established for a purely legislative or administrative purpose, it is part of the legislative or administrative system of the state, even though it has to perform duties which are judicial in character.'

The functions of the local valuation court were administrative rather than judicial. Similarly, in *General Medical Council v British Broadcasting Corporation* [1998] 3 All ER 426, the Court of Appeal held that the Professional Conduct Committee of the General Medical Council is not a court. The committee does have a judicial function but this is to exercise the self-regulatory power of the medical profession to maintain professional standards. The Committee is not exercising the judicial power of the state.

This concept of a court exercising the judicial power of the state is now incorporated into s19 of the Contempt of Court Act 1981.

4.2 Civil courts of trial

The system of civil courts that now operates in England and Wales is based on the system set up in the nineteenth century. However, there have been many modifications to jurisdiction and procedure, especially in the late twentieth century. The courts where cases are tried at first instance are the High Court, the Family Court and the County Court.

The High Court was created as part of the Supreme Court of Judicature in 1873. Up to 2013 there were three divisions in the High Court. These were:

- Queen's Bench Division;
- Chancery Division;
- Family Division.

Under the Crime and Courts Act 2013, a new Family Court has been created. This court has taken over the work of the Family Division and also of the family work done in the County Court and the Magistrates' Courts.

The High Court as a whole has jurisdiction to hear any civil case. However, each division has been given jurisdiction to hear certain types of cases so that judges with the relevant specialist knowledge can deal with them.

The modern County Courts were created by the County Courts Act 1846 to hear small cases. Initially the limit on its jurisdiction to hear claims was £20. This was raised at intervals to reflect inflation so that by 1981 the limit was £5,000. In 1991 this upper limit was removed, so that in theory the County Court can hear cases of any value.

We will now go on to consider the present-day jurisdiction of the High Court and the County Court in more detail.

4.2.1 Queen's Bench Division

This is the biggest division of the High Court. Its main jurisdiction is to try cases involving the law of contract and tort. In addition, it has three special courts attached to it. These are the Commercial Court, the Admiralty Court and the Technology and Construction Court.

The Queen's Bench Division is the only division in which cases can still be tried by a jury sitting with the judge. Even in this division this is now a rare occurrence, with only a very small number of jury trials each year. For further information on the use of juries in civil cases, see Chapter 8.

Commercial Court

This court has specialist judges to deal with insurance and banking and other commercial matters, for example the problems of the Lloyd's 'names' for the losses caused by large insurance claims. In this court a simplified speedier procedure is used and the case may be decided on documentary evidence.

Admiralty Court

This, as its name implies, deals with matters relating to shipping. The two most common matters dealt with are damage to cargo and collision of ships. The judge in the Admiralty Court sits with two lay assessors, who are chosen from Masters of Trinity House, and who are there to advise the judge on questions of seamanship and navigation.

Technology and Construction Court

The Queen's Bench Division also administers the Technology and Construction Court which hears cases which are technically complex. This includes building and engineering disputes and computer litigation. Cases can be referred to it by either the Queen's Bench Division or the Chancery Division.

4.2.2 Chancery Division

The principal business of this division consists of corporate and personal insolvency disputes, the enforcement of mortgages, partnership disputes, intellectual property rights, copyright and patent, disputes relating to trust property, disputed probate cases and administration of the estates of deceased persons. There is also a special Companies Court in the division which deals mainly with winding up companies. Juries are never used in the Chancery Division and cases are heard by a single judge.

4.2.3 Family Division

This division has jurisdiction to hear a wide range of matters connected with the family. Since the creation of the Combined Family Court in 2014 most of the work of the Family Division has been taken over by the Family Court. This includes all matrimonial cases, including divorce and declarations for nullity of marriage, and related issues such as disputes over matrimonial property. The Family Court also hears wardship and adoption cases and all proceedings relating to children under the Children Act 1989. As well, it has jurisdiction over any proceedings under the Child Abduction and Custody Act 1985. The Family Division of the High Court still deals with the most serious (usually international) cases.

4.2.4 County Court

There are about 200 County Courts around England and Wales, although the current Conservative government has announced that many of these will close over the coming years. These courts have jurisdiction to hear:

- claims based on the law of contract;
- claims based on the law of tort;
- claims for the recovery of land, e.g. landlord and tenant disputes;
- matters connected to trusts, mortgages and dissolution of partnerships: for all these there is a financial limit in that the amount of the fund or the value of the property involved cannot exceed £30,000;
- contentious probate proceedings where the net value of the estate is less than £30,000.

N.B. The County Court used to deal with cases relating to family law, but this work has been taken over by the Family Court.

There are financial limitations on the jurisdiction of the County Court. This can be seen in the above list. However, where the parties agree that the County Court should have jurisdiction then it is possible for larger claims to be dealt with here. Otherwise the case will have to be dealt with in the High Court which has unlimited jurisdiction. In fact, all claims for less than £25,000 have to be started in the County Court. In addition, personal injury cases of less than £50,000 must be started in the County Court, but where the claim is for more than £50,000 it should be tried in the High Court unless it is more suitable for trial in a County Court.

There used to be a geographical limitation although claims could be started in any County Court, but if a claim was defended it was usually transferred to the County Court for the district in which the defendant's address for service is situated. Under the Crime and Courts Act 2013, a single County Court was created so that it is now one court but sits in different towns and cities. This makes it easier for cases to be started without any geographical limitation.

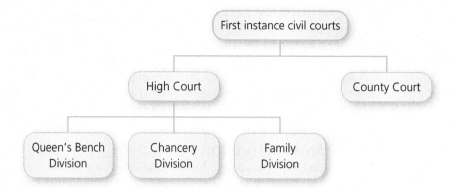

Figure 4.1 First instance civil courts

There is also a limitation in that defamation cases must be started in the High Court although it is then possible for such cases to be transferred for trial to the County Court where suitable.

4.2.5 Small claims

In 1973 a new procedure for small claims was started within the County Court. This was a more informal hearing which encouraged parties to take the case without the help of lawyers. Initially the limit on small claims was £75, but by 1979 it had increased to £500 and, by 1991, £1,000. In 1999 the limit was increased to £5,000, and, most recently, in 2013 the limit was increased to £10,000.

The small claims procedure allows the District Judge to be flexible in the way he deals with each case. To achieve this, District Judges are encouraged to be more inquisitorial and given training in how to handle small claims cases, so that they will take an active part in the proceedings, asking questions and making sure that both parties explain all their important points. Litigants are encouraged to take their own case so that costs are kept low. However, it is possible to have a lawyer to represent you at a small claims hearing but the winner cannot claim the costs of using a lawyer from the losing party.

4.2.6 The track system

The Woolf Report (see section 4.4) recommended that civil cases should be allocated to one of three tracks. These are based on the value of the amount claimed. The three tracks now are:

- small claims cases with a limit of £10,000;
- fast-track cases from £10,000 to £25,000;
- multi-track cases over £25,000.

Small claims track

This track kept the same principles as the earlier small claims court. However, the general limit now is £10,000, but parties with a larger claim can have their case dealt with as a small claims case if they agree. The limit for personal injury and housing cases is lower, at £1,000. All small claims cases are dealt with in the County Court. Where possible, the case is dealt with at one hearing with no pre-trial hearing. The judge has flexibility to run the proceedings in the way he thinks is the most suitable for each case.

Fast-track cases

The limits on these cases are normally £10,000 to £25,000 but cases for a greater value can be dealt with in this way if they are straightforward. In addition, claims which are for less than £25,000 may be dealt with as multi-track cases if they are thought to be too complex for the fast-track system. All fast-track cases are dealt with in the County Court. The aim is that all fast-track cases should be heard within 30 weeks of the case being set down for trial. The length of the hearing should be no more than one day. To save cost and delay, only one joint expert witness is allowed. There are also fixed costs for hearings.

Multi-track cases

These are for claims over £25,000 or for complex cases for a lesser amount. These can be started and heard in either the County Court or the High Court. The emphasis in multi-track cases is on case management by the judge. This should mean that issues are identi-fied and the judge can set timetables for any pre-trial procedure that is necessary.

Allocation of cases to the tracks

The allocation of each case to its proper track is based on answers given by the parties to an allocation questionnaire (Form N150). Once a defence is filed, the court sends this questionnaire to both parties. The main consideration in allocating a case to a track is the amount of the claim, but the allocation judge will also consider the complexity of the facts of the case, whether there are difficult issues of law involved, the amount of oral evidence, the time the hearing is likely to take and the wishes of the parties.

4.2.7 Transfer of cases between the County Court and the High Court

All small claims and fast-track cases must be started in the County Court and will be tried there. However, as we have seen, multi-track cases can be started in either the High Court or the County Court. There are various rules about when cases should be trans-ferred. Section 40 of the County Courts Act 1984 allows defamation claims and other contract and tort cases to be transferred from the High Court to the County Court. Under Rule 30.3 of the Civil Procedure Rules (CPR) the following criteria are considered:

1. the financial value of the claim and the amount in dispute, if different;
2. whether it would be more convenient or fair for hearings (including the trial) to be held in some other court;
3. the availability of a judge specialising in the type of claim in question;
4. the complexity of the facts, legal issues, remedies or procedures involved;
5. the importance of the outcome of the claim to the public in general; and
6. the facilities available at the court where the claim is being dealt with and whether they may be inadequate because of any disabilities of a party or potential witness.

In addition, a Practice Direction has been issued under Part 29 of the CPR, stating that certain types of proceedings are particularly suitable for trial in the High Court and, there-fore, should not normally be transferred to a County Court. These are cases involving:

1. professional negligence;
2. fatal accidents;
3. allegations of fraud or undue influence;
4. defamation;
5. malicious prosecution or false imprisonment;
6. claims against the police;
7. contentious probate claims.

This Practice Direction does not totally prevent the transfer of such cases to the County Court, especially where the parties agree to the trial taking place in the County Court.

Amount claimed	Where case is started	Where case is tried
Up to £10,000 *but* personal injury cases and housing cases only up to £1,000	County Court	County Court Small claims track
Between £10,000 and £25,000 *and* personal injury cases and housing cases from £1,000	County Court	County Court Fast track
Over £25,000 or complex cases of less value	County Court or High Court	County Court or High Court Usually tried in court where case was commenced
Exceptions: personal injury cases up to £50,000	County Court only	Cases over £50,000 are likely to be transferred to High Court
Defamation cases	High Court only	County Court can hear any value (even over £50,000) with the agreement of the parties

Figure 4.2 Starting and trying cases in the civil courts

ACTIVITY

Applying the law

Explain where the claims in the following situations may be started and tried.

1. A month ago Selina bought a washing machine for £350. It has developed several minor faults including a leak. Selina has complained to the shop where she bought the machine. They have offered to replace it with another machine of the same model, but they refuse to refund her money. Selina wants to return the machine and claim its cost. Advise Selina as to which court she must start proceedings in and to which track the case is likely to be allocated.
2. Tyler was seriously injured when a car mounted a pavement and hit him as he was waiting for a bus. He estimates his claim as being for about £85,000. Advise him as to which court(s) he may commence his claim in, the track to which it is likely to be allocated and in which court(s) it may be tried.
3. Victoria suffered minor injuries when a car in which she was a passenger crashed. She has been told that she is likely to get £12,000 in damages. Advise her as to which court she must start proceedings in and the track to which her case is likely to be allocated.
4. Wallace wishes to sue a local newspaper for defamation. He is prepared to limit his claim to £20,000. Advise him as to which court(s) he may commence his claim in, the track to which it is likely to be allocated and in which court(s) it may be tried.
5. Yves has had an extension built on to his house. The work has been done so badly that the foundations of the original house have been damaged and it has cost Yves £30,000 to put them right. Advise him as to in which court(s) he may commence his claim, the track to which it is likely to be allocated and in which court(s) it may be tried.

4.3 Problems in the civil justice system

During the second half of the twentieth century it was felt that taking a case to court was very expensive. There were also excessive delays, so that the average wait from issuing a claim in the County Court to the trial was three years, while for the High Court it was five years. Between 1950 and the year 2000, this problem of delay was considered on six occasions by different committees. These were:

- the Evershed Committee (1953);
- the Winn Committee (1968);
- the Cantley Committee (1979);
- the Civil Justice Review (1988);
- the Heilbron–Hodge Committee (1993); and
- the Woolf Review (1995–96).

The first three reports led to minor changes but these had little effect on the problems of delay and cost. The last three led to more major changes. In particular, the Woolf Report instituted the three-track system and a complete new set of CPR. This has led to a change in attitude of litigants and lawyers, from an adversarial stance of the two parties in a case to a more cooperative one.

4.3.1 The Civil Justice Review

The Civil Justice Review produced five consultation papers on different types of civil claim, covering personal injuries, small claims, the Commercial Court, enforcement of debt and housing cases.

The Review thought that delay was a matter of public concern for the following reasons:

1. it caused personal stress, anxiety and financial hardship to claimants and their families;
2. these pressures often led claimants to accept low settlement offers;
3. delay reduced the availability of evidence and eroded the reliability of the evidence which was available;
4. delay meant that compensation was delayed until long after it was needed;
5. it lowered public estimation of the legal system.

A major recommendation of the Civil Justice Review was that there should be no upper limit on the jurisdiction of the County Court. This was given effect through s1 of the Courts and Legal Services Act 1990 (CLSA 1990) which gave the Lord Chancellor power to confer jurisdiction on the County Courts and to allocate business between the High Court and the County Courts. And in 1991 the Lord Chancellor exercised this power to remove the upper limit on the County Court.

The Civil Justice Review also proposed various changes to combat delay, but virtually none of them was adopted immediately after the Review. Some of them on the timetable of cases were repeated in the Woolf Report and subsequently brought into effect. These were:

- laying down and enforcing a strict timetable for larger cases;
- giving court administrators targets for trials;
- the court taking control of the timetable.

4.3.2 The Heilbron–Hodge Committee

The Heilbron–Hodge Committee was set up by the Law Society and the Bar Council. The fact that the legal professions took this step underlines the dissatisfaction with the civil justice system. The Heilbron–Hodge Committee, which reported in 1993, started with the concept:

QUOTATION

'It is axiomatic that in any free and democratic society all citizens should be equal before the law. This means that all litigants, rich and poor, however large or however small is the subject matter of their litigation, should have access to a fair and impartial system of disputes resolution.'

'Civil Justice on Trial: The Case for Change' (1993), p 6, para 1.8(ii)

The Committee thought that the existing court procedures were 'unnecessarily technical, inflexible, rule-ridden, formalistic and often incomprehensible to the ordinary litigant'. They also pointed out that fear of the cost of litigation deterred people from using the courts, and that most people want their dispute resolved rather than have their 'day in court'.

One of the Committee's main recommendations was that the court should take over control of cases. It said:

QUOTATION

'Litigants and their lawyers need to have imposed upon them, within sensible procedural time-frames, an obligation to prosecute and defend their proceedings with efficiency and despatch. Therefore, once the process of the court is invoked, the court should have a more active and responsible role over the progress and conduct of cases.'

Many of their recommendations were aimed at simplifying procedures and some of these were put into effect by Practice Directions which were issued to all three divisions of the High Court in 1995.

Other recommendations were more far-reaching. These included a recommendation that the Queen's Bench Division and the Chancery Division of the High Court should be merged into one single division, but this solution was not adopted. Other recommendations were that more High Court Judges should be appointed; this was aimed both at avoiding the long waiting time for a case to be heard and at the overuse of Deputy High Court Judges. This recommendation was implemented by the Lord Chancellor's Department and over the period from 1993 to 2003 the number of High Court Judges was increased from 60 to 73. The number has since increased to over 100.

4.4 The Woolf Report

This enquiry was headed by Lord Justice Woolf. It started its deliberations in 1994 with an Interim Report being published in 1995 and a final report in 1996. It built on many of the recommendations of the Civil Justice Review and the Heilbron–Hodge Report. As in that Report, Lord Woolf highlighted the lack of court control over cases when he wrote in his report:

QUOTATION

> 'In particular there is no clear judicial responsibility for managing individual cases or for the overall administration of the civil courts.'
>
> *Interim Report of the Woolf Report 'Inquiry into Civil Justice,*
> *Access to Justice' (1995), p 7, para 1*

Lord Woolf also considered whether the High Court and the County Court should be amalgamated to form one civil court but concluded that this was not necessary provided that there was flexibility between the courts. He said:

QUOTATION

> '6. I have therefore considered whether to recommend the unification of the two courts. This would be an advance since it would produce a single, vertically integrated court. However, very much the same result could be achieved if the movement towards aligning the jurisdiction of the county courts and the High Court was continued and the powers of Circuit judges were to be extended. This would make it generally unnecessary to identify the criteria which mark the boundary between the jurisdiction.'
>
> *Interim Report of the Woolf Report 'Inquiry into Civil Justice, Access to Justice'*
> *(1995), Ch 12, para 6*

The Interim Report proposed:

- extending small claims up to £3,000 – this was brought into effect immediately and later extended to £5,000;
- a new fast track for straightforward cases up to £10,000 – when the track system came into force in 1999, some four years after the Interim Report, the upper limit was set at £15,000 and in 2009 increased to £25,000;
- a new multitrack for cases for higher value or complex cases with capping of costs;
- encouraging the use of alternative dispute resolution (ADR);
- giving judges more responsibility for managing cases;
- more use of information technology (IT);
- simpler documents and procedures.

The final Woolf Report 'Access to Justice' was published in July 1996. This extended the ideas of the Interim Report and set out key objectives which were:

- parties to be encouraged to explore alternatives to a court resolution of a dispute;
- a single set of rules governing proceedings in the High Court and the County Court;
- a shorter timetable for cases to reach court and for length of trials;
- more affordable litigation.

4.4.1 The track system

The track system was a key component of the Woolf Report. The intention of it is that cases should be dealt with in a way that is proportionate to the value of the claim and the importance of the issues in the case. Prior to the Woolf reforms it was found that for smaller claims the costs of cases were often higher than the value of the claim. By increasing the limit on the amount that could be dealt with as a small claim and introducing the fast track for intermediate value claims it was hoped that the cost would be considerably reduced.

The emphasis on case management in multitrack was also aimed at reducing cost and delay. Lord Woolf pointed out:

QUOTATION

'14. The new multi-track will itself straddle the High Court and the county courts. Within it cases will be handled by High Court judges, Circuit judges, Masters and District judges. The courts, through the procedural judges, will have responsibility for ensuring that cases are dealt with at the appropriate level.'

Interim Report of the Woolf Report 'Inquiry into Civil Justice, Access to Justice' (1995), Ch 12, para 14

4.4.2 Civil procedure

The Woolf Report led to a completely new set of CPR. These form a single procedural code so that the same rules apply in both the High Court and the County Court. The general objectives in making or altering the CPR are set out in s1(3) of the Civil Procedure Act 1997 as amended by the Courts Act 2003. This states:

SECTION

's 1(3) Any power to make or alter Civil Procedure Rules is to be exercised with a view to securing that –

(a) the system of civil justice is accessible, fair and efficient, and

(b) the rules are both simple and simply expressed.'

Within the CPR, Rule 1.1 sets out that the overriding objective of the CPR is to enable courts to deal with cases justly. Rule 1.2 explains that this includes:

1. ensuring that the parties are on an equal footing;
2. saving expense;
3. dealing with the case in ways which are proportionate to:
    - the amount of money involved,
    - the importance of the case,
    - the complexity of the issues, and
    - the financial position of each party;
4. ensuring that it is dealt with expeditiously and fairly; and
5. allotting to it an appropriate share of the court's resources, while taking into account the need to allot resources to other cases.

4.4.3 Case management

As already seen, case management is an important feature in multi-track cases. Rule 1.4 of the CPR sets out what is involved in case management:

'r 1.4 (1) The court must further the overriding objective by actively managing cases. (2) Active case management includes:

(a) encouraging the parties to co-operate with each other in the conduct of the proceedings;
(b) identifying the issues at an early stage;
(c) deciding promptly which issues need full investigation and trial and accordingly disposing summarily of the others;
(d) deciding the order in which issues are to be decided;
(e) encouraging the parties to use an alternative dispute resolution procedure if the court considers that appropriate and facilitating the use of such procedure;
(f) helping the parties settle the whole or part of the case;
(g) fixing timetables or otherwise controlling the progress of the case;
(h) considering whether the likely benefit of taking a particular step justifies the cost of taking it;
(i) dealing with the case without the parties needing to attend court;
(j) making use of technology; and
(k) giving directions to ensure that the trial of a case proceeds quickly and efficiently.'

This is a very comprehensive list which allows judges to decide what is necessary for each particular case and gives wide powers to ensure that cases are dealt with properly.

4.4.4 Pre-action protocols

In order to make sure that parties have taken all necessary steps before starting a case, pre-action protocols for different types of claim have been produced, giving very clear guidance on what a claimant needs to do. If a claimant does not adhere to these pre-action protocols then he may not be awarded his full costs at the end of the case, even though he wins the case.

4.4.5 Encouraging alternative dispute resolution

Rule 1.4(2)(e) of the CPR states that the court must encourage the parties to use an ADR procedure if the court considers that appropriate and, if so, facilitate the use of such procedure. Although the rule only states that the court should encourage ADR, the courts have taken a tough line. In *R (Cowl and others) v Plymouth City Council* [2001] EWCA Civ 1935 the Court of Appeal held that judicial review proceedings about the closure of an old people's home should be allowed to go ahead if a significant part of the issues could be resolved by ADR. Lord Woolf, giving judgment, said:

JUDGMENT

'the importance of this appeal is that it illustrates that, even in disputes between public authorities and members of the public for whom they are responsible, sufficient attention is paid to the paramount importance of avoiding litigation whenever that is possible'.

He stated that if necessary the court might have to hold, on its own initiative, an inter-parties hearing in which the parties could explain what steps they had taken to resolve the dispute without involvement of the court. This placed the lawyers on both sides under a heavy obligation to use ADR unless it really proved impossible.

The Court of Appeal showed the same tough attitude to the use of ADR instead of litigation in *Dunnett v Railtrack plc (in administration)* [2002] EWCA Civ 303; [2002] 2 All ER 850 where the court applied cost penalties for a failure to use ADR. What had happened was that the claimant had been granted leave to appeal, but in giving leave the trial judge advised both parties that they should consider the use of ADR. The defendant declined to mediate. On the hearing of the appeal the claimant's appeal was dismissed but the defendant was not awarded costs, because of his refusal to try ADR. Brooke LJ said:

JUDGMENT

'It is hoped that publicity will draw the attention of lawyers to their duties to further the overriding objective ... and to the possibility that, if they turn down out of hand the chance of alternative dispute resolution when suggested by the court, as happened on this occasion, they may have to face uncomfortable cost consequences.'

This case was the first time that a successful party was refused costs because they declined to mediate.

In *Cable & Wireless plc v IBM United Kingdom Ltd* [2002] EWHC 2059 (Comm) the judge held that a contractual term providing for mandatory ADR in the event of a dispute was capable of being enforced by a stay of any proceedings. However, this could only happen if there was sufficient certainty as to what type of ADR procedure should be used. The court stressed the overriding objective of the CPR and also the encouragement of ADR in case management under Rule 1.4(2)(e).

This very hard line on the use of ADR was considered as going beyond 'encouraging' ADR. Indeed, Khawar Qureshi, in an article 'Doors of the High Court are Opened by Fewer and Fewer' (*The Times*, 27 April 2004) pointed out that it could violate Article 6 of the ECHR – the right to a fair trial. The matter was considered further by the courts in the conjoined appeals of *Halsey v Milton Keynes General NHS Trust* and *Steel v Joy and another* [2004] EWCA Civ 576. In this case the Law Society was joined as an interested party and put forward arguments on the point of when ADR should be used. The Court of Appeal stressed the distinction between encouraging mediation strongly and ordering it and said:

JUDGMENT

'to oblige truly unwilling parties to refer their disputes to mediation would be to impose an unacceptable obstruction on their right of access to the courts'.

Lord Justice Lawton set out the relevant factors to be considered in deciding whether to impose a costs penalty for refusal to try ADR. He started by pointing out that an order to deprive a successful party of some or all of his costs because that party had refused to agree to ADR was an exception to the general rule that costs should follow the event. The burden was on the unsuccessful party to show why there should be a departure from the general rule. Relevant factors to be considered in such cases were:

- The nature of the dispute: some cases were unsuitable for ADR; these included cases where there was a point of law or interpretation in issue, claims involving fraud and cases where there was a claim for an injunction.

- The merits of the case: where a party reasonably believes that he has a watertight case then he may be justified in refusing to use ADR.
- Previous attempts to settle by other methods: although parties should realise that mediation often succeeded where other attempts to settle had failed.
- The cost of mediation: this is particularly important where the amount being claimed is relatively small.
- Delay: if mediation was suggested late in the case and would have the effect of delaying the trial then that was a good reason for refusing ADR.
- Whether mediation had a reasonable prospect of success.

So, the present position is that the court will continue to strongly encourage the use of ADR, while recognising that there are circumstances in which a refusal to attempt ADR is justified.

Position taken at mediation

In the *Earl of Malmesbury v Strutt and Parker* [2008] EWHC 424 (QB) it was held that not only should the court consider litigants' willingness to engage in mediation but also the position taken in such mediation. If one party takes an unreasonable position then there can be a costs penalty. The case involved negligence of estate agents who were acting on behalf of the Earl in negotiating leases of part of his land to Bournemouth Airport. The claim was for just over £87 million. Mediation was attempted, but Malmesbury's solicitors approached the mediation with a very high figure in mind and refused to budge during the courts of the mediation. The mediation failed.

At the trial of the case, the Earl won but was only awarded just under £1 million, not the £87 million claimed. This was because the judge applied a loss of capital calculation rather than a loss of income calculation. On the Earl's application for all the costs of the case, the judge, Jack J, considered the position that the parties had taken during the mediation. He said:

JUDGMENT

'As far as I am aware the courts have not had to consider the situation where a party has agreed to mediation but has then taken an unreasonable position in the mediation. It is not dissimilar in effect to an unreasonable refusal to engage in mediation … a party who agrees to mediation but then causes the mediation to fail by reason of his unreasonable position in the mediation is in reality in the same position as a party who unreasonably refuses to mediate.'

As a result the judge held that the position taken by the claimant's side in the mediation was an unreasonable one and only awarded the claimant a fraction of his costs. This was critical as the claimant's costs were more than the damages awarded to him. The total costs for both sides were £5.38 million.

4.4.6 Strict timetables

One of the key points of case management is that the courts should set timetables for the parties, and that these timetables should be strictly enforced. This has been done with a strictness that sometimes seems out of proportion.

CASE EXAMPLE

Vinos v Marks and Spencer plc [2001] 3 All ER 784

The claimant had suffered injuries at work. His solicitor negotiated with the defendants over a long period of time but no settlement was reached. A week before the expiry of the limitation period for issuing proceedings the solicitor issued a claim, but because of an oversight did not serve it on the defendants until nine days after the four-month period set out in the CPR for serving claims. The claimant applied for an extension of time to serve the proceedings. The Court of Appeal refused to give this.

It is noticeable in this case that the Court of Appeal was not prepared to apply Rule 3.10 of the CPR which provides:

> where there has been an error of procedure such as failure to comply with a rule or practice direction (a) the error does not invalidate any step taken in the proceedings unless the court so orders; and (b) the court may make an order to remedy the error.

The Court of Appeal held that the general words of this rule did not allow it to extend the period for service.

Later in the same year (2001) the Court of Appeal made another strict decision on time limits in *Godwin v Swindon Borough Council* [2001] EWCA Civ 1478; [2001] 4 All ER 641.

CASE EXAMPLE

Godwin v Swindon Borough Council [2001] EWCA Civ 1478; [2001] 4 All ER 641

The claim form actually arrived with the defendants in time but the 'deeming' provision in Rule 6.7(1) of the CPR meant that it was deemed to have arrived three days late. Even though there was evidence that it had arrived in time, the court ruled that the service of the claim was out of time and refused to remedy the situation. Again, the court refused to use other provisions in the CPR which would have allowed the case to go ahead. In particular, the court refused to use Rule 6.9 of the CPR which gives the court power to dispense with service altogether, as it felt that that would condone the failure to comply with the express terms of the rule about service.

In the next year the same point about service occurred in *Anderton v Clwyd County Council* [2002] EWCA Civ 933; [2002] 3 All ER 813 which involved five separate appeals on the point. The Court of Appeal again held that the deemed date of service under Rule 6.7(1) of the CPR could not be rebutted by evidence that the claim form had in fact been received earlier (and within the time for service). However, unlike in the case of *Godwin v Swindon Borough Council* (2001), it was prepared to use its power under Rule 6.9 of the CPR to dispense with service altogether. The court held that this could be done in exceptional circumstances where there had been an attempt to serve within the time limit, even though this was not successful.

However, in *Cranfield v Bridgegrove Ltd* [2003] EWCA Civ 656; [2003] 3 All ER 129, where the same point was again considered by the Court of Appeal, the court held that the principle established in *Godwin* (2001) was important. The court would only exercise its power to dispense with service under Rule 6.9 of the CPR in truly exceptional cases. The court would not normally exercise its discretion where there had been late service. So it can be seen that the time limits set down in the CPR are enforced very strictly.

4.4.7 Judgment in default and summary judgment

Default judgment

default judgment

Judgment given for the claimant because the defendant has failed to file documents in time

In cases where the defendant fails to file either an acknowledgement of service or a defence within the time limits, the claimant can normally ask the court to give judgment in the case in his favour. This is known as a **default judgment**. This means that the case ends at this point with a judgment for the claimant. However, the default judgment can be set aside if it was obtained in breach of the technical rules or if the defendant can show that he has a real prospect of successfully defending the claim or if it appears to the court that there is some other good reason why the default judgment should be set aside.

Summary judgment

This is where the defendant has both acknowledged service and filed a defence within the correct time limits, but the defence does not reveal a real defence. In such cases the court has power to give summary judgment for the claimant (Part 24 of the CPR). This can be done where the claimant applies for summary judgment or where the court identifies the case as being one where there is no real defence. The test applied by the court is whether the defendant has a real prospect of success.

It is also possible for the court to strike out a claim if it discloses no reasonable grounds for bringing the case.

4.4.8 Part 36 offers to settle

Under the CPR both the defendant and the claimant can make an official offer to settle the case. Prior to the Woolf reforms, only the defendant could do this by making a payment into court. If the claimant was then awarded less than the amount paid in, the claimant had to pay the defendant's costs of the case. Part 36 allows the court more discretion on what costs order should be made where there has been a Part 36 offer.

Part 36 offers have proved popular with both claimants and defendants and frequently lead to the case being settled.

4.4.9 Are the Woolf reforms a success?

Lord Woolf thought that a civil justice system should:

- be just in the results it delivers;
- be fair in the way it treats litigants;
- offer appropriate procedures at a reasonable cost;
- deal with cases at a reasonable speed;
- be understandable to those who use it;
- provide as much certainty as the nature of particular cases allows;
- be effective, adequately resourced and organised.

In fact, the great majority of civil legal disputes do not even get as far as lawyers, let alone into the courts. In 1984 the Oxford Socio-Legal Centre published research into personal injury cases (D Harris *et al.*, *Compensation and Support for Illness and Injury* (Clarendon Press, 1984)). This study was based on a national household survey which produced a random sample of 1,711 victims of accidents who had suffered some impairment for at least two weeks after their accident. Only 26 per cent of these had even considered claiming damages. Fourteen per cent had actually consulted a solicitor and most of these (12 per cent of the original sample, some 182 cases) had received damages. Of the 12 per cent where damages were obtained, in two in five cases a claim had been issued in the courts, but there was a court hearing in only five cases. This represented 2.7 per cent of the 182 who obtained damages, but only 0.2 per cent of the total sample of 1,711.

In 1999 Hazel Genn published a study (*Paths to Justice* (Hart Publishing, 1999)) in which she had surveyed 4,125 randomly selected adults to find out what experience they had had of any legal problems. She found that two out of every five people had experienced a problem which could have led to litigation. About 60 per cent of these tried to resolve the problem with advice, about one-third tried to resolve it without advice and about 5 per cent did nothing. Although people sought advice, they were unlikely to use the courts to resolve their dispute. Only two out of ten cases used legal proceedings or contacted an Ombudsman. In many of these cases the people in the survey had had cases taken against them. So very few of those in the survey actually initiated proceedings.

If the civil justice system was cheaper, quicker and simpler, one would expect that more people would be prepared to consider litigation if they could not achieve a satisfactory conclusion to their dispute by other means.

Fewer cases

In fact the number of cases heard at first instance decreased between 1990 and 2003. This trend started following the Civil Justice Review 1985 and the CLSA 1990 which made major changes to the distribution of work between the High Court and the County Court. The trend continued following the Woolf reforms.

There was a slight increase in County Court claims in the early 1990s, with the removal of the upper limit in that court. However, as Figure 4.3 shows, the overall trend was for fewer cases to be started, with the lowest year being 2003. After that there was a gradual increase to 2009. Since then the numbers decreased, with an increase again in 2015.

The decrease can be interpreted in two opposing ways. The first is that more cases are settled through negotiation and so fewer cases are started in the courts. This view would suggest that the Woolf reforms have been a success, as one of the changes in 'culture' that Lord Woolf wanted to bring about was that disputants should view litigation as a last resort and disputes should be settled by non-court means. The second point of view is that there are fewer cases because people increasingly perceive court proceedings as being slow, costly and complex. If this is the reason for the reducing numbers of cases then the Woolf reforms have failed in their objectives.

Research

The first substantial study carried out on the effect of the Woolf reforms was 'More Civil Justice? The Impact of the Woolf Reforms on Pre-action Behaviour' by Tamara Goriely, Richard Moorhead and Pamela Abrams (May 2002) which was published jointly by the Law Society and the Civil Justice Council. This study concentrated on pre-action behaviour and pre-action protocols and was based on interviews with 54 solicitors dealing with personal injury cases, clinical negligence cases or housing repair cases. The study found that in all three markets claimant work was concentrated in fewer, more specialist solicitor firms. This was mainly the result of Legal Services Commission policy rather than the Woolf reforms.

Year	1990	1994	1998	1999	2003	2007	2009	2011	2012	2015
Number of claims started in the Queen's Bench Division	350,000	157,453	114,984	72,161	14,191	18,505	18,600	13,928	14,454	10,366
Number of claims started in the County Court (excluding family cases)	3,034,923	2,487,377	2,010,606	1,760,308	1,347,414	1,555,486	1,879,000	1,553,983	1,394,230	1,565,927

Figure 4.3 Number of claims commenced in the Queen's Bench Division and the County Court

The study focused on fast-track cases. It showed:

- a less adversarial culture;
- a greater willingness to 'put cards on the table';
- Part 36 offers are popular;
- insurance companies were more prepared to settle;

but

- in personal injury cases front-loading of work meant that costs went up;
- generally the ratio of costs to damages remains the same as pre-Woolf – 68 per cent;
- delay has not improved because solicitors do more work before opening proper negotiations (because of the tight timetables once cases are started);
- overall the average time for settlement in personal injury cases was 13 months (similar to pre-Woolf) but the minimum time was longer, mainly because getting medical reports takes longer than before.

The study also found that there were problems in other areas, in particular inconsistent case management by judges and difficulties with conditional fee agreements (CFAs).

A study, 'Further Funding: A Continuing Evaluation of the Civil Justice Reforms' (LCD, August 2002) stated that the time between issue and hearing for small claims had risen slightly but 'may now be falling'. On costs the study concludes that there is 'conflicting evidence' and many of the claims for more expense are 'anecdotal'.

Suzanne Burn considered all the available evidence in 'The Woolf reforms in retrospect' (2003) *Legal Action* 8. She points out that it is difficult to isolate 'the Woolf factor' because there are a number of other factors that came into effect either at the same time as the Woolf reforms or within a short time afterwards. These include:

- the withdrawal of legal aid from certain types of civil claim, in particular personal injury cases;
- the widening of the scope of CFAs together with the ability to recover success fees and insurance premiums (see Chapter 7 for detailed information);
- the introduction of tougher standards and controls by both the Law Society and the Legal Services Commission;
- the implementation of the HRA 1998 in October 2000.

With the overlapping effects of these other changes and also the fact that there is only limited empirical research, Burn pointed out that measuring the success or otherwise of the Woolf reforms is difficult. However, she does state:

QUOTATION

'Certainly the total volume of litigation has fallen since April 1999. But this was a well-established trend going back many years. The rate of settlement between issue and trial has also increased ... and anecdotally the number of fast track trials, in particular, has dropped sharply in many courts. But the time taken for cases to get to trial has surprisingly improved very little post-April 1999 ... A factor in this is almost certainly the continuing under-resourcing of many County Courts which causes delays in issuing, allocation, listing and production of orders.'

Burn also highlighted other areas where there were still problems. These include the fact that the new CPR are very lengthy and too many amendments have been issued – some 32 amendments in four years, at the time Burn was writing. There is also the fact that small claims listings seem to have suffered as priority has been given to fast-track and multi-track conferences and trials. Increases in court fees and problems in the enforcement of judgments may also have played a part in reducing the number of small claims cases. In multi-track cases some practitioners told Burn that they had doubts about the usefulness of case management, with some claiming that case management 'takes extra time and cost, but adds little value'. The main complaints were that conferences were not arranged efficiently and judges often had not read the papers in advance.

Lack of IT
Lord Woolf's recommendations included that more use should be made of IT to make the court system more efficient. Burn felt very strongly that 'the lack of investment in the civil courts, particularly the County Courts greatly handicapped the development of an accessible, efficient, modern civil justice system in England and Wales'.

This point was also made by Lord Justice Brooke in May 2003. In a speech at a seminar in Leeds he said:

QUOTATION

'Far and away our greatest need is to introduce software systems which will enable court staff and judges to manage court business better in the civil and family courts. Today the courts are not networked … we are miles behind most government departments and modern private sector businesses … At present we rely on paper filing systems. It is not always easy to retain and motivate staff when files go missing, or get into a muddle quite so often. Nowadays court users have every reason to complain about some of the delays and inefficiencies that occur.'

In his report, 'Should the Courts be Unified' (Judicial Office, August 2008) Brooke LJ again commented on the need for good IT. He pointed out that the government has not given the Courts Service sufficient funding to meet the Woolf objectives. He stressed that the civil justice system was in crisis. Hazel Genn in the Hamlyn lectures in 2008 also stated that the whole civil justice system has been allowed to decline.

More recently Lord Justice Briggs authored the 'Civil Courts Structure Review' (Courts and Tribunals Judiciary, July 2016), in which he recommended that a new Online Court be created. This Online Court would involve litigants not being represented by lawyers, but digitally exchanging documents and information about their case, with the process being overseen by a judge. IT would therefore be central to the court's operation, and Lord Justice Briggs was hopeful that this would make access to the courts easier, quicker and cheaper for many.

In September 2016 the Lord Chancellor, Lord Chief Justice and Senior President of Tribunals released a report, 'Transforming Our Justice System' (Ministry of Justice, 2016), in which they committed to spending £700 million to modernise the court and tribunal systems. This report promised, by 2019, a greater use of IT and digitisation within the courts to increase transparency and efficiency throughout the justice system. It is yet to be seen whether this investment will finally address the problem identified by Lord Woolf.

Recent criticisms
In 2011 the government in its consultation paper, 'Solving Disputes in the County Court', pointed out that it was 15 years since the Woolf Report and the system has not kept pace with the 'major economic and social shifts that have taken place since'. It believes that

the system needs to focus more on dispute resolution and debt recovery, rather than the ideals of 'justice'. In particular, it pointed out that the costs of taking a case to court are often more than the amount claimed. The ideal is that disputes: 'should be resolved in the most appropriate forum, so that processes and costs are commensurate with the complexity of the issues involved'.

It proposed a range of options to achieve this, including:

- fixed costs (already used for traffic accidents under £10,000) to be extended to other personal injury claims for up to £25,000 or even £50,000;

- requiring all cases below the small claims limit to have attempted settlement by mediation, before being considered for a hearing;

- introducing mediation information/assessment sessions for claims above the small claims limit to try to divert more cases into ADR;

- increasing the upper level for small claims to at least £10,000.

These proposals were implemented by Parliament in the Crime and Courts Act 2013. The long-term impacts of these reforms are yet to be determined.

Critics

One of the main critics of the Woolf reforms throughout has been Professor Zander. From 1995 onwards he published articles and essays pointing out likely problems in the approach taken by Lord Woolf (see 'The Woolf Report: Forwards or Backwards for the New Lord Chancellor' (1997) 16 *Civil Justice Quarterly Review*, 208–227). With evidence now emerging that the reforms have not been as successful as hoped, Zander wrote that he:

QUOTATION

'remains of the view that on balance the disadvantages of the reforms outweigh the advantages. He believes that if Lord Woolf had presented his package of reforms with an admission that, in addition to the great upheaval involved, they would end by costing most litigants more, that they would not greatly reduce delays (if at all) and that they would hugely increase uncontrollable judicial discretion, it is doubtful whether they would have been implemented.'

M Zander, Cases and Materials on the English Legal System
(10th edn, LexisNexis Butterworths, 2007), p 140

In 2009, Zander reviewed the ten years from the Woolf reforms and pointed out that there was still a delay in cases. The delay had merely changed from after issue of the case to before starting a case. He also noted that the complexity of the rules had increased as the CPR are more than five times longer than the rule books preWoolf. Matters were made worse by the fact that there had been 49 updates in the ten years since the first issue of the CPR. Finally, on the issue of costs, he pointed out that there was universal agreement that costs have increased.

Cost

The cost of a court action is not always the most important issue for people when deciding to start a court case. This was shown by a research paper, 'What's Cost Got to Do With It? The Impact of Charging Court Fees on Users', Ministry of Justice Research Series 04/07 (2007). This found that the main reasons people take court proceedings were:

- 'getting a final decision' (especially for those going through a divorce or in child contact/residency cases); and

- 'getting justice'.

The great majority of individuals (93 per cent) considered alternative options before entering the court process to try to resolve their issue. Overall, two in three individuals used legal representation, but there were great differences depending on the type of case. Those in divorce proceedings were much more likely to have legal representation, especially for ancillary issues (89 per cent division of assets, 80 per cent child contact/residence), while for ordinary money claims only 17 per cent had legal representation.

The cost of going to court was ranked very low on the list of factors considered when going to court, especially in divorce cases. Seven out of ten people said that higher court fees would not have affected their decision to proceed to court.

Jackson Report
Although the cost of going to court was ranked very low, it is still worrying that the cost of cases has increased since the Woolf reforms. In 2008 Lord Justice Jackson was given the task of making recommendations to reform the cost system. The objective was:

QUOTATION

> 'to carry out an independent review of the rules and principles governing the costs of civil litigation and to make recommendation in order to promote access to justice at proportionate cost'.
>
> *Civil Litigation Costs Review (May 2009)*

In his Preliminary Report (May 2009) Jackson highlighted several problems in the present costs system. The main ones were:

- Should the rule that costs follow the event be changed?
- Should the existing range of fixed costs be extended?
- Is there any way that the high costs currently incurred in respect of processing personal injury claims can be reduced, while ensuring that proper compensation reaches claimants?
- The need to control the costs of 'heavy' litigation (high value commercial claims).
- Whether, where a party has been represented under a **conditional fee agreement** (CFA), success fees and after-the-event insurance premiums should be recoverable from the losing party.
- The need for a better method for assessing costs.

conditional fee agreement
An agreement under which the client pays nothing if he loses the case

In his final report, 'Review of Civil Litigation Costs', Lord Jackson stressed the need for costs to be proportionate to the claim. This recommendation was brought into force in April 2013 by new costs rules. CPR Rule 44.3(5) states:

SECTION

> 'Costs are proportionate if they bear a reasonable relationship to:
>
> (a) the sums in issue in the proceedings
> (b) the value of any non-monetary relief in issue in the proceedings
> (c) the complexity of the litigation
> (d) any additional work generated by the conduct of the paying party
> (e) any wider factors involved in the proceedings, such as reputation or public importance.'

Costs which are disproportionate may be disallowed by the trial judge. This is so even though the costs were reasonably or even necessarily incurred. The exact way in which the proportionality rule will work is left to the Court of Appeal to decide. There have been a number of appeals in relation to the new costs rules. In *Williams v Devon County Council* [2016] EWCA Civ 419, the Court of Appeal made clear that the:

JUDGMENT

'rules exist to enable the court to resolve the matters in issue, not to throw up unnecessary technical obstacles'.

The approach of the Court of Appeal to the issue of costs is exemplified in the case of *Mitchell v News Group Newspapers Ltd* [2013] EWCA Civ 1537. Here, the claimant filed his costs budget late, in breach of the CPR, which led to the original hearing being delayed. As a result, he was only allowed to recover his court fees, and not his wider legal costs, which were in excess of £500,000. The Court of Appeal noted that unless there was a 'good reason' for a court rule being breached, sanctions would be applied.

4.5 Enforcement of judgment

When the court awards damages to the claimant, payment of those damages is due immediately unless the court has ordered payment by instalments or postponed payment for some reason, possibly pending an appeal. One of the main problems in litigation is that if the other party does not pay, it is left to the claimant to take steps to enforce the judgment; the courts will not intervene unless the claimant initiates enforcement proceedings. Where the claimant starts enforcement proceedings the court does have various powers which can be used.

Enforcement by taking control of goods
This is where the claimant applies for an order that the court enforcement officer seizes goods belonging to the debtor and then sells them to raise money to pay for the judgment. This is the most common way of trying to enforce a judgment.

Attachment of earnings
If the debtor is working in regular employment, then it is possible to have an order made under the Attachment of Earnings Act 1971. This orders the debtor's employer to deduct money from the debtor's wages each week and send that money to the court. The court will decide a figure for the 'protected earnings' of the debtor, and the employer can only deduct from above that figure so that the debtor is left with enough money for essential living expenses.

Third-party debt orders
Where the debtor has a bank account or a savings account, or where the debtor is owed money by a third party, the claimant can ask the court to order the other party to pay enough of that money to the court to satisfy the judgment.

Bankruptcy proceedings
If the judgment is for more than £750 and a warrant of execution has already been issued without success, then the claimant may apply for the debtor to be declared bankrupt. If this occurs the debtor's assets are divided among his creditors in proportion to the amount owed to them.

Unpaid judgments

Despite all these methods of enforcement, some judgments will remain unpaid. Indeed, the claimant may well have incurred extra court costs in trying to enforce the judgment. This is particularly true of small claims. There is a register in which judgments which have not been paid can be entered. The judicial statistics show that, in 2006, 1,022,166 County Court judgments were entered. Only 128,665 had been paid in full by the end of the year, with another 89,620 being cancelled. These figures show that the vast majority of successful claimants do not receive the full amount of damages awarded to them.

John Baldwin in his report, 'Evaluating the Effectiveness of Enforcement Procedures in Undefended Claims in the Civil Courts', made the following points about the problems with enforcement:

- it was the most critical issue confronting the civil courts at the time of his report (March 2003);
- the system needs to be overhauled otherwise public confidence in the civil courts will be undermined;
- the key to improving enforcement is to ensure that courts have adequate information about the financial circumstances of defendants.

The government consulted widely on the problem of enforcement and issued a White Paper, 'Effective Enforcement', in March 2003. This suggested that there should be a register of judgment debts which included both High Court and County Court judgments. This was put into force by s98 of the Courts Act 2003. The White Paper also stressed the importance of improving the quality and quantity of information available on which creditors can base their decisions on which is the best method of enforcement to use in any particular case. As a result, the Tribunals, Courts and Enforcement Act 2007 included a new court-based mechanism to help the court gain access to information about the judgment debtor on behalf of the creditor.

ACTIVITY

Self-test questions

1. Identify five differences between civil and criminal cases.
2. What is meant by a court of first instance?
3. Name the three divisions of the High Court.
4. Name the tracks in civil cases and give the financial limits of each.
5. What report published in 1996 led to major changes in the civil justice system, including the establishing of the track system?
6. What were the key objectives set out in that report?
7. Explain what is involved in case management.
8. What are the advantages and disadvantages of pre-action protocols?
9. What has been the courts' approach to time limits in cases?
10. In what ways is enforcement going to be improved?

4.6 Tribunals

Tribunals operate alongside the court system and have become an important and integral part of the legal system. They have been referred to as the third pillar of the legal system – the administrative justice pillar: the civil justice system and the criminal justice system being the other two pillars. It should be noted that the parties in tribunal cases cannot go to court to resolve their dispute. This is different from the use of ADR procedures where the parties decide to use ADR instead of using the courts (see section 4.7). For tribunal cases the appropriate tribunal must be used.

It was mainly the development of the welfare state after 1945 that led to the creation of administrative tribunals. It was necessary to have a system that gave people a way of challenging administrative decisions made, usually by government departments, and thus allow individuals to have full access to the various rights given them under the welfare state and other legislation. There are also what are known as domestic tribunals which are set up by private bodies to resolve their own internal disputes. These are explained in section 4.6.5.

4.6.1 Administrative tribunals

These are tribunals that have been created by statute. As already stated, their main function is to resolve disputes between private individuals and government departments, usually in respect of a decision made by a department. This gives individuals a way of ensuring that any rights which have been granted through social, welfare, employment and other legislation are protected. There are many different rights. These may be related to social security, such as the right to a mobility allowance for those who are too disabled to walk more than a very short distance. Or they may be related to employment, for example the right to a payment if one is made redundant from work. There are also rights in education such as the right not to be excluded unnecessarily from school. There are also rights which are part of our basic human rights, for example the right not to be discriminated against because of one's sex, race or disability or the right not to be held in a mental hospital unnecessarily or the right of immigrants to have a claim for political asylum heard. Others are concerned with more technical points, such as the level of compensation payable when land has been compulsorily purchased; or appeals against the refusal to grant a licence in respect of chemical weapons. These are just a few examples; there are many more.

4.6.2 Tribunals, Courts and Enforcement Act 2007

Prior to the Tribunals, Courts and Enforcement Act 2007 there were about 70 types of tribunal, all of which operated separately from one other. There were different procedures for the various tribunals and no coherent system. The system was changed as a result of the Leggatt Report, 'Tribunals for Users: One System, One Service', in March 2001. The four main objects identified by the Leggatt Report were:

- the 70 or so tribunals should be made into one tribunals system;
- the tribunals should be made independent of the relevant government department;
- the training of chairmen and other members of tribunals should be improved;
- the system should be such that it will enable users to participate effectively and without apprehension in tribunal proceedings.

The Tribunals, Courts and Enforcement Act 2007 provided for the creation of a new simplified and unified framework for tribunals. It contained provision for the setting up of a First-tier Tribunal to hear cases at first instance and an Upper Tribunal to hear appeals. The move to incorporate most tribunals into this one system began in 2008.

First-tier Tribunal

Since the First-tier Tribunal deals with about 300,000 cases each year and has nearly 200 judges and 3,600 lay members, it operates in seven chambers. These are:

- Social Entitlement Chamber which covers a wide range of matters such as Child Support, Criminal Injuries Compensation and Gender Recognition;
- Health, Education and Social Care Chamber which includes the former Mental Health Review Tribunal which dealt with appeals against the continued detention of those in mental hospitals – this Chamber also deals with Special Educational Needs issues;
- War Pensions and Armed Forces Compensation Chamber;
- General Regulatory Chamber;
- Taxation Chamber;
- Land, Property and Housing Chamber;
- Asylum and Immigration Chamber.

Upper Tribunal

This appellate Tribunal is divided into four Chambers. These are:

- Administrative Appeals Chamber which hears appeals from the Social Entitlement Chamber, the Health, Education and Social Care Chamber, and the War Pensions and Armed Forces Compensation Chamber;
- Tax and Chancery Chamber;
- Lands Chamber;
- Asylum and Immigration Chamber.

From the Upper Tribunal there is a further possible appeal route to the Court of Appeal and from here to the Supreme Court.

As well as these appeal routes, tribunals are also subject to judicial review. The Queen's Bench Administrative Court has the power to hear applications for judicial review against tribunal decisions and can use its prerogative powers to quash a decision. This route should not normally be used where there is an appeal route available. However, it is the method to be used where there has been a breach of natural justice. The Upper Tribunal will also deal with some areas of judicial review.

Employment tribunals

Employment tribunals are not included in the new unified system. They remain separate and have their own appeal route. An appeal from an employment tribunal is to the Employment Appeal Tribunal, which is headed by a High Court Judge, and from there to the Court of Appeal. There is a final appeal to the Supreme Court.

The Tribunals Service is responsible for the administration of all tribunals including employment tribunals.

4.6.3 Composition and procedure

The proceedings are heard by a tribunal judge. For some topics two lay members will sit with the judge to make the decision. These lay members will have expertise in the particular field of the tribunal. For example, the lay members in a hearing about a claim to mobility allowance would be medically qualified, while there would be surveyors sitting on the Lands Tribunal. In an Employment Tribunal for an unfair dismissal claim, the two lay members would be one representative from an organisation for employers and one from an organisation for employees.

The selection of tribunal judges is carried out by the Judicial Appointments Commission (JAC). Vacant positions are advertised and candidates must apply, provide references and be interviewed.

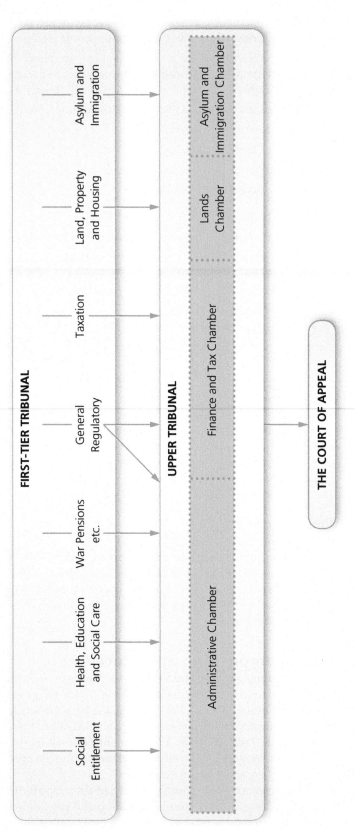

Figure 4.4 Structure of the tribunal system

Rules

Rules for the procedure in the various chambers have been issued. These all have common elements and are aimed at creating a harmonised system of rules for the new structure.

The Tribunals, Courts and Enforcement Act 2007 sets out that there should be 'proportionate dispute resolution' (s2(3)(d)). This is an encouragement to use an alternative form of dispute resolution. The Ministry of Justice is running two pilot schemes in an Early Dispute Resolution Project to see how different forms of ADR might be used instead of using the relevant tribunal. The pilot schemes are judicial mediation in complex disability, sex or race discrimination cases in employment tribunals and 'early neutral evaluation' in disability living allowance (social security) appeals.

4.6.4 Advantages and disadvantages of tribunals

Tribunals were set up to prevent the overloading of the courts with the extra cases that social, employment and other rights claims would generate. Having a separate system allows the courts to concentrate on mainstream civil claims.

For the applicant in tribunal cases the advantages are that such cases are dealt with more cheaply, more quickly and more informally than they would be if there were a court hearing. There is also the fact that the panel is often composed of a mix of legal expertise and lay expertise in the field concerned. However, all these claims need to be evaluated.

Cost-effectiveness

As applicants are encouraged to represent themselves and not use lawyers, it is true to say that tribunal hearings do not normally involve the costs associated with court hearings. It is also rare for an order for costs to be made by a tribunal, so that an applicant need not fear a large bill if he loses the case. However, applicants who are not represented have a lower chance of winning their case than those who are represented, so the saving on the cost of a lawyer may not be cost-effective.

Hazel Genn, in 'The Effectiveness of Representation at Tribunals' (1989), found that the success rate for those with lawyers was 49 per cent, while for those without lawyers it was 28 per cent. She also discovered that applicants lost most often when they appeared without representation against a legally represented respondent. She found that representation had an effect on the amount awarded in successful cases. The mean amount of award made in her study was £1,084 in cases where the applicant had legal representation, but only £449 in cases where the applicant received no advice from any source.

Although this study was on the old system of tribunals, it is possible that the same criticism will apply to the new system.

Speedy hearings

This was one of the original advantages of tribunal hearings but it is no longer true to say that cases will be dealt with speedily. Successive reports by the Council on Tribunals highlighted delays. These are caused by the vast volume of work that tribunals now face, together with the fact that any lay members sit only part-time. The use of lay members creates a particular problem if the case is complex and likely to last several days, as it can lead to proceedings being spread over separate days in several weeks.

Hopefully, the new system will be less prone to delay, especially with the encouragement of the use of ADR.

Simple procedure

It is true that this is a more informal hearing than in court. In addition, most cases are heard in private. These comments do not apply to Employment Tribunals, which are open to the public and tend to be more formal. However, for individuals presenting their own cases the venue is unfamiliar and the procedure can be confusing. The Leggatt Report highlighted the point that users may be disconcerted if the proceedings are totally unstructured, because they are then uncertain when to make particular points.

Where applicants are not represented the judge is expected to take an inquisitorial role and help to establish the points that the applicant wishes to make. This ideal is not always achieved, as shown by research into social security cases carried out by J Baldwin, N Wikeley and R Young in their study, 'Judging Social Security', published in 1992. They found that of the hearings they attended, the chairman's handling of the case could be described as 'good' or 'excellent' in 57 per cent of cases and 'adequate' in a further quarter of cases. However, in one-sixth of cases the chairman's conduct was open to serious criticism. This type of criticism has also been levelled at Employment Tribunals. In these cases an applicant in person may often find themselves opposed by a lawyer representing the employer, and so it is even more important that the proceedings should be kept simple and that the chairman should act inquisitorially to redress the balance.

The problem of the unrepresented applicant comes about because legal aid is not available for most tribunals. This may put an applicant at a disadvantage if the other side (often a government department or an employer) uses a lawyer.

KEY FACTS

Administrative tribunals

Function	To resolve disputes between private individuals and government departments over decisions made by the department To allow private individuals to enforce their rights, e.g. under employment law
Types of tribunal	First-tier Tribunal with seven chambers: • Social Entitlement • Health, Education and Social Care • War Pensions and Armed Forces Compensation • Taxation • Land, Property and Housing • General Regulatory • Asylum and Immigration Employment Tribunals
Panel	Panel of three: judge and two lay members with expertise in the area *or* One judge
Procedure	Usually informal and in private Employment Tribunals use a more formal procedure and are open to the public
Availability of publicly funded legal representation	Only available for a limited number of tribunals where the applicant's human rights are in issue, e.g. • mental health review tribunals • immigration cases
Appeals	To relevant chamber of Upper Tribunal and from there to Court of Appeal From Employment Tribunals there is an appeal to the Employment Appeals Tribunal and from there to the Court of Appeal
Control of tribunals	Judicial review

4.6.5 Domestic tribunals

These are effectively 'in-house' tribunals set up by private bodies, usually for their own internal disciplinary control. There are disciplinary tribunals to decide whether there has been a breach of professional conduct for professions and occupations including doctors, dentists, opticians, veterinary surgeons, osteopaths, accountants, solicitors, barristers and even footballers. There are also disciplinary committees for a wide range of other organisations including trade unions and universities. Each domestic tribunal must keep to the rules of natural justice and their decisions are subject to judicial review. In addition, for many professional disciplinary tribunals where the tribunal has decided to strike off a member from the professional register, there is an appeal route to the JCPC. For example, this applies to decisions of the disciplinary committee of the General Medical Council and also to other medical disciplinary tribunals.

4.7 Alternative dispute resolution

Using the courts to resolve disputes can be costly, in terms of both money and time. It can also be traumatic for the individuals involved and it may not lead to the most satisfactory outcome for the case. An additional problem is that court proceedings are usually open to the public and the press, so there is nothing to stop the details of the case being published in local or national newspapers. It is not surprising, therefore, that more and more people and businesses are seeking other methods of resolving their disputes. Alternative methods are referred to as ADR which stands for 'alternative dispute resolution'. This includes any method of resolving a dispute without resorting to using the courts. There are many different methods which can be used, ranging from very informal negotiations between the parties to a comparatively formal commercial arbitration hearing. The four main methods are:

- negotiation;
- mediation;
- conciliation; and
- arbitration.

4.7.1 Negotiation

Negotiation is the quickest and cheapest method of settling a dispute. It also has the advantage of being completely private. Anyone who has a dispute with another person can always try to resolve it by negotiating directly with them. If the parties cannot come to an agreement, they may decide to take the step of instructing trained negotiators. Even where the parties have referred the matter to their solicitors, it is usual for the solicitors to try to negotiate a settlement. In fact, even when court proceedings have been commenced the lawyers for the parties will often continue to negotiate on behalf of their clients. This is reflected in the high number of claims which are issued but are then settled out of court. Once lawyers are involved then there will be a cost element and, clearly, the longer negotiations go on, the higher the costs will be. One of the worrying aspects is the number of cases that drag on for years only to end in an agreed settlement literally 'at the door of the court' on the morning that the trial is due to start. It is this situation that ADR methods are aimed at preventing. This is reinforced by the CPR (see section 4.4.5).

4.7.2 Mediation

In mediation a neutral mediator helps the parties to reach a compromise solution. The role of a mediator is to act as a 'go-between'. He will consult with each party and see how much common ground there is between them. He will explore the position with each party, looking at their needs and will carry offers to and fro, while keeping confidentiality. This usually takes place at a neutral venue. The parties are given separate private rooms. The mediator will see each of the parties in their private rooms to explain the format of the day. Then there is usually a joint opening session in a larger room. After this the parties return to their private rooms (also known as caucuses) and the mediator will discuss each party's case with them privately and explore possible areas for compromise until either a solution is reached or it is obvious that an amicable resolution cannot be reached. Even if the mediation does not resolve the dispute, it is likely to narrow the issues and so make a court case shorter. Mediation can also take different forms and the parties can choose the exact method they want. The important point in mediation is that the parties are in control; they make the decisions.

A mediator will not usually tell the parties his own views of the merits of the dispute; it is his job to act as a 'facilitator', so that an agreement is reached by the parties. However, a mediator can be asked for his opinion of the merits and in this case the mediation becomes more of an evaluation exercise, which again aims at ending the dispute. Mediation is only suitable if there is some hope that the parties can co-operate. Companies who are used to negotiating contracts with each other are likely to benefit from this approach. Mediation is also often successful in divorce cases where there are disputes over the children or property.

4.7.3 Conciliation

This has similarities to mediation in that a neutral third party helps to resolve the dispute, but the main difference is that the conciliator takes a more active role. He will be expected to suggest grounds for compromise and the possible basis for a settlement. This is sometimes referred to as 'evaluative' mediation. As with mediation, conciliation does not necessarily lead to a resolution and it may be necessary to continue with a court action, though the conciliation process, even where unsuccessful, may well narrow the issues and avoid lengthy court cases. It is also similar to mediation in that the parties make the agreement. They remain in control throughout the proceedings; they do not have to accept the conciliator's suggestions.

Formalised settlement conference

This is a more formal method of approaching conciliation. It involves a 'mini-trial' where each side presents its case to a panel composed of a decision-making executive from each party and a neutral third party. Once all the submissions have been made, the executives, with the help of the neutral adviser, will evaluate the two sides' positions and try to come to an agreement. If the executives cannot agree, the neutral adviser will act as a conciliator between them.

An advantage of mediation and conciliation is that the decision need not be a strictly legal one sticking to the letter of the law. It is more likely to be based on commercial common sense and compromise. These methods will also make it more possible for companies to continue doing business with each other in the future. Some settlements may even include agreements about the conduct of future business between the parties, which is something that cannot happen when a court gives judgment. All forms of mediation and conciliation avoid the adversarial conflict of the courtroom and the winner/loser result of court proceedings as well as minimising the large-scale costs associated with a court case.

4.7.4 Online Dispute Resolution

In February 2015 a new Online Dispute Resolution (ODR) platform was created by the European Commission, on behalf of the EU. It was introduced into the UK by the Alternative Dispute Resolution for Consumer Disputes (Amendment) Regulations 2015, and the platform went live in February 2016. Because of this the ODR platform is now part of UK law. It is yet to be seen how it will be affected by the UK's decision to leave the EU.

The ODR platform will allow consumers to make a complaint against a trader where goods or services have been bought online. The complaint will be considered by an approved ADR provider. The Regulations mandate that all online traders who sell goods and services must provide consumers with a link on their website to the ODR platform, and an e-mail address on their website so that consumers have a first point of contact with the trader. If a trader does not provide this information, trading standards services can apply for a court order requiring them to comply.

4.7.5 Dispute resolution services

There are a growing number of dispute resolution services. One of the main ones is the Centre for Dispute Resolution (CEDR) which was set up in London in 1991. The centre has many important companies as members, including almost all of the big London law firms. Businesses say that using the Centre to resolve disputes has saved several thousands of pounds in court costs. The typical cost of a mediator is about £1,000 to £1,500 for a case. This compares with potential litigation costs which are usually well over £100,000 and in major commercial cases likely to be over £1 million. The Centre has a high success rate, with over 80 per cent of cases in which it is asked to act being settled. There are also mediation services aimed at resolving smaller disputes, for example those between neighbours. Most areas have local mediation schemes offering a free service that will try to help resolve disagreements between neighbours arising from such matters as noise or boundary fence disputes. Such services are run by trained volunteers who will not take sides or make judgments on the rights and wrongs of an issue. There are even online services offering dispute settlement via the internet.

In 2004 the Civil Mediation Council was set up to promote mediation in civil and commercial cases. It is working with the government on the expansion of court-based mediation schemes.

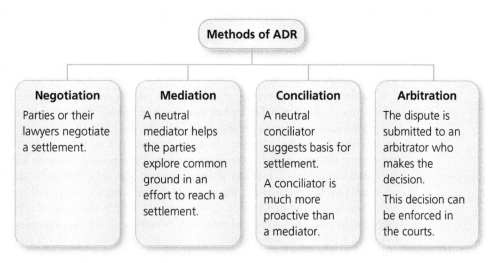

Figure 4.5 Different methods of ADR

4.7.6 Arbitration

Arbitration is where the parties agree to submit their claims to the judgment of an independent person instead of taking a court case. In fact arbitration was described by Sir John Donaldson as 'usually no more and no less than litigation in the private sector' (*Northern Regional Health Authority v Derek Crouch Construction Co Ltd* [1984] 1 QB 644 at 670). Arbitration is governed by the Arbitration Act 1996 and s1 of that Act sets out the principles behind it. This says:

SECTION

's 1 (a) the object of arbitration is to obtain the fair resolution of disputes by an impartial tribunal without unnecessary delay or expense;

(b) the parties should be free to agree how their disputes are resolved, subject only to such safeguards as are necessary in the public interest.'

So arbitration is the voluntary submission by the parties of their dispute to the judgment of some person other than a judge. The agreement to arbitrate will usually be in writing and indeed the Arbitration Act 1996 applies only to written arbitration agreements. The precise way in which the arbitration is carried out is left almost entirely to the parties' agreement. Under s33 of the Act the parties are free to adopt whatever procedures they think appropriate, but the arbitrator(s) must act fairly and impartially under the rules of natural justice. The procedures adopted must be suitable to the circumstances and avoid unnecessary delay and expense.

The agreement to go to arbitration can be made by the parties at any time. It can be before a dispute arises or when the dispute becomes apparent. Many commercial contracts include what is called a *Scott v Avery* (1843–1860) clause, which is a clause where the parties in their original contract agree that in the event of a dispute arising between them, they will have that dispute settled by arbitration. Alternatively, the agreement to go to arbitration can be made after the dispute arises. Arbitration is often used in commercial cases.

Staying court proceedings

Where there is an arbitration agreement in a contract, the Arbitration Act 1996 states that the court will normally refuse to deal with any dispute. If court proceedings are brought, the court will stay the proceedings and the matter must go to arbitration as agreed by the parties. In *Cable & Wireless plc v IBM United Kingdom Ltd* [2002] EWHC 2059 (Comm) the court extended this principle by holding that proceedings could be stayed not only where there was an arbitration clause but also where there was a contractual term providing for mandatory ADR in the event of a dispute.

The arbitrator

The Arbitration Act 1996 (s15) states that the parties are free to agree on the number of arbitrators, so that a panel of two or three may be used or there may be a sole arbitrator. If the parties cannot agree on a number then the Act provides that only one arbitrator should be appointed. The Act also says that the parties are free to agree on the procedure for appointing an arbitrator. In fact, most agreements to go to arbitration will either name an arbitrator or provide a method of choosing one and it is often provided in commercial contracts that the president of the appropriate trade organisation will appoint the arbitrator. There is also the Institute of Arbitrators which provides trained arbitrators for major disputes. In many cases the arbitrator will be someone who has expertise in the particular field involved in the dispute, but if the dispute involves a point of law the parties may decide to appoint a lawyer. If there is no agreement on whom or how to appoint, then, in the last resort, the court can be asked to appoint an appropriate arbitrator.

The arbitration hearing

The actual procedure is also left to the agreement of the parties in each case, so that there are many forms of hearing. In some cases the parties may opt for a 'paper' arbitration, where the two sides put all the points they wish to raise into writing and submit this together with any relevant documents to the arbitrator. He will then read all the documents and make his decision. Alternatively, the parties may send all these documents to the arbitrator, but before he makes his decision both parties will attend a hearing at which they make oral submissions to the arbitrator to support their case. If the parties wish, it is possible for witnesses to be called to give evidence. Where witnesses are asked to give evidence orally then this will not normally be given on oath. However, if the parties want, the witness can be asked to give evidence on oath and the whole procedure will be very formal. If witnesses are called to give evidence the Arbitration Act 1996 allows for the use of court procedures to ensure the attendance of those witnesses. The date, time and place of the arbitration hearing are all matters for the parties to decide in consultation with the arbitrator. This gives a great degree of flexibility to the proceedings; the parties can choose what is most convenient for all the people concerned.

The award

The decision made by the arbitrator is called an award and is binding on the parties. It can even be enforced through the courts if necessary. The decision is usually final, though s68 of the Arbitration Act 1996 allows it to be challenged in the courts on the ground of serious irregularity in the proceedings or on a point of law.

Advantages and disadvantages of arbitration

There are several advantages which largely arise from the fact that the parties have the freedom to make their own arbitration agreement and decide exactly how formal or informal they wish it to be. The main advantages are:

- the parties may choose their own arbitrator and can therefore decide whether the matter is best dealt with by a technical expert or by a lawyer or by a professional arbitrator;
- if there is a question of quality this can be decided by an expert in the particular field, saving the expense of calling expert witnesses and the time that would be used in explaining all the technicalities to a judge;
- the hearing time and place can be arranged to suit the parties;
- the actual procedure used is flexible and the parties can choose that which is most suited to the situation – this will usually result in a more informal and relaxed hearing than in court;
- the matter is dealt with in private and there will be no publicity;
- the dispute will be resolved more quickly than through a court hearing;
- arbitration proceedings are usually much cheaper than going to court;
- the award is normally final and can be enforced through the courts.

However, there are some disadvantages of arbitration, especially where the parties are not on an equal footing as regards the ability to present their case. This is because legal aid is not available for arbitration and this may disadvantage an individual in a case against a business; if the case had gone to court a person on a low income may have qualified for legal aid and so had the benefit of a lawyer to present his case. The other main disadvantages are:

- an unexpected legal point may arise in the case which is not suitable for decision by a non-lawyer arbitrator;
- if a professional arbitrator is used, his fees may be expensive;

- it will also be expensive if the parties opt for a formal hearing with witnesses giving evidence and lawyers representing both sides;
- the rights of appeal are limited;
- the delays for commercial and international arbitration may be nearly as great as those in the courts if a professional arbitrator and lawyers are used.

This problem of delay and expense has meant that arbitration has to some extent lost its popularity with companies as a method of dispute resolution. More and more businesses are turning to the alternatives offered by centres such as the Centre for Dispute Resolution or, in the case of international disputes, are choosing to have the matter resolved in another country. One of the problems was that the law on arbitration had become complex and the Arbitration Act 1996 is an attempt to improve the process. In general, it can be said that certain types of dispute are suitable for arbitration. This especially includes commercial disagreements between two businesses where the parties have little hope of finding sufficient common ground to make mediation a realistic prospect and provided there is no major point of law involved.

KEY FACTS

Different methods of dispute resolution

Method of dispute resolution and decision-maker	Procedure	Advantages	Disadvantages
Negotiation The parties themselves or through negotiators	Informal Usually through letters or email	Quick No cost Parties in control and agree to outcome	None
Mediation The parties with the help of a mediator	Mediator discusses case with each side in turn trying to find a solution which is acceptable to both parties	Cheaper than courts Parties in control and parties agree to outcome Private	Not binding May not lead to settlement
Conciliation The parties with the help of a conciliator	Mediator evaluates the case and gives opinion to parties	Cheaper than courts Parties in control and parties agree to outcome Private	Not binding May not lead to settlement
Arbitration The arbitrator	Use of arbitration may be agreed in advance with a *Scott v Avery* clause Can be paper proceedings or more formal like a court	Cheaper than courts *but* more expensive than mediation Binding	Can be formal Arbitrator's fee may be high Not suitable if dispute is on a point of law
Litigation in the courts A judge	Regarded as last resort Must follow CPR and timetables set by the court	Decision is final and binding	Expensive Lengthy Formal Adversarial Public hearing

4.7.7 Encouraging the use of alternative dispute resolution

There have been many moves to encourage the use of ADR over the past ten years. In particular this can be seen in the Woolf Report which included more use of ADR as one of its recommendations. This led to the provision in Rule 1.4(2)(e) of the CPR which states that case management includes encouraging the parties to use an ADR procedure if the court considers that appropriate and facilitating the use of such procedure.

Since 1996 a scheme for court-based mediation has been in operation at the Central London County Court. The original pilot scheme was aimed at claims for amounts between £3,000 and £10,000 and parties who agreed to take part were offered a mediation session within 28 days at a cost of £25 for each party. If the dispute could not be resolved by mediation, then it was referred to court for a court hearing in the normal way. However, the response to this scheme was disappointing. Professor Hazel Genn, evaluating the scheme in 1998, found that of the first 1,300 offers of mediation, only 4 per cent were taken up. In 38 per cent of cases the scheme was firmly rejected, with the other 58 per cent of cases failing to reply to the court offer. Despite this unpromising start, court-based mediation is now being used at a few other courts.

Further, since 2004 the Central London County Court has tried an automatic referral to mediation (ARM). If any of the parties to the case objects to the use of mediation, the District Judge may:

- direct that the case be listed for a hearing of the objections to mediation, but may still make the decision that the mediation should go ahead; or

- direct that a mediation appointment should proceed; or

- proceed with case management if he accepts that the opposition to mediation is justified.

In 2007 Hazel Genn and others evaluated both of the above mediation programmes in the Central London County Court. The results of the evaluation were reported in a research paper, 'Twisting Arms: Court Referred and Court Linked Mediation under Judicial Pressure', Ministry of Justice Research Series 01/07 (2007).

The two programmes were:

- an experiment in quasi-compulsory mediation (ARM) which ran in the court between April 2004 and March 2005; and

- the voluntary mediation scheme which had been operating in the court since 1996 (and had previously been evaluated in 1998).

The ARM scheme involved the allocation of 100 cases per month to mediation, with an opportunity to opt out – 82 per cent of the cases referred to mediation were personal injury (PI) cases. It was found there was a very high rate of objection. Overall, one or both of the parties objected in 81 per cent of cases. The objection rate was particularly high in PI cases. In non-PI cases the objection rate was only 45 per cent.

The settlement rate for those who did try ARM was initially 69 per cent but had fallen to 38 per cent by the end of the pilot period. In unsettled cases the view was that the unsuccessful mediation had added between £1,000 and £2,000 to the legal costs of the case. However, the majority of the cases in the ARM scheme settled out of court without going to mediation.

In respect of the voluntary mediation scheme, the 2007 evaluation found that since the 1998 evaluation the noticeable points were:

- a significant increase in demand after the decision in *Dunnett v Railtrack* in 2002;
- low rates of PI cases seeking mediation (only 40 out of 1,000 cases mediated between 1999 and 2004);
- low settlement rates – since 1998 the settlement rate was below 50 per cent each year with a low of 40 per cent in 2000 and 2003.

Employment cases

This is an area of law where ADR has long been used in the shape of ACAS (Advisory Conciliation and Arbitration Service). When any claim is filed at an Employment Tribunal, a copy of that claim is sent to ACAS who will then contact the two parties involved and offer to attempt to resolve the dispute without the need for the matter to go to a tribunal. ACAS has specially trained conciliation officers who have a great deal of experience of industrial disputes. The success of this service can be seen from the fact that over half of all claims filed are settled in this way. However, there is criticism that the amount paid in such settlements is less than would have been awarded by a tribunal. This suggests that employees are at a disadvantage and feel under pressure to settle.

In addition, since May 2001 ACAS has been offering a new, speedy and informal arbitration service for unfair dismissal cases. This uses a single arbitrator and is in private, but workers using the scheme must waive their rights to go to an Employment Tribunal.

So it can be seen that there is an increased awareness of the use of ADR in all sorts of disputes.

ACTIVITY

Critiquing the law

Quotation

'In some cases, a precedent is needed or publicity is needed to set an example or to show that a party is a "repeat offender". The organisation and use of ADR might result in "poor justice for the poor" or "discount justice".'

A Nylund, 'Access to Justice: Is ADR a Help or Hindrance?' in L Ervo and A Nylund (eds), The Future of Civil Litigation (Springer, 2014), p 330

ADR is a way in which individuals and businesses can resolve disputes more quickly, discretely and less expensively than relying upon court action. Each instance of ADR is unique and dealt with on its merits. However, the ELS is a common law system, and the basis of this system is precedent. ADR does not create precedent. Given this, consider these questions:

1. Will an increased reliance on ADR have a negative effect on the ELS and the doctrine of precedent, as fewer cases are being decided by the courts?
2. Could another disadvantage be that 'repeat offenders' use ADR precisely because 'precedent or publicity is lacking', meaning that their misbehaviour will not be corrected through a legal judgment, or advertised to the public?

ACTIVITY

Self-test questions

1. Why were administrative tribunals created?
2. What types of panel may be used in tribunals?
3. Explain the advantages and disadvantages of taking a case in a tribunal.
4. Which report on tribunals was published in 2001? What were its main recommendations and what reforms has the government introduced as a result?
5. How can the courts control the workings of tribunals?
6. Explain how mediation is normally conducted.
7. Why are mediation and conciliation popular ways of resolving disputes?
8. What is a *Scott v Avery* clause?
9. In what ways is the use of ADR being encouraged?

SAMPLE ESSAY QUESTION

Alisha has just separated from her husband. They have agreed that they should seek a divorce but they cannot agree on her husband's contact time with the children, or on the division between them of some of the furniture in their home.

Alisha has also just been dismissed from her job because she took a day off to care for her three-year-old son when he was ill. She believes that her employers have unfairly dismissed her.

She also has problems with building work which was carried out two months ago. A new flat roof over the kitchen has been leaking and there is water damage in the kitchen. She has written several times to the builders who did the work but they have ignored her letters. It has cost her £2,000 to have the roof put right and another £500 to have the damage to the kitchen dealt with.

Advise Alisha on the best method(s) of dispute resolution for the problems she faces.

Explain the main issues Alisha has which require advice:

- a dispute with her husband over the amount of contact time he should have with their children, and over the division of their furniture between them;
- a dispute with her former employer over whether she was lawfully dismissed from her job;
- a dispute with her builders over the adequacy of work she paid them to complete.

State the best methods for dispute resolution for Alisha's dispute with her husband:

- as this is a family dispute Alisha should consider ADR due to its privacy and the fact that the process is much cheaper than court proceedings;
- discuss the details and appropriateness of mediation;
- discuss the details and appropriateness of conciliation; and explain how these types of ADR could resolve Alisha's dispute.

> **State the best methods for dispute resolution for Alisha's dispute with her former employer:**
> - disputes relating to employment are heard at Employment Tribunals;
> - explain the composition of tribunals and their advantages to the court process;
> - explain the relationship between the tribunal system and the court hierarchy, especially in relation to appeals;
> - explain how ACAS operates as a method for dispute resolution in employment tribunals.

> **State the best methods for dispute resolution for Alisha's dispute with her builders:**
> - discuss and explain the track system in the civil courts – small claims, fast track, multi-track;
> - note that the total amount of the claim is £2,500 and the dispute is focusing on housing, so a fast-track claim in the County Court would be most appropriate;
> - explain the process of bringing a claim in the fast track;
> - focus on the relevant CPR and how they will apply.

> **CONCLUSION**

Figure 4.6 Essay map on ADR and civil courts

SUMMARY

Differences between civil and criminal law

- Civil law is concerned with rights and duties between individuals, businesses or organisations.
- Criminal law deals with behaviour which the state has forbidden.
- Civil trials are held in the County Court and the High Court.
- Criminal trials are held in the Magistrates' Courts and the Crown Court.
- Standard of proof is 'the balance of probabilities' in civil courts and 'beyond reasonable doubt' in criminal courts.

Civil courts

- The County Court deals with all claims of £25,000 and below. It can also deal with higher claims.
- The High Court has three divisions: Queen's Bench Division, Chancery Division and Family Division. It deals with claims of over £25,000.

Track system

All claims are assigned to one of three tracks:

- small claims – less than £10,000 (personal injury and housing claims less than £1,000);
- fast-track claims between £10,000 and £25,000;
- multi-track claims over £25,000 or complex cases for a lesser amount.

Problems of the civil justice system

Civil justice is thought to:

- be expensive;
- take too long;
- be too complex.

Woolf reforms were aimed at:

- the three-track system;
- encouraging the use of ADR;
- giving judges more responsibility for managing cases;
- more use of IT;
- simpler documents and procedures;
- avoiding the adversarial nature of civil litigation.

Enforcement of judgments can be through:

- seizing goods;
- attachment of earnings;
- third party debt order;
- bankruptcy proceedings.

Tribunals

- These operate alongside the court system. They deal with rights granted in areas such as welfare, employment, education and immigration.
- The Leggatt Report led to a restructuring of tribunals into First-tier and Upper Tribunals (Tribunals, Courts and Enforcement Act 2007).
- Some decisions are made by a judge and two lay members.

Alternative dispute resolution

- This is where the parties choose to resolve their dispute by using an alternative to the courts. The main ADR methods are negotiation, mediation, conciliation and arbitration.
- In negotiation, mediation and conciliation, the parties try to reach an agreed settlement. In arbitration the dispute is decided by an arbitrator.

Further reading

Book

Zander, M, *Cases and Materials on the English Legal System* (10th edn, Cambridge University Press, 2007), Ch 2.

Articles

Baldwin, J, 'Evaluating the effectiveness of enforcement procedures in undefended claims in the civil courts', [2003] *LCD Research Report* 3.

Burn, S, 'The Woolf reforms in retrospect' [2003] *Legal Action* 8.

Foyle, A and Singh, S, 'Arbitration: an introduction to the procedure' [2002] *NLJ* 1417–1418.

Genn, H and Genn, Y, 'The effectiveness of representation at tribunals' [1989] Faculty of Law, Queen Mary College, University of London.

Genn, H and others, 'Twisting arms: court referred and court linked mediation under judicial pressure' [2007] Ministry of Justice Research Series 01/07.

Hewitt, L and Hughes, S, 'The changing Face(book) of family law' [2013] *NLJ* 7555.

Miller, F, 'The adversarial myth' [1995] *NLJ* 743.

Newmark, C, 'In praise of ADR' [2002] *NLJ* 1896–1897.

Ramsay, J, 'Implementation of the costs reforms' [2013] *CJQ* 112.

Zander, M, 'Where are we heading with the funding of civil litigation?' [2003] *CJQ* 23.

Zander, M, 'Zander on Woolf' [2009] *NLJ* 367.

Internet links

Administrative Justice and Tribunals Council at: www.ajtc.gov.uk

Centre for Effective Dispute Resolution at: www.cedr.co.uk

HM Courts and Tribunals Service at: www.gov.uk/government/organisations/hm-courts-and-tribunals-service and www.tribunals.gov.uk

5

Criminal courts and procedure

AIMS AND OBJECTIVES

After reading this chapter you should be able to:

- Explain the role of the Crown Prosecution Service in bringing prosecutions in criminal cases
- Describe the system of advanced sentence indication at the Crown Court under the *Goodyear* rules
- Describe and distinguish the first instance and the appellate courts which hear criminal cases
- Classify crimes as summary, indictable only or either way, and explain where each must or may be tried
- Advise a defendant who is pleading not guilty to an either way offence whether he should elect trial at the Crown Court, and why or why not
- Discuss whether there is a general right to trial by jury and, if so, what the limitations on that right might be

5.1 Introduction

Most crimes are investigated by the police. Other agencies that might detect and investigate crimes include local authorities (e.g. trade description offences), the Health and Safety Executive (e.g. injuries or deaths that occur at work), the Serious Fraud Office (no explanation needed) and Revenue and Customs (e.g. for tax evasion). These agencies also deal with bringing prosecutions in these cases. However, our focus in this chapter is on those crimes investigated by the police and then prosecuted by the CPS; the majority of the offences that you will study in criminal law, in fact.

The powers of the police are extensive, as are the rules governing the exercise of those powers.

Figure 5.1 gives an overview of the prosecution process in England and Wales. It was taken from the Home Office Criminal Justice website and is a useful summary of the roles of the police, CPS and the courts. Terms used which may be unfamiliar to you at this stage are defined and explained throughout the chapter.

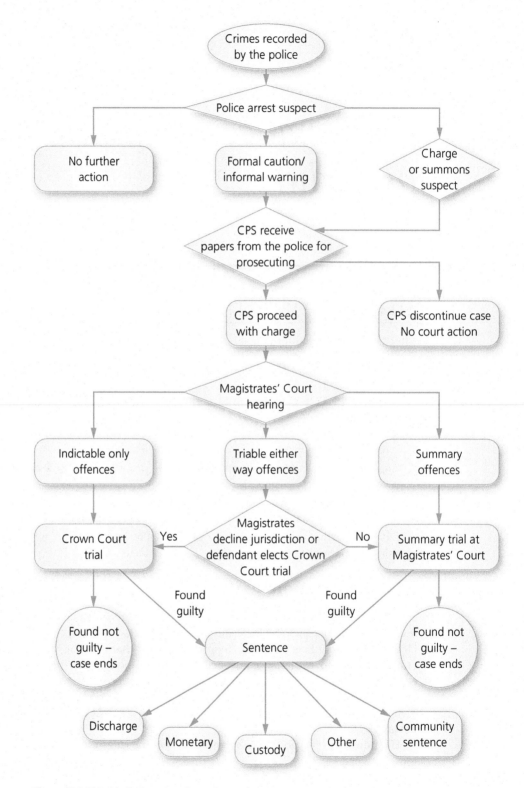

Figure 5.1 The criminal prosecution process

5.2 The Criminal Procedure Rules

In Chapter 4, you will have seen that the civil justice system was subject to a full scale review between 1994 and 1996 (see section 4.4, The Woolf Report) which resulted in a single set of rules governing civil proceedings. A similar type of review on criminal proceedings, headed by Lord Justice Auld, was completed in 2001. This report led to the simplification and codification of the practices and procedures in the criminal courts. The Criminal Procedure Rules 2005 (the CrimPRs) codified nearly 500 individual rules found in over 50 different places. Updated regularly by the Criminal Procedure Rules Committee, the full set is available at www.justice.gov.uk/courts/procedure-rules/criminal.

One example of the rules is provided here (CrimPR, r 1.1), and you may find it familiar as it broadly reflects the first rule of the CPR, although as you will see, it is then directed to matters arising only in criminal cases:

SECTION

'(1) The overriding objective of this new code is that criminal cases be dealt with justly.

(2) Dealing with a criminal case justly includes –
  (a) acquitting the innocent and convicting the guilty;
  (b) dealing with the prosecution and the defence fairly;
  (c) recognising the rights of a defendant, particularly those under Article 6 of the European Convention on Human Rights;
  (d) respecting the interests of witnesses, victims and jurors and keeping them informed of the progress of the case;
  (e) dealing with the case efficiently and expeditiously;
  (f) ensuring that appropriate information is available to the court when bail and sentence are considered; and
  (g) dealing with the case in ways that take into account –
    (i)   the gravity of the offence alleged,
    (ii)   the complexity of what is in issue,
    (iii) the severity of the consequences for the defendant and others affected, and
    (iv)   the needs of other cases.'

5.3 The Crown Prosecution Service

The CPS has a pivotal role in bringing prosecutions. The head of the CPS is the Director of Public Prosecutions (the DPP), currently Alison Saunders. The role of DPP was created in 1880 and initially was limited to responsibility for prosecutions in a very small number of complex cases. During most of the twentieth century, the majority of prosecutions were carried out by the police (either by in-house solicitors or by contract with local firms). However, the Royal Commission on Criminal Procedure 1981 (the Philips Commission) concluded that it was inappropriate for the police, who investigated cases, to make the decision whether or not to prosecute as well, and then conduct the proceedings. It also found that different police forces around the country used different guidelines to decide whether or not to prosecute, and individual police forces were putting forward too many weak cases, sometimes against the advice of lawyers, resulting in a high percentage of judge-directed acquittals. There was a culture of prosecuting wherever an accused person had been charged, irrespective of the strength of the evidence.

The CPS was set up in 1986. Its statutory responsibilities and duties are contained in the Prosecution of Offences Act 1985. Section 3(2) states that the function of the CPS is to take over criminal proceedings from the police (and other agencies) and proceed, where it is deemed appropriate, with the prosecution in court (but that does not necessarily mean that all offenders who have been charged by the police will be prosecuted in court, see below).

5.3.1 Code for Crown Prosecutors

Under s10 of the Prosecution of Offences Act 1985, the DPP must issue a Code for prosecutors, giving guidance on when proceedings should be commenced (or continued). The decision whether to proceed with a charge involves a Crown Prosecutor using two tests:

1. *The evidential test*

The evidential test under para 4.4 of the Code is, whether there is a realistic prospect of conviction.

CLAUSE

'4.5 The finding that there is a realistic prospect of conviction is based on the prosecutor's objective assessment of the evidence, including the impact of any defence and any other information that the suspect has put forward or on which he or she might rely. It means that an objective, impartial and reasonable jury or bench of magistrates or judge hearing a case alone, properly directed and acting in accordance with the law, is more likely than not to convict the defendant of the charge alleged. This is a different test from the one that the criminal courts themselves must apply. A court may only convict if it is sure that the defendant is guilty.

4.6 When deciding whether there is sufficient evidence to prosecute, prosecutors should ask themselves the following:

Can the evidence be used in court?
Prosecutors should consider whether there is any question over the admissibility of certain evidence. In doing so, prosecutors should assess:

(a) the likelihood of that evidence being held as inadmissible by the court; and

(b) the importance of that evidence in relation to the evidence as a whole.

Is the evidence reliable?
Prosecutors should consider whether there are any reasons to question the reliability of the evidence, including its accuracy or integrity.

Is the evidence credible?
Prosecutors should consider whether there are any reasons to doubt the credibility of the evidence.'

If the case does not pass the evidential test, it must not go ahead, no matter how important or serious it may be. If the case does meet the evidential test, Crown Prosecutors must decide if a prosecution is needed in the public interest.

2. *The public interest test*

CLAUSE

'4.8 It has never been the rule that a prosecution will automatically take place once the evidential stage is met. A prosecution will usually take place unless the prosecutor is satisfied that there are public interest factors tending against prosecution which outweigh those tending in favour. In some cases the prosecutor may be satisfied that the public interest can be properly served by offering the offender the opportunity to have the matter dealt with by an out-of-court disposal rather than bringing a prosecution.

4.9 When deciding the public interest, prosecutors should consider each of the questions set out below in paragraphs 4.12 (a) to (g) so as to identify and determine the relevant public interest factors tending for and against prosecution. These factors, together with any public interest factors set out in relevant guidance or policy issued by the DPP, should enable prosecutors to form an overall assessment of the public interest.

...

4.12 Prosecutors should consider each of the following questions:

a. How serious is the offence committed?
    The more serious the offence, the more likely it is that a prosecution is required ...
b. What is the level of culpability of the suspect?
    The greater the suspect's level of culpability, the more likely it is that a prosecution is required ...
c. What are the circumstances of and the harm caused to the victim?
    The circumstances of the victim are highly relevant. The greater the vulnerability of the victim, the more likely it is that a prosecution is required. This includes where a position of trust or authority exists between the suspect and victim ...
d. Was the suspect under the age of 18 at the time of the offence?
    The criminal justice system treats children and young people differently from adults and significant weight must be attached to the age of the suspect if they are a child or young person under 18 ...
e. What is the impact on the community?
    The greater the impact of the offending on the community, the more likely it is that a prosecution is required ...
f. Is prosecution a proportionate response?
    Prosecutors should also consider whether prosecution is proportionate to the likely outcome ...
g. Do sources of information require protecting?
    In cases where public interest immunity does not apply, special care should be taken when proceeding with a prosecution where details may need to be made public that could harm sources of information, international relations or national security. It is essential that such cases are kept under continuing review.'

When the CPS took over prosecutions in 1986, the practice of discontinuing cases in line with the Code, which before 1986 had been very rare, became more common. This is one of the reasons that the CPS did not enjoy particular popularity, especially within the police force. You should note that the Code does not require an examination of the **guilt** of the accused, but the **likelihood of conviction**: a factor which may influence the CPS to drop cases where the evidence is perceived as being weak. But because the police had previously not discontinued cases or downgraded offences in this way, tension between the police and the CPS grew.

Until 1999, it was the role of the police to compile the files for each investigated case and to arrange the date for the first appearance in court. The police **then** sent the file to the CPS. The CPS would review the evidence in the file and decide whether it justified the charge being laid by the police **after** the court date had been fixed. The CPS might discontinue the case, continue as per the charge or could downgrade the charge which involves substituting it with a lesser offence.

5.3.2 The Glidewell Report

In 1998, the Glidewell Report into the CPS ('The Review of the Crown Prosecution Service', Cm 3690 (1998)) had found that approximately 12 per cent of cases were discontinued. It identified serious tension between the police and the CPS, with a tendency for each party to blame the other if a case failed. Since 1986, Glidewell found, the CPS had become increasingly isolationist, and a rift in communication and co-operation had resulted. The main recommendation of the Glidewell Report was to place CPS representatives into police stations to form a single integrated unit in charge of assembling and managing the case files, able to call on the police to obtain more evidence where necessary. These changes seem to have succeeded. In the preface to the CPS Annual Report 2002–03, the DPP's letter to the Attorney General (to whom the DPP is answerable) indicated:

QUOTATION

'In magistrates' courts, the CPS secured a conviction in 98% of its prosecutions – around 978,000 defendants either pleaded or were found guilty. This is an increase of 45,000 on 2001–2002, and includes a 70% conviction rate in those cases where the defendant pleaded not guilty.

In the Crown Court, almost 90% of cases proceeding to hearing resulted in a conviction – around 72,000 defendants – an increase of almost 9,000 and 14% more than in 2001–2002. Almost 62% of defendants who pleaded not guilty in the Crown Court were convicted.'

As a result of the Glidewell recommendations, ss28 to 31 of the Criminal Justice Act 2003 provide that the CPS is responsible for determining the charge to be laid against suspects. This is called the Charging Programme, and during 2015–16, the CPS provided 283,736 pre-charge decisions (source: CPS 'Annual Report 2015–16', available at www. cps.gov.uk/publications/reports/index.html). CPS lawyers are placed in police stations and are also available through a 24-hour telephone service, CPS Direct, to work in partnership with the police to ensure that the right charging decision is made, building stronger cases and reducing the number of unsuccessful outcomes and ineffective trials. However, while discontinuance rates do improve year on year (from 16.2 per cent in 2001–02 steadily decreasing to 10.3 per cent in 2015–16) what this does mean is that about one case in every ten (at the Magistrates' Courts; the figure is even higher in the Crown Court) is not continued after charge. In addition, 3.8 per cent of cases result in an acquittal in the Magistrates' Courts after a trial, and 19.6 per cent of cases result in an acquittal at the Crown Court after a trial (set against a background of a 8.0 per cent conviction rate after a trial: most cases, however, do not proceed to trial because approximately 70 per cent of defendants plead guilty).

5.3.3 Victims' Right to Review

In June 2013, the CPS launched the Victims' Right to Review, or VRR, policy which enshrines a victim's right to request a review of any decision taken by the CPS not to charge a suspect or to stop a prosecution. This reflects a change in the criminal justice system over the past decade in respect of the role of the victim in the system, not just as a passive and unfortunate witness to an alleged offence, but as an active party to the proceedings, albeit represented by the CPS on behalf of the state. A VRR consists of a completely fresh examination of all the evidence and circumstances of a case, and if a charge is justified and there are no legal barriers to prosecution, proceedings will be continued and not stopped.

ACTIVITY

Self-test questions

1. Most crimes are investigated by local authorities.	True/False
2. The overriding objective of the CrimPRs is to deal with cases quickly.	True/False
3. Most criminal prosecutions are brought by the CPS.	True/False
4. The evidential test under the Code for Crown Prosecutors is whether it is in the public interest.	True/False
5. One of the key considerations of the public interest test is the likelihood of a significant sentence.	True/False

5.4 Advance sentence indication

5.4.1 Advance indication of sentence *not* plea-bargaining

The procedure we outline here is not plea-bargaining. Instead, it is where the defendant instructs his counsel to seek an indication from the judge of his current view of the maximum sentence which would be imposed on the defendant in the event of a guilty plea being entered at the time the indication is sought.

This is different from plea-bargaining because a bargained plea is where the defendant pleads guilty in exchange for an agreed reduction in sentence or he pleads guilty to a lesser offence on the same facts. It is not uncommon practice in other jurisdictions, and might in time be introduced here; the Attorney General of England and Wales consulted on the introduction of plea-bargaining in fraud cases in April 2008. In 2009 the Attorney General introduced guidelines which allowed for a limited 'plea negotiation framework' in fraud cases. To date, this framework has not been extended to other offences.

Plea-bargaining does provide benefits to prosecuting agencies. Guilty pleas help those agencies in meeting targets for convictions because they save the system time and the expense. However, plea-bargaining is not accepted in English law (the previous practice per *R v Turner* [1970] 53 Cr App R 352 has been abolished), and is highly controversial in the jurisdictions where it is practised. The victim of the crime (or his or her family) may feel justice has not been done because the offender has not pleaded guilty to the offence and the victim feels he or she has been subject to, or has not received, the full sentence for the crime. It is also true that any system of plea-bargaining can lead to a suspicion of over-charging. Furthermore, it does put a lot of pressure on a defendant to plead guilty to benefit from a reduction in sentence rather than risk being convicted following trial, and receive a higher sentence. Research carried out for the Runciman Report (M Zander and P Henderson, 'The Crown Court Study', Royal Commission on Criminal Justice Study 19, 1993, p 145) suggested that 11 per cent of defendants who pleaded guilty as a result of a plea-bargain (under the since abolished system) insisted later they were innocent but pleaded guilty to secure a lesser sentence.

5.4.2 The *Goodyear* rules

In *Goodyear* [2005] EWCA Crim 888, guidance was given by the Court of Appeal on the procedure to be adopted where a request is made for an advanced indication of sentence. First, there must be a written 'basis of plea'. This is a document in which the defendant sets out the facts on which a guilty plea would be entered. It is impossible for a judge to give any indication of sentence without knowing the basis of the plea. However, even if there is an agreed basis of plea, the judge has an unfettered discretion to refuse to give an advance indication of sentence and does not even have to give reasons for his decision. The judge might also reserve his position until such time as he feels able to give an indication.

Once an indication is given it remains binding on the judge who had given it and any other judge who becomes responsible for the case. If, after a reasonable opportunity to consider his position in light of the indication, the defendant does not plead guilty, the indication ceases to have effect. The hearing should take place in open court.

The new procedure does not apply in the Magistrates' Court – but there are mechanisms for obtaining an advance indication of the type of sentence being considered, subject to the type of crime charged (see section 5.8.3 below).

5.5 Courts exercising criminal jurisdiction

The courts mentioned below exercise criminal jurisdiction. Some of the courts are also capable of exercising civil jurisdiction and have therefore already been mentioned in Chapter 4. Where this is the case, the relevant information has not been repeated. The courts in the ELS can be classified as courts of *first instance* or *original jurisdiction* and courts of *appellate jurisdiction*. Simply, this means:

First instance or original	Hears trials
Appellate	Hears appeals

However, there is no single trial court and no single appellate court. In fact, the Crown Court has both original and appellate jurisdiction, as the following table shows:

	First instance	Appellate
Magistrates' Court	✓	✗
Crown Court	✓	✓
High Court, Administrative Court	✗	✓
Court of Appeal (Criminal Division)	✗	✓
Supreme Court	✗	✓

Our focus in this chapter is on the two courts of first instance. Brief mention will be made of the appeal courts here but you will find more detail in Chapter 6.

5.6 Appellate courts

In addition to the Court of Appeal and the Supreme Court, which we will come to presently, there are two courts of special jurisdiction worth a brief mention.

5.6.1 The Court of Justice of the European Union

Under Article 267 of the Treaty of Rome this court may be asked to give rulings concerning EU law. The status of the Court of Justice's rulings are unaffected by the vote to leave the EU in the June 2016 referendum. Its rulings remain binding on English courts until the UK leaves the Union. See Chapter 1.

5.6.2 The Judicial Committee of the Privy Council

The JCPC is the court of final appeal for the UK overseas territories and Crown dependencies (e.g. the Falkland Islands), and for those Commonwealth countries that have retained the appeal to the Judicial Committee (e.g. Saint Kitts and Nevis). In October 2003 New Zealand legislated to abolish appeals to the Privy Council in respect of all cases heard after the end of 2003.

In dealing with these appeals from courts outside the UK the business of this Committee is mainly civil. The Committee will not grant special leave for an appeal to be heard in criminal cases, unless there are exceptional circumstances. Leave to appeal will be granted only if there has been a substantial injustice and the accused has been denied a fair trial.

It was reported in *The Times* ('Death Under the Sun', 18 January 2000) that Trinidad & Tobago, Barbados, Guyana and Jamaica all signed up in principle to a new Court of Appeal to curtail the power of the Privy Council in criminal cases. The opinion of the Privy Council expressed in *Pratt* [1993] 4 All ER 769 may have made the Privy Council master of its own destruction. Death row inmates who have been in prison for more than five years had, in the Council's opinion, suffered 'inhuman or degrading treatment' and accordingly their sentences would be commuted to life. *Pratt* (1993) is a very unpopular judgment in these countries where the death penalty is widely supported. The Caribbean Court of Justice was created in 2001, and now is the final court of appeals for Caribbean countries.

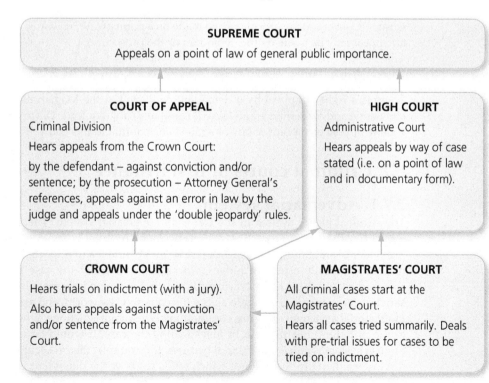

SUPREME COURT
Appeals on a point of law of general public importance.

COURT OF APPEAL
Criminal Division
Hears appeals from the Crown Court:
by the defendant – against conviction and/or sentence; by the prosecution – Attorney General's references, appeals against an error in law by the judge and appeals under the 'double jeopardy' rules.

HIGH COURT
Administrative Court
Hears appeals by way of case stated (i.e. on a point of law and in documentary form).

CROWN COURT
Hears trials on indictment (with a jury).
Also hears appeals against conviction and/or sentence from the Magistrates' Court.

MAGISTRATES' COURT
All criminal cases start at the Magistrates' Court.
Hears all cases tried summarily. Deals with pre-trial issues for cases to be tried on indictment.

Figure 5.2 Criminal court hierarchy

This aspect of the work of the Privy Council was unaffected by the creation of the Supreme Court.

5.6.3 The Supreme Court

The Supreme Court may hear appeals on matters of criminal law. These appeals may come either from the Court of Appeal (Criminal Division) or from the Administrative Court of the Queen's Bench Division. Certain conditions must be satisfied before the Supreme Court can hear appeals in criminal cases, and the details of this will be described in Chapter 6, which deals with the appeals system in greater depth.

5.6.4 The Court of Appeal (Criminal Division)

Originally, the Court of Appeal was created to hear civil cases only, but the Court of Criminal Appeal, as it was then known, was created in 1907, to hear appeals in criminal cases only. This court was replaced in 1966 by the Court of Appeal (Criminal Division) the name by which it is now known. The head of this court is the Lord Chief Justice. It has jurisdiction to hear appeals against sentence or conviction by persons convicted of offences at the Crown Court, but it does not deal with cases which have been heard by the Divisional Court of the Queen's Bench Division; these cases go direct to the Supreme Court. Again, you will understand this point more thoroughly when you have read Chapter 6 on the appeal procedures in the court system.

5.6.5 The High Court of Justice

You may find it odd to see the High Court mentioned here, as it was dealt with in Chapter 4 as a court which deals primarily with civil cases. However, as mentioned there, this court has jurisdiction in respect of offences which have been tried in the Magistrates' Courts and an appeal may be made on a point of law by way of case stated. Such an appeal may be made by the defendant or the prosecution.

5.6.6 The Crown Court – appellate jurisdiction

There is a right of appeal by a defendant convicted at the Magistrates' Court against conviction and/or sentence and leave is (uniquely) not required. The prosecution has no right to appeal on a point of law or against an acquittal to this court.

5.7 Criminal courts of first instance

5.7.1 Adversarial system

The criminal justice system in the UK is an adversarial system. The term adversarial means that there are two parties (adversaries) who represent their positions by presenting evidence and calling witnesses before an independent and impartial person or group of people (usually a jury or judge), who decides whether the case is proven to the standard required (in English criminal law, that is beyond reasonable doubt). Adversarial systems are more common across the common law world, and are compared with inquisitorial systems which are common in civil law jurisdictions, where a judge (or a group of judges) has the task of investigating the case. It would be wrong to say the English system is *purely* adversarial because, for example, the prosecution has a duty to disclose evidence to the defence which tends to show the defendant is not guilty, and also under the CrimPRs (above at section 5.2) the judge has a proactive role to direct the parties and give a timetable for the case to proceed to trial.

5.7.2 The Crown Court

Students often confuse the names and functions of the Crown Court and the County Courts. Try to memorise now the fact that the Crown Court is a court which exercises criminal jurisdiction, whereas the County Courts exercise civil jurisdiction.

The Crown Court sits in court centres throughout England and Wales. The Crown Court in London is referred to as the Central Criminal Court (known popularly as the Old Bailey). The Crown Court is regarded as one single court which sits in various parts of the country. It was created to replace the previous system of Assizes and Quarter Sessions.

The personnel of the court consists of all the judges of the High Court, Circuit Judges, Recorders and Justices of the Peace (JPs) (who will sit with a judge drawn from one of the other categories). Under the Courts Act 2003, District Judges (Magistrates' Court) (DJ(MC)) can also carry out functions as a judge of the Crown Court, such as interlocutory (pre-trial) matters.

A distinctive feature of the Crown Court is the use of the jury as part of the trial process. See further Chapter 8 on the jury system.

The Crown Court is the only court which has jurisdiction to hear all trials on indictment for offences wherever committed. It also has the power to sentence persons convicted by the magistrates. In the Crown Court, the jury determines questions of fact (what happened, to whom and when) and the judge decides questions of law (including the admissibility of evidence and directing the jury).

5.7.3 The Magistrates' Court

In addition to their work in civil cases (described in Chapter 9), the Magistrates' Courts deal with a vast quantity of criminal cases: 98 per cent of all criminal matters are dealt with by these courts. Magistrates have jurisdiction in respect of trials of **summary offences, either way offences** and they also have the task of carrying out preliminary matters (bail, remand and related matters) in every case in which a person is accused of an **indictable only offence**.

The terms in bold are explained in full at section 5.8 below, but before we examine these terms, we will briefly identify the personnel involved and the new system operating in this court.

Not surprisingly, the personnel of the Magistrates' Court consists of magistrates. There are two types:

1. Lay Magistrates, or JPs. These are generally lay (not legally qualified, although a legal qualification is not a bar to becoming a JP), unpaid (expenses only), volunteers who live within the local justice area and have been nominated or have applied to be on the Bench. Some training is provided, but a qualified Bench Legal Adviser (court clerk) advises them on legal matters.

2. Stipendiary Magistrates, now referred to as District Judges (Magistrates' Court), who have been solicitors or barristers for at least seven years (CLSA 1990 and Access to Justice Act 1999: see Chapters 10 and 11). The title of 'Justice of the Peace' is generally used when referring to lay judges but technically it may refer equally to a lay justice and to a DJ(MC).

There are approximately 17,500 lay magistrates, compared with approximately 140 DJ(MC)s, plus Deputy DJ(MC)s. Lay magistrates work part-time, sitting for 26 half-days per annum. DJ(MC)s are full-time and salaried.

5.8 Classification of criminal offences

Criminal offences are divided into three categories:

1. **Offences triable only on indictment**. These are tried only in the Crown Court. These are the offences which are considered too serious to be dealt with by the Magistrates' Courts and must be heard by a judge and jury. Examples of indictable only offences include murder, attempted murder, manslaughter and rape, serious offences against the person, e.g. causing grievous bodily harm with intent, and aggravated burglary. In the main, these are offences which were developed by the common law, rather than by statute. Indictable only offences are themselves divided into four classes according to the gravity of the offence, and then matched to a judge of the appropriate status. Thus, cases in Classes 1 and 2 which include murder, treason and rape, are usually heard by a High Court Judge with a jury. Cases in the other classes may be heard by a High Court Judge, a Circuit Judge or a Recorder, with a jury in every case where the defendant pleads not guilty.

2. **Summary offences**. These are dealt with summarily (literally briefly, without a jury) in the Magistrates' Courts. These are less serious offences, including many motoring offences under the Road Traffic Acts, taking a motor vehicle without consent and many other offences created by statute.

3. **Offences triable either way**. These are crimes which can be tried *either* summarily by the magistrates, *or* on indictment, i.e. before a judge and jury in the Crown Court. They are often referred to as **hybrid offences**. They include less serious assaults, criminal damage in excess of £5,000 and many of the offences contained in the Theft Act 1968 but excluding, among other things, blackmail and certain burglaries.

ACTIVITY

Self-test questions

Consider the following story, and the questions based on it.

Mrs Smith claims that one day last year, she saw Dan point a gun in the direction of his girlfriend, and pull the trigger. The gun failed to fire because the mechanism was faulty, but Dan had not been aware of that until after he had pulled the trigger. Dan is now being tried for the attempted murder of his girlfriend, under the provisions of the Criminal Attempts Act 1981. He claims that he did not point the gun in his girlfriend's direction as alleged and that Mrs Smith was mistaken or is lying. Second, he claims that the act of pointing a gun in this way is not legally capable of falling within the relevant section of the 1981 Act.

1. Who has decided whether Dan should be tried for this offence and by what procedure?
2. In which court would this case be tried and by whom?
3. Who will decide whether either Dan or Mrs Smith is lying about what happened?
4. Who will decide whether Dan's alleged actions are capable as a matter of law of being within the ambit of the Criminal Attempts Act 1981?

5.8.1 Indictable only offences

It is worth noting that *all* criminal offences start at the Magistrates' Court. The majority (98 per cent) also finish there and will not 'move up' to the Crown Court. The remaining 2 per cent therefore do go up to the Crown Court. This 2 per cent is made up of indictable only offences and either way offences to be tried on indictment. The term 'indictment' (pronounced 'inditement') merely means the document containing the charge. The term used in the Magistrates' Court is 'written charge'.

Traditionally, when faced with an indictable only offence, the magistrates undertook a preliminary hearing, known as committal proceedings, in which the magistrates had to be satisfied there was a case for the accused to answer. However, due to the complexity of committals, and to save court time, s51(1) of the Crime and Disorder Act 1998 abolished committals in indictable only offences.

Accordingly, although indictable only offences commence at the Magistrates' Court, as there are no committals, the role of the magistrates in such cases is to deal with legal aid (the Criminal Defence Service Fund: see Chapter 7), bail and remand. Note that a defendant charged with an indictable only offence does not enter his plea until the plea and case management hearing (PCMH) at the Crown Court. The PCMH is managed by the judge. The defendant enters his plea. If guilty, the judge proceeds to sentence. If not guilty, the parties inform the court of the main factual and legal issues in the case and the judge directs the parties with a timetable for the case to proceed, fairly and promptly, to trial. If the defendant wishes to receive an indication of sentence (section 5.4.2 above), this takes place at the PCMH.

5.8.2 Summary offences

Summary offences are dealt with only by the Magistrates' Courts. Offenders are not entitled to trial by jury in respect of these offences. There are literally hundreds of offences which are triable summarily only, many of them being motoring offences under the Road Traffic Acts. To avoid the court system being totally overwhelmed by minor traffic violations (most of which are non-recordable offences which means a defendant cannot be imprisoned upon conviction), it is possible for defendants in these cases to choose not to appear at court but to plead guilty by post. New fast-track traffic courts were established by the end of 2013 to handle these cases.

Because of the less serious nature of these offences, the magistrates are restricted in the type of sentence which they can impose. Generally, therefore, an offender can be given only a maximum of six months' imprisonment in respect of a summary offence. Similarly, the magistrates can impose a fine of only £1,000 in respect of summary offences, or such amount as is specified in the statute creating the offence, whichever is higher, up to an overall limit of £5,000.

The magistrates also have power to compensate victims of crime, by ordering a convicted person to pay an amount (again, up to £5,000) to the victim of the crime.

5.8.3 Offences triable either way

The third category of offences with which magistrates may deal is the group of offences known as 'either way' offences. In very basic terms, summary offences 'live' at the Magistrates' Court, indictable only offences 'visit' the Magistrates' Court but 'live' at the Crown Court; but either way offences are 'of no fixed abode'. The first thing that has to be done with an either way offence, therefore, is to find it a 'home'. The process starts with the plea.

Plea before venue

Remember that all criminal offences start at the Magistrates' Court. Under s17A Magistrates' Courts Act 1980 (as amended, most recently by the Criminal Justice Act 2003) a defendant charged with an either way offence will be first asked at the Magistrates' Court to indicate his plea.

If the defendant pleads guilty, the Magistrates' Court passes sentence or may commit the defendant for sentence at the Crown Court if the magistrates' sentencing powers are inadequate. A guilty plea obviously means there is no need for a trial, as a trial is a hearing to determine guilt. This provides the defendant with the earliest opportunity to plead guilty.

Mode of trial

If a defendant charged with an either way offence pleads not guilty, the magistrates proceed to a mode of trial hearing or, under the Criminal Justice Act 2003, an **'allocation' hearing**. This is a pre-trial hearing to decide which court will hear the trial; it is *not* a hearing to decide guilt or innocence.

Section 19 of the Magistrates' Courts Act 1980 governs the procedure to be followed by a Magistrates' Court in deciding whether a case involving an either way offence (to which the defendant has pleaded not guilty) should be tried summarily or on indictment. Under the new procedure ('allocation') the court is to be informed about, and must take account of, any previous convictions of the defendant in assessing whether the sentencing powers available to it are adequate. Certain cases involving children and serious or complex fraud cases are generally sent to the Crown Court immediately (ss51B and 51C Crime and Disorder Act 1998).

Under s20 Magistrates' Courts Act 1980, if the magistrates decide that the case is suitable for summary trial, defendants must be told that they can either consent to be tried summarily or, if they wish, they can choose to be tried on indictment. Before the Criminal Justice Act 2003, a defendant making this choice was informed that if he consented to be tried summarily, if convicted, he could have been committed for sentencing to the Crown Court for *any* either way offence. Now, it is generally no longer possible to be committed for sentence to the Crown Court once the magistrates have accepted jurisdiction. Defendants who elect summary trial can therefore not receive a sentence beyond the magistrates' powers.

The exception to this rule is where committal for sentence under s3A of the Powers of Criminal Courts (Sentencing) Act 2000 is available for specified violent or sexual offences carrying a sentence of imprisonment of ten years or more where the court is of the opinion that there is a significant risk to members of the public of serious harm occasioned by the commission by the defendant of further specified offences. The writer cannot foresee many situations in which the magistrates would have decided that such offences would be suitable for summary trial in any event.

Indication of sentence

Defendants also now have the opportunity of requesting an indication from the magistrates whether, if they pleaded guilty at that point, the sentence would be custodial or not. The Magistrates' Court will have a discretion whether or not to give an indication to a defendant who has sought one. Where an indication is given, defendants will be given the opportunity to reconsider their original indication as to plea. Where a defendant then decides to plead guilty, the Magistrates' Court will proceed to sentence. A custodial sentence will be available only if such a sentence was indicated. Where an indication of sentence is given and the defendant does not choose to plead guilty on the basis of it, the sentence indication is not binding on the magistrates who later try the case summarily, or on the Crown Court if the defendant elects trial on indictment.

Otherwise (i.e. where the defendant declines to reconsider his plea indication, or where no sentence indication is given) the defendant will be given the choice between accepting summary trial and electing trial on indictment.

Schedule 3, para 7 of the Criminal Justice Act 2003 amends s21 of the Magistrates' Courts Act 1980 so that, where the court decides that trial on indictment appears more suitable, it will proceed to send the case to the Crown Court in accordance with s51(1) of the Crime and Disorder Act 1998. There are no committals for either way offences to be tried on indictment.

Allocation guidelines

Under s170 of the 2003 Act, allocation guidelines are published to assist the magistrates to decide whether summary or trial on indictment is suitable. In March 2016, the Sentencing Council introduced new guidelines for Magistrates' Courts to help them determine whether a trial should be heard in a Magistrates' or Crown Court.

QUOTATION

'**Venue for trial**

It is important to ensure that all cases are tried at the appropriate level.

1. In general, either way offences should be tried summarily unless:

   - the outcome would clearly be a sentence in excess of the court's powers for the offence(s) concerned after taking into account personal mitigation and any potential reduction for a guilty plea; or
   - for reasons of unusual legal, procedural or factual complexity, the case should be tried in the Crown Court. This exception may apply in cases where a very substantial fine is the likely sentence. Other circumstances where this exception will apply are likely to be rare and case specific; the court will rely on the submissions of the parties to identify relevant cases.

2. In cases with no factual or legal complications the court should bear in mind its power to commit for sentence after a trial and may retain jurisdiction notwithstanding that the likely sentence might exceed its powers...

Where the court decides that the case is suitable to be dealt with in the magistrates' court, it must warn the defendant that all sentencing options remain open and, if the defendant consents to summary trial and is convicted by the court or pleads guilty, the defendant may be committed to the Crown Court for sentence.'

Sentencing Council, Allocation Guidelines, www.sentencingcouncil.org.uk/ wp-content/uploads/Allocation_Guideline_2015.pdf, March 2016

These are currently found in the Consolidated Criminal Practice Direction, Part II, Preliminary Proceedings, para 9A:

QUOTATION

'**Preliminary proceedings 9A: ALLOCATION (MODE OF TRIAL)**

II.9A.3 Certain general observations can be made:

(a) the court should never make its decision on the grounds of convenience or expedition;
(b) the court should assume for the purpose of deciding mode of trial that the prosecution version of the facts is correct.'

The starting point for the magistrates is therefore to consider dealing with the case summarily, but this is far from the end of the matter. Each either way offence is listed in the Practice Direction detailing common aggravating and mitigating features which might make the considered offence more suitable for trial at the Crown or Magistrates' Court respectively. It is important for you to grasp the significance of the mode of trial (allocation) procedure because, as you will see below, the right to elect trial by jury has been regarded as a cornerstone of our constitutional rights. It is a right not exercised as frequently as we may imagine, however, as Slapper and Kelly point out:

QUOTATION

'Most defendants charged with either way offences are tried by magistrates: 9% of cases go to the Crown Court because the magistrates consider their current sentencing powers to be inadequate [note that this was limited at the time of writing to six months maximum; now it is increased to 12 months, this percentage may in future be even lower]; 4% of cases go to the Crown Court because the defendants elect trial by jury.'

G Slapper and D Kelly, *The English Legal System* (7th edn, Cavendish, 2004), p 140

ACTIVITY

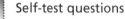

Self-test questions

Using the classification of criminal offences given in this chapter, identify the types of offences set out below, and state which of them will be tried by the Crown Court, and which by the Magistrates' Court:

1. manslaughter;
2. taking a motor vehicle without consent;
3. taking goods from a supermarket without paying for them;
4. deliberately causing damage to another person's property valued at £2,000.

5.8.4 The choice: Magistrates' Court or Crown Court?

A defendant charged with an either way offence where the magistrates have decided in the allocation hearing that the case is suitable for summary trial may consent to trial by the magistrates or may elect trial by jury. What factors influence his decision?

Stay at the Magistrates' Court	Elect the Crown Court
The maximum sentence is lower and post-trial committals for sentence have (on the whole) been abolished.	There may be considerable delay; time served on remand is taken off final sentence (if convicted) and remand prisoners have more rights than prisoners following conviction.
Conviction rate is higher on a not guilty plea (see the letter to the Attorney General in section 5.3.2).	Conviction rate is lower on a not guilty plea.
There is less publicity (journalists are not barred from the Magistrates' Court but are generally more interested in jury trials).	The CPS will review the files and may decide to drop the charge during the delay between allocation and the plea and directions hearing.
If convicted, the right to appeal to the Crown Court does not require leave (permission) and, as the Magistrates' Court has to give reasons for decisions, it is easier to discover errors in fact or law.	If convicted, D will need leave to appeal and it is difficult to persuade the Court of Appeal to overturn a jury verdict. On the other hand, no reasons are given by the jury so the Court of Appeal may be able to find the conviction unsafe where there is a trial judge error in directing the jury (even if it had no effect on jury deliberations).

Figure 5.3 Factors influencing a defendant's decision to elect trial by jury in an either way offence

Criminal court procedure, and in particular allocation of either way offences, can be rather tricky for students to grasp; especially students with no experience of the court system. Figure 5.4 should help, but we also strongly advise you to make the time to visit your local courts.

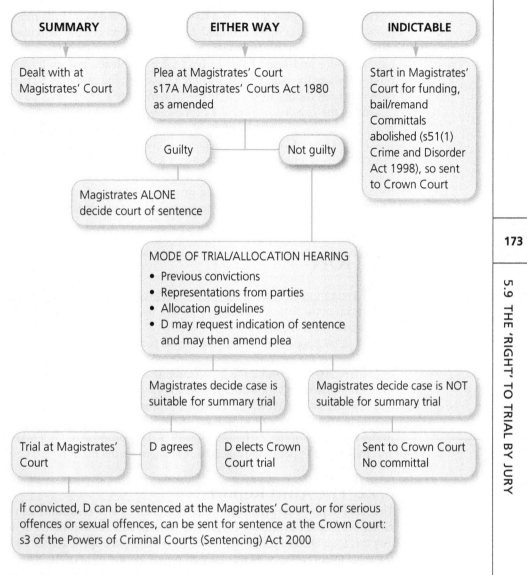

Figure 5.4 Criminal procedure

5.9 The 'right' to trial by jury

5.9.1 The Mode of Trial Bills

In November 1999, the Criminal Justice (Mode of Trial) Bill was introduced in the House of Lords (the legislative chamber of course). This exceptionally controversial Bill would have given effect to the unanimous recommendations of the Royal Commission on Criminal Justice (Runciman) 1993, the Review of Delay in the Criminal Justice System (Narey) 1997 and a government Consultation Paper. Both reports stated that the decision on mode of trial **should be entirely for the magistrates to make**. The defendant should not, said the reports, have the final decision on a not guilty plea to an either way charge to elect jury trial where the magistrates were of the opinion that the case was suitable for summary trial, i.e. if the magistrates felt the case should 'stay down' then it should 'stay down' and not be sent to the Crown Court.

Had it become law, this would have removed the defendant's right to elect jury trial in the only situation in the criminal justice system where the defendant has the right to choose (on a summary charge he cannot request a jury trial; for indictable offences, he has no choice and must have a jury trial if he pleads not guilty; but for either way offences where the magistrates are of the view that the case may be tried summarily, the defendant can choose to 'go up' to the Crown Court).

One of the reasons behind the proposal was to remove the practice of the 'cracked trial'. This is where a defendant pleads not guilty at the Mode of Trial hearing and elects trial at the Crown Court, but then enters a guilty plea at the Crown Court on the day of the trial. Why might he do this? Have a look at the grid above (under section 5.8.4) to see some of the factors that may influence a defendant to enter a late guilty plea (for example, he may have hoped the CPS might drop the charges). In addition, the delay between Mode of Trial and Plea and Directions might be as much as six months. As Slapper and Kelly point out:

QUOTATION

'The accuracy of testimony becomes less reliable the longer the gap between the original reception of the data [for example, the first time the witness makes his police statement] and his account of it in court.'

G Slapper and D Kelly, *The English Legal System* (7th edn, Cavendish, 2004,) p 159

In January 2000, the first Bill was defeated in the House of Lords, but in February 2000, the Criminal Justice (Mode of Trial) (No 2) Bill was introduced in the House of Commons; and rejected by the House of Lords in September of the same year. The government swiftly promised that a third Bill would be passed into law without the Lords' approval under the power of the Parliament Act 1911. This promise did not materialise, however, and the Queen's Speech in June 2001 was silent on the matter.

5.9.2 The Auld Report

The Auld Report was published in October 2001. It also recommended that allocation of either way offences should be for the Magistrates' Court alone, or in the event of a dispute, for a District Judge to decide, with a right of appeal to a Circuit Judge. This was the third major report which proposed removing the right of the defendant to elect trial by jury. However, to balance the procedure, committals for trial and post-trial committals for sentence would both be abolished. As you are aware above, some of these proposals have been enacted in the Criminal Justice Act 2003.

Auld recommendations accepted in the Criminal Justice Act 2003	Auld recommendations rejected in the Criminal Justice Act 2003
Committals for trial for all either way offences to be tried on indictment have been abolished.	The proposal to abolish the defendant's right to elect jury trial (not guilty plea; either way offence).
Posttrial committals for sentence have been abolished (on the whole).	
Magistrates are aware of the defendant's previous convictions in making the allocation decision.	

Figure 5.5 The Auld recommendations and the Criminal Justice Act

5.9.3 The Criminal Justice Act 2003
Risk of jury tampering
Section 44 of the Criminal Justice Act 2003 provides for a trial to be conducted without a jury where there is a 'real and present danger' of jury tampering, or continued without a jury where the jury has been discharged because of jury tampering. The court must be satisfied that the risk of jury tampering would be so substantial (notwithstanding any steps, including police protection, that could reasonably be taken to prevent it) as to make it necessary in the interests of justice for the trial to be conducted without a jury.

It is considered that it is far harder to intimidate a judge than to threaten a jury member. You may wish to note that this is the reason behind the abolition of juries in certain trials in Northern Ireland in 1973. Lord Diplock had chaired a Royal Commission in 1972 ('Report of the Commission to Consider Legal Procedures to Deal with Terrorist Activities in Northern Ireland', Cmnd 5185) and thus we call single-judge courts in that jurisdiction 'Diplock' courts.

Section 44 came into force, by SI, in July 2006 and the first order for a jury-less trial was made by the Court of Appeal in 2009. Towards the end of the first trial of a number of defendants charged with armed robbery at Heathrow Airport in 2004, a re-trial had been ordered because the jury of nine could not deliver a majority verdict (see Chapter 8 on majority verdicts). At the re-trial, the jury had to be discharged because there was evidence that two jurors had been approached and the judge could not continue alone because he had seen highly prejudicial but inadmissible evidence. Before the third trial, the prosecution requested a trial without a jury. The judge agreed that there was a real and present danger of jury tampering but directed that a package of measures be put in place (which would have cost £1.5 million and involved 32 police officers for six months) to reduce the risk to an acceptable level. On the prosecution application to the Court of Appeal, an order was granted to hold the third trial before a judge alone (see *R v Tworney* [2009]).

In *R v KS* [2010] EWCA Crim 1756, however, trial by judge alone was refused even though there had been jury tampering because the tampering had been opportunistic and the Court of Appeal thought better arrangements to separate juries from the public (e.g. during smoking breaks) would avoid it in future.

5.9.4 Do we have the 'right' to elect jury trial?
The short answer is 'no'. There is no specific statutory or recognised legal 'right' to trial by jury, but trial by one's peers has been a tradition for so long that the public and some Members of Parliament strongly oppose any invasion into that perceived right. The government's two Mode of Trial Bills were defeated and despite three Royal Commission reports supporting their view, the government conceded in the Criminal Justice Act 2003 that allowing magistrates to have the only and final say in court of trial was not worth the political cost.

After much wrangling between the Houses of Commons and Lords, the Criminal Justice Act 2003 did, in theory only, remove this right in serious or complex frauds, and where there is jury tampering. As we saw, however, s43 requires an SI to give it effect and there was no confidence that the affirmative resolution procedure would be passed. The government therefore decided to pass primary legislation to tackle part of this problem. The Fraud (Trials without a Jury) Bill 2006–07 attempted to enable the government to implement s43 of the Criminal Justice Act 2003 without getting the approval of the Houses of Parliament. The Bill did not get through the enactment process before the end of the parliamentary year, and there was no specific mention of the provisions in the Queen's Speech at the opening of the 2007–08 parliamentary session. In light of the historic efforts to remove certain trials from the jury, this is unlikely to be the end of the matter.

However, there was one small victory for the previous Labour government. The Domestic Violence, Crime and Victims Act 2004 contains the following provisions:

- The defendant may be tried before a jury on a sample count (s19(1)). (A sample or specimen count is a single offence in circumstances where the alleged conduct has been repeated on several occasions but there are thought to be too many charges to be heard in one trial. For example, a defendant may be charged with one or two sample counts of fraud or downloading indecent images of children from the internet; but the prosecution alleges there are many more offences committed in the same way.)

- If the defendant is convicted by the jury of the sample count.

- The defendant may then be tried by the judge without a jury for the other offences (s17(2)) and sentenced accordingly.

The background to the proposed changes are neatly summarised by the legal correspondent for the *Daily Telegraph*, Joshua Rozenberg:

QUOTATION

'The story began in 1996, when Philip Richard Kidd, 49, the headmaster of a primary school in Derbyshire, was convicted of indecently touching girls while they were in the classroom. He was sentenced to 15 months' imprisonment for four offences, three against one girl and one against another.

These were just specimen charges. In all, Kidd had been accused of 17 offences involving eight girls, a factor that the judge took into account when deciding the length of his sentence. But that meant Kidd was being sentenced on offences for which he had not been convicted.

Ruling subsequently on Kidd's appeal, the Lord Chief Justice, Lord Bingham, said that defendants should no longer be sentenced on charges that were neither admitted nor proved – convenient and economical though it might be to try a defendant for specimen offences.

Kidd's sentence was upheld – 15 months was not excessive even for four offences – but, from now on, said the Court of Appeal, defendants would have to be tried on all the charges the prosecution wanted to bring. Some defendants would now face more counts, but the Lord Chief Justice said that this need not be "unduly burdensome or render the trial unmanageable".'

Daily Telegraph, 1 April 2004, Media section, p 18

The decision of the Court of Appeal presented the government with a problem: time and resources could not always be expended in proving each of hundreds of counts of indecent assault or minor fraud; but unless the defendant was convicted on each and every one, he would not receive a sentence which reflected the totality of his criminal conduct. This is why the new two-stage trial process explained above was recommended. However, the proposal is not uniformly supported:

QUOTATION

'The definition [of the term "sample"] provided in the Bill simply leaves it up to the court to decide, saying that a count, or charge, is to be regarded as a sample if the judge "considers that the sample count is a sample of the other counts" ...

And what ... if the defendant is acquitted on the sample counts? In principle, the remaining charges should be dropped. But the Bill does not say this. It would be up to the judge to decide.

There is nothing in the Bill to stop the prosecution having another go ... courts should be required to direct an acquittal on all remaining counts: to do otherwise would leave more defendants effectively facing double jeopardy.

[Vera Baird, QC, a Labour backbencher] sees no difficulty in having t?
by a jury, whose members would be told that the defendant had alread?
similar charges. Again, a guilty plea would seem likely.

But her main concern is the law of unintended consequences.
becomes law, people will soon be singing the praises of trial by judg

There is no doubt that a judge is speedier and cheaper than a f?
will also have to give reasons.

"The question will then be asked: why do we need 10 of these counts to be trie?
if the other 190 are being tried by a judge? Let's do them all by judge", the MP says. "It wi?.
be the beginning of the end for juries – again".'

Daily Telegraph, 1 April 2004, Media section, p 18

ACTIVITY

Critiquing the law

Quotation

'[T]rial by jury is more than an instrument of justice and more than one wheel of the constitution: it is the lamp that shows that freedom lives.'

Lord Devlin, Trial by Jury (Stevens & Sons, 1956), p 164

Lord Devlin's statement is a strong defence of the jury system. He believed that the jury system was central to the operation of British democracy. Yet it is also true that there are many democratic countries throughout the world that do not have a jury system. Issues of fact and law are decided by judges or magistrates alone. Indeed, even in the English legal system the vast majority of criminal cases are not heard in front of a jury. The jury is also nearly non-existent in civil cases as well.

With this in mind, re-read the details of the jury system in this chapter. Consider the following thinking points:

1. What do you think the main advantages of the jury system are?
2. Do you think that the criticisms of the jury system are fair?
3. Do you think that judges should be able to replace juries in the English legal system? Why?
4. If you had an opportunity to reform the jury system, what changes would you make?

KEY FACTS

Criminal courts and procedure

CrimPRs	The Criminal Procedure Rules	A single set of rules governing criminal procedure in both courts of first instance and appeals. Available (including the updates) online.
The Crown Prosecution Service	Governed by …	Prosecution of Offences Act 1985.
	Code for Crown Prosecutors	Stage One – the evidential test. Stage Two – the public interest test.
	Changes	Glidewell. Criminal Justice Act 2003. Advice in person and CPS Direct.

Advance sentence indication	Definition	D seeks the judge's view on maximum sentence in the event of a guilty plea.
	Guidelines	*R v Goodyear* [2005] EWCA Crim 888.
	Procedure	Crown Court only agreed basis of plea D requests. Judge has unfettered discretion to give an indication, defer or refuse. Binding on judge and other judges, but for a 'reasonable' time.
Courts of criminal first instance	Magistrates' Court	All cases start at the Magistrates' Court. 98% of all criminal matters dealt with to completion. All crimes triable summarily. Allocation hearings for either way offences (right to elect jury trial?). Indictable only offences are sent to the Crown Court. No committals (Crime and Disorder Act 1998 and Criminal Justice Act 2003).
	Crown Court	Trials on indictment.
Appellate Courts	Crown Court	See Chapter 6.
	High Court Administrative Court	
	Court of Appeal (Criminal Division)	
	Supreme Court	
	CJEU	
	Privy Council	

SAMPLE ESSAY QUESTION

'It is odd that most lay people think criminal trials are tried before a jury. Quite simply, most aren't, and there is no such "right" to trial by jury either.' Discuss.

> Start by explaining that the only criminal trial court where there is a jury is the Crown Court. Explain that most criminal matters are dealt with to completion at the Magistrates' Court (about 98 per cent). At the very most therefore, only 2 per cent could ever be tried before a jury.

> Next, you might wish to point out from the CPS statistics that 73 per cent of defendants at the Crown Court plead guilty, so statistically, trials before juries amount to less than 0.5 per cent of criminal matters.

In respect of the 'right' to elect, explain that there is no such right for a summary case and that indictable offences have to go to the Crown Court (so again, there is no 'right'). The only time a defendant has a say is for an either way offence; and that the decision is initially for the magistrates anyway (if he feels the case must 'go up', then it is sent to the Crown Court). It is only where the magistrates are of the view that the case may be tried summarily that a defendant can 'elect' Crown Court trial.

It is also worth mentioning there may be a jury-less trial under s44 Criminal Justice Act 2003 where there is a real and present danger of jury tampering (*R v T and others* [2009] EWCA Crim 1035), and there can be a judge-only trial after a jury has tried sample counts under ss17–19 Domestic Violence, Crime and Victims Act 2004.

CONCLUDE

Figure 5.6 Essay map on the 'right' to trial by jury

SUMMARY

- Criminal courts are those courts where criminal liability and/or sentence are assessed.
- Most crimes are investigated by the police.
- Most charges are laid by the CPS and most prosecutions are brought by the CPS. Decisions to proceed to trial are made by a Crown Prosecutor according to the two tests in the Code for Crown Prosecutors:
  - the evidential test;
  - the public interest test.
- Criminal courts in England and Wales do not currently operate a system of plea bargaining, but an accused may request and receive an advanced indication of sentence under the *Goodyear* rules.
- Criminal trials are held in either the Magistrates' Court (before magistrates) or the Crown Court (before a judge and jury, or, rarely, a judge only).
- Criminal cases are either tried on indictment or summarily, but criminal offences are classified as indictable only, summary or hybrid (either way).
- Hybrid, or either way, cases must be allocated a court of trial or sentence.

- Indictable only offences start in the Magistrates' Court but are tried/sentenced at the Crown Court.
- Summary offences are dealt with at the Magistrates' Court.
- Hybrid offences may be tried either on indictment or summarily according to the magistrates' and the defendant's decision.
- Some trials on indictment may (rarely) take place without a jury.

Further reading

Articles

Cammiss, S, ' "I will in a moment give you the full history": mode of trial, prosecutorial control and partial accounts' [2006] *Crim LR* 38.

Cammiss, S and Stride, C, 'Modelling mode of trial' [2008] *Brit J Criminal* 482.

Herbert, A, 'Mode of trial and magistrates' sentencing powers: will increased powers inevitably lead to a reduction in the committal rate?' [2003] *Crim LR* 314.

Jeremy, D, 'The prosecutor's rock and hard place' [2008] *Crim LR* 925.

Jones, D and Brown, J, 'The relationship between victims and prosecutors: defending victims' rights? A CPS response' [2010] *Crim LR* 212.

Julian, RF, 'Judicial perspectives on the conduct of serious fraud trials' [2007] *Crim LR* 751.

Julian, RF, 'Judicial perspectives in serious fraud cases: the present status of and problems posed by case management practices, jury selection rules, juror expertise, plea bargaining and choice of mode of trial' [2008] *Crim LR* 764.

Padfield, N, 'Shining the torch on plea-bargaining' [2009] *CLJ* 11.

Vamos, N, 'Please don't call it "plea bargaining" ' [2009] *Crim LR* 617.

Wilcock, P and Bennathan, J, 'Overhauling criminal procedures: part 1' [2004] 154 *NLJ* 778–779 and part 2 [2004] 154 *NLJ* 862–863.

Internet links

Crown Prosecution Service at: www.cps.gov.uk/

Ministry of Justice Code of Practice for Victims of Crime at: www.gov.uk/government/publications/the-code-of-practice-for-victims-of-crime

Ministry of Justice Statistics on criminal offences and convictions at: www.gov.uk/government/collections/criminal-justice-statistics-quarterly

6

Appeals

AIMS AND OBJECTIVES

After reading this chapter you should be able to:

- Identify the purpose of an appeal
- Explain the hierarchy of the courts
- Describe the rules governing appeals in civil cases
- Distinguish the appeals available to the prosecution in criminal cases and those available to the defence
- Describe the power of the Court of Appeal when determining an appeal against conviction
- Explain and illustrate the role of the Criminal Cases Review Commission

Before we examine the court hierarchy and the appeal system in detail, you need to consider: what is the purpose of an appeal? You cannot evaluate the effectiveness of the appeals system without considering whether it meets its aims.

- What is the aim of an appeal?
- Is that aim the same for criminal and civil cases?
- Should there be any restriction on which party can appeal?
- Should there be any restrictions on how many times either party may appeal?

Lord Woolf wrote in his Report 'Access to Justice' (see Chapter 4) that there are two main purposes of an appeals system. The first is the private one of doing justice in individual cases by correcting wrong decisions. The second is the public one of engendering public confidence in the administration of justice by making those corrections and in clarifying and developing the law. Of course, the report focused on the civil justice system, but you might reflect that a similar purpose could be stated to apply in relation to criminal cases. Bear these aims in mind as you progress through this chapter as well as any you considered in response to the thinking points above.

6.1 Appeals in civil proceedings

6.1.1 The Access to Justice Act 1999

The Access to Justice Act 1999 (AJA 1999) made it clear that being able to bring an appeal in civil cases is not an automatic right for the losing party. This may strike you as rather restrictive, but it must be borne in mind that the rules have to achieve a balance between the rights of the individual wishing to prove his case, and the pressure on the time and resources of the court system.

The AJA 1999 and Part 52 of the CPR provide a common and harmonised set of rules for civil appeals. Section 54 of the AJA 1999 provides that before an appeal can be heard, permission to appeal must be granted. Section 55 provides that there should generally be only one appeal in any case, rather than cases progressing, almost automatically, through the court hierarchy, as occurred in the past. The 1999 Act also provides for a great deal of flexibility in deploying judges to hear appeals.

The appeal regime in civil cases was subjected to detailed analysis in *Tanfern Ltd v Gregor Cameron-Macdonald* [2000] 2 All ER 801. This case stated that, unlike appeals in criminal cases (see section 6.2 below), where an appeal lies to the next **court** in the hierarchy, appeals in civil cases generally lie to the next **judge** in the hierarchy.

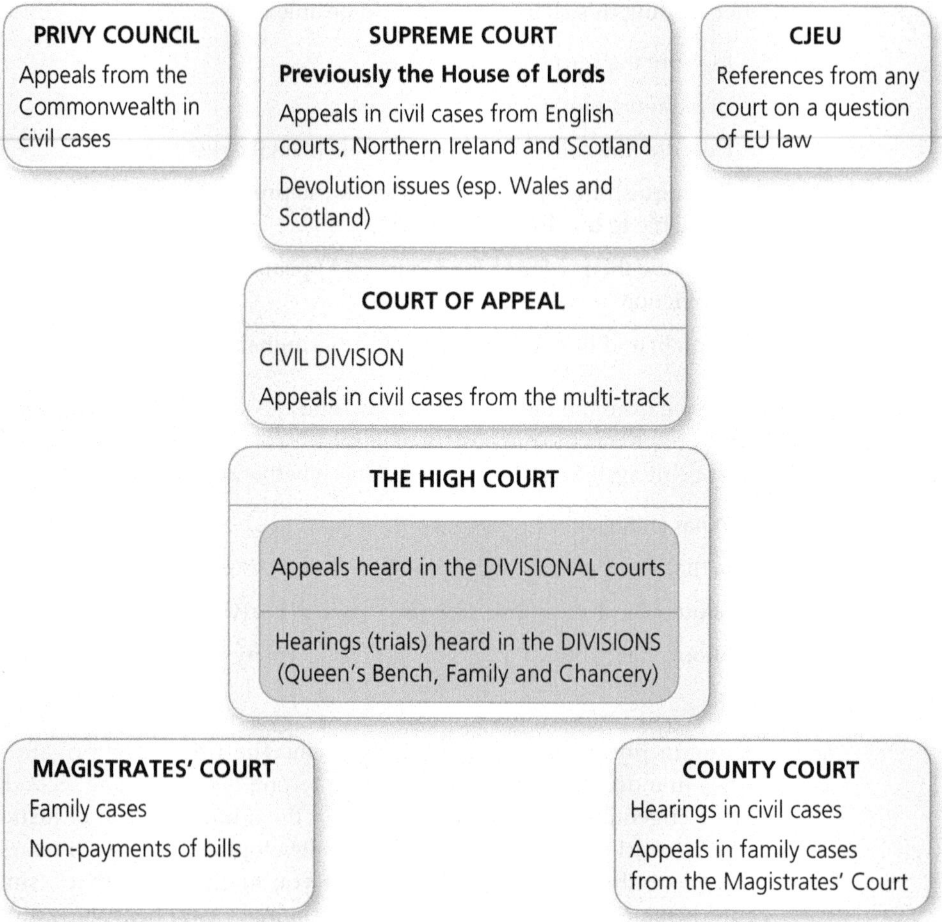

PRIVY COUNCIL
Appeals from the Commonwealth in civil cases

SUPREME COURT
Previously the House of Lords
Appeals in civil cases from English courts, Northern Ireland and Scotland
Devolution issues (esp. Wales and Scotland)

CJEU
References from any court on a question of EU law

COURT OF APPEAL
CIVIL DIVISION
Appeals in civil cases from the multi-track

THE HIGH COURT
Appeals heard in the DIVISIONAL courts
Hearings (trials) heard in the DIVISIONS (Queen's Bench, Family and Chancery)

MAGISTRATES' COURT
Family cases
Non-payments of bills

COUNTY COURT
Hearings in civil cases
Appeals in family cases from the Magistrates' Court

Figure 6.1 Appeals in civil proceedings

Permission to appeal is generally always required, which will be granted only where there is a 'real prospect of success or some other compelling reason'. The appeal court's role is to review the decision of the lower court; it will not conduct a full re-hearing of the case. It will allow an appeal where:

- the decision of the lower court was wrong; or
- it was unjust because of a serious procedural or other irregularity in the proceedings of the lower court.

The appeal court also has all the power of the lower court; it may also affirm, set aside or vary any order or judgment made or given by the lower court, may refer any claim or issue for determination by a lower court, may order a new trial or hearing and may make a costs order.

Appeals from	Heard by	Appeal to
County Court, small claims	District Judge	Circuit Judge
County Court, fast track	District Judge	Circuit Judge
County Court, fast track	Circuit Judge	High Court Judge
County Court, multi-track	District Judge	Circuit Judge
County Court, multi-track	Circuit Judge	High Court Judge
High Court, multi-track	High Court Judge	Court of Appeal

There are also new rules governing subsequent (called 'second-tier') appeals. The relevant point of principle or practice must be an important one and the Court of Appeal must consider that the appeal would raise an important point of principle or practice, or that there is some other compelling reason for it to hear this second appeal. These rules concerning second appeals may also be seen as being harsh, but as Brooke LJ pointed out in *Tanfern v Gregor Cameron-Macdonald* (2000):

JUDGMENT

'All courts are familiar with the litigant, often an unrepresented litigant, who will never take "no" for an answer, however unpromising his/her cause.'

and accordingly:

JUDGMENT

'The decision of the first appeal court is now to be given primacy.'

Self-test questions

1. Under the rule explained above, where will the following appeals be heard?
   - An appeal from a District Judge in a County Court?
   - An appeal from a Circuit Judge in a County Court?
   - An appeal from a High Court Judge in the High Court?
   - An appeal from a District Judge hearing a multi-track case at the County Court?
2. When is permission to appeal required?
3. Under what circumstances will the appeal court allow an appeal?
4. What are the general rules concerning second appeals?

6.1.2 The Court of Appeal (Civil Division)

The Court of Appeal was established by the Judicature Act 1873 and, with the High Court and Crown Court, makes the Senior Courts of England and Wales. You may think it is odd that these courts are called 'senior' when the Supreme Court is superior to them, but this is because the 1873 Act intended for the previous House of Lords' appellate capacity to be abolished and for the Court of Appeal to be the final appeal court. A change of government saw the reintroduction of the House of Lords as the final appeal court by the Judicature Act 1875, however. The House of Lords' appellate jurisdiction was replaced by a new Supreme Court of the UK in October 2009.

The Court of Appeal consists of 39 Lords Justices of Appeal, the Lord Chief Justice, the President of the Family Division of the High Court, the Vice-Chancellor of the Chancery Division of the High Court and the Master of the Rolls. In addition, High Court Judges may be invited to sit at the Court of Appeal. Judges sit in threes, but, for very important cases, they may sit in fives. The Civil Division generally sits in four or five courts each day; so you can see it is a very busy court. In 2016, the Civil Division disposed of more than 5,000 cases, including hearings applying for permission to appeal.

The new appeal rules introduced under the AJA 1999 above in May 2000 did not affect civil appeals to the House of Lords, now the Supreme Court of the UK, which are governed by the Supreme Court rules and Practice Directions.

6.1.3 The Supreme Court of the UK

The Supreme Court hears appeals in civil cases from:

- the High Court (explained further below);
- the Court of Appeal Civil Division (explained further below);
- courts in Northern Ireland and Scotland.

The Supreme Court consists of 12 Justices of the Supreme Court. The Supreme Court replaced the Appellate Committee of the House of Lords in October 2009.

Appeals to the Supreme Court

Appeals from the High Court are heard by the Court of Appeal (Civil Division) unless under ss12–15 of the Administration of Justice Act 1969 (as amended by the Criminal Justice and Courts Act 2015), the case is able to 'leap-frog' the Court of Appeal and go straight to the Supreme Court. The conditions to be satisfied in order for the 'leap-frog' procedure to be used are:

1. The trial judge must be satisfied that a point of law of general public importance is involved and one or more of three conditions are met:

    a. the appeal raises issues of national importance, or

    b. the result of the proceedings is so significant (whether considered on its own or together with other proceedings or likely proceedings) that, in the opinion of the judge, a hearing by the Supreme Court is justified, or

    c. the judge is satisfied that the benefits of earlier consideration by the Supreme Court outweigh the benefits of consideration by the Court of Appeal.

2. The Supreme Court gives **leave to appeal**.

leave to appeal

Permission to appeal

Appeals from decisions of the Court of Appeal lie to the Supreme Court, but in order to limit the workload of the Justices, permission to appeal must be given by one of these courts. There are also certain classes of cases in which any further appeal from the Court of Appeal is prohibited by statute, e.g. an appeal from a County Court in probate proceedings. In all other cases, an appellant may seek permission to appeal from the Court of Appeal and, if this is refused, he is free to apply to the Supreme Court for permission.

Appeals to the Supreme Court in civil matters usually concern questions of law, although appeals on questions of fact are possible. Generally speaking, the Supreme Court will only hear appeals involving matters of general public importance, although this is not a statutory requirement, in contrast to criminal cases. Where a case does involve an issue which is of general public importance, this will increase the likelihood of permission to appeal being granted.

6.1.4 Other appeals in civil cases

The Privy Council

In dealing with appeals from courts outside the UK, the business of this committee is mainly civil. It is also the final appeal court for the Channel Islands and the Isle of Man. It also has jurisdiction to hear appeals from prize courts (i.e. the Queen's Bench Division, which has considered the ownership of a ship or aircraft captured by an enemy), ecclesiastical courts and medical tribunals. The Committee may also have special cases referred to it by the Crown.

The Supreme Court has taken over the Privy Council's domestic jurisdiction within the UK, including the function of being the court of final appeal for determining 'devolution issues' under the UK devolution statutes of 1998 (Northern Ireland, Scotland and Wales).

The CJEU

Under Article 267 of the Treaty of Rome this court may be asked to give rulings concerning EU law. This role will continue until the UK leaves the EU. See Chapter 1.

6.2 Appeals in criminal proceedings

The system of appeals in criminal cases is often the subject of considerable discussion. One reason for this was the emergence in the 1990s (and since) of cases of serious miscarriages of justice, where innocent people had been imprisoned for crimes they did not commit. Partly as a result of the discovery of such cases, the criminal justice system was subject to a Royal Commission which reported in 1993 (the Runciman Commission) and which made a number of recommendations for improvement; those dealing with appeals were made by the Criminal Appeal Act 1995.

Other controversy includes the right of the prosecution to appeal against an acquittal. Generally, if the court (Magistrates' Court or the jury in the Crown Court) has found the defendant not guilty, it is not possible for the prosecution to 'have another go'. However, in October 1999 and as a result of the Macpherson Report concerning the Stephen Lawrence murder and the Law Commission recommendations, this 'rule against double jeopardy' was abolished in the Criminal Justice Act 2003.

6.3 Prosecution appeals

6.3.1 Section 36 Criminal Justice Act 1972

The prosecution can refer a point of law to the Court of Appeal for clarification following an acquittal, but this will not affect the validity of the acquittal in any way. It is not the prosecution who makes the referral, but the Attorney General. The person who was acquitted, the previous 'defendant', has the right to present argument, but is not in any danger by doing so as the acquittal is unaffected even if the Court of Appeal finds that the law was wrongly applied and the defendant should have been convicted.

6.3.2 Section 36 Criminal Justice Act 1988

Following a conviction and sentence (so naturally not an acquittal) in the Crown Court, the Attorney General can use s36 of the Criminal Justice Act 1988 to refer an 'unduly lenient sentence' to the Court of Appeal. If the Court of Appeal agrees, it has the power to increase the sentence.

6.3.3 Sections 54 and 55 Criminal Procedure and Investigations Act 1996

This was the first time power was given to the prosecution to appeal against a jury acquittal, where a person has been convicted of intimidating one of the jurors in an attempt to secure that acquittal. The power requires the prosecution to ask the High Court to certify that, but for the other's interference, there would not have been an acquittal. If it would be contrary to the interests of justice, the court may refuse to grant the prosecution's request. The power has never been exercised.

6.3.4 Appeals against a judge's erroneous decision – Criminal Justice Act 2003

As a result of the Auld Report ('A Review of the Criminal Courts of England and Wales', 2001), the prosecution may appeal against a judicial ruling which effectively terminates the prosecution's case (and therefore the case as a whole collapses) before the jury delivers its verdict. For example, the trial judge may agree with a defence submission at the close of the prosecution case that there is not enough evidence against the defendant and the judge makes a finding of 'no case to answer'. The rationale of this new power under ss57–61 Criminal Justice Act 2003 is to balance the defendant's rights to appeal in similar circumstances. For example, say a trial judge rules that the defence that the defendant is relying on is not automatism, which would lead to a full acquittal if successful, but is instead the defence of insanity. Rather than risk the chance of being detained in a secure mental institute (which sometimes follows the finding of insanity) the defendant changes his plea to guilty. The defendant could then appeal against his conviction (even though he pleaded guilty) on the ground that the trial judge's decision erred in law. A prosecution appeal in parallel circumstances is felt necessary to ensure that justice for the victims is done despite a trial judge's error of law, which is unfortunately not a rare occurrence.

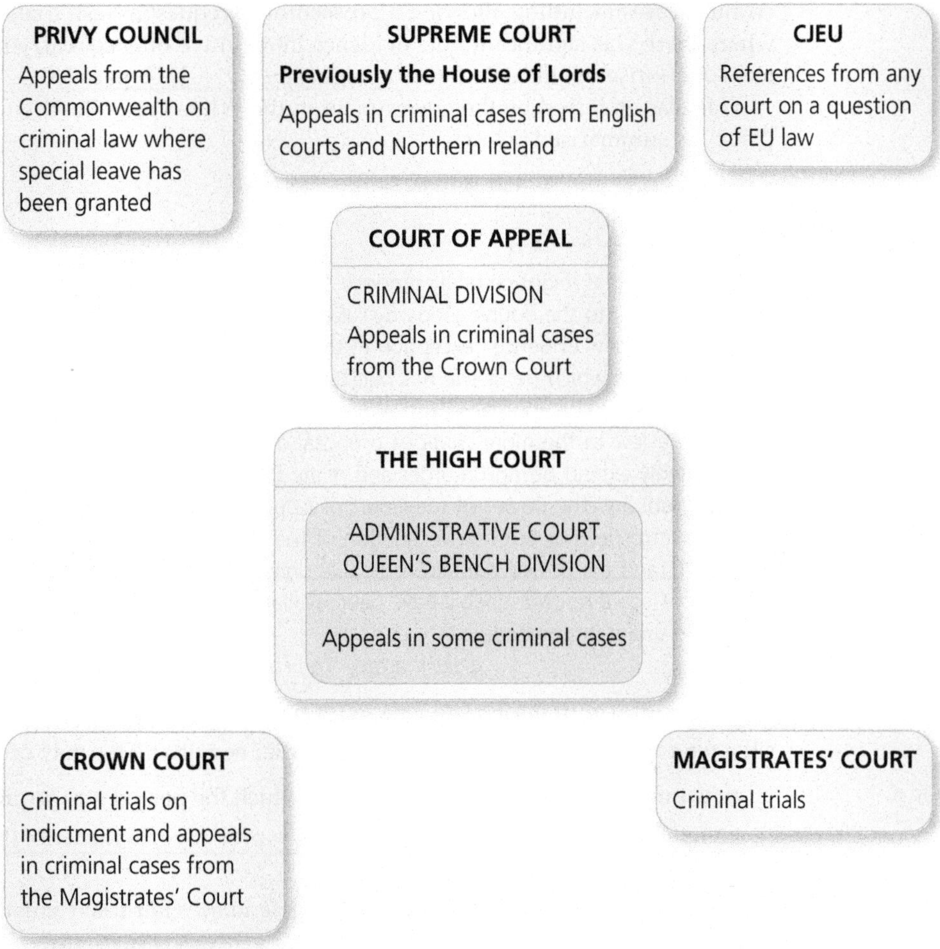

Figure 6.2 Appeals in criminal proceedings

6.3.5 Abolition of the rule against double jeopardy – Criminal Justice Act 2003

autrefois acquit

A plea made by the defendant which states he should not be tried because he has previously been tried and acquitted of the same or a similar crime

double jeopardy

To be put in jeopardy twice for the same offence. It is associated with the plea of *autrefois acquit*

There is a well-established common law doctrine of *autrefois acquit*. This is a special plea, available to a defendant, that he has been previously acquitted of the same or a very similar offence. It is designed to prevent the defendant from being prosecuted for a second time after having been acquitted (so-called 'cherry picking' by the prosecution). It is not an absolute rule and inroads were made on the principle even before the Criminal Justice Act 2003. For example, there could be a re-trial in a Magistrates' Court following a successful prosecution appeal by way of case stated to the Queen's Bench Divisional Court. The Supreme Court also has the power to restore a conviction that (usually) the Court of Appeal has set aside following the defendant's appeal from the Crown Court against his conviction. The plea of *autrefois acquit* is more commonly referred to as the rule against **double jeopardy**.

The Law Commission's Report, 'Double Jeopardy and Prosecution Appeals' (Law Com No 267 (2001), recommendation 1, p 122) proposed a partial abolition of the rule, recommending limiting prosecution appeals against acquittals to murder cases only. The Auld Report (2001) also made a series of recommendations concerning appeals in criminal cases including allowing a prosecutor to request a fresh trial after an acquittal where there was significant new evidence in all grave offences carrying life or a 'long term of imprisonment as Parliament might specify' (Ch 12, para 63).

This was endorsed by the government in the White Paper 'Justice for All', Cm 5563 (2002), as summarised below:

QUOTATION

'one reform that might certainly produce a few more convictions of guilty people is the proposed change to the double jeopardy rules. As expected, the White Paper accepts the argument for a "new evidence" exception to the old rule that a person may not be tried again for an offence of which he or she has been acquitted. In relation to the offences to which the exception would be applicable, the White Paper prefers the approach advocated by Auld and in this Review to the more cautious proposal of the Law Commission; the exception would accordingly extend beyond murder and related offences to include rape, manslaughter and armed robbery. The power of the Court of Appeal to quash an acquittal and order a re-trial will be retrospective, but re-investigation of the offence will require the personal consent of the DPP, and the power will be exercisable only where there is compelling new evidence of guilt that could not reasonably have been available for the first trial. Only one re-trial will be possible under this procedure.'

L Lustgarten, 'The Future of Stop and Search' [2002] Crim LR 601

Sections 75 and 76 of the Criminal Justice Act 2003 enacted these changes, making it possible for a re-trial to take place despite an earlier acquittal. This may occur if there is:

- new (not adduced in the proceedings in which the person was acquitted); *and*
- compelling (reliable, substantial and highly probative) evidence of the acquitted person's guilt; *and*
- it is in the public interest (including the defendant's fair trial rights) (s78).

Examples of new evidence might include DNA or fingerprint tests, new witnesses to the offence coming forward (even if they are not able to give direct evidence, provided their evidence is admissible and highly probative; see *R v A* [2008] EWCA Crim 2908) or even a confession made by the defendant before the double jeopardy rule was abolished (see *Dunlop* [2006] EWCA Crim 1354). Probative means 'of value in proving the case'.

The measures also amend the law to permit the police to reinvestigate a person acquitted of serious offences in these circumstances, to enable the prosecuting authorities to apply to the Court of Appeal (s77) for an acquittal to be quashed, and for a re-trial to take place where the Court of Appeal is satisfied that the new evidence is highly probative of the case against the acquitted person. There are 30 offences which are 'qualifying offences' for the purposes of the abolition of the rule, including: murder, attempted murder, soliciting murder, manslaughter, kidnapping, rape, attempted rape, various sexual offences under the Sexual Offences Act 2003, offences concerning Class A drugs, serious criminal damage and arson offences, war crimes and terrorism offences. There are some safeguards aimed at preventing the possible harassment of acquitted persons in cases where there is not a genuine question of new and compelling evidence, by requiring the personal consent of the DPP both to the taking of significant steps in the reopening of investigations – except in urgent cases – and to the making of an application to the Court of Appeal (s76(3)). The DPP will take into account both the strength of the evidence and the public interest in determining whether a reinvestigation or application to the court is appropriate.

Possibly the most controversial, but least surprising, aspect is the retrospective application of the rules under s75(6). This means that the prosecution may apply for a re-trial after an acquittal even where the acquittal occurred before the Criminal Justice Act 2003 came into force. In 2011, Gary Dobson and David Norris were convicted after jury trial for the murder of Stephen Lawrence in 1993 after Dobson's original acquittal (from 1996) had been quashed by the Court of Appeal.

ACTIVITY

Self-test question

Explain whether, and if so, how, the prosecution can appeal from the Crown Court:

- against an unduly lenient sentence;
- on a point of law following an acquittal;
- to request a re-trial following an acquittal;
- against a jury-tampered acquittal;
- against a trial judge's ruling that terminated the prosecution's case.

6.4 Defence appeals

We now turn to the system of appeals for defendants in criminal cases. What must be borne in mind is that the **mode of appeal is always governed by the place of original trial**. This means that if a case was originally tried in the Magistrates' Court, then the route which an appeal will take will differ from that taken by a case which has been tried before a judge and jury at the Crown Court.

6.4.1 Appeal following summary trial

The route for an appeal against a decision of the magistrates in a criminal case is initially *either* to the Crown Court *or* to the Administrative Court of the Queen's Bench Division of the High Court.

To the Crown Court

The defendant may appeal to the Crown Court concerning a question of fact or law, i.e. he may dispute either the evidence or a decision on a point of law or both. The prosecution does not have a right of appeal from the Magistrates' Court to the Crown Court.

If the defendant pleaded not guilty before the magistrates, then there is a right of appeal against conviction or sentence or both. However, if the defendant originally pleaded guilty, then there is no appeal against conviction, only against sentence.

The appeal will take the form of a complete re-hearing (called a 'trial de novo') with witnesses but without a jury, and the Crown Court may vary the original decision, or confirm it, and has the power to increase the sentence given by the magistrates, but it cannot exceed the Magistrates' Court's sentencing limits.

By way of further appeal, either the prosecution or the defence may require the Crown Court to 'state a case' for the opinion of the High Court.

To the High Court

Both the prosecution and the defence have the right to appeal from the Magistrates' Court to the Administrative Court, but only on the grounds that the magistrates' decision was wrong in law or that they exceeded their jurisdiction by making an order which was outside their powers. This is not a re-hearing of the case with witnesses; instead, the magistrates 'state the case' in writing and the court works from these written documents.

This procedure is known as an appeal 'by way of case stated'. The Administrative Court may confirm or alter the magistrates' decision. If the prosecution succeeds at this stage, the Administrative Court can direct the magistrates to convict and pass sentence on the defendant. Further appeal by either party is possible, from the Administrative Court direct to the Supreme Court. However, before that Court will hear such an appeal, the Administrative Court must certify that a point of law of general public importance is involved, *and* leave to appeal must be obtained from either court, as required by s1 of the Administration of Justice Act 1960 as amended.

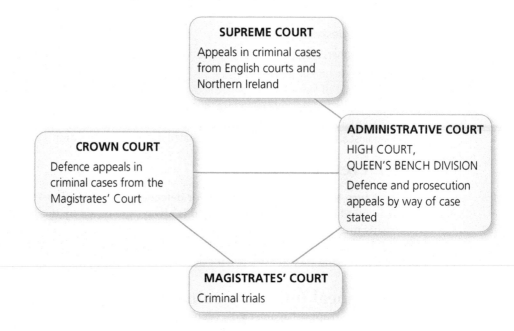

Figure 6.3 Appeals following summary trial

6.4.2 Appeal following trial on indictment
From decisions of the Crown Court, appeal lies to the Court of Appeal (Criminal Division).

Leave to appeal
Under the Criminal Appeal Act 1968 as amended, a defendant who wishes to appeal against conviction and/or sentence must apply for and be granted leave (permission) to appeal to the Court of Appeal. When an appeal against sentence is made to the Court of Appeal (Criminal Division), the court can dismiss the appeal or vary the sentence, although it cannot increase it. (But see above on the court's power to increase sentence on an appeal by the prosecution.)

There are a number of reasons for the leave restriction on the defendant's right to appeal against the outcome of a trial. You will recall that your attention has been drawn to the fact that a balance has to be struck between ensuring that the liberty of the individual is protected and that people are not wrongly convicted of offences, and ensuring that the appeal system is not so overloaded that injustice results from the long waiting period for appeals to be heard.

Probably most of the defendants who are convicted of indictable offences would wish to argue that the jury's finding of fact was wrong and to appeal on this basis. But there is a reluctance on the part of the Court of Appeal to question the facts as found by the jury, and so this avenue of appeal is restricted by the requirement of leave. Similarly, many defendants would probably wish to argue that their sentence should not be so severe, and so the possibility of appeal against sentence is limited, in order to ensure that only meritorious appeals reach the Court of Appeal.

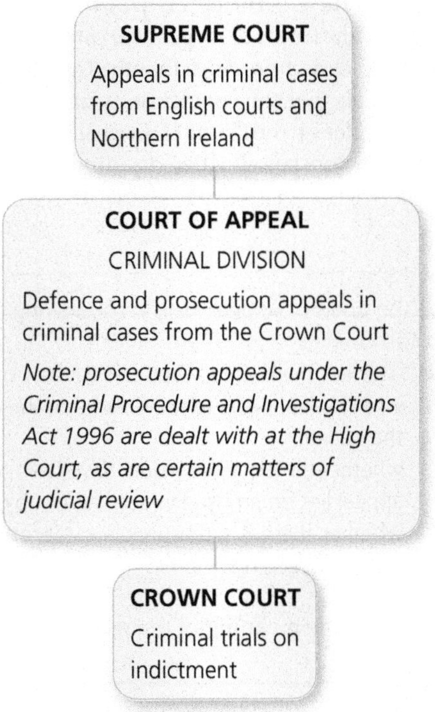

SUPREME COURT

Appeals in criminal cases from English courts and Northern Ireland

COURT OF APPEAL

CRIMINAL DIVISION

Defence and prosecution appeals in criminal cases from the Crown Court

Note: prosecution appeals under the Criminal Procedure and Investigations Act 1996 are dealt with at the High Court, as are certain matters of judicial review

CROWN COURT

Criminal trials on indictment

Figure 6.4 Appeals following trial on indictment

Appeal to the Supreme Court

From the Court of Appeal, further appeal by the defendant to the Supreme Court is possible, but there are statutory requirements that must be met before that Court will hear such appeals. These are contained in the Criminal Appeal Act 1968. Section 33 of that Act (as amended) stipulates that an appeal will only lie to the Supreme Court if the Court of Appeal certifies that the case involves a point of law of general public importance and it appears that the point is one which ought to be considered by the Supreme Court, and either the Court of Appeal or the Supreme Court gives leave for the appeal to proceed.

There is what may seem to be a rather anomalous difference between appeals in these cases, in that in civil cases there is no statutory requirement that the case involves a question of general public importance, whereas this is a prerequisite for criminal cases. In practice, it is likely that only those civil cases which do contain a point of law of general public importance will be heard by the Supreme Court, but the technical difference is still there.

A defence application in *Dunn v R* [2010] EWCA Crim 1823 in respect of s33 (above) failed. The defence argued that the Court of Appeal's decision whether or not to certify a question (that a point of law of general public importance, etc.) breached the European Convention because the Court of Appeal was effectively reviewing its own decision, which could give rise to the appearance of bias; and a refusal to certify a question means there is no possibility of a second appeal. The Court of Appeal held, however, that there was no bias because the Court was not reviewing its own decision, but assessing whether the case involved a question of general public importance; and in any event the Convention did not contain a guarantee of a right to appeal, or any guarantee of a second appeal.

Powers of the Court of Appeal (Criminal Division)

The powers of the Court of Appeal are carefully prescribed by statute. The Criminal Appeal Act 1968 as amended provides that the Court of Appeal shall allow an appeal against conviction if it feels that the conviction is **unsafe**, and in all other cases, the appeal must be dismissed. Under s4, the Court of Appeal has a discretion to hear new evidence and it must consider the factors below when deciding how to exercise its discretion:

SECTION

'4 (2) The Court of Appeal shall, in considering whether to receive any evidence, have regard in particular to

(a) whether the evidence appears to the Court to be capable of belief;

(b) whether it appears to the Court that the evidence may afford any ground for allowing the appeal;

(c) whether the evidence would have been admissible in the proceedings from which the appeal lies on an issue which is the subject of the appeal; and

(d) whether there is a reasonable explanation for the failure to adduce the evidence in those proceedings.'

Let us consider the meaning of the word unsafe mentioned above. We start with a think point:

Which is worse, in your opinion (*read this carefully – it is not the usual question of wrongly acquitting a guilty person or wrongly convicting an innocent person*):

1. for a guilty person to be released because the evidence against him was obtained improperly; or

2. for a guilty person's conviction to be upheld despite the fact that the prosecution evidence against him was improperly obtained?

What sometimes worries students doing exercises like this is the lack of clear answers forthcoming from the tutor. There is no definitive answer to the questions posed above. Different people (academics, practitioners, lawyers, lay people and so on) have different perspectives on both the question and the answer.

However, does the Court of Appeal have to choose option (1), (2) or neither? The answer lies in the decision of the Court of Appeal in *R v Mullen* [1999] 2 Cr App R 143.

CASE EXAMPLE

R v Mullen [1999] 2 Cr App R 143

In late December 1988, the police lawfully searched the defendant's flat, finding explosives, power units for detonating various types of bomb, a number of ready-made car bombs, blasting incendiary devices, mortar bomb equipment, firearms and ammunition. The prosecution alleged that the defendant was responsible for renting the flat for the use of the IRA (Irish Republican Army, an illegal organisation in the UK).

The defendant later said he had been unaware of any IRA involvement until mid-December 1988 when he tried to withdraw from the scheme but he was threatened to continue with it. A few days later, the defendant flew to Zimbabwe where he had already obtained a residence permit by falsely claiming he had not been convicted of any crime in any country and falsely giving his occupation as journalist. The London police immediately contacted the Zimbabwe Central Intelligence Organisation (CIO) to see if the defendant could secretly be deported from Harare to London. The London police and Zimbabwean authorities agreed that the aim of their plan was 'foolproof return of Mullen to London' even though it was not certain at that time that the 'evidence was sufficient'. The defendant was brought back to the UK from Zimbabwe in early 1989 by a Zimbabwean immigration officer. At Gatwick Airport, English police boarded the plane, arrested the defendant and took him for interview. On deportation, he had been denied access to a lawyer, contrary to Zimbabwean law and internationally recognised human rights laws.

In June 1990, the defendant was convicted of conspiracy to cause explosions likely to endanger life or cause serious injury to property and was sentenced to 30 years' imprisonment. He appealed on the ground that the circumstances of his deportation from Zimbabwe to England prior to his trial rendered his conviction unsafe. No challenge was made about the conduct of the trial itself and he accepted that if it had been fair to try him, he had been properly convicted.

The Court of Appeal allowed his appeal, holding that:

1. abuse of pre-trial process can cause a conviction to be unsafe;
2. a safe conviction is a lawful conviction;
3. 'unsafe' bears a broad meaning.

Therefore the answer to the question above is (2). The Court of Appeal decided that it would be wrong to uphold Mullen's appeal even though he had not directly appealed on the basis of his innocence. It appears from the judgment that it is worse to uphold the conviction if the evidence was obtained unfairly, and therefore it is better to allow the appeal of a guilty person where the evidence obtained against him was obtained unfairly. Do you agree?

Since the enactment of the HRA 1998, the relationship between the meaning of 'unsafe' and the meaning of 'unfair' under Article 6(1) ECHR has not been clarified. Would proceedings that fall foul of Article 6 automatically render a conviction unsafe? In *R v Togher* [2001] 3 All ER 463; [2001] 1 Cr App R 33, the Court of Appeal stated that if a defendant had been denied a fair trial, it was almost inevitable that his conviction would be regarded as unsafe. This was the first consideration of this question after the ECHR became part of domestic law under the HRA 1998.

ACTIVITY

Self-test questions

1. What is the single ground for allowing an appeal against conviction in the Court of Appeal?
2. What does the term 'leave to appeal' mean?
3. Explain when a defendant requires leave to appeal to the Court of Appeal.
4. Under what circumstances will the Supreme Court hear an appeal from the Court of Appeal in a criminal case?

6.5 The Supreme Court

The Supreme Court hears appeals in criminal cases from

- the High Court;
- the Court of Appeal Criminal Division (explained above);
- Northern Ireland.

Appeals from the Administrative Court go direct to the Supreme Court

Before the Supreme Court will hear such an appeal, the Administrative Court must certify that a point of law of general public importance is involved, and leave to appeal must be obtained from either court, as required by s1 of the Administration of Justice Act 1960 as amended.

From the Court of Appeal to the Supreme Court

Section 33 of the Criminal Appeal Act 1968 as amended stipulates that an appeal will lie to the Supreme Court only if the Court of Appeal certifies that the case involves a point of law of general public importance and it appears that the point is one which ought to be considered by the Supreme Court and either the Court of Appeal or Supreme Court gives leave for the appeal to proceed.

6.6 Other courts

The Privy Council

The JCPC must grant special leave for an appeal to be heard in criminal cases. This special leave will not be given unless there are exceptional circumstances, a substantial injustice has occurred and the accused has been denied a fair trial.

The CJEU

In the same way that this court may be asked to give rulings concerning civil law, so references may be made to it for the interpretation of EU law where this involves criminal law.

ACTIVITY

Critiquing the law

In the 1760s, the famed English jurist William Blackstone formulated a principle in his *Commentaries on the Laws of England*. Blackstone declared:

Quotation

'better that ten guilty persons escape than that one innocent suffer'.

Blackstone's formulation expresses an assumption in favour of a system that would let the guilty walk free over a system that would convict innocent people. Thus the system needs to be weighted in favour of the suspect, as it is better to let a suspect walk free if there is uncertainty as to whether they committed the crime, than to risk convicting an innocent person.

Wrongful convictions give the impression that the system is weighted too much in favour of the state and aims to convict an individual for a crime, without taking the time to ensure that the individual is actually guilty. However, it must be understood that a miscarriage of justice can also involve not convicting a guilty defendant. Both types of miscarriages of justice affect the wider public. If innocent people are jailed this undermines our faith in the legal system and its ability to find the truth. If manifestly guilty defendants are not convicted our faith in the legal system is as undermined, as we do not see the law giving the victims and their families the justice they deserve.

'Justice' here refers to the ideal that the innocent will not be convicted of crimes that they have not committed, and those guilty of crimes will be convicted. However, as we have seen, that ideal is not always met. This is why the trial systems include safeguards to protect the innocent and punish the guilty. One of these safeguards is the law of appeals.

With this in mind, re-read the details of criminal appeals in this chapter. Consider the following thinking points:

1. Do you think that the system of criminal appeals is weighted too much in favour of the defence?
2. Do you think the fact that the defence has more possibilities for an appeal than the prosecution is fair?
3. If you had an opportunity to reform the system of criminal appeals, what change would you make?

6.7 The Criminal Cases Review Commission

Appeals have strict time limits. You may have seen how long it took for the defendant in *Mullen* (1999) above to have his conviction quashed. This is because his application to appeal was too late and he had to apply to appeal out of time. In such cases, unless leave to appeal out of time is granted, wrongly convicted offenders may serve years in prison on an unsafe conviction. This is a miscarriage of justice. How can the Court of Appeal get to reconsider miscarriages of justice where the appeal is time-barred? Or what if the defendant has already appealed and his appeal was dismissed, but doubts remain about the safety of the conviction? And what if the medical or forensic evidence used to convict the defendant has subsequently been discredited?

Under the old law (s17 of the Criminal Appeal Act 1968), only the Home Secretary was empowered to request the Court of Appeal to review such a miscarriage of justice. He was able to refer any case tried on indictment to the Court of Appeal 'if he thinks fit'. In 1993, the Royal Commission on Criminal Justice, the Runciman Commission, recommended:

QUOTATION

'the responsibility for reopening cases [should be] removed from the Home Secretary and transferred to a body independent of the Government'.

The Home Secretary had rarely exercised his power. At Ch 11, para 5, the Runciman Commission stated:

QUOTATION

'The available figures for the number of cases referred by the Home Secretary to the Court of Appeal under section 17 of the Criminal Appeal Act 1968 show that the power is not often exercised. From 1981 to the end of 1988, 36 cases were referred to the Court of Appeal as a result of the doubts raised about the safety of the convictions concerned. This represents an average of between 4 and 5 cases a year. In the years 1989–92, 28 cases have been referred, including a number of cases stemming from the terrorist incidents of the early 1970s and inquiries into the activities of the West Midlands serious crimes squad. We were told by the Home Office that it receives between 700 and 800 cases a year which are no longer before the courts and where it is claimed that there has been a wrongful conviction. (The figure for 1992 was 790 of which 634 involved a custodial sentence.) Plainly, therefore, a rigorous sifting process is applied, and only a small percentage of cases end in a reference to the Court of Appeal under section 17:

Year	No of cases referred	No of appellants	Results
1989	3	6	6 convictions quashed
1990	7	20	19 convictions quashed
			1 re-trial*
1991	10	12	10 convictions quashed
			1 re-trial*
			1 appeal pending
1992	8	11	10 appellants pending
			1 appeal dismissed

[* – Both the re-trials resulted in the defendant's acquittal.]'

Section 17 of the Criminal Appeal Act 1968 was repealed and under ss8–12 of the Criminal Appeal Act 1995 the s17 procedure was replaced with a new statutory body, independent of the government, called the Criminal Cases Review Commission (CCRC). The Commission is not a court and does not decide the appeal. It refers cases to the appropriate court: cases originally heard at the Crown Court are referred to the Court of Appeal; cases originally heard at the Magistrates' Court are referred to the Crown Court, so the new system includes referring doubtful summary convictions.

The role of the CCRC

The role of the CCRC is, *inter alia*:

- to review and investigate cases of suspected wrongful convictions and/or sentence in England and Wales; and
- to refer cases to the appropriate court whenever it feels that there is a real possibility that the conviction, verdict, finding or sentence will not be upheld.

To establish that there is a real possibility of an appeal succeeding regarding a conviction, there has to be an argument or evidence which has not been raised during the trial, or exceptional circumstances. To establish that there is a real possibility of an appeal succeeding against sentence, there has to be a legal argument or information about the individual or the offence which was not raised in court during the trial or at appeal.

References by the CCRC take effect as if they were appeals by the convicted person and, once the reference has been made, the CCRC has no further involvement. The CCRC may investigate cases of its own accord, or individuals may ask the Commission to investigate but, in either event, normal rights of appeal must ordinarily have been exhausted before the Commission can intervene (although failure to do this is not an absolute bar). The first case referred to the Court of Appeal by the Commission was *R v Matten*, *The Times*, 5 March 1998, where the conviction of a Somali seaman was overturned, over 20 years after the Home Secretary had failed to see any reason to reopen the case under s17. In *Matten*, Rose LJ specifically recognised the role of the CCRC as:

JUDGMENT

'a necessary and welcome body without which the injustice in this case might never have been identified'.

On 30 July 1998, the Court of Appeal famously allowed the appeal and quashed the conviction of Derek Bentley who was hanged on 28 January 1953. Bentley had been convicted in 1952 as an accessory to the murder of a policeman by his friend. After an unsuccessful appeal, Bentley was hanged while the murderer was sentenced to detention at Her Majesty's pleasure because he was only 16. The trial judge had summed up in a pro-prosecution manner, failing to point out the standard (beyond reasonable doubt) and burden (on the prosecution) of proof; he even kept secret from the jury that Bentley had a mental age of 11. The representations made to the Home Secretary to exercise his power under s17 of the 1968 Act had failed to stir him into action; but the CCRC felt differently and the Court of Appeal, in quashing Bentley's conviction, agreed:

JUDGMENT

'the summing-up in the present case had been such as to deny the appellant that fair trial which was the birthright of every British citizen'.

[1999] Crim LR 330

Despite the heavy workload of the CCRC and the criticism that it prioritises cases rather badly (for example, Derek Bentley had been hanged 46 years before the appeal; while other cases where the defendants were still in prison were in the backlog) the value of the CCRC in referring miscarriages of justice cannot be doubted:

QUOTATION

'In the six years from when it started work to March 31, 2003, the Commission received a total of 5,762 applications for review. 5,115 reviews have been completed, 365 cases were under review and 282 were in the pending trays. The vast majority of applications were deemed ineligible for a referral to a court of appeal. The number of cases referred was 196, of which 133 had been determined. The outcomes of the referrals are interesting. 77 convictions were quashed (i.e. 64 per cent of the total of convictions) and 44 (36 per cent of the total) upheld. Ten sentences were varied and two upheld.'

[2003] Crim LR 663

Over an eight-year period, the Home Secretary had referred a total of 36 cases. In its first ten years, the CCRC referred 528, 341 of which resulted in convictions being quashed. Although the CCRC is not limited to referring cases which have been tried on indictment, the difference in the approach to the review of miscarriages of justice in the ELS is revealing.

That said, the CCRC is not without its critics. It is funded by the government and its case workers are government appointees, giving an appearance of bias. It also has no independent investigatory powers.

ACTIVITY

Self-test questions

1. The CCRC is an appeal court.   True/False
2. The CCRC replaced s17 of the Criminal Appeal Act 1968.   True/False
3. The Home Secretary made over 150 referrals of suspected miscarriages of justice to an appeal court between 1990 and 1992.   True/False
4. The CCRC has made over 350 referrals of suspected miscarriages of justice to an appeal court since it was established.   True/False

ACTIVITY

Critiquing the law

The CCRC has been hailed by many as a success. But what does it tell you about the criminal justice system, and the system for appeals in English law, that the CCRC is needed today? Is not the very existence of the CCRC an admission that criminal trials lead to innocent people being convicted, and that these people are then not helped by the appeals process? How much confidence does this give you in the justice system?

KEY FACTS

Appeals in criminal cases

Prosecution appeals	Following summary trial	1. By way of case stated to the Administrative Court
	Following trial on indictment	1. Attorney General's reference on a point of law 2. Attorney General's reference against an unduly lenient sentence 3. Against a jury-tampered acquittal for which a person has been convicted 4. Against an erroneous decision by the trial judge which effectively terminates the prosecution 5. For a re-trial following an acquittal (the abolition of the double jeopardy rule)
Defence appeals	Following summary trial	1. Against conviction and/or sentence to the Crown Court 2. By way of case stated to the Administrative Court
	Following trial on indictment	1. Against conviction, to the Court of Appeal 2. Against sentence, to the Court of Appeal
Appellate courts	Crown Court	Appeal by the defendant from the Magistrates' Court
	High Court	Appeals by the defendant or prosecution to the Administrative Court by way of case stated
	Court of Appeal	Appeals by the defendant or prosecution following trials on indictment
	Supreme Court	Appeals by the defendant or prosecution either from the Administrative Court or the Court of Appeal

CCRC	Not an appeal court	Refers cases tried summarily or on indictment to an appeal court where it feels there is a real possibility that the conviction, verdict, finding or sentence will not be upheld

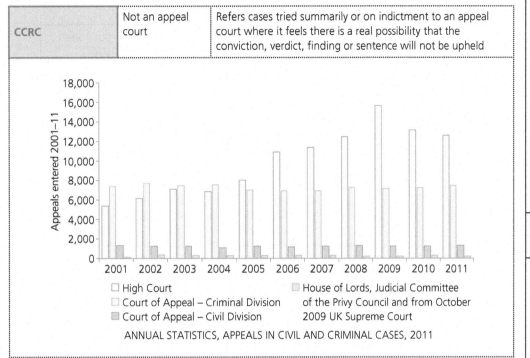

ANNUAL STATISTICS, APPEALS IN CIVIL AND CRIMINAL CASES, 2011

SAMPLE ESSAY QUESTION

Critically comment on the differences between the appeal rights of the prosecution and defence in criminal matters.

Although the essay does involve giving a detailed explanation of the appeal rights of each party, from summary trial as well as trial on indictment, you are asked to comment critically, so you do need to consider the comparability of the rights of the prosecution and the defence, and consider what restrictions, if any, exist.

Start at the Magistrates' Court. Only the defendant can appeal to the Crown Court, against conviction and/or sentence, and there is no leave requirement. The prosecution cannot appeal against an acquittal. Either the prosecution or the defence may appeal to the High Court by way of case stated, the grounds of which are limited. Appeal from the High Court to the Supreme Court is possible, but leave is required and there must be a point of law of general public importance.

At first glance, the defendant has more powers of appeal following trial on indictment than the prosecution.

Explain the defendant's appeal route to the Court of Appeal against conviction and/or sentence; but point out that leave is always required.

Explain what appeals the prosecution might bring and whether those appeals can affect D's acquittal (e.g. to refer a point of law for clarification, no; against an unduly lenient sentence, obviously not; against a jury tampered acquittal, possibly; to quash an acquittal to bring a retrial, yes). Add comment on the abolition of the double jeopardy rule.

CONCLUDE

Figure 6.5 Essay map on appeals

SUMMARY

- Either party may bring an appeal in a civil or a criminal case, but appeals are generally not available as of right; the appeal must usually be on a point of law rather than fact and permission (leave) granted.

- Appeals 'go up' the hierarchy, either from judge to judge in seniority or from court to court. There are Acts of Parliament, rules of court (including but not restricted to the CPRs and CrimPRs, see Chapters 4 and 5) and Practice Directions which provide for the exact procedures governing:

  - appeal requirements;
  - the subject matter of appeals; and
  - the power(s) of the appeal court.

- Appeals in civil matters usually proceed from judge to judge and then may go from the High Court (Divisional Courts) or Court of Appeal to the Supreme Court.

- Appeals in criminal matters go from:

  - the Supreme Court;
  - the Crown Court to the Court of Appeal and then may go to the Supreme Court.

- The prosecution is, on the whole, unable to appeal against an acquittal, but a defendant may, in certain circumstances, appeal against conviction and/or sentence. Under the Criminal Justice Act 2003, however, the Court of Appeal can quash an acquittal and an acquitted person may be retried for a criminal offence, abolishing the plea of *autrefois acquit*.

- On a defence appeal, the Court of Appeal may reduce sentence and must allow an appeal against conviction if that conviction is unsafe.

Further reading

Book

Elks, L, *Righting Miscarriages of Justice? Ten Years of the Criminal Cases Review Commission* (Justice, 2008).

Articles

Dennis, I, 'Prosecution appeals and retrial for serious offences' [2004] *Crim LR* 619.

Dennis, I, 'Convicting the guilty: outcomes, process and the Court of Appeal' [2006] *Crim LR* 955.

Hamer, D, 'The expectation of incorrect acquittals and the "new and compelling evidence" exception to double jeopardy' [2009] *Crim LR* 63.

O'Doherty, S, 'New trials for old crimes' [2009] 173(30) *CL and J* 469.

Ormerod, D, Waterman, A and Fortson, R, 'Prosecution appeals: too much of a good thing?' [2010] *Crim LR* 169.

Spencer, JR, 'Quashing convictions for procedural irregularities' [2007] *Crim LR* 835.

Taylor, N and Ormerod, D, 'Mind the gaps: safety, fairness and moral legitimacy' [2004] *Crim LR* 266.

Internet links

Amalgamated websites for legal system and procedural matters including the courts at: www.justice.gov.uk

Criminal Cases Review Commission at: www.justice.gov.uk/about/criminal-cases-review-commission

For an up-to-date list of the judiciary at: www.judiciary.gov.uk

Key statistics on courts and appeals at: www.gov.uk/government/collections/judicial-and-court-statistics

Practice Directions of the Supreme Court at: www.supremecourt.uk/procedures/practice-directions.html

Rules of the Supreme Court at: www.supremecourt.uk/procedures/rules-of-the-court.html

Supreme Court at: www.supremecourt.uk

7

Funding

After reading this chapter you should be able to:

▪ Understand the need for publicly funded help with legal costs

▪ Identify the key component of the government's current legal aid scheme

▪ Discuss the problems of publicly funded legal aid

▪ Understand the role and working of conditional fee agreements

7.1 Access to justice

When faced with a legal problem, the average person will usually need expert help from a lawyer or someone with expertise in the particular type of legal difficulty. Most often the need is just for advice, but some people may need help in starting court proceedings and/or presenting their case in court. For the ordinary person who needs to seek legal assistance there are three main difficulties. These are:

▪ lack of knowledge;

▪ fear of lawyers; and

▪ cost.

The lack of knowledge is not only of the law and legal system, but also of where the nearest solicitor is located and which solicitor specialises in the law involved in the particular problem. The second problem is that many people have a fear of dealing with lawyers. Clients may feel intimidated through fear of the unknown. The final difficulty of cost arises because solicitors charge from about £100 an hour for routine advice from a legal executive in a small local firm to over £600 an hour for work done by a top city firm of solicitors in a specialist field. If the matter can be resolved with just one hour's advice, then the cost is not too great for most people. However, many matters are complicated and will take several hours of work. The cost can quickly run into several thousand pounds.

Where a person cannot get the help they need, it is said that they are being denied access to justice. Access to justice involves both an open system of justice and also being able to fund the costs of a case. There have been various schemes aimed at making the law more accessible to everyone. For example, the national network of Citizens' Advice Bureaux was started in 1938 and now operates in most towns. More recently, the Law Society relaxed rules so that solicitors are allowed to advertise and inform the public of the areas of law in which they specialise. And in the last few years the government has provided an online information service. This gives information on the solicitors available in different areas of the country.

However, the problem of cost still remains a major hurdle. Justice Darling once said:

JUDGMENT

'The law courts of England are open to all men like the doors of the Ritz hotel.'

In other words, the courts are there for anyone to use, but cost may prevent many people from seeking justice. The cost of a civil case in the High Court may run into hundreds of thousands of pounds. Even in the cheaper County Court, the costs are likely to be more than the amount of money recovered in damages. There is the additional risk in all civil cases that the loser may have to pay the winner's costs. Cost is also vital in criminal cases where a person's liberty may be at risk. It is, therefore, essential that they should be able to defend themselves properly.

The need for access to justice was recognised in the early twentieth century but it was not until the middle of that century that a publicly funded system was first set up in England.

7.2 Public funding

7.2.1 History

Until 1949 there was very little help available for those who could not afford to pay for their own lawyer. It was truly a situation of one law for the poor and one for the rich. In criminal cases defendants were able to get representation in court under the Poor Prisoners' Defence Acts of 1903 and 1930, but even this was far from satisfactory. It only gave access to lawyers in limited cases. During the second half of the twentieth century a government-funded scheme of legal aid and advice was developed. Originally the aim was to provide a scheme which allowed the poor and those of 'modest means' access to justice so that the poorer members of society could obtain advice and be represented in the courts.

The government-funded legal aid and advice system began after the report by the Rushcliffe Committee in 1945. This was the era of the development of the Welfare State and access to legal services was viewed as being as important as access to medical services and education. The Rushcliffe Committee set out a number of general principles on the public funding of legal expenses. The main principles were:

1. Legal aid should be available in all courts and in such a manner that would enable persons to have access to the professional help that they required.

2. The provision of legal aid should not be limited to people 'normally classed as poor' but should also include those of moderate means.

3. The scheme should be means tested so that those who could not afford to pay anything would receive aid free of charge and there should be an increasing scale of contributions for those who could afford to pay something towards costs, but could not afford to finance a case completely on their own.

4. The cost of the scheme should be borne by the state, but it should not be administered by the state; the legal profession should be responsible for the administration.

5. There should be a merits test to be judged by legal practitioners, not by a government agency.

6. Lawyers acting for legally aided clients should receive 'adequate' pay.

The government accepted the proposals in principle and enacted the Legal Aid and Advice Act 1949. Under this Act the Law Society (the governing body of solicitors) was given responsibility to 'make arrangements … with the approval of the Lord Chancellor … for securing that legal aid and legal advice are available'.

The initial scheme covered only civil cases. It was not until 1964 that the scheme was extended to criminal cases. Other parts of the scheme were gradually set up. For example, advice of up to two hours, free of charge to the poorest or at reduced rates to those of modest means, became available under the Green Form scheme set up by the Legal Advice and Assistance Act 1972. Also, following the Police and Criminal Evidence Act 1984, duty solicitor schemes in police stations and Magistrates' Courts were established. The entire system was consolidated in the Legal Aid Act 1988 when the handling of civil legal aid was taken from the Law Society and given to the specially created Legal Aid Board. Applications for criminal legal aid were dealt with by the criminal courts, usually by the clerk in the Magistrates' Court.

Eligibility

When the scheme started in 1949 it was estimated that about 80 per cent of the population was eligible to receive help with civil cases. This was in line with the principle of the Rushcliffe Committee that the scheme should be available not only to the poor but also to those of moderate means. However, because the financial limits for qualifying did not keep pace with inflation, the number qualifying gradually went down to about 48 per cent by 1978. In 1979 the limits were increased considerably so that once more nearly 80 per cent of the population qualified. This did not last long. The amount being spent on legal aid increased so rapidly that the government made severe cuts to the financial limits in order to save money. This meant that in the 1990s only about 48 per cent of the population were eligible to receive help, and many of these had to pay large contributions towards their funding. Following the reforms of the AJA 1999, the number of people eligible for legal aid continued to fall. Only the poorer members of society were eligible. Under the current system brought in by the Legal Aid, Sentencing and Punishment of Offenders Act 2012 (LASPO 2012) the number of those eligible for legal aid is still falling.

7.2.2 The Access to Justice Act 1999

Under the AJA 1999, there was a major reform of the legal aid system. The Act established a Legal Services Commission which had overall control over public funding of both civil and criminal cases and established two services. These were:

- the Community Legal Service for civil matters; and
- the Criminal Defence Service for criminal matters.

A system of granting contracts to service providers was set up. However, in March 2010, the House of Commons Committee of Public Accounts criticised the Legal Services Commission for its financial management. As a result in 2012 the government decided to abolish the Legal Services Commission and bring legal aid under the control of the Ministry of Justice. This was done by passing the LASPO 2012.

7.3 The Legal Aid, Sentencing and Punishment of Offenders Act 2012

The LASPO 2012 abolished the Legal Services Commission. The administration of legal aid since April 2013 has been operated by the Legal Aid Agency which comes under the umbrella of the Ministry of Justice. An independent civil servant is the Director of Legal Aid Casework and the decisions on granting legal aid are made by them and their team.

The Legal Aid Agency has various different types of services available in civil cases. These include:

- Legal Help whereby advice can be given;
- Help at Court where someone can speak for you in court but does not officially represent you;
- Family Mediation – both help (advice) and representation in mediation proceedings;
- Legal Representation which gives full legal services for the case including representation in court or tribunal.

7.3.1 Service providers

The system works by the government making contracts with providers of legal services so that the providers can do legal work and be paid from government funds. Providers include law firms and not-for-profit organisations, such as the Citizens Advice Bureau (CAB) offering advice on legal matters.

7.3.2 Criteria for civil legal aid services

The Act gives the Lord Chancellor the power to set criteria for making civil legal aid services available. It also sets out the factors the Lord Chancellor must consider when setting the criteria. These factors are set out in s10(3) of the Act. They include:

- the likely cost of providing the services and the benefit which may be obtained by them;
- the availability of resources to provide the services;
- the importance for the individual of the matters in relation to which the services would be provided;
- the availability of other services, such as mediation;
- where the services are sought by an individual in relation to a dispute, the individual's prospect of success in the dispute;
- the public interest.

Chris Grayling, the then Lord Chancellor, exercised his power to set out criteria for making legal aid services available to individuals through issuing guidance in 2013. These criteria have proven to be extremely controversial, as they aimed to restrict the circumstances in which legal aid was to be granted. The Lord Chancellor set a very high threshold to reach in order for legal aid to be granted:

QUOTATION

'The overarching question to consider is whether the withholding of legal aid would make the assertion of the claim practically impossible or lead to an obvious unfairness in proceedings. This is a very high threshold.'

Lord Chancellor's Exceptional Funding Guidance (Non-Inquests), 2013, para 19

The legality of this guidance was challenged in the courts. In the case of *R (Gudanavicene and others) v The Director of Legal Aid Casework; The Lord Chancellor* [2014] EWCA Civ 1622, the Court of Appeal ruled that the Exceptional Case Funding Guidelines were unlawful as it set the bar for the provision for legal aid too high. The Court of Appeal held that s10(3) of the LASPO required legal aid to be granted where failure to provide such legal aid would constitute a breach of EU law or the ECHR.

As a result of this judgment, the guidance was revised, but has been subject to further challenges. In 2016, the Court of Appeal in *The Director of Legal Aid Casework; The Lord Chancellor v IS* [2016] EWCA Civ 464 ruled that the revised guidance was lawful, overturning a High Court decision which had held that the guidance was 'inherently unlawful' and therefore void. It is certain that further appeals and cases will be brought challenging the guidance under s10(3).

7.3.3 Availability of legal aid

Originally legal aid was available for most types of civil case. Just a few categories of case were excluded, in particular small claims, defamation and most tribunal cases. The AJA 1999 continued to provide legal services for most types of civil case, although it did exclude personal injuries cases, except for those caused by clinical negligence.

Under the system set up by the LASPO 2012, the starting point is that legal aid is not available for civil cases unless it is a category specifically mentioned in the Act or other regulations. This has also proven controversial. Schedule 1 of the Act sets out the categories for which legal services will be provided under the Legal Aid Agency. These categories include:

- cases involving children's rights, e.g. care, supervision and protection of children;
- mental health and mental capacity issues;
- community care and facilities for the disabled;
- domestic violence and certain other family matters;
- *habeas corpus*;
- immigration rights;
- loss of home and homelessness;
- equality issues;
- inquests.

Clinical negligence cases are restricted to those where a child has been severely disabled while in the womb or during birth.

Section 9(2) of the LASPO gave the Lord Chancellor power to add to, or 'vary or omit' the categories listed in Schedule 1. The Lord Chancellor attempted to amend Schedule 1 in order to introduce a 'residency test'. This would have meant that only those who are lawfully resident in the UK at the time of the application and have been resident in the UK for at least 12 months would be able to claim civil legal aid. The Supreme Court unanimously ruled that the Lord Chancellor's actions were unlawful in *R (The Public Law Project) v Lord Chancellor* [2016] UKSC 39. This was because the Lord Chancellor was given the power to add or remove categories from the list in Sch 1; he was not given power to determine who could access legal aid for those categories.

Excluded matters

Part 2 of Sch 1 of the LASPO 2012 sets out categories which are excluded from legal aid services. These include:

- personal injury and death;
- any claim in negligence;
- trespass to the person, goods or land;
- defamation;
- trust law issues;
- conveyancing;
- making of wills.

These last four categories have always been excluded, and negligence claims causing personal injury were excluded under the AJA 1999. However, the current system excludes a much wider range of categories.

7.4 Government funding in civil cases

The funding for legal aid comes from the government's budget. This means that a specific amount is made available each year. Also the amount set has to be considered against all the other claims on the budget, such as hospitals and health care and education. As a result the government cannot afford to make legal aid available to everyone. In order to qualify there is a strict means test.

7.4.1 Means testing

A person applying for government-funded advice or representation must show that he does not have enough money to pay for his own lawyer. In order to decide if the applicant is poor enough to qualify for government-funded help, his income and capital are considered.

People receiving certain benefits such as Income Support or Income-Based Job Seekers' Allowance or Universal Credit are passported into the legal scheme. This means they automatically qualify, assuming their disposable capital is below the set level. For all other applicants their gross income is considered first. If a person's gross income is above a set amount per month then they do not qualify.

Disposable income

If the person's gross income is below the set amount per month, then their disposable income has to be calculated by starting with their gross income and taking away:

- tax and National Insurance;
- housing costs;
- childcare costs or maintenance paid for children;
- an allowance for themselves and for each dependant.

If the amount left after making all deductions is below a set level the applicant qualifies for legal aid. If the amount left is above the set level the person will not qualify for legal aid.

For Legal Help, Help at Court, Family Mediation and Legal Representation in Immigration cases the income limits in 2016 were £2,657 gross income and £733 disposable income. For these services the applicant does not have to pay any contribution towards their funding. However, no one who is above the limits can use any of these services.

For Legal Representation those above the minimum set limits are eligible provided they are not above a set maximum income. Those with incomes between the minimum and maximum levels will have to pay a contribution towards the costs of the case. This idea is shown in diagram form in Figure 7.1.

Note that the figures for the limits on income are increased slightly most years. You will be able to find the current figures on the website www.gov.uk/legal-aid.

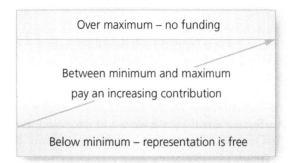

Figure 7.1 Minimum and maximum limits for legal aid

Disposable capital
Disposable capital is the assets of the person, such as money in a bank or savings account, stocks and shares or expensive jewellery. In order to qualify for funding there is a maximum limit for disposable capital of £8,000 (£3,000 in immigration cases). If the assets are over £8,000 they must use their own money to fund any legal case, although once they have spent the money in excess of £8,000 they can become eligible for funding.

Where a person owns a home the value of that home is taken into account in deciding the disposable capital. This is so even though the person may have a large mortgage. Only the first £100,000 of any mortgage is deducted from the value of the home. This rule means that people are regarded as having too much disposable capital because of the value of the house, but in reality they have no spare money.

7.4.2 Problems with funding of civil cases
'Advice deserts'
There is evidence that not enough legal service providers have contracts. This is partly due to the smaller numbers of contracts made with providers by the Legal Services Commission (and now by the Legal Aid Agency) and also to the fact that many solicitors are finding that the rates of pay are so low, it is not economically viable for solicitors to continue in the scheme. This has created what have been called 'advice deserts'.

The problem of advice deserts was considered by the Constitutional Affairs Select Committee as long ago as 2004. In the evidence to the Committee, even the Legal Services Commission (then responsible for legal aid) acknowledged:

QUOTATION

'It is clear that there are parts of England and Wales in which the need for publicly funded legal services is not currently being met.'

Select Committee on Constitutional Affairs, Fourth Report of session 2003–04
'Civil Legal Aid: Adequacy of Provision', para 50

In its report the Select Committee gave the position in Northumberland as an example. There were no housing law advisers and no one with a contract for immigration law in Northumberland. Furthermore, there were only two contracts for employment law in the area. People have to travel a long way to see a lawyer. This can be expensive and is difficult for people on low incomes, those caring for small children or those who have a disability which makes it difficult to travel.

Since 2004 the position has been getting worse as more solicitors have stopped doing government-funded legal work. With so few legal service providers in certain areas, people who want help may have to travel long distances to find it.

The continuing lack of lawyers to do certain types of case was confirmed by a survey carried out in 2008–09 by the Legal Action Group. For example, they quote one person from South Wales as saying she had: 'contacted dozens of solicitors in the last month, but no help was forthcoming as none specialised in welfare benefits'.

The annual report for the Legal Services Commission also showed how the numbers of law firms doing legal aid work had decreased. When the Legal Services Commission started in 2000, there were about 5,000 law firms doing legal aid work. By 2016 there were only 1,500 firms.

Eligibility levels

Even where there are enough legal services providers in an area, only people with very low levels of income and capital can qualify for help. As far back as 2004 the Select Committee on Constitutional Affairs which investigated the adequacy of the provision of civil legal aid pointed out:

QUOTATION

'At present, the legal aid system is increasingly being restricted to those with no means at all. There is a substantial risk that many people of modest means but who are home-owners will fall out of the ambit of legal aid. In many cases this may amount to a serious denial of access to justice.'

'Civil Legal Aid: Adequacy of Provision', para 105

The financial limits have become increasingly restrictive so that this statement is even truer today. In addition, under the current system there is no provision for those whose income falls just above the limits.

Non-availability

As set out in section 7.3.3, funding is not available for all civil claims. Most claims in tort are now excluded. Any such case has to be paid for privately or through a CFA (see section 7.5). This works well where there is damage to property or where people have suffered minor injuries, but it can be argued that it creates difficulties for people who have been left with serious disabilities. They need all the help they can get to make sure they receive adequate compensation.

In employment issues the only cases eligible to receive legal aid funding are where there is an equality issue. For other employment issues no help is available. It can be argued that people bringing employment claims against large companies are disadvantaged by being unable to receive public funding to bring their case. The company will be able to afford a lawyer and will be at an advantage in the case.

Public funding in civil cases

Managing body	Legal Aid Agency
Different levels of help and representation available	• Advice only. • Legal Representation – covers all aspects of case. • Support Funding – partial funding of a very high-cost case.
Means test	Strict means test on gross income, disposable income and disposable capital for all services.
Merits test for Legal Representation	Whether the case has a reasonable chance of success and the damages will be worth more than the costs. Other criteria including: • Can the matter be funded in another way? • Are there funds available?
Problems	• Number of solicitors is decreasing. • Financial level of eligibility excludes people of modest means. • Capping of fund together with increasing criminal expenditure means that less is available for civil cases. • Only available for specified types of cases.

7.5 Private funding

As pointed out at the beginning of this chapter, it is possible to pay privately for legal advice and representation. However, the costs are high, particularly where a civil case goes to court. The main problem is that it is not possible to predict exactly how long a case will last, and, therefore, what the costs are likely to be. For example, will the other side admit liability or will they fight the case? If so, will they try to delay the hearing for as long as possible? Another major problem is that if the case is lost, then the claimant may be ordered to pay the other side's costs. In order to help people to fund cases privately and to avoid unforeseen expense, the government introduced CFAs.

7.5.1 Conditional fee agreements

Conditional fees must not be confused with contingency fees. Contingency fees are the system used in the USA for private funding of civil claims. They operate on the basis that, if the case is won, the lawyer will be paid a percentage of the damages awarded to the claimant. In this country there was always concern that this system of paying a percentage of the winnings to the lawyer gives the lawyer too great a financial interest in the outcome of the litigation. It is thought that it promotes 'ambulance chasing' in which lawyers almost literally follow an injured person to hospital in order to get the right to take the case. In addition, it may tempt some lawyers to use unethical means to ensure that they win the case. However, damages-based agreements (effectively contingency fees) have continued to be allowed under the LASPO 2012.

Conditional fees do not give the lawyer a stake in the amount of the damages. Instead, the lawyer and the client agree a success fee which will be paid to the lawyer if the case is won. The amount of the damages is irrelevant. CFAs were first allowed by s58 of the CLSA 1990. They were originally limited to personal injury cases, insolvency cases and human rights cases. Although the 1990 Act paved the way for conditional fees, it took five years before the Conditional Fee Agreements Regulations 1995 (SI 1995 No 1674) set out the details of how the system was to work. So the first such agreements were not actually used until 1995. In 1998, the government extended the use of conditional fees to all civil cases where there was a money claim (excluding any family matters).

The AJA 1999 amended s58 of the CLSA 1990 so that they could also be used in civil claims where there was no money claim (e.g. a claim for an injunction).

7.5.2 How conditional fees work

The solicitor and client agree on the fee that would normally be charged for such a case. The agreement will also set out what the solicitor's success fee will be if he wins the case. Many CFAs will be made on the basis that if the case is lost, the client pays nothing. Because of this sort of agreement, the scheme is often referred to as 'no win, no fee'. However, some solicitors may prefer to charge a lower level fee, for example half the normal fee, even if the case is lost. If the case is won the client has to pay the normal fee plus the success fee.

7.5.3 Success fee

The success fee could be up to 100 per cent of the normal fee. However, most agreements will include a 'cap' on the success fee, which prevents it from being more than 25 per cent of the damages (amount of money) that the client wins as compensation. This protects the client from having to pay more than he or she won as compensation. Even so, it can mean that the client is left with very little of their damages. This is easier to understand by looking at the examples given in the key facts table, above (Public funding in civil cases).

Agreement	
Normal fee	£4,000
Fee if case is lost	Nil
Success fee	£2,000
Cap on success fee	25% of damages
Possible results of case	**Client pays**
Case is lost	Nothing
Case is won: client gets £50,000 damages	£6,000 (£4,000 + £2,000)
Case is won: client gets £6,000 damages	£5,500 (£4,000 + £1,500*)
*This £1,500 is because the success fee cannot be more than 25% of the damages.	

Figure 7.2 Illustration of conditional fees

Under the LASPO 2012, the Lord Chancellor is able to set a limit on the maximum percentage for the success fee, so it is unlikely that solicitors will be able set a success fee of 100 per cent in future.

Under s58 of the CLSA 1990, a winning claimant used to be able to claim the success fee back from the losing defendant. This has been amended by the LASPO 2012 so that s58(6) of the CLSA now states:

SECTION

'A costs order made in proceedings may not include provision requiring the payment by one party of all or part of a success fee payable under a conditional fee agreement.'

So now the position is that a winning claimant has to pay any success fee themselves.

7.5.4 Insurance premiums

Although the client will often not have to pay anything to his own lawyer if the case is lost, he will usually have to pay the costs of the other side. This can leave the client with a very large bill to pay. To help protect against this, it is possible to insure against the risk. This type of insurance is known as 'after-the-event' (ATE) insurance. So, if the case is lost, your insurers will pay the other side's costs.

In order to get insurance it is necessary to pay a premium (a sum of money) to the insurance company. Premiums for ATE insurance are usually quite expensive. This premium usually has to be paid in advance of the decision in the case. This can cause problems to people who cannot afford the cost of the premium.

It used to be possible for a winning claimant to be able claim the cost of ATE back from the defendant. This has been changed by the LASPO 2012 and the cost of ATE insurance can no longer be claimed back. The claimant has to fund it himself.

7.5.5 Are conditional fees working?

CFAs have helped thousands of people to bring cases to court and obtain justice. One area in which they have been particularly useful for claimants has been in defamation cases. Legal aid has never been available for such cases and only the rich could risk pursuing defamation claims. CFAs have enabled ordinary people to take such cases.

However, there are problems with CFAs. Low value cases are not attractive to lawyers who need to be able to make a profit for their legal business to survive. Lawyers are also more likely to take on cases where there is a very high chance of success.

The LASPO 2012 has made CFAs less attractive for two reasons:

- the cost of ATE insurance can no longer be claimed back from the defendant by a claimant who wins the case;
- success fees can no longer be claimable from the defendant by a claimant who wins the case.

These two points mean that a winning claimant will have to bear more of the cost of taking a case. As a result, a large proportion of the amount of damages they receive may well be used up by their costs.

Conditional fee agreements

How CFAs work	• The client and solicitor agree on the normal fee and on a success fee if the case is won. • The success fee can be up to 100% of the normal fee (although this has been limited in some areas). • If the case is lost, most clients will pay nothing to their own solicitor. • ATE insurance is usually taken out to protect against the risk of paying the other's costs if the case is lost.
Advantages of CFAs	• Provide access to justice for those who cannot get government funding and cannot afford to pay in the normal way. • Client will feel confident in solicitor's commitment to case. • Hopeless cases will not be taken on, saving court time.
Disadvantages of CFAs	• Clients cannot afford to pay insurance premiums or other expenses. • Consumers may be subjected to high-pressure sales tactics. • Consumers do not understand the risks and liabilities of CFAs and may be misled by sales persons. • Some claims end in 'zero gain'. • Solicitors do not want to take on high-risk claims or low-value claims: this can deny access to justice.

7.6 Advice in civil cases

When people have a legal problem the first thing they want is advice. The Legal Advice Agency has a website offering legal advice. There are also lawyers and other bodies which provide legal advice and help. The main ones of these are Citizens Advice Bureaux (CABx) and law centres, but there are others which can offer specialist advice on certain topics, for example the RAC and the AA offer members some help in traffic matters, while trade unions will help members with legal problems in work-related matters. There are also charities such as Shelter which offer advice to people with housing problems. The legal profession also offers assistance with schemes run by solicitors or barristers which provide free advice. This is often referred to as *pro bono* work (see section 7.6.6).

7.6.1 Civil Legal Advice

The Legal Services Commission had established Community Legal Advice Centres (CLACs). These were a one-stop service providing advice on debt, welfare benefits, community care, housing and employment. It was intended that there would eventually be about 75 CLACs. In 2013 the Ministry of Justice renamed Community Legal Advice 'Civil Legal Advice'. It introduced a new free online service. Individuals are able to check online whether they are eligible for legal aid. If they are, the online service gives details of how to contact Civil Legal Advice either online or through a face-to-face meeting with a legal provider.

7.6.2 Service providers

People can also get advice from a solicitor or a not-for-profit organisation that holds a contract with the government to give advice in civil cases. For example, some CABx have contracts. To receive advice from a service provider under the government-funded schemes, the person has to come within the financial limits explained in section 7.4.1 above.

7.6.3 Other advice agencies

Apart from government-funded schemes, there are a number of different advice schemes available. The main ones are CABx and law centres. However, there are other agencies which offer advice on specific legal topics. These include trades unions which will help members with work-related legal problems. There are also charities such as Shelter which offers advice to people with housing problems. These will offer advice free to anyone who has a problem of the type they deal in.

7.6.4 Citizens Advice Bureaux

CABx were first set up in 1938 and today there are about 1,000 throughout the UK with a bureau existing in many towns. They give general advice free to anyone on a variety of issues mostly connected to social welfare problems and debt, but they also advise on some legal matters. They can also provide information on which local solicitors do legal aid work or give cheap or free initial interviews. Many have arrangements under which solicitors may attend at the bureau once a week or fortnight to give more qualified advice on legal matters.

One of the most used CABx is the one in the Royal Courts of Justice on The Strand in London. With the decrease in the availability of legal aid for civil cases, this CAB is handling large numbers of enquiries – about 14,000 per year. In cases where there is a litigant in person in the Court of Appeal, the Court of Appeal Judges will often suggest that the litigant in person should get advice from the CAB.

As well as being available for anyone to get advice, some CABx have contracts to provide government-funded advice.

7.6.5 Law centres

These offer a free, non-means tested legal service to people in their area. The first law centre opened in North Kensington in 1970. This stated its aims as providing:

> a first class solicitor's service to the people ... a service which is easily accessible, not intimidating, to which they can turn for guidance as they would to their family doctor, or as someone who can afford it would turn to his family solicitor.

Their aim is to provide free legal advice (and sometimes representation) in areas where there are few solicitors. Many of their clients are disadvantaged.

Funding

Law centres have always struggled to secure enough funding. Recent cuts by local authorities in their budgets have meant the withdrawal or reduction of funding from this source. As a result some law centres have had to close. Funding also comes from the Legal Aid Agency. Some centres have received funds from the Big Lottery Fund where the law centre is part of a community project.

In 2016 there were 44 law centres operating. The website of the Law Centres Federation at www.lawcentres.org.uk provides information about Law centres.

7.6.6 Schemes run by lawyers

Some solicitors offer a free half-hour first interview. Local CABx will have a list of solicitors who offer the service. Another service by solicitors is the Accident Legal Advice Service (ALAS) which is aimed at helping accident victims claim compensation. In addition, the Law Society runs Accident Line – a free telephone service to put accident victims in contact with solicitors who do personal injury work.

Bar Pro Bono Unit

Since 1996 volunteer barristers have staffed the Bar Pro Bono Unit. This Unit gives free advice to those who cannot afford to pay and who cannot get legal aid. They will give advice on any area of law and will also where necessary represent the client in court proceedings.

Free Representation Unit (FRU)

This is also staffed by volunteer barristers. It was founded in 1972 and provides representation for:

- cases in the employment tribunals;
- social security appeals; and
- claims for criminal injury compensation.

These are areas of law where legal aid is not available.

Until recently the FRU operated only in London. However, it is trying to set up Units in Nottingham, Birmingham and Manchester.

7.6.7 Insurance

Another way of funding a court case is by legal insurance. Most motor insurance policies offer cover (for a small amount extra) for help with legal fees in cases arising from road accidents and there are also policies purely for insurance against legal costs.

KEY FACTS

Where to get advice in civil cases

Government-funded schemes	Advice agencies	Lawyers
Legal Aid Agency website offering advice	CABx	Some solicitors offer a free half-hour first interview
Telephone service	Law centres	Bar Pro Bono Unit
CLACs	Legal insurance	Pay privately for advice
Legal aid advice scheme – means tested and only available to those on low incomes		

7.7 Legal aid in criminal cases

Legal advice and representation are recognised as basic human rights for those charged with a criminal offence. This is set out in Article 6 of the ECHR which states:

ARTICLE

'Art 6(3) Everyone charged with a criminal offence has the following minimum rights: ...

(b) to have adequate time and facilities for the preparation of his defence;

(c) to defend himself in person or through legal assistance of his own choosing or, if he has not sufficient means to pay for legal assistance, to be given it free when the interests of justice so require.'

In order to comply with Article 6(3)(c) legal aid funding from the Legal Aid Agency is available in criminal cases, but it is subject to two tests:

- merits;
- means.

7.7.1 Merits test

For criminal cases in both the Magistrates' Courts and the Crown Court the merits test is whether it is in the interests of justice for the defendant to receive funding. What are known as the 'Widgery criteria' lay down the factors to be considered in deciding this. These are:

1. whether the individual would, if any matter arising in the proceedings is decided against him, be likely to lose his liberty or livelihood or suffer serious damage to his reputation;
2. whether the determination of any matter arising in the proceedings may involve consideration of a substantial point of law;
3. whether the individual may be unable to understand the proceedings or to state his own case;
4. whether the proceedings may involve the tracing, interviewing or expert cross-examination of witnesses on behalf of the individual; or
5. whether it is in the interests of another person that the individual is represented.

In point 1 of this list, the stress is on whether the defendant is likely to be given a custodial sentence. For example, theft carries a maximum sentence of seven years' imprisonment. However, first-time offenders charged with a small theft are never given a custodial sentence, so they would not meet the test of being likely to lose their liberty. However, a defendant charged with stealing from work might be at risk of losing his job and so might qualify under the 'likely to lose livelihood' part of these criteria. The more serious the offence charged, the more likely there is a risk of loss of liberty, so defendants charged with offences such as rape or a serious assault will always come within this test.

Point 3 makes sure that those who are not capable of understanding the proceedings or being able to ask questions or put their own case are given representation. This covers those who have a disability such as deafness, or mental illness affecting their understanding. It also applies to those who do not speak English sufficiently well to present their own case.

The last point, whether it is in the interests of another person that the individual is represented, is necessary to protect victims in alleged sex abuse cases from being questioned directly by the defendant and other similar situations.

7.7.2 Means test

Some defendants are 'passported' into the legal aid scheme. This means that they automatically pass the means test. It applies to anyone under 18 or any adult who is in receipt of certain benefits such as Income Support, Income-Based Job Seeker's Allowance or Universal Credit. For all other defendants there is a means test.

The initial means test considers all of the defendant's income and also that of his or her partner. It then gives a weighting for any dependants the defendant has and adjusts the income accordingly. If the adjusted income is £12,475 or less (all figures are for 2016), the defendant will receive funding and will not have to pay any contribution. If the adjusted income is more than £12,475 but less than £22,325 then a full means test is applied. This takes into account tax and National Insurance payments, annual housing and childcare costs and maintenance being paid to any former partners and any children. An adjusted living allowance is also given depending on the size of the defendant's family. If the defendant qualifies under this means test then funding is available but for Crown Court cases the defendant may have to pay a contribution to the cost of the case.

Anyone whose income is above the limits set will not receive any funding for a case in the Magistrates' Courts. However, they will still be able to receive funding for a Crown Court case but will have to pay a contribution during the proceedings or at the end of the case. The defendant's capital is also taken into account in deciding whether a contribution should be paid. About one in every four defendants in the Crown Court has to pay a contribution.

7.7.3 Advice and assistance for individuals in custody

Any person who is arrested and held in custody at a police station has the right to legal advice. Since 2008 much of the advice has been given over the phone, though sometimes a duty solicitor will attend at the police station. In the 1990s reliance on telephone advice was viewed as a defect of the system, but telephone advice has now become the government's preferred method of action for duty solicitors.

7.7.4 The Public Defender Service

The AJA 1999 allowed the Legal Services Commission to set up a service, within the Criminal Defence Service, of employed lawyers to defend people charged with an offence. This concept of a public defender system has been controversial. It means that the state is both prosecuting and defending in cases. This must mean that there is a potential conflict of interest. Such public defender schemes have existed in the USA and Canada for some time and there has been research in both these countries, but this has shown conflicting results (see C Frazer, 'The Criminal Defence Service: Lessons from Abroad' [2001] *NLJ* 670).

The first five Public Defender Service (PDS) offices (Birmingham, Cheltenham, Liverpool, Middlesbrough and Swansea) were set up in England and Wales in 2001, with another one (Pontypridd) being opened in 2002 and two more (Chester and Darlington) in 2003.

An evaluation of the PDS, 'Evaluation of the Public Defender Service in England and Wales', by L Bridges, E Cape, P Fenn, A Mitchell, R Moorhead and A Sherr (Stationery Office, 2007) was published at the beginning of 2007. This found that there were positive aspects to the use of the PDS. In particular, lawyers from the service were more likely to attend at a police station to advise clients being held there. Where this happened, clients were less likely to be charged with an offence than those who used lawyers from private practice.

However, defendants who were charged and represented by the PDS were more likely to plead guilty in the Magistrates' Courts. This did not appear to have any advantage for the defendant in the way of pleading to a lower level offence or receiving a lesser sentence than those represented by private lawyers.

The evaluation found that the cost effectiveness of the PDS was not as good as for private firms. During the first three years of its operation the average case costs for the PDS ranged from between 40 per cent to just over 90 per cent higher than costs of private firms. As a result of this, four of the offices were closed down in 2007 as not being cost-effective.

The remaining four offices remain open and are now managed by the Legal Aid Agency.

ACTIVITY

Critiquing the law

In March 2016, over 20 senior lawyers and directors of legal aid charities wrote a letter to *The Guardian* newspaper. In this letter they stated that:

Quotation

'Every day, our members and the people we support see the impact of the measures implemented in the Legal Aid, Sentencing and Punishment of Offenders Act. We believe the legal aid reforms have had a severe impact on the ability of vulnerable people to access justice since they came into effect on 1 April 2013 ... the cuts have limited access to justice for some of those who need legal aid the most. Too much effort has focused on the point of crisis rather than prevention, and the number of people who have no choice but to represent themselves in court has risen sharply.'

Throughout this chapter, you have read about the different rules and criteria used to determine whether individuals can access legal aid from the state. Having to go to court to seek justice, or to defend yourself from an accusation, is inordinately expensive. Re-read the details about civil and criminal legal aid in this chapter and consider the following thinking points:

- How easy do you think it is to apply for legal aid, given the existence of means testing?
- Consider the rules for eligibility for means tested legal aid. How complicated do they seem?
- Do you think it is right that people have to get legal advice from free advice centres and clinics, rather than from the state via legal aid?
- The LASPO 2012 has tightened the rules on legal aid, with an aim to cutting the overall legal aid budget. How do you think this will affect access to justice?

SAMPLE ESSAY QUESTION

Without publicly funded advice and representation, access to justice would be denied to many people. Discuss.

> **Explain the concept of access to justice**
>
> **and**
>
> **discuss problems in access to justice such as:**
> - high cost of using lawyers;
> - complexity of law and procedure;
> - fear of approaching a lawyer and lack of knowledge of where to find a lawyer.

> **Briefly explain the system of public funding in civil cases:**
> - means tested;
> - representation merits tested;
> - certain areas of law excluded e.g. personal injury cases.

Briefly explain the system of public funding in criminal cases:

- means tested;
- merits – interests of justice.

Advice can be obtained by telephone and internet.

Discuss problems of the system such as:

- low limits on income and capital mean that majority of population do not qualify for public funding;
- certain areas of law excluded;
- fewer lawyers have contracts for legal aid work;
- 'advice deserts' – the lack of sufficient lawyers/advice agencies in certain areas/topics of law;
- reintroduction of means testing for defendants in the Crown Court.

Discuss other methods providing access to justice:

- CFAs for civil cases;
- advice agencies providing free help;
- *pro bono* work by lawyers.

Look at wider issues especially allowing non-lawyers to run law firms – 'Tesco's law' (Legal Services Act 2007).

CONCLUSION

Figure 7.3 Essay map on funding

SUMMARY

History

■ Public funding for legal advice and funding has been available since 1949.

Present system

■ The present system was set up by the LASPO 2012.

■ The system is administered by the Legal Aid Agency.

■ The Agency deals with funding for both civil and criminal cases.

■ The Agency contracts with legal service providers: these can be legal professionals or not-for-profit agencies.

Public funding in civil cases

- It is only available for specified types of case – these include cases involving welfare of children, human rights and social welfare cases.
- It is means tested with free help being available to those with low levels of disposable income and capital. It is not available to those above certain limits of disposable income and capital. Those in between the two limits have to pay contributions.
- Problems with the system are that only those on low incomes are eligible; it is difficult to find solicitors as fewer have contracts to do legal aid work and some areas of the country have very limited services.

Public funding in criminal cases

- Advice is available for those detained in police stations; this often by telephone but for some cases a duty solicitor will attend.
- In four areas the PDS is available to represent defendants.
- For representation there is a merits test for cases – is it in the interests of justice?
- There is a means test for both Magistrates' Courts and Crown Court.

Private funding

- Anyone can pay a legal professional for advice and/or representation but privately funding a court case can be very expensive.
- CFAs (no win, no fee) may be used to fund civil cases: under these a basic fee is agreed and on top of that a success fee is to be paid if the case is won. ATE insurance is used to protect claimants from costs of losing.

Advice agencies

- There are various organisations which offer free advice. The main ones are CABx and law centres.

Further reading

Book

Newman, D, *Legal Aid Lawyers and the Quest for Justice* (Bloomsbury, 2008).

Articles

Gilg, J-Y, 'Carolyn Regan: legal aid is the fourth plank of the welfare state' [2009] *SJ* 10.
Peysner, J, 'Tail wags dog: contingency fees' [2013] *CJQ* 112.
Willman, S, 'Access to justice or Tesco's law?' [2006] 156 *NLJ* 1537.

Internet links

Information on legal aid at: www.gov.uk/legal-aid
Legal Aid Agency at: www.gov.uk/government/organisations/legal-aid-agency
Parliamentary Select Committee reports at: www.parliament.uk

8

Juries

AIMS AND OBJECTIVES

After reading this chapter you should be able to:

- Understand the qualifications and selection of jurors
- Understand the role of juries in criminal cases
- Understand the limited role of juries in civil cases
- Discuss the advantages and disadvantages of using juries in criminal cases
- Discuss the advantages and disadvantages of using juries in civil cases

8.1 Introduction

History

Juries have been used in our legal system for over 1,000 years. There is evidence that they were used even before the Norman Conquest, but it was not until after 1215 that juries became the usual method of trying criminal cases. This was as a result of the fact that trial by ordeal was condemned by the Church and, in 1215, Magna Carta included the recognition of a person's right to trial by 'the lawful judgment of his peers'. Originally juries were used for providing local knowledge and information and acted more as witnesses than decision-makers. However, by the late fifteenth century juries had become independent assessors and assumed their modern role as deciders of fact.

8.1.1 The independence of the jury

The independence of the jury as deciders of fact became firmly established following *Bushell's Case* [1670] Vaugh 135.

CASE EXAMPLE

Bushell's Case [1670] Vaugh 135

Several jurors refused to convict Quaker activists of unlawful assembly. The trial judge would not accept the not guilty verdict, and ordered the jurors to resume their deliberations without food or drink. When the jurors persisted in their refusal to convict, they were fined and committed to prison until the fines were paid. On appeal, the Court of Common Pleas ordered the release of the jurors, holding that jurors could not be punished for their verdict.

This case established that the jury is the sole arbiter of fact and a judge cannot challenge its decision. This rule remains today and a more modern example demonstrating that judges must respect the independence of the jury is *R v McKenna* [1960] 2 All ER 326. In that case the judge at the trial had threatened the jurors, who had been deliberating for about two-and-a-quarter hours, that if they did not return a verdict within another ten minutes they would be locked up all night. The jury then returned a verdict of guilty within six minutes, but the defendant's conviction was quashed on appeal because the judge had put undue pressure on the jury. This was explained by the Court of Criminal Appeal when Cassels J said:

JUDGMENT

'It is a cardinal principle of our criminal law that in considering their verdict, concerning as it does, the liberty of the subject, a jury shall deliberate in complete freedom, uninfluenced by any promise, unintimidated by any threat. They still stand between the Crown and the subject, and they are still one of the main defences of personal liberty. To say to such a tribunal in the course of its deliberations that it must reach a conclusion within ten minutes or else undergo hours of personal inconvenience and discomfort, is a disservice to the cause of justice.'

It is worth noting that this case took place before majority verdicts were allowed. It was also at the time when the jurors were not allowed to separate after they had started their deliberations. If they did not reach a decision by night time they had to remain in the jury room. So the threat of the judge to lock them up was a very real threat. In recent times, if a jury needs more than one day to reach its decision, the members are sent to a hotel overnight and then brought back to the court in the morning to resume their discussions.

8.1.2 Modern-day use of the jury

Juries can be used in the following courts:

- the Crown Court for criminal trials on indictment (a panel of 12 is used);
- the High Court, Queen's Bench Division but only for certain types of cases (see section 8.4) (a panel of 12 is used);
- the County Court for similar cases to the Queen's Bench Division (a panel of eight is used);
- Coroners' Courts (a panel of between seven and 11 is used).

The main use is in the Crown Court, but even here a jury will be used in only about one-third of cases. This is because two-thirds of defendants plead guilty and so no jury is required for those cases. Juries are very rarely used in the civil courts.

8.2 Jury qualifications

8.2.1 Basic qualifications

The qualifications for jury service were revised in 1972 following the Morris Committee Report on jury service. Before this date there was a property qualification, which meant that in order to be a juror it was necessary to be the owner or tenant of a dwelling. This restriction had the effect that many women and young people were prevented from serving on a jury as they were less likely to own or rent property. The Morris Committee thought that being a juror should be the counterpart of being a citizen. As a result, the qualifications for jury service were widened in the Criminal Justice Act 1972 and based on the right to vote.

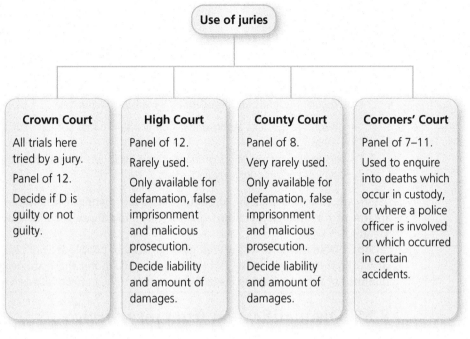

Figure 8.1 The use of juries

The present qualifications are set out in s1 of the Juries Act 1974 (as amended) which states:

SECTION

's 1 (1) Subject to the provisions of this Act, every person shall be qualified to serve as a juror in the Crown Court, the High Court and the County Courts and be liable accordingly to attend for jury service when summoned under this Act if –

(a) he is for the time being registered as a parliamentary or local government elector and is not less than eighteen nor more than seventy six;
(b) he has been ordinarily resident in the United Kingdom, the Channel Islands or the Isle of Man for any period of at least five years since attaining the age of thirteen;
(c) he is not a mentally disordered person; and
(d) he is not disqualified for jury service.'

To qualify for jury service, a person must:

- be aged between 18 and 75;
- be an elector; and
- have lived in the UK for at least five years.

Schedule 1 to the Juries Act 1974 sets out what is meant by 'mentally disordered person'. This was amended by the Criminal Justice Act 2003 so that mentally ill people are disqualified whereas previously they were ineligible. Although the definition is the same as under the old law, there have been criticisms that it is too wide. Schedule 1 defines a 'mentally ill person' as:

SECTION

'1. A person who suffers or has suffered from mental illness, psychopathic disorder, mental handicap or severe mental handicap and on account of that condition either –

(a) is resident in a hospital or similar institution; or
(b) regularly attends for treatment by a medical practitioner.

2. A person for the time being under guardianship under section 7 of the Mental Health Act 1983.
3. A person who, under Part 7 of that Act, has been determined by a judge to be incapable of administering his property and affairs.'

There are criticisms that this definition does not distinguish between those receiving treatment for mild depression from their GP and those sectioned under the Mental Health Act 1983.

Apart from mentally disordered persons, certain people are not permitted to sit on a jury even though they are within the basic qualifications; these are people who are disqualified or for various reasons lack the capacity to act effectively as a juror.

8.2.2 Disqualification from jury service

Some criminal convictions will disqualify a person from jury service. The type of sentence and the length of a prison sentence decide whether the person is disqualified and the period for which that disqualification lasts.

Disqualified permanently are those who at any time have been sentenced to:

- imprisonment for life, detention for life or custody for life;
- detention during Her Majesty's pleasure or during the pleasure of the Secretary of State;
- imprisonment for public protection or detention for public protection;
- an extended sentence;
- a term of imprisonment of five years or more or a term of detention of five years or more.

Disqualified for ten years are those who have:

- at any time in the last ten years served a sentence of imprisonment;
- had a suspended sentence passed on them;
- had a community order or other community sentence passed on them.

In addition, anyone who is currently on bail in criminal proceedings is disqualified from sitting as a juror. If a disqualified person fails to disclose that fact and turns up for jury service, he may be fined up to £5,000.

8.2.3 Excusal from jury service

Until April 2004 there was a category of people who were ineligible for jury service. This included judges and others who had been involved in the administration of justice within the previous ten years. This category was abolished by the Criminal Justice Act 2003. This means that judges, lawyers, police etc. are eligible to serve on juries. Many people feel that this could lead to bias or to a legally well-qualified juror influencing the rest of the jury. When Lord Justice Dyson (from the Court of Appeal) was summoned to attend as a juror in June 2004, the Lord Chief Justice, Lord Woolf, issued observations to judges who are called for jury service. These point out:

- a judge serves on a jury as part of his duty as a private citizen;
- excusal from jury service will be granted only in extreme circumstances;
- deferral of jury service to a later date should be sought where a judge has judicial commitments which make it particularly inconvenient for him to do jury service at the time he was called to do so;
- at court, if a judge knows the presiding judge or other person in the case, he should raise this with the jury bailiff or a member of the court staff if he considers it could interfere with his responsibilities as a juror;
- it is a matter of discretion for an individual judge sitting as a juror as to whether he discloses the fact of his judicial office to the other members of the jury;
- judges must follow the directions given to the jury by the trial judge on the law and should avoid the temptation to correct guidance which they believe to be inaccurate as this is outside their role as a juror.

The point about letting the court know when someone involved in the case is personally known to the juror is also relevant to practising lawyers who are called for jury service. It was noticeable that when a Queen's Counsel was summoned for jury service at the Central Criminal Court (the Old Bailey) in the summer of 2004, he was prevented from sitting in each case that he was called for, on the ground that he knew one or more people involved in each trial.

Before April 2004 mentally ill people were also in the ineligible category. Now, as already seen above, they are disqualified from jury service under the 2003 Act.

The right to be excused jury service

Also prior to April 2004, people in certain essential occupations, such as doctors, had a right to be excused jury service if they did not want to do it. The Criminal Justice Act 2003 also abolished this category. This means that doctors and other medical staff are no longer able to refuse to do jury service, though they can apply for a discretionary excusal. However, for full-time serving members of the forces there is discretion to excuse from service if the commanding officer certifies that it would be prejudicial to the efficiency of the service.

8.2.4 Discretionary excusals

Anyone who has a problem which makes it very difficult for them to do their jury service may ask to be excused or for their period of service to be deferred (put back to a later date). The court has a discretion to grant such an excusal but will do so only if there is a sufficiently good reason. Such reasons include being too ill to attend court or suffering from a disability that makes it impossible for the person to sit as a juror, or being a mother with a small baby. Other reasons could include business appointments that cannot be undertaken by anyone else, examinations or holidays that have been booked. In these situations the court is most likely to defer jury service to a more convenient date, rather than excuse the person completely. This is stated in the current guidance for summoning officers which is aimed at preventing the high number of discretionary excusals which used to occur previously. The overall principle states:

'The normal expectation is that everyone summoned for jury service will serve at the time for which they are summoned. It is recognised that there will be occasions where it is not reasonable for a person summoned to serve at the time for which they are summoned. In such circumstances the summoning officer should use his/her discretion to defer the individual to a time more appropriate. Only in extreme circumstances, should a person be excused from jury service.'

'Guidance for Summoning Officers when Considering Deferral and Excusal Applications', HMCS, 2003, para 4

If a person is not excused from jury service he must attend on the date set or he may be fined up to £1,000 for non-attendance.

8.2.5 Make-up of jury panels

There used to be concerns that jury panels were not representative of the population. In a study by J Baldwin and M McConville, *Jury Trials* (Clarendon, 1979), it was found that women were very under-represented, making up only 27 per cent of jury members. Ethnic minorities were also very under-represented with only 28 of the 3,912 jurors in the study coming from an ethnic minority. Census figures for the area suggested that there should have been between ten and 15 times that number. There were also fewer lower-working class on the panels than there were in the local population.

In 1993 *The Crown Court Study* by M Zander and P Henderson (Royal Commission on Criminal Justice Research Study No 19, HMSO), found juries to be more balanced. Fifty-three per cent of jurors were male and 5 per cent of jurors were from ethnic minorities. This latter figure compared fairly well with the 5.9 per cent in the population according to the 1991 census.

More recently, a study by Cheryl Thomas, 'Diversity and Fairness in the Jury System' (Ministry of Justice Research Series 02/07, 2007), looked at juries in 2003 and 2005. This choice of years allowed the research team to look at possible effects of the changes to jury qualifications made by the Criminal Justice Act 2003 as these came into effect in 2004.

The report found that there was a marked increase in the proportion of those summoned who served on a jury. In 2003 only 54 per cent did so. In 2005 the figure was 64 per cent. This suggests that there are now fewer discretionary excusals. However, the figures for 2005 showed that 5 per cent of summonses were returned as not deliverable and 10 per cent were not responded to.

The report found that, in both years, the juries studied were representative in gender, age and race. The only under-representation found by the study was of lower classes and unemployed. The changes to eligibility made by the Criminal Justice Act 2003 did not affect the socio-economic make-up of juries, with one exception. This was that the proportion of serving jurors that were 65–69 years of age doubled from 3 per cent in 2003 to 6 per cent in 2005. This change is clearly the result of the fact that people in this age group can no longer claim discretionary excusal, which they could do prior to the changes made by the Criminal Justice Act 2003.

8.2.6 Police and prosecutors on jury service

The Criminal Justice Act 2003 made all police and lawyers eligible to sit on a jury. There have been challenges to this on the basis that it breaches the human right to a fair trial.

In *R v Abdroikof: R v Green: R v Williamson* [2007] UKHL 37 the House of Lords considered appeals in three cases where there had been either a police officer or a prosecuting lawyer as a member of the jury. The facts of these three cases are given below.

Basic qualifications for jury service:
- be aged between 18 and 75;
- be an elector; and
- have lived in the UK for at least five years.

But may be unable to sit for one of reasons below:

Mentally disordered

Cannot sit on jury Criminal Justice Act 2003 Sch 1.

Disqualified

Permanently:
- imprisoned for life;
- imprisoned for public protection;
- serving an extended sentence;
- serving a term of imprisonment of five years or more.

For ten years:

At any time in the last ten years:
- served a sentence of imprisonment;
- had a suspended sentence passed on them;
- had a community order;
- is on bail.

Excusal

Full-time serving members of the forces may have right to be excused.

Discretionary excusal

Where there is a good reason why person cannot sit, e.g. too ill.

Figure 8.2 Qualifications for jury service

CASE EXAMPLE

R v Abdroikof [2007] UKHL 37

The defendant was tried for attempted murder. When the jury was considering its verdict, the foreman of the jury sent a note to the judge revealing that he was a serving police officer. He was concerned that, if required to report for duty at the Notting Hill Carnival on the following Bank Holiday Monday when the court was not sitting, he might meet one or more police officers who had been called to give evidence at the trial. With the acquiescence of defending counsel, who had not previously known of the foreman's occupation, the juror was directed not to report for police duty on the Monday.

R v Green [2007] UKHL 37

The defendant was searched by police. In the course of the search the officer put his hand into the appellant's pocket and pricked his finger on a used syringe. The appellant was charged with offences of assault occasioning actual bodily harm and having a bladed or pointed article. He was convicted. There was a major conflict of evidence between the police and the defendant about what had happened in the incident.

Some time after the trial, by chance, the appellant's solicitor discovered that a police officer had been a member of the trial jury. This officer was, at the time of the trial, posted within the same Operational Command Unit as the officer who had searched the defendant. In addition both officers had once served in the same police station at the same time although they did not know one another.

R v Williamson [2007] UKHL 37

The defendant was charged with two offences of rape. A senior Crown Prosecutor was summonsed for jury duty. Before the trial began he wrote to the court informing them that he worked for the CPS. He was a Higher Court Advocate and had acted as prosecuting counsel in cases in many local courts, including the trial court. His job at the time of the trial was to advise the police on charging out of hours.

This letter was passed to defending counsel, who challenged the use of the juror, contending that the court should not only do what is right but should be seen to have done what is right. Defending counsel argued there was the potential for bias and relied on the appellant's right to a fair trial under Article 6 of the ECHR. The judge ruled that he had to operate within the law passed by Parliament. Under the Criminal Justice Act 2003 the prosecutor was eligible to sit and the judge could see no objection to this in the light of the current legislation.

House of Lords' decision in R v Abdroikof: R v Green: R v Williamson

The House of Lords by a majority of three to two allowed the appeals in the cases of Green and Williamson, though Williamson was remitted to the Court of Appeal for consideration of any application for a re-trial. The appeal in the case *Abdroikof* was unanimously dismissed by the Law Lords.

The majority decision in the cases of *Green* and *Williamson* was based on the problem of appearance of bias. Lord Bingham pointed out that this was an important principle when he said:

JUDGMENT

'In his extempore judgment in *R v Sussex Justices, Ex p McCarthy* [1924] 1 KB 256, 259, Lord Hewart CJ enunciated one of the best known principles of English law: "…it is not merely of some importance but is of fundamental importance that justice should not only be done, but should manifestly and undoubtedly be seen to be done".'

In the case of *Green* there was a crucial dispute on the evidence between the appellant and the police sergeant who searched him. The fact that the sergeant and the juror, although not personally known to each other, shared the same local service background was an important consideration. Lord Bingham pointed out:

JUDGMENT

'In this context the instinct (however unconscious) of a police officer on the jury to prefer the evidence of a brother officer to that of a drug-addicted defendant would be judged by the fair-minded and informed observer to be a real and possible source of unfairness, beyond the reach of standard judicial warnings and directions. The second appellant was not tried by a tribunal which was and appeared to be impartial. It cannot be supposed that Parliament intended to infringe the rule in the *Sussex Justices* case, still less to do so without express language.'

In the case of *Williamson* there was a broader issue as to whether a trial in which there was a juror who was professionally committed to one side only of an adversarial trial process could ever be seen to be fair. Lord Bingham said:

JUDGMENT

'It must, perhaps, be doubted whether Lord Justice Auld or Parliament contemplated that employed Crown prosecutors would sit as jurors in prosecutions brought by their own authority. It is in my opinion clear that justice is not seen to be done if one discharging the very important neutral role of juror is a full-time, salaried, long-serving employee of the prosecutor … The third appellant was entitled to be tried by a tribunal that was and appeared to be impartial, and in my opinion he was not.'

Minority judgments were given by Lord Rodger and Lord Carswell, both of whom would have dismissed all three appeals. Lord Rodger explained his view when he said:

JUDGMENT

'For my part, I consider that, although the fair-minded and informed observer would see that it was possible that a police officer or CPS lawyer would be biased, he would also see that the possibility of the jury's verdict being biased as a result was no greater than in many other cases. In other words, the mere presence of these individuals, without more, would not give rise to a real possibility that the jury had been unable to assess the evidence impartially and reach an unbiased verdict.'

Abdroikof was not a case which turned on a contest between the evidence of the police and of the appellant. The Lords in their judgment thought that it would have been hard to suggest that the case was one in which unconscious prejudice, even if present, would have been likely to operate to the disadvantage of the appellant. Accordingly all five Law Lords were in agreement that this appeal should be dismissed.

Following the decision in *Abdroikof* the Court of Appeal heard five conjoined appeals in *R v Khan* [2008] EWCA Crim 531. None was successful, but two interesting points arose from the cases. First there appears to be inconsistency in what is felt to be apparent bias. In *Green* (one of the cases decided in the *Abdroikof* judgment), the appeal was allowed because a police officer juror had worked in the same borough and had once worked at the same police station as a police witness. Yet it was held there was no apparent bias in *Hanif and Basish Khan* (one of the five cases in the *Khan* judgment) where a police officer juror had known a key prosecution witness for ten years and worked with him on three cases (over two years earlier), although they were never stationed in the same police station.

The other point is that the Court of Appeal (Criminal Division) stated that in looking at the judgment of the House of Lords in *Abdroikof* they had:

'not found it easy to deduce on the part of the majority of the committee clear principles that apply where a juror is a police officer'.

The case of *Hanif and Khan* went to the ECtHR. This court ruled that having a police officer, who knew one of the prosecution witnesses, on the jury was a breach of Article 6(1) of the ECHR – the right to a fair trial. The tribunal that tried *Hanif* was not independent.

At the original trial the officer had alerted the judge to the fact that he knew one of the prosecution witnesses. However, the trial judge had ruled that this did not matter. The case continued with the police officer juror being the foreman of the jury and the defendant was convicted.

In its judgment, the ECtHR surveyed 14 other jurisdictions in Europe and elsewhere where jury trial is used. They found that police officers are banned from being jurors in all but two of those jurisdictions. Those two are Belgium and New York, but in both the defendant has the right to 'peremptory challenge'. This means that the defence can object to any juror and have him or her removed from the jury before the trial starts without having to give a reason. This right no longer exists in England, though it did before 1988.

The ECtHR did not rule on the wider issue of whether having a police officer on a jury without being able to challenge them was itself a breach of Article 6. But as JR Spencer puts it 'The tenor of the judgment suggests that, if it had been obliged to decide the point, it would have ruled that the mere presence of any police officer on a jury is enough to violate the defendant's right to a fair trial' ([2012] 71(1) *CLJ* 254 at 257). It seems likely that allowing police officers on juries will continue to be challenged in future cases.

8.3 Selection at court

Names are selected at random from the electoral registers for the area which the court covers. This is done through a computer selection at the Central Summoning Bureau. It is necessary to summons more than 12 jurors as most Crown Courts have more than one courtroom, so that several jury panels will be needed. In addition, it is not known how many of those summonsed for jury service are disqualified or may be excused from jury service. In fact, at the bigger courts more than 150 summonses may be sent out each fortnight.

Those summonsed must notify the court if there is any reason why they should not or cannot attend. All others are expected to attend for two weeks' jury service, though, of course, if the case they are trying goes on for more than two weeks they will have to stay until the trial is complete. Where it is known that a trial may be exceptionally long, such as a complicated fraud trial, potential jurors are asked if they will be able to serve for such a long period.

8.3.1 Lack of capacity

A judge at the court may discharge a person from being a juror for lack of capacity to cope with the trial. This could be because the person does not understand English adequately or because of some disability which makes them unsuitable as a juror. This includes the blind, who would be unable to see plans and photographs produced in evidence. Section 9B(2) of the Juries Act 1974 (which was added into the 1974 Act by s41 of the Criminal Justice and Public Order Act 1994) makes it clear that the mere fact of a disability does not prevent someone from acting as a juror. The judge can only discharge the juror if he is satisfied that the disability means that that juror is not capable of acting effectively as a juror.

In June 1995 a deaf man was prevented from sitting on a jury at the Old Bailey despite wishing to serve and bringing with him a sign language interpreter. The judge pointed out that that would mean an extra person in the jury room and this was not allowed by law. He also said that the way in which witnesses gave evidence and the tone of their voice was important: 'A deaf juror may not be able to pick up these nuances and to properly judge their credibility.'

In *McWhinney* 1999 Woolwich Crown Court unreported, the controversy surfaced again. Mr McWhinney, aged 39, who was the Chief Executive of the British Deaf Association, was summonsed for jury duty. He was described as 'an intelligent, hard-working, responsible man who has made a great contribution to life'. Despite this he was discharged from serving when it was realised that he was profoundly deaf. The only reason for this was that he would have had to have a sign interpreter with him in the jury room and there is no provision for any additional person to be present during a jury's deliberations.

8.3.2 Vetting

In criminal cases, once the list of potential jurors is known, both the prosecution and the defence have the right to see that list. In some cases it may be decided that this pool of potential jurors should be 'vetted', that is checked for suitability. There are two types of vetting. The first is where routine police checks are made on prospective jurors to eliminate those disqualified. In *R v Crown Court at Sheffield, ex p Brownlow* [1980] 2 All ER 444 the defendant was a police officer and the defence sought permission to vet the jury panel for convictions. The judge gave permission but the Court of Appeal, while holding that it had no power to interfere, said that vetting was 'unconstitutional' and a 'serious invasion of privacy' and not sanctioned by the Juries Act 1974. However, in *R v Mason* [1980] 3 All ER 777, where it was revealed that the Chief Constable for Northamptonshire had been condoning widespread use of unauthorised vetting of criminal records, the Court of Appeal approved of this type of vetting. Lawton LJ pointed out that, since it is a criminal offence to serve on a jury while disqualified, the police, by checking for criminal records, were only doing their normal duty of preventing crime. Further, the court said that, if in the course of looking at criminal records convictions were revealed which did not disqualify, there was no reason why these should not be passed on to prosecuting counsel, so that this information could be used in deciding to stand by individual jurors (see section 8.3.4 for information on the right of stand by).

The second type of vetting is where a wider check is made on a juror's background and political affiliations. This practice was brought to light by the 'ABC' trial in 1978 where two journalists and a soldier were charged with collecting secret information. It was discovered that the jurors had been vetted for their loyalty. The trial was stopped and a new trial ordered before a fresh jury. Following these cases the Attorney General in 1980 published guidelines on when political vetting of jurors should take place. These guidelines were revised in 1988 in a Practice Note (*Jury: Stand By; Jury Checks*) [1988] 3 All ER 1086 and state:

1. vetting should be used only in exceptional cases involving:
   (a) national security where part of the evidence is likely to be given in camera (in private);
   (b) terrorist cases;

2. vetting can only be carried out with the Attorney General's express permission.

8.3.3 At court

The jurors are usually divided into groups of 15 and allocated to a court. At the start of a trial the court clerk will select 12 out of these 15 at random. If there are not enough jurors to hear all the cases going scheduled for that day at the court, there is a special power to select anyone who is qualified to be a juror from people passing by in the streets or from local offices or businesses. This is called 'praying a talesman'. It is very unusual to use this power but it was used at Middlesex Crown Court in January 1992 when about half the jury panel failed to turn up after the New Year's holiday and there were not sufficient jurors to try the cases.

8.3.4 Challenging

Once the court clerk has selected the panel of 12 jurors, these jurors come into the jury box to be sworn in as jurors. At this point in criminal cases, before the jury is sworn both the prosecution and defence have certain rights to challenge one or more of the jurors. There is no right to challenge in a civil case. There are two challenges which can be made and, in addition, the prosecution have a special right of 'stand by'. These are:

1. To the array

This right to challenge is given by s5 of the Juries Act 1974 and it is a challenge to the whole jury on the basis that it has been chosen in an unrepresentative or biased way. This challenge was used successfully against the 'Romford' jury at the Old Bailey in 1993 when, out of a panel of 12 jurors, nine came from Romford, with two of them living within 20 doors of each other in the same street. In *R v Danvers* [1982] Crim LR 680 this method of challenging a jury was also used. In this case the defendant was of an ethnic minority background but all the jurors were white, so the defence used a challenge to the array on the basis that the jury did not reflect the ethnic composition of the area from which the jury was empanelled. The Court of Appeal held that in law there was no requirement that the jury should be ethnically mixed. Also in *R v Ford* [1989] 3 All ER 445 it was held that if the jury was chosen in a random manner then it could not be challenged simply because it was not multi-racial.

2. For cause

This involves challenging the right of an individual juror to sit on the jury. To be successful the challenge must point out a valid reason why that juror should not serve on the jury. An obvious reason is that the juror is disqualified, but a challenge for cause can also be made if the juror knows or is related to a witness or defendant. If such people are not removed from the jury there is the risk that any subsequent conviction could be quashed. This occurred in *R v Wilson and R v Sprason*, *The Times*, 24 February 1995:

CASE EXAMPLE

R v Wilson and R v Sprason, *The Times*, 24 February 1995

The wife of a prison officer was summonsed for jury service. She asked to be excused attendance on that ground, but this request had not been granted. She served on the jury which convicted the two defendants of robbery. Both defendants had been on remand at Exeter prison where the juror's husband worked. The Court of Appeal said that justice must not only be done but must be seen to be done and the presence of Mrs Roberts on the jury prevented that, so the convictions had to be quashed.

3. Prosecution right to stand by jurors

This is a right that only the prosecution can exercise. It allows the juror who has been stood by to be put to the end of the list of potential jurors so that they will not be used on the jury unless there are not enough other jurors. The prosecution does not have to give a reason for 'standing by', but the Attorney General's guidelines issued in 1988 make it clear that this power should be used sparingly.

When the prosecution uses this right, it has to make the decision to use it on the information provided through the vetting procedure. It cannot question the prospective juror in court. The system in the USA allows both prosecution and defence to question jurors to ensure that they are not biased or pre-judging the case, but this courtroom questioning is not allowed in our legal system.

8.3.5 Aids for the jury

All potential jurors are sent a leaflet when they are summonsed to do jury service. This leaflet gives them information on the selection process, including the right of challenge and the prosecution right to stand by jurors. The leaflet also tells them to inform the clerk of the court if they find that they know someone in the case to which they are assigned. At the start of their jury service at the court they are shown a video which explains the layout of the court and where the judge and lawyers and other people sit in it. Other essential matters are explained to them, such as the need to elect a foreman. Since 2004 they are also warned in criminal cases that if any one of them is concerned about the attitude and behaviour of another juror, for example because they are showing racial bias against a defendant, they must report this before the verdict is given. See section 8.7 for further information on this.

8.4 Juries in civil cases

Although juries in civil cases are very rare, it is still possible to have a trial by jury in certain civil cases. Where this occurs a jury in the High Court will have 12 members, while a jury in the County Court will have eight members. Juries in civil cases are now used only in very limited circumstances, but where they are used they have a dual role. They decide whether the claimant has proved his case or not; then, if they decide that the claimant has won the case, the jury also goes on to decide the amount of damages that the defendant should pay to the claimant.

Until 1854 all common-law actions were tried by jury, but from 1854 the parties could agree not to use a jury and gradually their use declined. Then in 1933 the Administration of Justice (Miscellaneous Provisions) Act limited the right to use a jury, so that juries could not be used in disputes over breach of contract. Juries continued to be used for all defamation cases and could also be used for other actions in tort.

KEY FACTS

Full measure

Basic qualifications	18–75 Registered as an elector Lived in UK for at least five years since 13th birthday	s1 Juries Act 1974 Jurors are randomly selected from the registers of electors by computer
Those not qualified	Mentally disordered persons include those who through mental illness are: • resident in a hospital or • regularly attend a doctor for treatment • under guardianship under s7 of the Mental Health Act 1983 or • judged to be incapable of administering his property and affairs	Sch 1, para 1 to the Criminal Justice Act 2003

Disqualified	• A life sentence • Imprisoned for public protection • An extended sentence • A custodial sentence of five or more years	All these are disqualified for life
	• A custodial sentence of less than five years • A suspended sentence • A community sentence or order	These are disqualified for ten years
Discretionary excusals	Full-time serving members of the forces if prejudicial to the efficiency of the service Those unable to do jury service for a good reason, e.g. illness	Normal expectation is that everyone will do jury service Deferral of service used rather than excusal
Lack of capacity	Unable to be an effective juror, e.g. too disabled or blind or unable to understand English Deafness is a lack of capacity if a sign interpreter is required	Can be discharged from service by the judge at the court *McWhinney* (1999) 13th person not allowed in jury room
Can be vetted	Vetting normally limited to checking for disqualifying convictions Vetting for background only allowed in case of: • national security • terrorism	Attorney General's guidelines (1988)
Can be challenged	To the array For cause Prosecution right of stand by	s5 Juries Act 1974 Attorney General's guidelines (1988)

8.4.1 Defamation cases

In 1971 the Faulks Committee was set up to consider the role of the jury in defamation cases. In its report, 'The Laws of Defamation', Cmnd 5709 (1974), it concluded that juries should no longer be allowed as of right in defamation cases. Instead there should be a discretion for a trial by jury to be allowed in certain types of cases.

The reasons it gave for recommending trial by judge alone as the normal method of trial in defamation cases included the following:

- in many cases there were matters to be decided where a judge was more competent, e.g. technical legal concepts such as fair comment and qualified privilege;
- judges gave their reasons for their decision whereas juries did not;
- juries were unpredictable;
- juries had difficulties with more complex cases;
- trial by jury was more expensive.

However, the Faulks Committee did concede that in a small number of cases trial by jury might be preferable. It pointed out:

QUOTATION

'We recognise it to be undesirable, that a judge sitting alone should be embroiled in a matter of political, religious or moral controversy. The same might be true where any party has been outspokenly critical of the Bench. Broadly, where the issue is whether the words were true or false and the subject is one that raises strong feelings among the general public so that a judge alone might be suspected, however mistakenly, of prejudice conscious or unconscious, we should expect that trial by jury might be awarded – but that in cases which did not involve such controversial questions a judge alone would be more likely to be selected.'

para 503

However, Parliament did not implement the recommendations of the Faulks Committee. Trial by jury in defamation cases continued to be a right where either party wanted it until 1981.

The present rules for when juries may be used in civil cases are set out in s69 of the Senior Courts Act 1981 for High Court cases and s66 of the County Courts Act 1984 for cases in that court. Section 69 of the Senior Courts Act 1981 states:

SECTION

's 69(1) Where, on the application of any party to an action to be tried in the Queen's Bench Division, the court is satisfied that there is in issue –

(a) a charge of fraud against that party; or

(b) a claim in respect of libel, slander, malicious prosecution or false imprisonment; or

(c) any question or issue of a kind prescribed for the purposes of this paragraph the action shall be tried with a jury, unless the court is of the opinion that the trial requires any prolonged examination of documents or accounts or any scientific or local investigation which cannot be conveniently made with a jury.

…

(3) An action to be tried in the Queen's Bench Division which does not by virtue of subsection (1) fall to be tried with a jury shall be tried without a jury unless the court in its discretion orders it to be tried with a jury.'

When the Bill which was to become the Senior Courts Act 1981 was going through Parliament, the government proposed an amendment which would have made trial by jury unavailable where the probable length of the case meant that it could not be conveniently tried by a jury. The case of *Orme v Associated Newspapers Group Ltd* 31 March 1981 unreported, had led to the attempt to make this amendment. In *Orme* the case had lasted more than 100 days (the then longest ever libel case). The amendment was voted against. However, in deciding applications for trial without a jury under s69, the courts have taken the word 'conveniently' to refer to the efficient administration of justice. This has allowed them to consider the probable length of the case as well as the other matters set out in s69. This was shown in *Goldsmith v Pressdram Ltd* [1987] 3 All ER 485 when Lawton LJ said:

JUDGMENT

'[a] trial by jury inevitably takes much longer than a trial by judge alone. If the trial is made much longer because of the time taken up by the jury examining documents, then an element of inconvenience arises.'

All the cases listed in s69(1) of the Senior Court Act 1981 involve character or reputation and it is for this reason that jury trial has been retained. However, even for these cases a jury trial can be refused by the judge if the case is thought to be unsuitable for jury trial because it involves complicated documents or accounts or scientific evidence. There have been libel cases in which the court has decided that the matter should be tried by a judge alone. This occurred in *Goldsmith v Pressdram Ltd* (1987) even though the alleged defamation involved suggesting that the claimant had committed a criminal offence.

CASE EXAMPLE

Goldsmith v Pressdram Ltd [1987] 3 All ER 485

The claimant was a director of a number of large international companies. The defendants published an article in the satirical magazine *Private Eye*, alleging that the claimant had been involved in secret share dealings. The defendants applied for the case to be tried by a judge alone, on the basis that their defence would involve detailed examination of complex multiple transactions carried out by the claimant. The claimant resisted this application, but the judge made an order for trial by judge alone. The claimant appealed against this decision to the Court of Appeal, which upheld the order for trial by judge.

The Court of Appeal did not think that the fact that the alleged defamation concerned criminal conduct was enough to outweigh the problems of lengthy examination of documents. Lawton LJ said:

JUDGMENT

'It is true that the allegation against Sir James [the claimant] is an unpleasant one. It charges him with criminal offences. His reputation, honour and integrity are, to some extent, in issue, but ... the fact that honour and integrity are under attack in a case is not an overriding factor in favour of trial with a jury ... This case, although it may be of importance to Sir James, cannot be said to be one affecting national interest or national personalities. It is a long way from such a case and, having regard to its undoubted complexity and the difficulties which a jury will have in following the detail of evidence, in my judgment the discretion of the court should not be exercised in favour of the [claimant].'

Another defamation case in which the defendants applied for jury trial but it was refused was *McDonald's Corporation v Steel and Morris* 1997 unreported (but see *The Times*, 20 June 1997). In the event, this case became the longest ever trial (partly because the defendants conducted their own defence without lawyers). Hearing for the trial took 313 days (from June 1994 to November 1996) and the judge then took another seven months to consider his judgment.

In *Beta Construction Ltd v Channel Four TV Co Ltd* [1990] 2 All ER 1012 the defendants had admitted liability in a libel action and the only matter to be decided was the amount of damages. This was going to involve a long and complicated examination of the claimants' accounts and other documents, as it was necessary to consider actual and estimated losses of their net profits. The claimants wanted the damages decided by a jury while the defendants wanted them to be assessed by a judge alone. The Court of Appeal upheld the decision not to use a jury. The court also set down factors to be considered whether a jury could conveniently decide a case where there would be 'prolonged examination of documents or accounts'. These were:

- the extent to which the presence of a jury might add to the length of the trial;
- the extent to which the presence of a jury might add to the cost of the trial by reason of its increased length and the necessity of photocopying a multitude of documents for use by the jury;
- any practical difficulties which a jury might cause, such as the physical problem of handling in the confines of a jury box large bundles of bulky documents;
- any special complexities in the documents or accounts which might lead a jury to misunderstand the issues in the case.

It is probable that with the use of computers in the courtrooms, the second and third points above are no longer valid.

Malicious prosecution

This is one of the other torts for which s69 of the Senior Court Act 1981 preserves a right to trial by jury unless the circumstances set out in the section are present. There are very few cases for malicious prosecution but in *Oliver v Calderdale Metropolitan Borough Council, The Times,* 7 July 1999 CA a judge at Halifax County Court rejected an application for jury trial by the claimant. The Court of Appeal upheld this decision, pointing out that there was no automatic right to jury trial. There was a presumption in favour of trial by jury but this could be displaced if any of the circumstances in subsection (3) were present. In the present case the claimant said he had suffered physical and psychological injury as a result of the malicious prosecution. There was clearly a significant dispute as to the claimant's psychological state and the case required close examination of the whole of the claimant's medical records. This made the case unsuitable for trial by jury.

8.4.2 Damages in defamation cases

In a defamation case, as in any civil case in which they are used, the jury decides the amount of damages. Until 1990 the Court of Appeal was unable to change this award. However, in the 1980s there were several high-profile cases in which juries gave extremely large awards of damages. These included:

- £300,000 to Koo Stark against the *Daily Mirror* for alleging that she had had a relationship with Prince Andrew;

- £500,000 to Jeffery Archer against the *Daily Star* for alleging that he had had sex with a prostitute (this was eventually repaid when Jeffery Archer was later convicted of committing perjury in the defamation case);

- £650,000 to Sonia Sutcliffe for an article in *Private Eye* which alleged that she had cashed in on the notoriety of her husband who had been convicted of several murders (the Yorkshire Ripper); the Court of Appeal did order a re-trial in this case so that the award of damages did not stand and Sonia Sutcliffe later accepted £60,000 in an out-of-court settlement.

These large awards led to a provision being included in the CLSA 1990 which allowed changes to be made to the appeal rules. As a result, since 1993 the Court of Appeal has on many occasions reduced over-large awards of damages. The first case in which this occurred was *Rantzen v Mirror Group Newspapers* [1993] 4 All ER 975 where the claimant had been awarded £250,000, the award was reduced to £110,000. The Court of Appeal said that the question to be asked was whether a reasonable jury could have thought the award was necessary to compensate the claimant and re-establish her reputation.

In later cases the Court of Appeal reduced awards by even greater amounts. In *John v Mirror Group Newspapers* [1996] 2 All ER 35, the Court of Appeal reduced a 'manifestly excessive' award of £350,000 to £75,000. The court also stressed that awards of libel damages should not be higher than awards for serious personal injury. Sir Thomas Bingham MR said:

JUDGMENT

'It is in our view offensive to public opinion, and rightly so, that a defamation [claimant] should recover damages for injury to reputation greater, perhaps by a significant factor, than if that same [claimant] had been a helpless cripple or an insensate vegetable. The time has in our view come when judges, and counsel, should be free to draw the attention of juries to these comparisons.'

8.4.3 Juries in personal injury cases

In other civil cases in the Queen's Bench Division of the High Court the parties can apply to a judge for trial by jury, but it is very rare for such a request to be granted. This follows the case of *Ward v James* [1965] 1 All ER 563 where the claimant was claiming for injuries caused in a road crash. In that case the Court of Appeal laid down guidelines for personal injury cases. These were, first, that normally personal injury cases should be tried by a judge sitting alone because such cases involved assessing compensatory damages which had to have regard to the conventional scales of damages. Second, that there had to be exceptional circumstances before the court would allow a jury to be used in such a case. Lord Denning explained the reasons for judges to make the decision on the amount of damages for personal injury:

JUDGMENT

'Recent cases show the desirability of three things. First, *assessability*: In cases of grave injury, where the body is wrecked or the brain destroyed, it is very difficult to assess a fair compensation in money, so difficult that the award must basically be a conventional figure, derived from experience or from awards in comparable cases. Second, *uniformity*: There should be some measure of uniformity in awards so that similar decisions are given in similar cases; otherwise there will be great dissatisfaction in the community, and much criticism of the administration of justice. Third, *predictability*: Parties should be able to predict with some measure of accuracy the sum which is likely to be awarded in a particular case, for by this means cases can be settled peaceably and not brought to court, a thing very much to the public good. None of these three is achieved when the damages are left at large to the jury.'

The decision in *Ward v James* (1965) effectively halved the number of civil jury trials. Before 1966 about 2 per cent of Queen's Bench Division cases were tried by jury, whereas in the years immediately following the case only about 1 per cent of Queen's Bench Division cases were tried by jury. Now there are very small numbers of trials by jury in the Queen's Bench Division; and since 1965 none of these has been in a personal injury case. In fact, there has been only one personal injury case since *Ward v James* (1965) in which the court granted trial with a jury. This was the following:

CASE EXAMPLE

Hodges v Harland and Wolff Ltd [1965] 1 All ER 1086

The claimant was operating an air compressor in the course of his work. The spindle on the machine was not properly guarded and it caught the claimant's trousers and tore away his penis and scrotum. He was left with the urge for sexual activity but was unable to perform the sexual act. He applied for the case to be tried with a jury and the Court of Appeal granted this.

It seems that the Court of Appeal was anxious to dispel fears that its decision in *Ward v James* (1965) had shown an intention to abolish the use of juries in civil cases. This was shown by Lord Denning's judgment in which he said:

JUDGMENT

'Naturally enough, we have been referred to the recent decision of this court in *Ward v James*. It is a mistake to suppose that this court in that case took away the right to trial by jury. It was not this court but Parliament itself which years ago took away any absolute right to trial by jury but left it to the discretion of the judges … What *Ward v James* did was this. It laid down the considerations which should be borne in mind by a judge when exercising his discretion: and it is apparent that, on those considerations, the result will ordinarily be trial by judge alone.'

Although the Court of Appeal granted trial by jury in *Hodges v Harland and Wolff* (1965) there have been very few applications for trial by jury in personal injury cases and the courts have not granted trial by jury in these. In *Singh v London Underground* 1990 unreported, a request for a jury to try a personal injury case arising from the King's Cross underground fire was refused. It was held that the case was unsuitable for jury trial because it involved such wide issues and technical points. The case of *H v Ministry of Defence* [1991] 2 All ER 834 further reinforced the rule in *Ward v James* (1965). In that case the defendant was a soldier who had received negligent medical treatment necessitating the amputation of part of his penis. He applied for jury trial, but it was held that jury trial for a personal injury claim would only be allowed in very exceptional circumstances and this case was not such a one. The court said that an example of when jury trial might be appropriate was where the injuries resulted from someone deliberately abusing their authority and there might well be a claim for exemplary damages.

KEY FACTS

Civil juries

Right to jury trial	Only in cases of: • fraud • malicious prosecution • defamation • false imprisonment	s69(1) Senior Courts Act 1981 s66 County Courts Act 1984
Limitation on right	Where there is need for: • prolonged examination of documents or accounts • any scientific or local investigation not suitable for jury	s69(1) Senior Courts Act 1981 *Beta Construction Ltd v Channel Four TV Co Ltd* (1990)
Right of appeal against jury award	Court of Appeal may reduce damages	*Rantzen v Mirror Group Newspapers* (1993)
Discretionary trial by jury	May be ordered by court *but* No such order made since 1965	s69(3) Senior Courts Act 1981 *Ward v James* (1965) *Hodges v Harland and Wolff Ltd* (1965)

8.5 Juries in Coroners' Courts

In these courts a jury of between seven and 11 members may be used to enquire into deaths. Under the Coroners and Justice Act 2009 where:

1. **a.** the death was a violent or unnatural one, or

   b. the cause of death is unknown;

2. the death resulted from an act or omission of a police officer;

3. the death was caused by a notifiable accident, poisoning or disease.

Where a jury is used in the Coroners' Court then its role is to decide on how the death was caused. The verdicts a jury can give include:

- death by unlawful killing;
- death from natural causes;

- death from dependence on drugs or through drug abuse;
- death by misadventure (accident); or
- that the deceased killed himself.

8.6 Juries in criminal cases

indictment
The document setting out the criminal charges against the defendant

The most important use of a jury today is in the Crown Court where it decides whether the defendant is guilty or not guilty. There are two categories of offence which can be tried with a jury at the Crown Court. The first of these is indictable-only offences which are the most serious offences and must be tried on **indictment** at the Crown Court.

The second category is triable either way offences which may be sent from the Magistrates' Court to the Crown Court for trial (see Chapter 5 for more detail). Jury trials, however, account for only about 1 per cent of all criminal trials. This is because 98 per cent of cases are dealt with in the Magistrates' Court and of the cases that go to the Crown Court, about two out of every three defendants will plead guilty. Also, some of the cases at the Crown Court where the defendant is pleading not guilty may be dismissed by the judge without any trial. This happens when the CPS withdraws the charges. This might occur because the prosecution now has evidence which shows that the defendant is not guilty or the prosecution may feel that its case is too weak to continue with the prosecution.

It is also worth noting that, where the defendant has a choice of being tried in the Magistrates' Court or by a jury at the Crown Court, only about one out of every 20 defendants chooses to go to the Crown Court.

At the Crown Court the trial is presided over by a judge and the functions are split between the judge and jury. The judge decides points of law and the jury decides the facts. At the end of the prosecution case, the judge has the power to direct the jury to acquit the defendant if he decides that in law the prosecution's evidence has not made out a case against the defendant. This is called a **directed acquittal** and occurs in about 10 per cent of cases.

Trial without a jury

Recent legislation has made provision for trials in special circumstances to be conducted in the Crown Court by a judge alone without a jury. Section 44 of the Criminal Justice Act 2003 allows the prosecution to apply for trial by judge alone where there is evidence of 'a real and present danger that jury tampering would take place'. It must also be shown that it is necessary in the interests of justice for the trial to be conducted without a jury. The first trial without a jury was approved in *R v Twomey and others* [2009] EWCA Crim 1035.

CASE EXAMPLE

R v Twomey and others [2009] EWCA Crim 1035

The defendants were charged with various offences connected to a large robbery from a warehouse at Heathrow. Three previous trials had collapsed and there had been a 'serious attempt at jury tampering' in the third trial. The prosecution applied to a single judge for the trial to take place without a jury. The judge refused but the Court of Appeal overturned this decision, ordering that the trial should take place without a jury.

Also the Domestic Violence, Crime and Victims Act 2004 allows for trial by judge alone for some counts where the defendant is charged with a large number of linked offences. However, this can only occur if the defendant has been tried and found guilty by a jury of some of the counts (see section 8.10.4 for more details).

8.6.1 Verdicts

Where the trial continues then the defence case is put and at the end of the case the judge sums up the case to the jury and directs it on any law involved. The jury retires to a private room and makes the decision on the guilt or innocence of the accused in secret. Initially the members of the jury must try to come to a unanimous verdict, that is one on which the jurors are all agreed. The judge must accept the jury verdict, even if he or she does not agree with it. This long-established principle goes back to *Bushell's Case* (1670). The jury does not give any reasons for its decision.

Majority verdicts

If after at least two hours (longer where there are several defendants) the jury has not reached a verdict, the judge can call the jurors back into the courtroom and direct them that he can now accept a majority verdict. Majority verdicts have been allowed since 1967. Where there is a full jury of 12, the verdict can be 10–2 or 11–1 either for guilty or for not guilty. If the jury has fallen below 12 for any reason such as the death or illness of a juror during the trial, then only one can disagree with the verdict. That is, if there are 11 jurors the verdict can be 10–1; if there are ten jurors it can be 9–1. If there are only nine jurors the verdict must be unanimous. A jury cannot go below nine members.

Majority verdicts were introduced because of the fear of jury 'nobbling', that is jurors being bribed or intimidated by associates of the defendant into voting for a not guilty verdict. When a jury had to be unanimous, only one member needed to be bribed to cause a 'stalemate' in which the jury was unable to reach a decision. It was also thought that the acquittal rates in jury trials were too high and that majority decisions would result in more convictions.

Where the jury convicts a defendant on a majority verdict the foreman of the jury must announce the numbers, both agreeing and disagreeing with the verdict in open court. This provision is contained in s17(3) of the Juries Act 1974 and is aimed at making sure the jury has come to a legal majority, and not one, for example, of eight to four, which is not allowed. Originally this section was interpreted as meaning that the foreman had to announce both the majority for conviction and the number of those who did not agree with the verdict. In *R v Reynolds* [1981] 3 All ER 849 the foreman announced only the number for the conviction (ten), but did not announce that two disagreed. The Court of Appeal quashed the conviction.

However, in *R v Pigg* [1983] 1 All ER 56, the House of Lords held that, provided that the foreman announced the number who had agreed with the verdict, and that number was within the number allowed for a majority verdict, then the conviction was legal. It did not matter that the foreman had not also been asked how many disagreed with the verdict. More than one-fifth of convictions by juries each year are by majority verdict.

It is not known how many acquittals are by majority verdict as the fact that it was a majority decision is not announced by the foreman when the verdict is given.

8.7 Secrecy of the jury room

The jury discussion takes place in secret and there can be no inquiry into how the jury reached its verdict. This is because s8 of the Contempt of Court Act 1981 makes disclosure of anything that happened in the jury room contempt of court which is a criminal offence.

SECTION

's 8(1) Subject to subsection (2) below, it is a contempt of court to obtain, disclose or solicit any particulars of statements made, opinions expressed, arguments advanced or votes cast by members of a jury in the course of their deliberations in any legal proceedings.

(2) This section does not apply to any disclosure of any particulars –

    (a) in the proceedings in question for the purpose of enabling the jury to arrive at their verdict, or in connection with the delivery of that verdict; or

    (b) in evidence in any subsequent proceedings for an offence alleged to have been committed in relation to the jury in the first mentioned proceedings, or to the publication of any particulars so disclosed.'

The section was brought in because newspapers were paying jurors large sums of money for 'their story'. This is obviously not desirable. In *Attorney General v Associated Newspapers Ltd* [1994] 1 All ER 556, the House of Lords held that s8 applies even where the information which is disclosed is obtained from a third party.

CASE EXAMPLE

Attorney General v Associated Newspapers Ltd [1994] 1 All ER 556

The *Mail on Sunday* published details of the jury's deliberations in the Blue Arrow fraud case. The information had been obtained from two members of the jury by an independent researcher who later gave transcripts of the interviews to a journalist. The convictions of the newspaper, its editor and the journalist concerned under s8 were upheld by the House of Lords. It ruled that the word 'disclose' in s8 applied to both the revelation of deliberations by jurors and any further disclosure by publication. It did not matter that the information of what happened in the jury room had come indirectly through another person.

However, the total ban on finding out what happened in the jury room means that it is difficult to discover whether jurors have understood the evidence in complex cases. The Runciman Commission (1993) recommended that s8 should be changed to allow research into the workings of juries. It was thought that in particular there should be research into the influence that jurors with criminal convictions may have on jury verdicts. However, Lord Justice Auld, in his review of the criminal justice system (2001), disagreed and thought that s8 should remain (Ch 5, paras 82–87).

The use of social media on the internet has also led to contempt of court as in *Attorney General v Fraill and Seward* [2011] EWCA Crim 1570.

CASE EXAMPLE

Attorney General v Fraill and Seward [2011] EWCA Crim 1570

Fraill was a member of the jury trying the case against Seward and her co-defendant, Knox. Seward was acquitted and, whilst the jury was still deliberating the charges against Knox, Fraill contacted Seward via Facebook and disclosed information about the jury's deliberations. Fraill also conducted internet research about Knox. Fraill admitted contempt of court through disclosing information and also her internet research. Seward was found guilty of soliciting information about the jury's deliberations. Fraill was committed to prison for 18 months and Seward given a suspended sentence.

In this case the Court of Appeal also commented on the use of the internet by jurors to conduct research. This problem is discussed more fully in the next section.

8.7.1 Common law rule

A further protection of the secrecy of the jury room is the fact that the appeal courts will not look into any alleged irregularities in the jury room once the verdict has been given. This is a long-standing common law rule as dating from the case of *Vaise v Delaval* [1785] 1 TR 11; 99 ER 944, KB in which the court refused to consider **affidavits** (sworn written statements) from two jurors indicating that they had decided on their verdict by tossing a coin.

The reason given by the court for refusing to consider the affidavits was to protect the jurors from self-incrimination for what Lord Mansfield described as 'a very high misdemeanour'. Since that case the courts have refused to admit evidence of what occurred in the jury room. The rule was applied in *R v Thompson* [1962] 1 All ER 65.

affidavit

A written statement of facts which the maker has sworn are true

CASE EXAMPLE

R v Thompson [1962] 1 All ER 65

After the defendant had been convicted, but before sentence had been passed, one of the jurors told a member of the public that a majority of members of the jury had been in favour of an acquittal until the foreman of the jury produced a list of the defendant's previous convictions. The defendant appealed against his conviction but the Court of Criminal Appeal refused to accept evidence of what happened in the jury room and upheld the conviction.

The rule also applies in civil cases. The rationale for the rule was explained by Atkin LJ in *Ellis v Deheer* [1922] 2 KB 113:

JUDGMENT

'The reason why that evidence is not admitted is twofold, on the one hand it is in order to secure the finality of decisions arrived at by the jury, and on the other to protect the jurymen themselves and prevent their being exposed to pressure to explain the reasons which actuated them in arriving at their verdict. To my mind it is a principle of highest importance in the interests of justice to maintain, and an infringement of the rule appears to me a very serious interference with the administration of justice.'

However, in *Ellis v Deheer* (1922), the Court of Appeal did allow an application for a new trial of a civil case. This was because the foreman had not given the verdict which the jury had agreed on. The other members of the jury had not raised the matter when the verdict was given because they were placed in a position in the courtroom where they could not hear what the foreman said. The Court of Appeal held that their decision did not infringe the rule as the jurors could not see or hear what was taking place when the verdict was announced.

The Court of Appeal has also ruled that it is permissible to investigate any happenings outside the jury room, even though these may affect the jury's deliberations. This occurred in the somewhat unusual case of *R v Young* [1995] 2 WLR 430:

CASE EXAMPLE

R v Young [1995] 2 WLR 430

The defendant was charged with the murder of two people. The jury members had to stay overnight in a hotel as they had not reached a verdict by the end of the first day of discussion. During this stay at the hotel four members of the jury held a seance using a Ouija board to try to contact the dead victims and ask who had killed them. The next day the jury returned a verdict of guilty. When the fact that the Ouija board had been used became known, the defendant appealed and the Court of Appeal quashed the verdict and ordered a re-trial of the case. The court felt able to inquire into what had happened as it was in a hotel and not part of the jury discussions in the jury room.

Internet research

In *R v Karakaya* [2005] EWCA Crim 346, where the case was adjourned overnight when the jury was deliberating, a juror did an internet search and brought the information into the jury room. The printouts of the internet material were discovered by the jury bailiff. The Court of Appeal held that this contravened the fundamental rule that no evidence was to be introduced after the jury had retired to consider its verdict and the conviction was quashed as being unsafe.

Judges do direct jurors not to look at the internet for information, but it seems that the use of internet research by jurors is becoming more common. In Cheryl Thomas' research, 'Are Juries Fair?' (2009), she found that 12 per cent of jurors admitted they had looked on the internet for information about cases they were trying. The risk of using the internet is that the information may be prejudicial to the defendant. For example, doing a search on a defendant's name may find newspaper reports of previous convictions, which the jury should not know about. Also defendants have been known to upload highly personal information regarding their own behaviour and even crimes, on to social networking sites.

In *Attorney General v Fraill and Seward* (2011) the Court of Appeal committed Fraill to prison for contempt of court as she had both disclosed information about the jury's deliberation and conducted internet research regarding one of the defendants. The Court emphasised that jurors promise on oath or by affirmation to return a true verdict according to the evidence. This promise underpins the jury system. So, enquiries made by jurors on the internet have the potential to undermine the jury system and public confidence in it. The jury's deliberations must be based exclusively on the evidence given in court.

As a result of concerns about jurors conducting their own research on the cases they are trying, the Criminal Justice and Courts Act 2015 was passed. This Act creates new criminal offences which prohibit jurors from conducting their own research on the cases they are trying, prohibit jurors from sharing that research with other jurors, prohibit jurors from deciding the case with reference to evidence that was not introduced in court and prohibit jurors from sharing any details of their deliberations. These are serious offences, triable in the Crown Court, with a maximum punishment of two years' imprisonment.

Consultation on jury room secrecy

In 2005 a consultation paper, 'Jury Research and Impropriety', CP 04/05 was issued proposing allowing 'sensitively conducted' research into jury discussions. The 'Summary of Responses' to this consultation was published in November 2005. This showed:

- the majority of respondents were in favour of allowing some form of research into the approach of juries to cases they tried;
- about 75 per cent of respondents were against allowing an independent party access to the deliberating room;
- most respondents rejected the idea of using CCTV to research jury deliberations;
- about 75 per cent of respondents considered that, following *R v Mirza* [2004] 1 All ER 925, it was unnecessary to amend the common law rule whereby the court would not inquire into jury discussions in the jury room.

The government's conclusion was that further research into the jury decision-making process would be valuable. However, this could be done within the confines of the present law: for example by using shadow juries. In fact, Cheryl Thomas' research 'Diversity and Fairness in the Jury System' (Ministry of Justice Research Series 02/07

2007), used case simulation with real jurors, supplemented by a study of jury verdicts in real cases when researching the impact of race on decision making.

The government stated it was not, in principle, against amending s8 of the Contempt of Court Act 1981 to allow jury research, but no change has been made to the law.

8.7.2 Human rights and jury secrecy

In the appeals of *R v Connor: R v Mirza (Conjoined appeals)* [2004] UKHL 4 the question was raised whether the refusal to admit evidence of any irregularity in the jury room was an infringement of the right to a fair trial under Article 6 of the ECHR (the right to a fair trial). The House of Lords (Lord Steyn dissenting) ruled that it did not. Two separate cases were considered in the appeal. These were:

CASE EXAMPLE

R v Connor and Rollock [2004] UKHL 4

The two defendants were jointly charged with wounding. They were both convicted by a majority verdict of 10–2. Five days after the verdict (but before sentence was passed) one of the jurors wrote to the Crown Court, stating that while many jurors thought it was one or other of the defendants who had committed the stabbing, they would convict both in order to 'teach them a lesson'. The complaining juror said that, when she argued that the jury should have considered which defendant was responsible, her co-jurors had refused to listen and remarked that if they did that it could take a week considering verdicts in the case.

R v Mirza [2004] UKHL 4

The defendant was a Pakistani who settled in the UK in 1988. He had an interpreter to help him in the trial and during the trial the jury sent notes asking why he needed an interpreter. He was convicted on a 10–2 majority. Six days after the jury verdict, one juror wrote to the defendant's counsel, alleging that from the start of the trial there had been a 'theory' that the use of an interpreter was a 'ploy'. The juror also said that she had been shouted down when she objected and reminded her fellow jurors of the judge's directions.

The House of Lords dismissed both appeals. It held that the common law rule which protected jurors' confidentiality and which precluded the court from admitting evidence of what had happened in the jury room after the verdict had been given was still effective. It also held that this rule was compatible with Article 6.

On the human rights point Lord Hope pointed out what had been said by the ECtHR in *Gregory v United Kingdom* [1997] 25 EHRR 577:

JUDGMENT

'The court acknowledges that the rule governing the secrecy of jury deliberations is a crucial and legitimate feature of English trial law which serves to reinforce the jury's role as the ultimate arbiter of fact and to guarantee open and frank deliberations among jurors on the evidence which they have heard.'

Lord Hope accepted that in the later case of *Sander v United Kingdom* [2000] 31 EHRR 1003 the majority decision of the ECtHR did not repeat this observation. However, it was referred to by Sir Nicholas Bratza in his dissenting opinion in *Sander v United Kingdom* (2000). Lord Hope, in *R v Connor: R v Mirza* (2004), pointed out that, in view of that dissent, the European Court did not depart from the rule in any respect in *Sander* and that nothing was said in the judgment which cast doubt on the validity of the rule.

When deciding that the rule should remain in English law the Lords pointed out:

- confidentiality was essential to the proper functioning of the jury process;
- there was merit in finality;
- jurors had to be protected from harassment.

The Lords did accept that there might be exceptional circumstances where it would be right to inquire into what occurred in the jury room. Lord Slynn said:

JUDGMENT

'The admission of evidence as to what happened in the jury room cannot be allowed without seriously detracting from the advantages which flow from the present system and which, in my view, need to be protected. If a case arose when all the jurors agreed that something occurred which in effect meant that the jury abrogated its functions and eg decided on the toss of a coin the case might be, and in my opinion would be, different. In the present case everything that happened is said to have happened in the jury room.'

Lord Steyn dissented. He would have allowed the appeal in *Mirza* (2004). He thought that s8 of the Contempt of Court Act 1981 did not affect the Court of Appeal's jurisdiction to receive evidence it regarded as relevant to the disposal of an appeal. On the human rights aspect he thought that there was a breach of Article 6 where there was known to have been a real risk of racial bias affecting the decision. In these exceptional circumstances he held that the appeal court should admit evidence of what had occurred in the jury room.

8.7.3 Practice Direction

Following the House of Lords' decision in *Connor and Mirza* (2004) a Practice Direction (*Crown Court: Guidance to Jurors*) [2004] 1 WLR 665 has been issued. This sets out:

QUOTATION

'Trial judges should ensure that the jury is alerted to the need to bring any concerns about fellow jurors to the attention of the judge at the time and not wait until the case is concluded. At the same time, it is undesirable to encourage inappropriate criticism of fellow jurors, or to threaten jurors with contempt of court.'

ACTIVITY

Essay writing

Critically discuss whether it is right or necessary to protect the secrecy of deliberations in the jury room.

8.8 Research into juries

The rigid rule that jury discussions must be kept secret has meant that research into how juries reach a verdict has been limited. Much of the research into how juries reach a verdict has been done by using a 'shadow' or a 'mock' jury. A shadow jury is one which sits in the courtroom and when the real jury withdraws to consider its verdict so does the shadow jury, but this is not in secret but in front of cameras. A mock jury is where the jury members watch a simulated case (or listen to a tape recording) and then deliberate on the verdict in front of cameras. In each case 12 people are selected in the same way as a real jury would be.

In 1974 the Oxford Penal Research Unit conducted a study with shadow juries looking at 30 cases. They found that the shadow juries took their task very seriously. S McCabe and R Purves wrote in *The Shadow Jury at Work* (Blackwell, 1974, pp 62–63):

QUOTATION

'The "shadow" juries showed considerable determination in looking for evidence upon which convictions could be based; when it seemed inadequate, they were not prepared to allow their own "hunch" that the defendant was involved in some way in the offence that was charged to stand in the way of an acquittal...

There was little evidence of perversity in the final decisions of these 30 groups. One acquittal only showed that sympathy and impatience with the triviality of the case so influenced the "shadow" jurors' view of the evidence that they refused to convict. One other unexpected acquittal seemed to be wholly due to dissatisfaction with the evidence.'

Other research on jury verdicts has been carried out by asking the judge and/or lawyers in the case whether they agreed with the jury verdict or not. This method of research was used by J Baldwin and M McConville in their research *Jury Trials* (Clarendon, 1979). They selected a random sample of 500 defendants who had been tried at Birmingham Crown Court and compared the actual verdict with the views of the judge, prosecuting solicitor, defence solicitor, the police and the defendant. Their findings were that jury decisions seemed to be unsatisfactory in a surprising number of cases. They found that one-quarter of acquittals were thought to be doubtful or highly questionable by three or more of the respondents. Even more worrying was the fact that about one in 20 convictions was also thought to be doubtful or highly questionable.

The same method of questioning other participants in the trials was used by researchers carrying out investigations for the Runciman Commission (1993). They looked into about 800 cases across the country over a two-week period in the Crown Court Study (M Zander and P Henderson, 'Royal Commission on Criminal Justice,' Research Study No 19, 1993). Questionnaires were given to judges, prosecuting and defence lawyers, the police and jurors. The questions to the jurors were carefully framed to make sure that there was no breach of s8 of the Contempt of Court Act 1981. Jurors were asked 'How difficult was it for you to understand the evidence?' Ninety-one per cent thought that it was either 'not at all difficult' or 'not very difficult'. Over 90 per cent of jurors also thought that the jury as a whole had understood the evidence. However just under 10 per cent of jurors admitted that they had had difficulty. When the foremen of juries were questioned on the same point, they thought that a small number of jurors (0.2 per cent) could not understand English sufficiently well to follow a case. The foremen also thought that about 1 per cent of jurors could not understand the details of a case, while another 1 per cent could not understand any case. These may be small numbers, but it is still worrying that in some cases a defendant's future is being decided by some members of the public who do not understand the case.

The other participants in the study were asked whether they thought that the jury's verdict was surprising. The results were not as pessimistic as those revealed by Baldwin and McConville, although there were still thought to be questionable verdicts. Prosecution and defence lawyers and the judges thought that between 2 and 4 per cent of jury decisions were surprising and inexplicable. The police thought that 8 per cent of the verdicts were inexplicable.

Recent research

The most recent research into the jury system in England and Wales has been by Cheryl Thomas. She has published two reports 'Diversity and Fairness in the Jury System' (Ministry of Justice Research Series 02/07, 2007) and 'Are Juries Fair?' (Ministry of Justice Research Series 1/10, 2010). The 2007 jury service study provides the most detailed look at representation among serving jurors that has been conducted to date for Crown Courts in England and Wales. The jury service study was conducted in the three Crown Courts during 2003, prior to the introduction of new juror eligibility rules in 2004. The study established that jury pools at individual courts closely reflected the local population in terms of gender and age:

QUOTATION

'88 per cent of all the juries had either a 6:6, 7:5 or 8:4 gender split: and there were no all-male or all-female juries in any of the courts. These findings strengthen the conclusion ... that the under-representation of women among serving jurors is yet another myth of jury service.'

The study also found that black and minority ethnic (BME) were reasonably represented:

QUOTATION

'In all three courts, BME representation in the jury pool fluctuated on a weekly basis, but overall there was no significant under-representation of BME jurors, and the fluctuations included both under and over-representation of BME jurors in relation to the BME population levels in the local areas.'

The 2010 study 'Are Juries Fair?' looked at various aspects of the use of juries. One area was jurors' understanding of cases. A series of simulated trials was used in order to test understanding. A total of 797 jurors in three different areas all saw the same simulated trial and heard exactly the same judicial directions on the law.

The jurors were first asked whether they thought they had understood the directions. In two of the areas, Blackfriars, London and Winchester, over two-thirds of the jurors felt they were able to understand the directions. In Nottingham only just under half of the jurors felt they had understood the directions.

The jurors' understanding of the directions was then tested. This showed that only 31 per cent of the jurors had actually understood the directions fully from the legal terms used by the judge. When the jurors were given a written summary of the instructions, the number who fully understood increased to 48 per cent.

This study showed that, even with a written summary, less than half of jurors fully understood the judge's directions.

Australian research

Jurors' understanding of cases was also considered in Australian research, 'Child Sexual Assault Trials: A Survey of Juror Perceptions' (New South Wales Bureau of Crime Statistics and Research, Bulletin 102, September 2006). The Australian research was into 32 trials about child abuse. It involved aspects such as how jurors thought the child witness had been treated in the case as well as their understanding of the case. It revealed that some jurors did not know what verdict had been given in the case they had just tried.

The jurors were given a questionnaire immediately after the verdict had been given; 277 jurors took part. The first question asked 'What was the verdict in this case?' Only in one-quarter of the trials did all the jurors give the correct answer. In the other cases at least one juror gave an incorrect version of the verdict. In one case four jurors said that the accused had been found guilty when he had actually been found not guilty.

The researchers pointed out that it was possible that jurors were expressing their own view of what they thought the verdict should have been. However, they go on to state that it seemed some jurors were confused, unclear or uncertain about the verdict. This raises the worry that, if jurors do not know what the verdict was immediately after that verdict has been given, there must be doubts about how much of the case the jurors had understood. The findings of this survey are in contrast to a recent small-scale research into judges' opinions of jurors' understanding of fraud cases.

Serious fraud trials
In this research, 'Judicial Perspectives on the Conduct of Serious Fraud Trials', by Robert Julian [2007] *Crim LR* 751–768, nine judges who had tried a serious fraud case were interviewed as to their opinions of the role of the jury in such cases. The judges were of the opinion that the jurors in such cases had understood the case. Indeed most judges said that they were more likely to agree with the jury's verdict in a complex fraud case than in other cases.

8.9 Advantages of trial by jury

8.9.1 Public confidence
On the face of it, asking 12 strangers who have no legal knowledge and without any training to decide what may be complicated and technical points is an absurd idea. Yet trial by jury is considered as one of the fundamentals of a democratic society. The right to be tried by one's peers is the bastion of liberty against the state and has been supported by eminent judges. For example, Lord Devlin said that juries are 'the lamp that shows that freedom lives'. The tradition of trial by jury is very old and people seem to have confidence in the impartiality and fairness of a jury trial. This can be seen in the objection to proposals to limit the right to trial by jury (see section 5.9).

The use of a jury is viewed as making the legal system more open. Justice is seen to be done as members of the public are involved in such a key role and the whole process is public. It also helps to keep the law clearer as points have to be explained to the jury and it enables the defendant to understand the case more easily. It prevents the criminal justice system from being completely dominated by professional judges. This is considered important as judges are perceived by the public as being remote from everyday life.

8.9.2 Jury equity
Since juries are not legal experts they are not bound to follow the precedents of past cases or even Acts of Parliament. Also, juries do not have to give reasons for their verdict. In view of these two facts it is possible for them to decide cases on their idea of 'fairness'. This is sometimes referred to as 'jury equity'. It is likely to occur where a jury believes the law to be unfair and, as a result, refuses to convict the defendant. In some instances the government has amended the law following a jury verdict showing disapproval of the existing law. The clearest example is *Ponting's Case* 1984, unreported:

CASE EXAMPLE

Ponting's Case 1984, unreported

A civil servant was charged under the old wide-ranging s2 of the Official Secrets Act 1911. He had leaked information on the sinking of the ship, the *General Belgrano*, in the Falklands war to a Member of Parliament. He pleaded not guilty, claiming that his actions had been in the public interest. The jury refused to convict him even though the judge ruled that there was no defence. The case prompted the government to reconsider the law and amend s2 of the 1911 Act.

A more recent example of jury equity is the case of the Kingsnorth six. In 2008 a jury at Maidstone Crown Court found six defendants who caused damage to the Kingsnorth coal-fired power station not guilty of criminal damage. The six had relied on a defence in s5 of the Criminal Damage Act 1971 of protection of property. They claimed that their actions were in order to prevent damage from global warming.

8.9.3 Panel of 12

It is thought that having 12 people making the decision is fairer than having one person deciding the verdict. Twelve people will bring a much wider set of experiences to a case than one person can do. In addition, any biases should be cancelled out. The random selection of 12 people to each jury panel also helps to prevent bias. It is also thought that honesty and reputation are best assessed by 12 ordinary people. For example, in the law of theft the test for dishonesty has to be established according to the standards of ordinary people. In other areas of law the test may involve deciding what is reasonable in the circumstances; for example in the law on self-defence. This is a matter on which a panel of 12 ordinary people can make the decision.

8.10 Disadvantages of trial by jury

8.10.1 Racial composition and bias

Although jurors have no direct interest in a case, and despite the fact that there are 12 of them, they may still have prejudices which can affect the verdict. Some jurors may be biased against the police. This is one of the reasons why those with certain criminal convictions are disqualified from sitting on a jury. In particular there is the worry that some jurors are racially prejudiced. This is worrying as the random selection of jury panels can produce a jury which does not contain anyone from the defendant's ethnic minority group. This was the situation that occurred in *R v Ford* [1989] 3 All ER 445. The defendant asked the judge to order that a new panel be selected but the judge refused. The defendant appealed and the Court of Appeal ruled that the judge could not interfere with the empanelling of the jury simply because it did not produce a racially mixed panel. Lord Lane LCJ said:

JUDGMENT

'The conclusion is that, however well intentioned the judge's motive might be, the judge has no power to influence the composition of the jury, and that it is wrong for him to attempt to do so. If it should ever become desirable that the principle of random selection should be altered, that will have to be done by way of statute and cannot be done by any judicial decision.'

The point was raised again in *R v Smith* [2003] EWCA Crim 283. In this case the defence submitted that the decision in *Ford* (1989) could not stand in the light of the implementation of the HRA 1998 which incorporated Article 6 of the ECHR, giving a right to a fair trial. The defence asked the Court of Appeal to declare s1 of the Juries Act 1974 to be incompatible with the 1998 Act. The Court of Appeal rejected this argument, saying:

JUDGMENT

'We do not accept that it was unfair for the appellant to be tried by an all-white jury or that the fair-minded and informed observer would regard it as unfair. We do not accept that, on the facts of this case, the trial could only be fair if members of the defendant's race were present on the jury. It was not a case where consideration of the evidence required knowledge of the traditions or social circumstances of a particular racial group. The situation was an all too common one, violence late at night outside a club, and a randomly selected jury was entirely capable of trying the issues fairly and impartially.'

The Court of Appeal referred to the decision of the ECtHR in *Gregory v United Kingdom* [1997] 25 EHRR 577 where evidence of racial bias had come to light during the course of the trial. In that case there was held to have been no breach of Article 6 since the trial judge had dealt with the matter in an adequate way. The Court of Appeal in *Smith* (2003) pointed out that the ECtHR in *Gregory* (1997) had not impugned the legitimacy of the jury system or the procedure by which juries are selected in this country. The Court of Appeal also pointed out that in *Gregory* (1997) there was reference to 'personal impartiality being assumed until there is evidence to the contrary'.

However, where there is proof of bias then the courts have taken a different view on the fairness of trials. In *Sander v United Kingdom* [2000] 31 EHRR 1003; [2000] Crim LR 767 the ECtHR ruled that there had been a breach of Article 6 of the ECHR.

CASE EXAMPLE

Sander v United Kingdom [2000] 31 EHRR 1003; [2000] Crim LR 767

During the trial one juror wrote a note to the judge, raising concern over the fact that other jurors had been openly making racist remarks and jokes. The judge asked the jurors to 'search their consciences'. The next day the judge received two letters, one signed by all the jurors (including the juror who had made the complaint) in which they denied any racist attitudes and a second from one juror who admitted that he may have been the one making racist jokes. Despite the discrepancy between the two letters, the judge allowed the case to continue. The ECtHR held that in these circumstances the judge should have discharged the jury as there was an obvious risk of racial bias.

The possibility of racial bias was shown by the research into juries by Baldwin and McConville in 1979 in which the legal professionals in the cases had serious doubts about the correctness of convictions in one out of every 20 convictions. It was apparent that black defendants were more likely to fall into this 'doubtful' conviction category than white defendants (see section 8.8).

This risk of racial prejudice was the reason that the Runciman Commission recommended that up to three jurors should be drawn from ethnic minority cases in certain cases where either the defendant or a victim was from an ethic minority and there was some special and unusual feature to the case. Lord Justice Auld also made the same recommendation in his review of the criminal justice system in 2001. However, the government rejected this proposal. The reasons for the rejection were set out in the White

Paper, 'Justice for All', Cm 5563 (2001). Paragraph 7.29 stated that it was thought wrong to interfere with the composition of the jury as this would potentially:

- undermine the fundamental principle of random selection and would not achieve a truly representative jury of peers;
- assume bias on the part of excluded jurors when no prejudice has been proved;
- place the selected minority ethnic jurors in a difficult position – they might feel that they are expected to represent the interests of the defendant or victim;
- generate tensions and divisions in the jury room instead of reaching consensus on the guilt or innocence of the accused based on the evidence put before it;
- place undue weight on the views of the especially selected jurors; and
- place a new burden on the court to determine which cases should attract an 'ethnic minority quota' and provide a ground for unmeritorious appeals.

Another way of preventing bias and allowing 'justice to be seen to be done' could be to reinstate the defence's right of peremptory challenge (a right which existed up to 1988 under which the defence could challenge a certain number of jurors without having to give a reason and remove them from the jury panel). This would allow defendants a limited choice over who sits on a jury and might create a racially mixed jury.

Research

Possibly the worries about the racial make-up of juries are no longer valid. Cheryl Thomas found in her study, 'Diversity and Fairness in the Jury System' (Ministry of Justice Research Series 02/07, 2007) that black and ethnic minority groups were reasonably represented in jury panels. Research was also conducted into the impact of race on decision making. This was carried through case simulations with jurors, supplemented by a study of jury verdicts in real cases. The main finding of the case simulation study was that the verdicts of racially mixed juries did not discriminate against defendants because of their race. The outcomes were very similar for white, Asian and black defendants.

In 'Are Juries Fair?' (2010) Cheryl Thomas looked at whether there was bias in cases where a defendant from a black ethnic minority was tried by an all-white jury. This was done by using two main methods:

- case simulations (mock trials) which used 41 juries with 478 jurors;
- analysis of over half a million charges tried in the period 1 October 2006 to 31 March 2008.

In the mock trials no racial discrimination was shown. The verdicts from the real cases during 2006–08 showed only small differences based on the defendant's ethnicity. White and Asian defendants both had a 63 per cent jury conviction rate; black defendants had a 67 per cent jury conviction rate.

However, there are still occasional cases that show a possibility of racial bias occurring. An example is *R v Heward* [2012] EWCA Crim 890 in which a juror sent a note to the trial judge saying 'To Judge, I believe that the members of the jury are being unfair and supporting their own race.' Before the judge could call the jury back into court and give them further instructions, the jury reached its verdict. The judge decided not to inquire any further. The Court of Appeal held that despite a verdict having been reached, the judge was under a duty to ensure that the verdict had been reached without bias. They quashed the conviction saying that they were left with the suspicion that 'the impartial observer would perceive the real risk of bias'.

8.10.2 Media influence

Media coverage may influence jurors. This is especially true in high-profile cases, where there has been a lot of publicity about the police investigations into a case. This occurred in the case *R v West* [1996] 2 Cr App R 374 in which Rosemary West was convicted of the murders of ten young girls and women, including her own daughter. From the time the bodies were first discovered, the media coverage was intense. In addition, some newspapers had paid large sums of money to some of the witnesses in order to secure their story after the trial was completed. One of the grounds on which Rosemary West appealed against her conviction was that the media coverage had made it impossible for her to receive a fair trial. The Court of Appeal rejected the appeal, pointing out that otherwise it would mean that if 'allegations of murder were sufficiently horrendous so as to inevitably shock the nation, the accused could not be tried'. They also said that the trial judge had given adequate warning to the jurors to consider only the evidence they heard in court.

In *R v Taylor and Taylor* [1994] 98 Cr App R 361 the defendants successfully appealed against their convictions because of high-profile, misleading and, in some instances, untrue press reports on the case.

CASE EXAMPLE

R v Taylor and Taylor [1994] 98 Cr App R 361

Two sisters were charged with the murder of another woman. The prosecution case was that one of the sisters, Michelle, had been having an affair with the victim's husband. The press printed misleading stills from a video of the victim's wedding in which Michelle appeared to be giving the bridegroom a passionate kiss. In fact, the full video showed her coming along the receiving line at the reception and giving him what was described as a 'peck on the cheek'. They also printed inaccurate sensational headlines such as 'Love Crazy Mistress Butchered Rival Wife Court Told' when the court had not been told that. The Court of Appeal quashed the sisters' convictions. The coverage of the trial by the media had created a real risk of prejudice against the defendants. As a result, their convictions were regarded as unsafe and unsatisfactory.

8.10.3 Perverse verdicts

In section 8.9.2 we considered the idea of jury equity where a jury refuses to follow the law and convict a defendant. However, it can be argued that this merely leads to a perverse verdict which does not reflect the evidence and is not justified. An example was the case of *R v Randle and Pottle*, *The Independent*, 26 March 1991.

CASE EXAMPLE

R v Randle and Pottle, *The Independent*, 26 March 1991

Twenty-five years after the spy George Blake escaped from prison, the defendants were charged with helping him to escape. They had published a book, *The Blake Escape: How We Freed George Blake and Why*, in which they admitted that they had helped him to escape. They had also discussed the matter in the media and made admissions of guilt. At the trial the judge told the jury that the defendants had no defence. Despite this the jury acquitted them, possibly as a protest over the lapse of time between the offence and the prosecution.

Another case in which the jury acquitted despite clear evidence was *R v Kronlid and others* (1996). In this case four female defendants were charged with causing over £1 million worth of damage to an aircraft. The women admitted breaking into a hangar and using hammers to damage the £10 million aircraft. However, they denied the charges, claiming that they were using reasonable force to prevent a greater crime. They said that disarming the jet, which had been bought by the Indonesian government, would prevent it from being used against the civilian population in East Timor. The jury found all the defendants not guilty.

To try to prevent perverse verdicts, the Auld Report (2001) on the criminal justice system recommended that where a judge thought it appropriate, the jury should be required to answer questions and declare a verdict in accordance with those answers. The report also recommended that juries should not have the right to acquit defendants in defiance of the law or in disregard of the evidence. These recommendations have not been implemented by the government. There was severe criticism of the recommendation. Professor Zander, in his comments to the Lord Chancellor's Department on this recommendation, said:

> I regard this proposal as wholly unacceptable – a serious misreading of the function of the jury. The right to return a perverse verdict in defiance of the law or the evidence is an important safeguard against unjust laws, oppressive prosecutions or harsh sentences. In former centuries juries notoriously defied the law to save defendants from the gallows. In modern times the power is used, sometimes to general acclaim, sometimes to general annoyance, usually one imagines to some of each.

Some perverse verdicts may be seen as just and equitable. This occurred in the case of *R v Gilderdale* (2010) (unreported) where a mother who assisted her daughter's suicide was charged with attempted murder. The daughter had been ill for a number of years and she had begged her mother to help her. The mother pleaded guilty to assisting suicide but the prosecution insisted on continuing with a charge of attempted murder. The jury found the mother not guilty of attempted murder. The judge passed a sentence of a one-year's conditional discharge on the assisting suicide charge.

ACTIVITY

Essay writing

Critically discuss whether the prosecution should be able to appeal against an acquittal on the ground that it was a perverse decision.

8.10.4 Fraud trials

Fraud trials in which complex accounts are used in evidence can create special problems for jurors. Even jurors who can easily cope with other evidence may have difficulty understanding a fraud case. These cases are also often very long, so that the jurors have to be able to be away from their own work for months. A long fraud trial can place a great strain on jurors. Such cases also become very expensive, both for the prosecution and for the defendants. The Roskill Committee in 1986 suggested that juries should not be used for complex fraud cases.

In 1998, the Home Office issued a Consultation Document, 'Juries in Serious Fraud Trials', inviting views on whether the system for trying fraud trials should be changed. One of the points in the document was the fact that the Court of Appeal had quashed the decision in the Blue Arrow fraud trial because the case had become unmanageable. The Court of Appeal had held that there was a significant risk of a miscarriage of justice because of the volume of evidence and the complexities of the issues which had to be decided by the jury. No further action was taken on the consultation paper, but at the end of 1999 Lord Justice Auld was asked to review the criminal justice system. This review (2001) recommended that fraud cases should be heard by a judge and two lay people taken from a special panel.

Following the review's recommendations, the government issued the White Paper 'Justice for All'. In this it stated:

QUOTATION

'4.28 A small number of serious and complex fraud trials, many lasting six months or more, have served to highlight the difficulties in trying these types of cases with a jury. Such cases place a huge strain on all concerned and the time commitment is a burden on jurors' personal and working lives. As a result it is not always possible to find a representative panel of jurors.

4.29 As well as this, the complexity and unfamiliarity of sophisticated business processes means prosecutions often pare down cases to try and make them more manageable and comprehensible to a jury. This means the full criminality of such a fraud is not always exposed, and there are risks of a double standard between easy to prosecute "blue-collar" crime and difficult to prosecute "white-collar" crime.

4.30 We have concluded that there should be a more effective form of trial in such cases of serious fraud. The Auld report recommended that the judge should have the power to direct such fraud trials without a jury, sitting with people experienced in complex financial issues or, where the defendant agrees, on their own. We recognise that the expertise of such people could help the trial proceed. However, identifying and recruiting suitable people raises considerable difficulties, not least because this would represent a substantial commitment over a long period of time.'

Criminal Justice Act 2003

The government proposed that serious fraud cases should be tried by a judge alone. It estimated that there would be only about 15–20 such trials a year. This proposal was contained in the Criminal Justice Bill 2002–03. The original Bill contained two measures aimed at limiting jury trials. One proposal would have allowed a defendant to apply for a trial to be conducted without a jury. This was defeated by the House of Lords and withdrawn by the government. The other was a provision allowing the prosecution to apply for trial without a jury where:

- the trial was likely to be lengthy or complex; or
- there was a danger of jury tampering.

This was defeated by the House of Lords, but the government reinstated it. The House of Lords voted against it again. Finally, a compromise was reached whereby there are provisions in the Criminal Justice Act 2003 for the prosecution to apply for trial by a judge alone in:

- complex fraud cases (s43); or
- cases where there has already been an effort to tamper with a jury in the case (s44).

However, s43 was abolished by s133 of the Protection of Freedoms Act 2012, without ever having been brought into effect.

Domestic Violence, Crime and Victims Act 2004

The government then put forward yet another way of restricting jury trial. This was in the Domestic Violence, Crime and Victims Act 2004. The effect of ss17–20 of that Act is that, where there are a large number of counts on the indictment, there can be a trial of sample counts with a jury. Then, if the defendant was convicted on those, the remainder could be tried by a judge alone. The prosecution has to apply to a judge to make such an order and there are three conditions which must be met:

the number of counts included in the indictment is likely to mean that a trial by jury of all those counts would be impracticable;

a sample of all counts must be tried by a jury;

it must be in the interests of justice for such an order to be made.

When considering the application a judge must have regard to any steps which might reasonably be taken to facilitate a trial by jury. This is being called a two-tier trial, but the idea behind it is that those who commit multiple offences should be convicted and punished for *all* their offences.

Small-scale research into judges' opinions of jurors' understanding of fraud cases has been carried out ('Judicial Perspectives on the Conduct of Serious Fraud Trials', by Robert Julian [2007] *Crim LR* 751–768). Nine judges who had tried a serious fraud case were interviewed as to their opinions of the role of the jury in such cases.

The judges were of the opinion that the jurors in such cases had understood the case. Indeed most judges said that they were more likely to agree with the jury's verdict in a complex fraud case than in other cases. Several also thought that judge-alone trials would be longer than those with a jury as the prosecution would be more likely to go for lengthy indictments and pursue more complex points.

8.10.5 High acquittal rates

Juries are often criticised on the ground that they acquit too many defendants. The figure usually quoted in support of this is that about two-thirds of those who plead not guilty at the Crown Court are acquitted. However, this figure does not give a true picture of the workings of juries as it includes cases discharged by the judge and those in which the judge directed an acquittal.

The statistics for 2015–16 show that a total of over 99,000 defendants were prosecuted at the Crown Court during the year. Over 70,000 of these defendants pleaded guilty to all the charges against them. Almost 30,000 pleaded not guilty to all charges. Of these 30,000 pleading not guilty, 72 per cent were found not guilty. However, the majority of these acquittals were by the judge and not the jury. Fifty-seven per cent of these defendants were discharged by the judge without a jury even being sworn in.

These were cases where the prosecution offered no evidence. In another 3 per cent the judge directed the jury to acquit the defendant. So, when these cases are excluded, it can be seen that the jury acquitted in 40 per cent of the cases. Of the cases in which the jury decides the verdict, they convict in more cases than they acquit. This statistic has remained broadly similar for a number of years, as shown by Figure 8.3.

Year	Percentage convicted by jury	Percentage acquitted by jury
2004	64.0	36.0
2006	69.6	30.4
2008	69.7	30.3
2010	66.5	33.5
2012	69.4	30.6
2014	58.4	41.6

Figures from 2004–12 are based on the *Judicial Statistics* published for each year. Figures for 2014 are based on the Criminal Justice System Annual Report.

Figure 8.3 Conviction and acquittal rates of juries

8.10.6 Other disadvantages

The compulsory nature of jury service is unpopular, so that some jurors may be against the whole system, while others may rush their verdict in order to leave as quickly as possible. Jury service can be a strain, especially where jurors have to listen to horrific evidence. Jurors in the Rosemary West case were offered counselling after the trial to help them cope with the evidence they had had to see and hear.

Jury 'nobbling' does occur and in some cases jurors have had to be provided with police protection. In order to try to combat this, the Criminal Procedure and Investigations Act 1996 allows for a re-trial to be ordered if, in any case, someone is subsequently proved to have interfered with the jury, although in actual fact there have not yet been any prosecutions under this Act. Also, as seen in section 8.10.4, the Criminal Justice Act 2003 has a provision for allowing trial to continue by a judge alone where there has been interference with a jury.

The use of juries makes trials slow and expensive. This is because each point has to be explained carefully to the jury and the whole procedure of the case takes longer. However, this has to be balanced against the advantage of the procedure of using a jury making the trial more open and understandable.

Standards of dishonesty

Use of a jury in cases involving dishonesty may lead to inconsistent verdicts between different juries. This is because jurors in dishonesty cases are directed to consider whether the defendant's behaviour was dishonest according to the standards of ordinary people. In 2009 Emily Finch and Stefan Fafinski carried out online research into people's ideas of dishonesty. They gave a series of situations and asked people to state whether they thought the behaviour involved was dishonest. They found that people's perception of what was dishonest varied widely, with 3 per cent not even considering taking a DVD from a shop without paying as being dishonest. Although as the survey was conducted online, it may be that respondents were not always careful with their answers.

ACTIVITY

Critiquing the law

Quotation

'[T]rial by jury is more than an instrument of justice and more than one wheel of the constitution: it is the lamp that shows that freedom lives.'

Lord Devlin, Trial by Jury (Stevens & Sons, 1956), p 164

Lord Devlin made a full-throated defence of the importance of the jury to democracy in 1956. This view places the jury as being of fundamental importance to the protection of freedoms in the ELS. Yet many democratic countries around the world do not use a jury system, and as you have seen in this chapter, the jury is far from common in the majority of civil and criminal cases. With this in mind, consider the following thinking points:

- Does the jury really help protect democracy and freedom?
- Is the importance of the jury overstated today, given it is used in relatively few cases?
- Do you think that the jury is fit for purpose, or should it be replaced by a different method for determining the truth in legal cases?

8.11 Alternatives to trial by jury

Despite all the problems of using juries in criminal cases, there is still a strong feeling that they are the best method available. However, if juries are not thought suitable to try serious criminal cases, what alternative form of trial could be used?

Trial by a single judge

This is the method of trial in the majority of civil cases in which it is generally regarded as producing a fairer and more predictable result. Trial by a single judge is also used for some criminal trials in Northern Ireland; these are called the Diplock courts and were brought in on the recommendation of Lord Diplock to replace jury trial because of the special problems of threats and jury 'nobbling' that existed between the different sectarian parties.

However, there appears to be less public confidence in the use of judges to decide all serious criminal cases. The arguments against this form of trial are that judges become case-hardened and prosecution-minded. They are also from a very elitist group and would have little understanding of the background and problems of defendants. Individual prejudices are more likely than in a jury where the different personalities should go some way to eliminating bias. But, on the other hand, judges are trained to evaluate cases and they are now being given training in racial awareness. This may make them better arbiters of fact than an untrained jury.

A panel of judges

In some continental countries cases are heard by a panel of three or five judges sitting together. This allows for a balance of views, instead of the verdict of a single person. However, it still leaves the problems of judges becoming case-hardened and prosecution-minded and their elitist background. The other difficulty is that there are not sufficient judges and our system of legal training and appointment would need a radical overhaul to implement this proposal. It would also be expensive.

A judge plus lay assessors

Under this system the judge and two lay people would make the decision together. This method is used in the Scandinavian countries. It provides the legal expertise of the judge, together with lay participation in the legal system by ordinary members of the public. The lay people could either be drawn from the general public, using the same method as is used for selecting juries at present, or a special panel of assessors could be drawn up as happens in tribunal cases. This latter suggestion would be particularly suitable for fraud cases.

A mini-jury using six members

Finally, if the jury is to remain, then it might be possible to have a smaller number of jurors. In many continental countries when a jury is used there are nine members. For example, in Spain, which reintroduced the use of juries in certain criminal cases in 1996, there is a jury of nine. Alternatively, a jury of six could be used for less serious criminal cases that at the moment have a full jury trial – this occurs in some American states.

ACTIVITY

Self-test questions

1. In which courts can juries be used?
2. What are the basic qualifications for jurors?
3. For what reasons are certain people disqualified from jury service?

4. What is meant by a 'discretionary excusal' and when will one be given?
5. Explain:

   (a) challenging to the array;
   (b) challenging for cause;
   (c) prosecution's right of standby.

6. When can a jury be used in civil cases?
7. Why are juries considered unsuitable for deciding personal injury cases?
8. What is a majority verdict and what is the law about announcing such verdicts in court?
9. What two factors ensure the secrecy of the jury room?
10. Explain how research into juries has been carried out.

SAMPLE ESSAY QUESTION

Juries give a voice to the general public in the administration of justice, protecting defendants from unfair convictions (the principle of jury equity). It is therefore right that as many people as possible are eligible for jury service and are only rarely able to excuse themselves from serving. Discuss.

State the qualifications for jury service:

- 18–75;
- voter;
- resident for at least five years in UK.

Mentally disordered people cannot serve.

Criminal conviction may disqualify a person from jury service.

Member of the armed forces may be excused.

Explain the pre-2003 limitations on jury service:

- those in the administration of justice were ineligible for jury service;
- certain groups had the right to be excused, e.g. MPs, people in the medical profession, those aged 65 to 70.

Discuss the removal of these limitations including points such as:

- changes have made more people eligible for jury service;
- should judges/police etc. serve on juries?
- is there a risk of prosecution bias?

Discuss use of discretionary excusals:

- pre-2003 large numbers were given discretionary excusals;
- post-2003 discretionary excusals are less likely to be given – jury service may be deferred instead;
- could this lead to unwilling jurors who may rush decisions?

Explain and discuss the principle of jury equity:

- use case examples;
- discuss whether having a wider range of people serving on a jury is likely to affect jury equity.

CONCLUSION

Figure 8.4 Essay map on juries

SUMMARY

Juries are used in the

- Crown Court (12);
- High Court (12) (only for cases of defamation, malicious prosecution, false imprisonment);
- County Court (8 – this is very rare);
- Coroners' Court (7–11).

Jury qualifications and selection

- must be aged between 18 and 75;
- must be an elector; and
- must have lived in the UK for at least five years;
- must not be mentally disordered or disqualified;
- only serving members of the armed forces can be excused service;
- other people may be given a discretionary excusal if they have difficulty in doing jury service, e.g. physically incapable of attending court;
- jury panels may be vetted;
- jurors can be removed from the panel if they have not been chosen randomly or if there is a reason why an individual juror should not serve.

Role of jury

- in criminal cases they decide the facts and give a verdict of guilty or not guilty;

- in civil cases, they decide liability and also the amount of damages;
- in Coroners' Courts they enquire into certain deaths;
- the jury is an independent decider of fact; a court cannot interfere with its finding of fact.

Advantages of jury trial
- public confidence;
- jury equity;
- a panel of 12 should lead to cancelling out of bias.

Disadvantages of jury trial
- bias may exist, especially racial bias;
- jurors may be influenced by media stories about the case;
- juries give perverse verdicts;
- fraud trials are too complicated for jurors to understand;
- juries acquit too many defendants;
- jurors may be 'nobbled';
- jury service is unpopular;
- the use of a jury makes a trial longer and more expensive.

Further reading

Book
Zander, M, *Cases and Materials on the English Legal System* (10th edn, Lexis-Nexis, 2003) Ch 5.

Articles
Coen, M and Hefferman, L, 'Juror comprehension of expert evidence: a reform agenda' [2010] *Crim LR* 195.

Darbyshire, P, 'The lamp that shows that freedom lives: is it worth the candle?' [1991] *Crim LR* 740.

Darbyshire, P, 'What can we learn from published jury research? Findings for the Criminal Courts Review 2001' [2001] *Crim LR* 970.

Devlin, Lord, 'The conscience of the jury' [1991] 107 *LQR* 398.

Ferguson, P, 'Whistleblowing jurors' [2004] *NLJ* 370.

Julian, R, 'Judicial perspectives on the conduct of serious fraud trials' [2007] *Crim LR* 751–768.

Thomas, C, 'Fairness in the jury system' [2007] Ministry of Justice Research Series 02/07.

Thomas, C, 'Avoiding the perfect storm of juror contempt' [2013] *Crim LR* 483.

Internet links
Ministry of Justice research series at: www.justice.gov.uk

9

Lay magistrates

AIMS AND OBJECTIVES

After reading this chapter you should be able to:

- Understand the selection of lay magistrates
- Understand the role of lay magistrates in the justice system
- Describe the role of the magistrates' clerk
- Discuss the advantages of using lay magistrates
- Discuss the disadvantages of using lay magistrates

9.1 Introduction

In our legal system, there is a tradition of using lay people, that is people who are not legally qualified, in the decision-making process in our courts. Today this applies particularly to the Magistrates' Courts and the Crown Court. However, in the past lay people were also frequently used to decide civil cases in the High Court and the County Court, and today there are still some cases in which a jury can be used in the civil courts. There are also lay people with expertise in a particular field who sit as part of a panel as lay assessors. This occurs in the Patents Court and the Admiralty Court in the High Court as well as in tribunals. However, the greatest use of lay people in the legal system is lay magistrates.

9.1.1 Lay magistrates

mode of trial
The procedure held in the Magistrates' Court for deciding whether the defendant will be tried at the Magistrates' Court or the Crown Court

There are around 17,500 lay magistrates sitting as part-time judges in the Magistrates' Courts. Another name for a lay magistrate is Justice of the Peace (JP). They sit to hear cases as a bench of two or three magistrates. The size of the panel has been limited to a maximum of three, whereas before 1996 there could be up to seven magistrates sitting together to hear a case. A single lay magistrate sitting on his own has limited powers. He can issue search warrants and warrants for arrest. He can also sit to decide **mode of trial** proceedings for offences triable either way when the decision as to whether the case will be tried in the Magistrates' Court or the Crown Court is made. From 2015, a single magistrate also has powers to try and sentence very low-level criminal offences (see section 9.7.1).

As a bench of two or three magistrates, they play a very large role in the legal system, dealing with about 98 per cent of all criminal cases.

9.1.2 District Judges

There are also qualified judges who work in Magistrates' Courts. These are called District Judges (Magistrates' Court). Prior to 1999, they used to be called stipendiary magistrates. They can sit on their own to hear any of the cases that come before the court. Under s16(3) of the Justices of the Peace Act 1979 they have the same powers as a bench of lay magistrates. In 2016 there were around 140 District Judges working in the judicial system.

9.2 History of the magistracy

The office of JP is very old, dating back to the twelfth century at least. In 1195 Richard I appointed 'keepers of the peace'. By the mid-thirteenth century the judicial side of their position had developed and by 1361 the title 'Justice of the Peace' was being used. By this time JPs already had the power to arrest suspects and investigate crime. In 1382 they were given the power to punish offenders. A statute in 1363 provided that the justices should meet at least four times a year in each county. These meetings, which became known as Quarter Sessions, continued to be held until they were abolished in 1971.

Over the years JPs were also given many administrative duties, for example being responsible for the poor law, highways and bridges, and weights and measures. In the nineteenth century elected local authorities took over most of these duties, though some remnants remain, especially in the licensing powers of the Magistrates' Courts. The poor quality of the local JP in London and the absence of an adequate police force became a matter of concern towards the end of the eighteenth century. This led to seven public offices with paid magistrates being set up in 1792. This was the origin of the modern DJ(MC). Until 1839 these professional magistrates were in charge of the police as well as hearing cases in court. Outside London the first appointment of a paid magistrate was in Manchester in 1813. In 1835 the Municipal Corporations Act gave a general power for boroughs to request the appointment of a stipendiary magistrate (now District Judge). At the beginning a paid magistrate did not have to have any particular qualifications, but from 1839 they could be appointed only from barristers. Solicitors did not become eligible to be appointed as stipendiary magistrates until 1949. Today District Judges need to be legally qualified as a barrister or solicitor and must have five years' experience in the law (see section 11.4 for details). In addition Chartered Institute of Legal Executives (CILEx) Fellows with five years' experience in law are eligible to be appointed as Deputy District Judges and can then be promoted to District Judge.

9.3 Qualifications for lay magistrates

In the foreword to the 'National Strategy for the Recruitment of Lay Magistrates', the Lord Chancellor wrote:

QUOTATION

'Magistrates are recruited from members of the local community. No formal qualifications are required, but applicants are expected to demonstrate common sense, integrity, intelligence and the capacity to act fairly. They perform a valuable service on behalf of their communities and their role is pivotal to the administration, not only of local justice, but to our judicial system as a whole.'

Although no formal qualifications are required, certain qualities are required and there are some limitations on who can be appointed. These are set out in sections 9.3.1 to 9.3.5.

9.3.1 Age

Lay magistrates must be aged between 18 and 65 on appointment. Until 2000 it was unusual for anyone over the age of 60 to be appointed but the Lord Chancellor recognised that there were many people who, having retired at 60, had the time for the commitment to magistrates' duties which they did not have when they were working. He increased the age limit and now will consider a person who is over the age of 60. In such cases an appointment is more likely to be made if the person is especially well qualified or their appointment would improve the overall composition of the Bench. The lower age range was reduced to 18 in 2003, but it is unusual for a person under 27 to be considered as it is felt that they will not have enough experience. However, since 2004 a few younger magistrates have been appointed.

Before 1906 there was a property qualification which meant that magistrates had to be home owners or tenants of property above a certain value. Also, before 1919 the Bench was an all-male affair with women becoming eligible for appointment only in 1919. Today there are no property qualifications and women now make up almost half of the magistracy.

9.3.2 Limitations

However, there are some people who are not eligible to be appointed. The important factor is that candidates should be of good standing in the local community. So people with serious criminal convictions are disqualified from becoming a magistrate, though a conviction for a minor motoring offence will not automatically disqualify a candidate. Undischarged bankrupts are also disqualified. Those involved in enforcement of the law, such as police officers, civilians working for the police and traffic wardens are ineligible. This is because their work is incompatible with sitting as a magistrate. Members of the armed forces are also ineligible. Close relatives of those working in the local criminal justice system will not be appointed as magistrates in that area as it would not appear 'just' if, for example, the wife of a local police officer were to sit to decide cases. However, there is no bar on them being appointed as a lay magistrate in another area. Close relatives who are both lay magistrates will not be appointed to the same Bench.

The magistracy does try to be inclusive, so people with disabilities may be appointed provided that those disabilities do not prevent them from carrying out the duties of a magistrate. In 1998 a pilot scheme was started to see if it was feasible for visually impaired people to sit as magistrates. This was successful and since 2001 visually impaired magistrates have been appointed.

9.3.3 Six key personal qualities

The only qualifications that lay magistrates need are the six key personal qualities that the Lord Chancellor set out in 1998. These are:

- good character;
- understanding and communication;
- social awareness;
- maturity and sound temperament;
- sound judgment;
- commitment and reliability.

Aspiring lay magistrates should have certain 'judicial' qualities. It is particularly important that they are able to assimilate factual information and make a reasoned decision on it. They must also be able to take account of the reasoning of others and work as a team.

9.3.4 Area

Up to 2003 it was necessary for lay magistrates to live within 15 miles of the commission area for the court in which they sat. In 2003 the Courts Act abolished commission areas. Instead there is now one commission area for the whole of England and Wales. However, the country is divided into local justice areas. These areas are specified by the Lord Chancellor and lay magistrates are expected to live or work within or near to the local justice area to which they are allocated.

9.3.5 Commitment

The other requirement is that lay magistrates are prepared to commit themselves to sitting at least 26 half-days each year. This is quite an onerous commitment and in the 'National Strategy for the Recruitment of Lay Magistrates' published by the Lord Chancellor in October 2003 it was suggested that the minimum number of days sitting might be reduced to 24 half-days. This has not happened. In fact, it is normal for lay magistrates to sit more than the minimum 26 half-days.

9.3.6 Allowances

Lay justices are not paid for sitting as magistrates but they are entitled to certain payments. These are:

- a travelling allowance;
- a subsistence allowance; and
- a financial loss allowance.

The magistrate can only claim for actual expenses incurred or actual loss.

9.4 Selection and appointment of lay magistrates

Between about 1,700 and 2,200 new lay magistrates are usually appointed each year. Until 2013 the Lord Chancellor appointed all lay magistrates. From 2013 this power has been transferred to the Lord Chief Justice, who in turn delegates this power to the Senior Presiding Judge for England and Wales. Until 2004, there was an exception for the area of the Duchy of Lancaster, where lay justices were appointed by the Chancellor for the Duchy. This right was abolished by s10 of the Courts Act 2003, and today the Lord Chief Justice makes all appointments. This is done 'on behalf of and in the name of Her Majesty'. The Lord Chief Justice is assisted in this by Advisory Committees who recommend candidates for appointment.

9.4.1 Recruitment

In the past, many applicants for the magistracy had their names put forward by existing magistrates, local political parties, trade unions, charities or other local organisations. This ensured that applicants were well known in the local community. Today, the emphasis is on encouraging applicants to apply directly and making the appointment system more open.

The 'National Strategy for the Recruitment of Lay Magistrates' (2003) included a list of objectives for improving recruitment. The most important of these were:

- to continue to develop ways of recruiting magistrates from a wide spread of people, particularly from groups currently under-represented nationally;
- to continue to develop a socially diverse Bench that will be representative of all sectors of society;
- to consider ways of building more flexibility into court sittings, so those magistrates with other responsibilities are able to meet at least the minimum number of required sittings;
- to target employers and encourage them to release staff who are magistrates to enable them to fulfil their duties;
- to revise existing methods of recruitment advertising and consider alternative possibilities.

Proposed actions were listed under each of these objectives and given a high, medium or low priority. There were only two proposed actions which were given a high priority. These were to develop a campaign aimed at employers and to direct recruitment campaigns through various media outlets, including local newspapers and radio, and specific publications – among others, those representing specific target groups.

These two priorities underline the main problems in recruiting. The first is that most people are unaware that they can apply to become a magistrate and that no formal qualifications are required. The second is the fact that many employers will not give paid time off for duties, although magistrates can claim loss of earnings as expenses. The third is that applicants are worried that they may lose out on promotion if they take time off to act as a magistrate. Employers are legally obliged to allow employees time off to act as a magistrate, but it does not prevent this problem.

9.4.2 Advisory committees

The procedure used by the Advisory Committees for identifying suitable candidates is that they encourage applications from people. To get applications they may advertise in local papers or on the radio and they may hold 'open' days to explain the work of magistrates to potential applicants.

Each Advisory Committee either has a formal Sub-Committee to interview applicants or will set up an interview panel for this task. Advisory Committees are made up of one-third non-magistrates and two-thirds serving magistrates. There is usually a two-stage interview process. At the first interview the panel tries to find out more about the candidate's personal attributes, in particular looking to see if they have the six key qualities required. The interview panel will also explore the candidate's attitudes on various criminal justice issues such as youth crime or drink-driving. The second interview is aimed at testing candidates' potential judicial aptitude and this is done by a discussion of at least two case studies which are typical of those heard regularly in Magistrates' Courts. The discussion might, for example, focus on the type of sentence which should be imposed on specific case facts.

Once suitable candidates have been identified, the Advisory Committee then has to ensure that the Bench broadly reflects the community which it serves, taking account of:

- gender;
- ethnic origin;
- geographical spread; and
- occupation.

The intention is to create a panel that is representative of all aspects of society. A candidate who is personally suitable may not be recommended for appointment because their appointment would increase an imbalance which already exists on the Bench. For example, there may already be too many magistrates from a particular occupational background, so that an applicant who is in the same occupation will not be recommended. The Advisory Committee then submits names of suitable candidates to the Senior Presiding Judge of England and Wales (who is acting on behalf of the Lord Chief Justice). He will then appoint new magistrates from this list. Once appointed, magistrates may sit until the age of 70.

Political affiliation

A major discussion point used to be to what extent, if any, the political views of a candidate should be considered. In 1966 the then Lord Chancellor, Lord Gardiner, issued a directive to Advisory Committees, telling them to bear in mind people's political allegiances in order to achieve a balance. At the time this caused a stir, but the reason behind it was to try to achieve better balanced panels of magistrates.

In 1998 the Lord Chancellor issued a Consultation Paper, 'Political Balance in the Lay Magistracy', considering whether the political views of applicants should be considered at all. After consulting he reluctantly decided that political balance was the most practicable method of ensuring a good social balance on the Bench.

However, in 2003 the Lord Chancellor announced that he would no longer use voting patterns and political affiliation as a means of trying to ensure that magistrates reflected their local community. Instead indicators using a mix of occupational, industrial and social groupings as shown by the 2001 census would be used.

9.5 Training of lay magistrates

The training of lay magistrates is supervised by the Magistrates' Committee of the Judicial College. This Committee has drawn up a syllabus of the topics which lay magistrates should cover during the course of their training. The Auld Review (2001) recommended that the Judicial Studies Board should be made responsible for 'devising and securing the content and manner of training for all magistrates'. The government accepted this recommendation.

Under the Courts Act 2003 a unified courts administration came into effect in April 2005. This combines the management of the Magistrates' Court with the Crown Court, County Court and higher courts. It has had an effect on the training of magistrates as the 2003 Act abolished the 42 independent Magistrates' Court Committees. In their place there are 42 unified areas (effectively covering the same areas as the Committees) but with responsibility for all the courts within their area under the direction of Her Majesty's Courts Service. This Service is overseen by the Ministry of Justice.

In June 2004 the Judicial Studies Board issued a consultation paper, 'Proposals for the Organisation and Management of Magistrates' Training in the Unified Courts Administration'. It set out five key goals for the new training system. It should:

- uphold judicial independence;
- contribute towards public confidence in the magistracy;
- enable the Judicial Studies Board to establish minimum standards for the content, design and delivery of magistrates' training that can be monitored and quality assured;
- be efficient and effective; and
- support recruitment, retention and succession planning of magistrates and staff.

Since 1998 magistrates' training has been monitored more closely. There were criticisms prior to then that, although magistrates were required to attend a certain number of hours of training, there was no assessment of how much they had understood. In 1998 the Magistrates New Training Initiative was introduced (MNTI1). In 2004 this was refined by the Magistrates National Training Initiative (MNTI2). The framework of training is divided into four areas of competence, the first three of which are relevant to all lay magistrates. The fourth competence is for chairmen of the Bench. The four areas of competence are:

1. Managing yourself – this focuses on some of the basic aspects of self-management in relation to preparing for court, conduct in court and ongoing learning.

2. Working as a member of a team – this focuses on the team aspect of decision making in the Magistrates' Court.

3. Making judicial decisions – this focuses on impartial and structured decision making.

4. Managing judicial decision making – this is for the chairman's role and focuses on working with the legal adviser, managing the court and ensuring effective, impartial decision making.

Section 19(3) of the Courts Act 2003 sets out a statutory obligation on the Lord Chief Justice to provide training and training materials. Training was formerly delivered by Bench Training and Development Committees (BTDCs). The Justice of the Peace Rules 2016 established two new committees which replaced the BTDCs. The Justices' Training, Approvals, Authorisations and Appraisals Committee (JTAAAC) undertakes its functions in respect of adult and youth justices. The Family Training, Approvals, Authorisations and Appraisals Committee (FTAAAC) undertakes the same functions in respect of family justices. The new committees will take effect from April 2017.

9.5.1 Training for new magistrates

There is a syllabus for new magistrates which is divided into three parts. These are:

1. Initial introductory training – this covers such matters as understanding the organisation of the Bench and the administration of the court and the roles and responsibilities of those involved in the Magistrates' Court.

2. Core training – this provides the new magistrate with the opportunity to acquire and develop the key skills, knowledge and understanding required of a competent magistrate.

3. Activities – these will involve observations of court sittings and visits to establishments such as a prison or a probation office.

The training programme for new magistrates should normally follow the pattern set out in Figure 9.1.

Mentors

Each new lay justice keeps a Personal Development Log of their progress. They also have a mentor, who is an experienced magistrate, to assist them. The initial introductory training is covered before the new magistrate starts sitting in court. They will also take part in a structured courtroom observation of cases on at least three occasions. These should be arranged so that they see different aspects of the work and should include preliminary decisions such as bail, a short summary trial and sentencing.

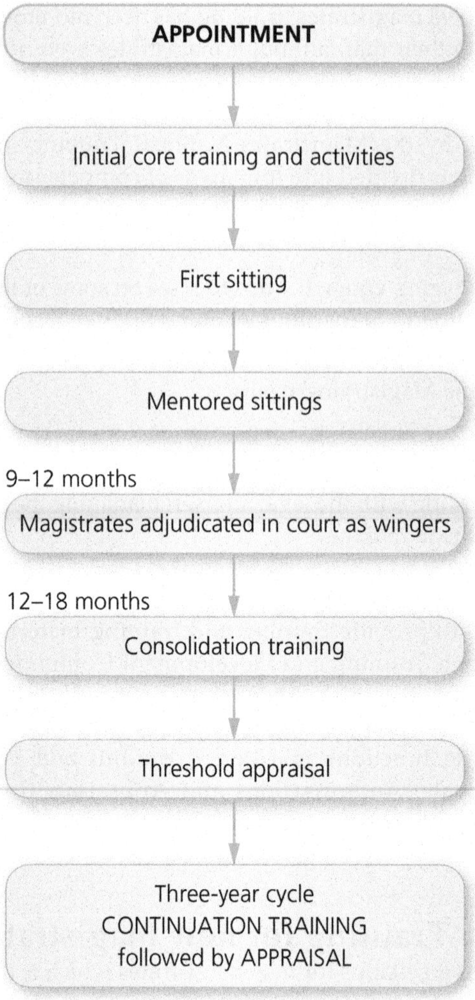

```
┌─────────────────────────────┐
│         APPOINTMENT          │
└─────────────────────────────┘
               │
               ▼
┌─────────────────────────────┐
│ Initial core training and    │
│         activities           │
└─────────────────────────────┘
               │
               ▼
┌─────────────────────────────┐
│         First sitting        │
└─────────────────────────────┘
               │
               ▼
┌─────────────────────────────┐
│       Mentored sittings      │
└─────────────────────────────┘
 9–12 months   │
               ▼
┌─────────────────────────────┐
│ Magistrates adjudicated in   │
│     court as wingers         │
└─────────────────────────────┘
 12–18 months  │
               ▼
┌─────────────────────────────┐
│    Consolidation training    │
└─────────────────────────────┘
               │
               ▼
┌─────────────────────────────┐
│     Threshold appraisal      │
└─────────────────────────────┘
               │
               ▼
┌─────────────────────────────┐
│       Three-year cycle       │
│    CONTINUATION TRAINING     │
│    followed by APPRAISAL     │
└─────────────────────────────┘
```

Figure 9.1 New magistrates' training and appraisal pathway

Training sessions

These are organised and carried out at local level within the 42 areas. Much of the training is delivered by Justices' Clerks. The Judicial Studies Board intends that most training should still be delivered locally. However, the structure takes into account the need to collaborate regionally and nationally where appropriate. In particular, the training of Youth and Family Panel Chairmen will be delivered nationally for areas which do not have enough such Chairmen needing training to run an effective course locally.

Appraisal

After their initial training, magistrates will start by sitting in the ordinary Magistrates' Court. They will be what are called 'wingers', that is, one of the two magistrates who sit on either side of the chairman of the Bench. During the first two years of sitting in court, the new magistrate is expected to attend about seven or eight training sessions. During the same period between eight and 11 of the sessions in which the new magistrate sits as a member of the Bench will be mentored.

After two years, or whenever it is felt that the magistrate is ready, there will be an appraisal to check whether the competencies have been achieved. Any magistrate who cannot show that they have achieved the competencies will be given extra training. If they still cannot achieve the competencies then the matter is referred to the local training committee, who may recommend to the Lord Chancellor that the magistrate be removed from sitting on the Bench.

After that, each magistrate should be appraised at least once every three years. When magistrates become more experienced they may be appointed to the Youth Court Bench or the Family Court Bench. There is additional training and appraisal for these roles. Finally, a magistrate may be appointed as chairman. Again, there is additional training for this role.

Post-sitting reviews

These were introduced by MNTI2 and are intended to provide an opportunity for the Bench of three to sit down together with the legal adviser to identify what went well and what they would like to do differently in future.

Summary

Overall, the training of lay magistrates has greatly improved. Much of their training is aimed at sentencing and they are also given a sentencing handbook (see Chapter 12 for further information). Despite this there are criticisms that sentences are inconsistent between different lay Benches (see section 9.10.3). Another area in which training is important is on deciding bail applications. Again, there are criticisms that there is a wide variation between Benches on the granting or refusal of bail. The main point of the training is that it is not intended to make the magistrates lawyers. They have a legal adviser who can advise them on the law when a legal point is at issue. As well as being given training on the type of cases they will hear, lay magistrates are also given training on equal treatment. As set out in the training pack provided by the Judicial Studies Board, this covers:

QUOTATION

'recognising the effects of discrimination on the basis of race, creed, colour, religion, ethnicity, gender, class, disability, or sexual orientation which can lead to unequal treatment of people in magistrates' courts'.

9.6 Resignation and removal of lay justices

This is governed by s11 of the Courts Act 2003 (as amended) which states:

SECTION

's 11(1) A lay justice may resign his office at any time.

(2) The Lord Chancellor, with the concurrence of the Lord Chief Justice, may remove a lay justice from his office by an instrument on behalf and in the name of Her Majesty –

    (a) on the ground of incapacity or misbehaviour,

    (b) on the ground of a persistent failure to meet such standards of competence as are prescribed by a direction given by the Lord Chancellor with the concurrence of the Lord Chief Justice, or

    (c) if he is satisfied that the lay justice is declining or neglecting to take a proper part in the exercise of his functions as a justice of the peace.'

9.6.1 Retirement

Lay magistrates must retire from sitting on the Bench when they reach the age of 70. When a lay magistrate resigns or retires, their name is placed on what is known as the supplemental list. While they are on this list they are still entitled to use the title 'Justice of the Peace'. The explanatory notes to the Courts Act 2003 explain that the supplemental list is now intended to be a recognition of the service given by lay magistrates.

9.6.2 Removal

The Lord Chancellor, with the concurrence of the Lord Chief Justice, has powers to remove lay magistrates in the circumstances set out in s11(2) above. Incapacity will include situations where a magistrate becomes too ill to sit but does not resign. Removal for misbehaviour usually occurs when a magistrate is convicted of an offence. There are about ten such removals each year. However, on occasions in the past there have been removals for such matters as taking part in a CND march or transvestite behaviour. There was considerable criticism of the Lord Chancellor's use of his power of removal in such circumstances. Today, the Lord Chancellor (which is solely a political office) must seek the agreement of the Lord Chief Justice to remove a magistrate. Therefore, it is unlikely that such behaviour today would lead to removal from the Bench.

The power under s11(2)(b) of removal for persistent failure to meet the required standards of competence reinforces the training initiative (MNTI2). It overcomes the problems of the old system whereby magistrates could continue to sit on the Bench regardless of whether they had understood their training. This is the first time that this power has been specifically set down by statute.

The power under s11(2)(c) allows the Lord Chancellor, with the concurrence of the Lord Chief Justice, to remove magistrates who refuse to fulfil their obligations to sit a certain number of times. It also allows magistrates to be removed if they refuse to operate a law enacted by the government.

9.7 Magistrates' duties

Magistrates have a very wide workload which is mainly connected to criminal cases, although they also deal with some civil matters, especially family cases.

9.7.1 Criminal cases

Ninety-eight per cent of all criminal cases are tried in the Magistrates' Court. As well as dealing with all these, magistrates also deal with preliminary hearings in the remaining 2 per cent of criminal cases. This will involve early administrative hearings and bail applications.

In 2009 the magistrates' recruitment website on www.direct.gov.uk explained the role in the following way:

QUOTATION

'As a magistrate, you will sit in your local magistrates' court dealing with a wide range of less serious criminal cases and civil matters. Some of your duties will include:

- determining whether a defendant is guilty or not and passing the appropriate sentence
- deciding on requests for remand in custody
- deciding on applications for bail
- committing more serious cases to the Crown Court

With experience and further training you could also go on to deal with cases in the family and youth courts.'

In criminal cases the role of lay magistrates has increased through the statutory downgrading of offences. Over the past 25 years a number of offences which were triable either way have been made summary offences and triable only in the Magistrates' Court; for example, drink-driving and driving while disqualified. It is also thought that the magistrates' workload has also increased through the CPS charging the lower of two possible charges against the defendant, again making the case triable only in the Magistrates' Court. However, to set against this, some less serious offences may be dealt with through an out-of-court disposal of a fixed penalty or police caution.

The Criminal Justice and Courts Act 2015 introduced a new single justice procedure whereby cases may be brought against defendants charged with summary only non-imprisonable offences. These cases will be dealt with by a single magistrate 'on the papers'. This means that neither the prosecutor nor defendant will attend court, but instead the defendant can contact the court in writing, rather than having to attend in person. This procedure will be used to deal with a number of straightforward and uncontested criminal cases. It has the potential to reduce the workload for magistrates and make the court operate more efficiently.

An important point to note is that, where a defendant pleads not guilty, the magistrates both decide on guilt or innocence and, if they find the defendant guilty, also pass sentence. This is in contrast to the Crown Court where the two roles of deciding the verdict and passing sentence are kept separate. In the Crown Court the jury decides on guilt or innocence. If it finds the defendant guilty the judge then passes sentence.

Crown Court appeals
Lay magistrates also sit at the Crown Court to hear appeals from the Magistrates' Court to hear cases where the defendant is appealing to the Crown Court against his conviction. In these cases the lay justices form a panel with a qualified judge.

9.7.2 Civil cases
Many civil matters are also dealt with in the Magistrates' Court. These include the enforcing of debts owed to the utilities (gas, electricity and water), non-payment of council tax and non-payment of television licences. In addition, they hear appeals from the refusal to grant a licence for the sale of alcohol (Licensing Act 2003) or for a licence to operate a Hackney cab (taxi). Until 2003 magistrates actually had to grant all licences to sell alcohol, including licences for one-off situations, such as extended hours for a bar for a graduation ceremony! This work took up a large amount of their time and it was felt that, as it was mainly administrative in nature, it would be better for local authorities to have the power to grant a licence and magistrates should only deal with appeals where a licence had been refused.

9.7.3 Youth Court
Specially nominated and trained justices form the Youth Court panel to hear criminal charges against young offenders aged 10 to 17 years old. The panel must usually include at least one man and one woman.

Magistrates in the Youth Court have the power to sentence young offenders to a maximum of two years' detention and training.

9.7.4 Family Court
Magistrates used to sit in a special panel on a 'Family Proceedings Court', dealing with a wide range of issues affecting family and children. Following the Crime and Courts

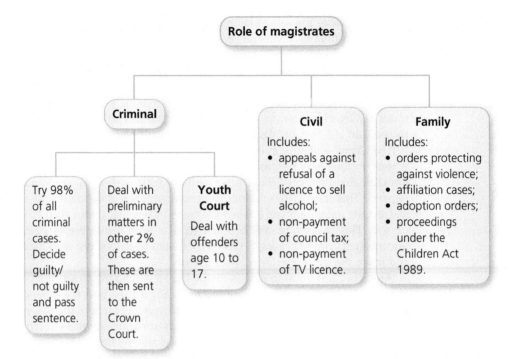

Figure 9.2 Role of magistrates

Act 2013 the powers of the Family Proceedings Court were transferred to the new Combined Family Court. In Family Court proceedings a bench of two or three lay magistrates (which will be gender balanced wherever possible) will deal with the more straightforward cases. More serious cases are heard by District Judges or High Court Judges. The magistrates for this court have special training and under the Courts Act 2003 the Lord Chancellor has the power to make rules on:

- the grant and revocation of authorisation of magistrates to sit as a member of the Family Court;
- the appointment of chairmen of these courts;
- the composition of the Bench in these courts.

These powers are intended to ensure that only trained and suitable magistrates sit in the Family Courts.

KEY FACTS

Lay magistrates

Qualifications	• No formal qualifications required. • 18–65 on appointment. • No serious convictions: not an undischarged bankrupt. • Six key personal qualities. • Live (or work) within or near to the local justice area in which they sit.

Selection/ appointment	Candidates encouraged to apply directly.
	Adverts are used to encourage applications from wide range.
	Local advisory committees interview and make recommendations to Lord Chief Justice.
	Lord Chief Justice appoints.
	Tries to obtain a balance by taking into account: • gender • ethnic origin • geographical spread • occupation.
Training	Judicial Studies Board (now Judicial College) has a strengthened role in training (Courts Act 2003).
	Most training carried out locally by legal advisers (magistrates' clerks) but some training is to be carried out nationally.
	MNTI2: • training sessions • mentors • appraisal • post-sitting reviews.
Role	Criminal cases: • deals with 98% of all criminal cases • also first hearing in other 2% • decide bail applications • decide verdict • pass sentence.
	Civil cases such matters as: • appeals against refusal of a licence to sell alcohol • non-payment of council tax • non-payment of TV licence.
	Youth Court.
	Family Court.
Retirement/ removal	Retire at 70.
	Can resign at any time.
	Removal is by the Lord Chancellor, with the concurrence of the Lord Chief Justice, for: • incapacity or misbehaviour • persistent failure to meet standards of competence • declining or neglecting to take a proper part in the exercise of his functions as a JP.
	(s11 Courts Act 2003)

9.7.5 Immunity from suit

Under the CLSA 1990 lay magistrates have immunity from being sued for anything they do in their judicial capacity in good faith. So even if an act is in excess of their jurisdiction, they cannot be sued if they believed that they were acting within their powers.

9.8 The magistrates' clerk

Every Bench is assisted by a clerk, or as they are now often referred to, a legal adviser. The senior clerk in each court has to be qualified as a barrister or solicitor for at least five years. Since 2010 all legal advisers have to be legally qualified. The Judicial College is responsible for training legal advisers. The clerk's duty is to guide the magistrates on questions of law, practice and procedure. This is set out in s28(3) of the Justices of the Peace Act 1979 which says:

SECTION

's 28(3) It is hereby declared that the functions of a justices' clerk include the giving to the justices … at the request of [them], of advice about law, practice or procedure on questions arising in connection with the discharge of [their] functions … and that the clerk may, at any time when he thinks he should do so, bring to the attention of the justices any point of law, practice or procedure that it or may be involved in any question so arising.'

At the same time as the implementation of the HRA 1998 in October 2000, a Practice Direction was issued requiring any legal advice given by the legal advisers to the justices to be given in open court.

QUOTATION

'8 At any time, justices are entitled to receive advice to assist them in discharging their responsibilities. If they are in any doubt as to the evidence which has been given, they should seek the aid of their legal adviser, referring to his/her notes as appropriate. This should ordinarily be done in open court. Where the justices request their adviser to join them in the retiring room, this request should be made in the presence of the parties in court.

Any legal advice given to the justices other than in open court should be clearly stated to be professional and the adviser should subsequently repeat the substance of the advice in open court and give the parties an opportunity to make any representations they wish on that professional advice. The legal adviser should then state in open court whether the professional advice is confirmed or, if it is varied, the nature of the variation.'

Practice Direction [2000] 4 All ER 895

This enforces the decisions in the earlier cases of *R v Sussex Justices, ex p McCarthy* [1924] 1 KB 256 and *R v Eccles Justices, ex p Fitzpatrick* [1989] 89 Cr App R 324.

CASE EXAMPLE

R v Sussex Justices, ex p McCarthy [1924] 1 KB 256

The defendant was being tried in the Magistrates' Courts on a charge of dangerous driving. The clerk to the justices was a member of a firm of solicitors who were representing the claimant in a civil case arising from the collision in the driving incident. When the magistrates retired to decide the case, the clerk retired with them. However, he was not asked for any advice and he did not inform the magistrates about the civil case. Despite the fact that the clerk did not take any part in the decision making, the Divisional Court quashed the decision. Giving judgment in this case, Lord Hewitt CJ said:

JUDGMENT

'It is not merely a matter of some importance but it is of fundamental importance that justice should not only be done but manifestly and undoubtedly be seen to be done.'

In *R v Eccles Justices, ex p Fitzpatrick* (1989) the Divisional Court quashed a decision and sent the case back to be dealt with by a new Bench because the clerk had retired with the justices for 25 minutes of the 30 minutes they were absent from court. The court said that any request for the clerk to retire with the justices must be made clearly and in open court.

The role of the legal adviser was substantially increased following the Narey Report, 'Review of Delay in the Criminal Justice System' (1997). This had recommended that clerks be given a wider role as case managers and with the power to do all the matters that a single justice can do. However, when the Crime and Disorder Act 1998, which implemented these proposals, was going through Parliament, there was some disquiet that the clerks' role was going to be too wide and erode the function of the justices. This point of view was put by Lord Bingham during the Second Reading in the House of Lords when he said:

QUOTATION

'To send a defendant to prison is a judicial act; it is not an order which anyone not exercising judicial authority should make, and it is certainly not a matter of administration.

...I object to the possibility that some of these powers might by rule be exercised by the justices' clerk because such a rule would erode the fundamental distinction between the justices and the justices' legal adviser ... If the justices' clerk were to be entrusted with these important decisions and judgements, judicial in character, the time would inevitably come when people would reasonably ask whether he or she should not be left to get on and try the whole case.'

As a result, s49(3) was inserted into the 1998 Act to prevent certain functions being delegated to clerks. The Justices' Clerks Rules 1999 (SI No 2784) set out what they can do. This includes dealing with routine administrative matters, but also issuing warrants for arrest, extending police bail and adjourning criminal proceedings if the defendant is given bail on the same terms as originally set by the justices.

9.9 Advantages of using lay magistrates

9.9.1 Cross-section of society

The system involves members of the community and provides a wider cross-section on the Bench than would be possible with the use of professional judges. This is particularly true of women, with 53 per cent of magistrates being women against 28 per cent of professional judges. Also, ethnic minorities are reasonably well represented in the magistracy. The numbers of ethnic minority magistrates have increased gradually and about 11 per cent of the magistracy are from an ethnic minority. This compares very favourably to the professional judiciary where less than 5 per cent are from ethnic minority backgrounds.

The relatively high level of ethnic minority magistrates is largely a result of campaigns to attract a wider range of candidates. In an effort to encourage those from ethnic minorities to apply, adverts are placed in such publications as the *Caribbean Times*, the

Asian Times and the *Muslim News*. There has also been a shadowing programme aimed at people from ethnic minorities under which potential applicants for the magistracy were able to shadow a sitting magistrate in order to discover what the role entailed. Although the gender and racial mix of the lay magistracy is good, there is still concern about the age and social background of magistrates. A report, 'The Judiciary in the Magistrates' Courts' (2002), commissioned jointly by the Home Office and the Lord Chancellor's Department found that lay magistrates:

- were drawn overwhelmingly from professional and managerial ranks; and
- 40 per cent of them were retired from full-time employment.

This trend continues as recent statistics show that 55 per cent of all lay magistrates are between 60 and 70 years of age, with less than 4 per cent being under 40. Although they are not a true cross-section of the local community and have little in common with the young working-class defendants who make up the majority of defendants, lay magistrates are more representative than District Judges in the Magistrates' Courts. The same report pointed out that in comparison with lay magistrates District Judges were:

- younger, but
- mostly white and male.

Davies, Croall and Tyrer, in their book *Criminal Justice*, raised the question of what would a more demographically representative panel achieve?

QUOTATION

'What more would a more representative magistracy achieve and just what, or who, should it represent? A representative magistracy on the grounds of demographic characteristics alone may not make different decisions in relation to either guilt or sentencing from the current magistracy. Women magistrates appear no more sympathetic, for example, to female offenders who often come from very different socio-economic backgrounds (see for example, Eaton 1986) [*Justice for Women?* Open University Press], and there is little evidence of any direct bias on the grounds of social status in respect of business offenders (see, for example, Croall 1991) ['Sentencing the Business Offender' 30(4) *Howard Journal* 280].'

M Davies, H Croall and J Tyres, Criminal Justice (2nd edn, Longman, 1998) p 177

So, it can be argued that the make-up of the magistracy is irrelevant provided those who are magistrates perform their role well. However, it is important that justice is not only done, but also seen to be done. As lay magistrates are seen as representatives of the community in the legal system, then it is critical that the make-up of benches should reflect the make-up of the local community.

9.9.2 Local knowledge

Lay magistrates used to have to live within 15 miles of the area covered by the commission, so that they should have local knowledge of particular problems in the area. Under the Courts Act 2003 there is no longer a formal requirement that they should live in or near the area in which they sit as a magistrate, although the explanatory notes for the Act say:

QUOTATION

'It is envisaged, however, that Advisory Committees (who advise the Lord Chancellor on appointments of lay magistrates) will continue, under guidance from the Lord Chancellor, to recommend that lay magistrates be assigned to the local justice area in which they reside unless there is a good reason to do otherwise (for example, should an applicant find it easier to sit where he or she works rather than where he or she lives).'

However, as most magistrates come from the professional and managerial classes, it is unlikely that they live in or have any real knowledge of the problems in the poorer areas. Their main value is that they will have more awareness of local events, local patterns of crime and local opinions than a professional judge from another area.

In addition, during the last ten years, some 150 Magistrates' Courts have been closed, with further closures planned. This causes problems of access and attendance as in some areas people have long journeys to their 'local' court. It also means that the advantage of lay magistrates having local knowledge is being lost.

9.9.3 Cost

The use of unpaid lay magistrates is cheap. The report 'The Judiciary in the Magistrates' Courts' (2000) found that at that time the cost of using lay magistrates was £52.10 per hour, whereas the cost of using District Judges in the Magistrates' Courts was £61.78 an hour. When this is multiplied by the number of hours of work carried out by lay magistrates in the course of the year, it is obvious that the cost of replacing them with professional judges would be several millions of pounds. In addition, there would also be the problem of recruiting sufficient qualified lawyers.

The cost of a trial in the Magistrates' Court is also much less than a trial in the Crown Court. This is partly because cases in the Crown Court are more complex and therefore likely to take longer, but even so it is clear that the cost both to the government and to defendants who pay for their own lawyer is much higher.

9.9.4 Legal adviser

Since 1999 all newly appointed magistrates' clerks have to be legally qualified and since 2010 all legal advisers must be legally qualified. This brings a higher level of legal skill to the Magistrates' Court. The availability of a legal adviser gives the magistrates access to any necessary legal advice on points that may arise in any case. This overcomes any criticism of the fact that lay magistrates are not themselves legally qualified. In addition, the training of lay magistrates is improving, with MNTI1 and MNTI2 and the strengthened role of the Judicial Studies Board in their training.

9.9.5 Few appeals

Comparatively few defendants appeal against the magistrates' decisions, and many of the appeals that are made are against sentence, not against the finding of guilt. In most years there are only about 5,000 or so appeals to the Crown Court from the Magistrates' Courts against conviction. Of these only about 40 per cent (2,000 or so) are allowed. There are also between 6,000 and 7,000 appeals to the Crown Court against sentence each year. Of these under 50 per cent are allowed. These are very small numbers out of the two million cases dealt with by Magistrates' Courts each year.

There are also only a very small number of appeals to the Queen's Bench Divisional Court on a point of law: about 100 cases each year. Just under half of these are successful. These figures show that, despite the amateur status of lay magistrates, they do a remarkably good job.

9.10 Disadvantages of lay magistrates

9.10.1 Middle-aged, middle class

Lay magistrates are often perceived as being middle-aged and middle class. The report 'The Judiciary in the Magistrates' Courts' (2002) showed that this was largely true. It found that 40 per cent of lay magistrates were retired and also that they were over-whelmingly from a professional or managerial background. Current figures show that less than 1 per cent of magistrates are under the age of 30, and over 80 per cent of magistrates are over the age of 50. However, as already discussed at section 9.9.1, lay magistrates are from a wider range of backgrounds than professional judges.

9.10.2 Prosecution bias

It is often said that lay magistrates tend to be prosecution biased, believing the police too readily. However, part of the training is aimed at eliminating this type of bias. There is also the fact that the magistrates will see the same CPS prosecutor or designated case worker frequently and this could affect their judgment. Another point is that there is a lower acquittal rate in Magistrates' Courts than in the Crown Court.

9.10.3 Inconsistency in sentencing

Magistrates in different areas often pass very different sentences for what appear to be similar offences. This has been an ongoing problem for many years. For example, the government's White Paper, 'Justice for All', set out differences found in the Criminal Statistics for 2001 when it gave these following examples:

- For burglary of dwellings, 20 per cent of offenders are sentenced to immediate custody in Teesside, compared with 41 per cent of offenders in Birmingham. Thirty-eight per cent of burglars at Cardiff Magistrates' Courts receive community sentences, compared with 66 per cent in Leicester.

- For driving while disqualified, the percentage of offenders sentenced to custody ranged from 21 per cent in Neath Port Talbot (South Wales) to 77 per cent in Mid North Essex.

- For receiving stolen goods, 3.5 per cent of offenders sentenced at Reading Magistrates' Court received custodial sentences, compared with 48 per cent in Greenwich and Woolwich (South London) and 39 per cent at Camberwell Green (South London).

Again in 2004, figures showed that matters had not improved. There were still some major differences in the way magistrates in different areas of the country sentenced defendants. For example, magistrates in Sunderland discharged 36.4 per cent of all defendants, whereas only 9.2 per cent of defendants in Birmingham were discharged. Another example is that in Newcastle magistrates sentenced only 7.2 per cent of defendants to an immediate custodial sentence whereas in Hillingdon in West London, the magistrates sentenced 32 per cent of defendants to an immediate custodial sentence.

Figures for 2010 show similar inconsistencies. The highest percentage of offenders being given a custodial sentence was in Bristol (11.1 per cent), followed by Peterborough (11.0 per cent). At the other end of the scale only 0.1 per cent of offenders appearing in Dinefwr Magistrates' Courts were given custodial sentences. Bristol also imposed the highest percentage of community sentences at 32.2 per cent, whilst in Dinefwr it was 6.6 per cent. The overall figures for Bristol show that out of 5,687 offenders sentenced, 630 were given a custodial sentence and 1,831 a community sentence. In Dinefwr out of 1,169 offenders sentenced only one was given a custodial sentence and 79 a community sentence. These figures do not take into account what types of offences were involved, but the figures for Bristol seem to be excessively high. This is so even when compared to other city areas with similar number of offenders, such as Coventry where, out of 7,162 offenders, 492 were given a custodial sentence (6.8 per cent) and 1,043 were given community sentences (14.4 per cent).

9.10.4 Reliance on the clerk

The lack of legal knowledge of the lay justices should be offset by the fact that a legally qualified clerk is available to give advice. However, this will not prevent inconsistencies in sentencing since the clerk is not allowed to help the magistrates decide on a sentence. In some courts it is felt that the magistrates rely too heavily on their clerk.

KEY FACTS

Advantages and disadvantages of using lay magistrates in the legal system

The points in this table are balanced against each other, so you will see the advantages and disadvantages of the same facts:

Advantages	Disadvantages
Cross-section of local people Good gender balance Improving ethnic balance Much better cross-section than District Judges	Not a true cross-section 40% are retired people Majority are from professional or managerial background Older than District Judges
Live (or work) locally and so know the area and its problems Cheaper than using professional judges as they are only paid expenses Cheaper than sending cases to the Crown Court	Unlikely to live in the poorer areas and so do not truly know the area's problems
Improved training through MNTI2 and the increased role of Judicial College Have legal adviser for points of law Very few appeals	There are inconsistencies in sentencing and decisions on bail

ACTIVITY

Self-test questions

1. What powers does a single lay magistrate have?
2. Who is disqualified from being a lay magistrate?
3. What are the six key personal qualities that the Lord Chancellor sets out for lay magistrates?
4. How often do lay magistrates normally sit in court?
5. What initiatives have been taken to encourage applications from a wide range of people?
6. What is the role of the Advisory Committee in selecting and appointing magistrates?
7. Outline the training of lay magistrates.
8. On what grounds can the Lord Chancellor remove a lay magistrate from the post?
9. What are the roles of magistrates in criminal cases?
10. Apart from criminal cases, what other cases can magistrates deal with?

SAMPLE ESSAY QUESTION

In 1997, the academic Penny Darbyshire criticised the English magistracy for being 'too white, too middle class and too old'. However, the changes to the selection and appointment procedures since then have rendered that criticism largely redundant. Discuss.

State the qualifications needed to be appointed a lay magistrate.

No formal qualifications except:

- aged 18 to 65;
- live in or near area to which they are appointed;
- six key qualities.

Explain the selection process including:

- make own application;
- role of local advisory committees;
- Lord Chief Justice makes final selection trying to balance gender, ethnic background, occupation and political affiliation.

Compare the present qualifications and selection process with the previous ones, e.g.:

- wider age group (was 21 to 60 and rarely appointed under 27);
- often were nominated by local group such as chamber of commerce – this favoured middle class;
- present system much more open;
- government's National Strategy for Recruitment (2003);
- advertised widely.

Consider the present make-up of magistrates, e.g.:

- statistics showing percentage of ethnic minorities;
- are there too many middle class?
- problems with time off from work – does this lead to high percentage of lay magistrates being retired people?
- examples of very young magistrates being appointed.

CONCLUSION

Figure 9.3 Essay map on lay magistrates

SUMMARY

■ Lay magistrates are non-lawyers who sit in panels of two or three to hear cases in the Magistrates' Courts.

Qualifications

■ No formal qualifications are required.

■ Must be between the ages of 18 and 65 and be of good standing in the local community.

■ Magistrates are expected to live or work in or near the local justice area for which they are appointed.

■ Key personal qualities are required.

Selection

■ Apply by filling in an application form.

■ Local advisory committees interview candidates and identify those who are suitable.

■ The Lord Chief Justice then appoints new magistrates from these people.

■ The aim is to keep a balance of gender, ethnic origin, geographical spread and occupation.

Training

■ Training is supervised by the Magistrates' Committee of the Judicial College.

■ Magistrates are trained in three areas of competence.

■ Each new magistrate is assigned a mentor and they will be appraised on the competences.

Magistrates' role

■ Try about 98 per cent of all criminal cases.

■ Deal with preliminary matters in the other 2 per cent of cases before the case goes to the Crown Court for trial.

■ Sit with a qualified judge at the Crown Court to hear appeals from the Magistrates' Court.

■ Deal with some civil matters such as non-payment of council tax or TV licence.

■ In the Youth Court they hear criminal cases involving those aged 10 to 17.

■ In the Family Court they deal with issues affecting family and children.

Advantages of using lay magistrates

■ It involves a cross-section of society in the legal system.

■ They are a much wider cross-section than professional judges.

■ They have local knowledge.

■ It is cheaper to use lay magistrates than to use professional judges.

■ Their lack of legal knowledge is compensated for by their legal adviser.

■ There are comparatively few appeals from decisions by Magistrates' Courts.

Disadvantages of using lay magistrates

- Tend to be middle-aged and middle class.
- They are perceived as being biased towards the police and prosecution.
- They are inconsistent in sentencing.
- They rely too heavily on their clerk.

Further reading

Book

Darbyshire, P, *Darbyshire on the English Legal System* (9th edn, Sweet & Maxwell, 2008) Ch 15.

Articles

Darbyshire, P, 'An essay on the importance and neglect of the magistracy' [1997] *Crim LR* 627.

Herbert, A, 'Mode of trial and magistrates' sentencing powers' [2003] *Crim LR* 314.

Robson, G, 'The lay magistracy: no time for complacency' [2002] 166 *Justice of the Peace* 624.

'The Judiciary in the Magistrates' Courts', Home Office and Lord Chancellor's Department, December 2000.

Internet links

Annual court statistics at: www.justice.gov.uk

Magistrates' Association at: www.magistrates-association.org.uk

Ministry of Justice research series at: www.justice.gov.uk

Statistics for magistrates at: www.judiciary.gov.uk

10

The legal professions

AIMS AND OBJECTIVES

After reading this chapter you should be able to:

- Identify the members of the legal professions
- Explain the different routes to qualification as a Chartered legal executive, a solicitor and a barrister
- Analyse the statistics available on the legal professions to examine the distribution of lawyers in terms of demographics, geography, types of work and specialisms
- Distinguish the representative functions of the Law Society and the Bar Council from the regulatory and disciplinary roles of the Solicitors' Regulation Authority and Bar Standards Board respectively
- Advise a client on how to make a complaint about the provision of legal services
- Explain what the letters QC stand for
- Explain the effects of the Legal Services Act 2007 on the work, regulation and organisation of the legal professions
- Identify what the future might hold for the legal professions

People working in legal services

Legal work involves a great many different personnel, who perform widely varying roles. In the course of your involvement with the law you may encounter 'paralegal' workers, qualified legal executives, licensed conveyancers, notaries and different types of legal clerks. There are also many non-lawyers who specialise in the law, such as accountants who work in tax and revenue law. However, the terms 'lawyer' and 'legal profession' are generally understood to describe those who belong to a professional regulatory body, as listed in Figure 10.1.

When the terms 'lawyer' or 'legal profession' are used, however, they are usually describing solicitors or barristers. Solicitors traditionally provide a wide range of legal services as the 'front-line' lawyers. They provide general legal advice, prepare cases for court and can also conduct litigation. Barristers are specialist legal advisers and on the whole conduct litigation (advocacy) in the courts. However, as you will

Profession	Representative body	Regulatory body
Solicitors	Law Society	Solicitors' Regulation Authority (SRA)*
Barristers	Bar Council	Bar Standards Board (BSB)
Legal executives	Chartered Institute of Legal Executives (CILEx)	ILEX Professional Standards Ltd (IPS)
Licensed conveyancers	Council For Licensed Conveyancers*	
Patent attorneys	Chartered Institute of Patent Attorneys (CIPA)	Intellectual Property Regulation Board (IPReg)
Trade mark attorneys	Institute of Trade Mark Attorneys (ITMA)	
Law costs draftsmen	Association of Costs Lawyers	Costs Lawyer Standards Board
Notaries	Master of the Faculties	

* The two bodies marked with an asterisk are also currently 'licensing authorities' which means they can license ABSs (see section 10.2.3 below).

Figure 10.1 The eight regulated legal services professions

see, this overview is simplistic and the changes made to the legal profession since the mid-1980s have blurred the distinction between solicitors and barristers (and perhaps between those and legal executives and paralegals too). For example, 30 years ago, the demarcation between the role of the barrister and that of the solicitor was clear; solicitors rarely undertook advocacy work outside the Magistrates' and County Courts; the code of professional conduct for solicitors prohibited them from advertising, and solicitors enjoyed a monopoly in conveyancing (that is, the legal work associated with the buying and selling of property). All this has changed in the intervening period of time, and as you read this chapter you will discover how many of these aspects of the professions have altered and are continuing to change. Your attention is drawn to the Legal Services Act 2007 which permits the establishment of alternative business structures (or ABSs). This means that, for the first time, non-lawyers are able to manage and/or own a business that offers legal services to the public. From a commercial perspective, this is very significant across the legal services sector.

10.1 Paralegals and legal executives

'Paralegal' is a term difficult to define precisely. Many of the personnel who work in a law firm may have a job title of this description; but they may or may not have any formal legal qualifications. There is one recognised paralegal qualification offered by the CILEx for those candidates who work in the legal field but do not satisfy the entry requirements to take the CILEx diploma courses (see Figure 10.2 below). Otherwise, the term paralegal is a rather general one that does not necessarily denote how involved in the practice of law they are; they may or may not attend court or even meet clients. They may not even be a fee earner. That is not to say that paralegals lack importance. Many of the more straightforward issues (such as the form-filling required to enter a CFA; or the routine searches carried out when a house is being sold and so on) are time-consuming but not necessarily complex so are therefore best carried out by a paralegal, rather than a qualified and higher salaried lawyer. In June 2013, the Legal Education and Training

Review (LETR, or more commonly just called 'letter'), a review commissioned by the SRA, the BSB and IPS (for a guide to the acronyms, see Figure 10.1 above) delivered its final recommendations, which included:

CLAUSE

'**Recommendation 21**
Work should proceed to develop higher apprenticeship qualifications at levels 5–7 as part of an additional non-graduate pathway into the regulated professions, but the quality and diversity effects of such pathways should be monitored.

Recommendation 22
... Regulated entities must however ensure that policies and procedures are in place to deliver adequate levels of supervision and training of paralegal staff, and regulators must ensure that robust audit mechanisms provide assurance that these standards are being met. To ensure consistency and enhance opportunities for career progression and mobility within paralegal work, the development of a single voluntary system of certification/licensing for paralegal staff should also be considered, based on a common set of paralegal outcomes and standards.

Recommendation 23
Consideration should be given ... to the role of voluntary quality schemes in assuring the standards of independent paralegal providers outside the existing scheme of regulation. The Legal Services Board may wish to consider this issue as part of its work on the reservation and regulation of general legal advice.'

These recommendations seek to balance the need for flexible entry routes to a career in the legal professions with the need to ensure consistent and high standards of legal services.

CILEx is the awarding body for fully qualified legal executives. (This is also a term often used of a person who is a Fellow of CILEx. Fellowship is a legal qualification in its own right, but it can also be a step towards qualification as a solicitor.) CILEx defines itself as the third branch of the legal profession and it has 20,000 members. The Institute was established in 1963 to provide education and training for salaried non-solicitors doing paid legal work in law firms while they work. It received Royal Charter in 2011. Chartered legal executives undertake many legal activities that solicitors do, so in practice it may be impossible to distinguish a solicitor from a Chartered legal executive.

The entry requirements to start the CILEx qualifications are four GCSE passes in academic subjects including English, or two A levels and one GCSE, or three AS levels or NVQ level 3. However, applicants aged 21 or over can register as mature students. Even without formal qualifications, enrolment can be on the basis of business, commercial, academic or other experience. Full membership of the Institute generally takes four years but, during this time, the student is earning money working in a law firm. After becoming a Fellow, it is possible to go on and qualify as a solicitor (see Figure 10.2).

Unlike solicitors, who are granted certain rights of audience automatically on qualification, Chartered legal executives do not, and must gain an additional qualification under the CILEx Advocacy Qualification Scheme which allows members and fellows rights of audience to represent clients in court. Advocacy Certificates can be awarded in the following three areas:

- criminal proceedings;
- family proceedings;
- civil proceedings.

For further information on higher rights in general, see section 10.2.3 under Rights of Audience.

10.1.1 Training routes to become a solicitor

Solicitor law degree route	Solicitor non-law degree route	CILEx route fellowship to solicitor
A levels or other access qualification degree	A levels or other access qualification	GCSEs, A levels or other access qualification or other accreditation of prior learning or experience
Law degree (usually an LLB (Hons)) provided it is a *qualifying law* degree (QLD), which means that it includes study of the 7 foundation subjects*	Degree in any subject (a non-QLD)	CILEx Professional Diploma and employment under the supervision of a solicitor, chartered legal executive, barrister or licensed conveyancer for three years
	Common Professional Examination (also called the Graduate Diploma in Law). Study of the 7 foundation subjects* in law plus an extended project	ILEX Professional Higher Diploma (with continued employment as above)
Join as student member of the SRA	Join as student member of the SRA	Fellowship of the Institute (on successful completion of a portfolio which meets the criteria for work-based learning from the qualifying employment period)
Legal Practice Course	Legal Practice Course	Legal Practice Course
Training contract	Training contract	
Professional Skills Course (during the training contract)	Professional Skills Course (during the training contract)	Professional Skills Course
Application to be entered on the Roll of Officers of the Supreme Court: this is admission to the profession as a qualified solicitor	Application to be entered on the Roll of Officers of the Supreme Court: this is admission to the profession as a qualified solicitor	Application to be entered on the Roll of Officers of the Supreme Court: this is admission to the profession as a qualified solicitor

* Contract Law, the Law of Torts, Public (also called Constitutional and Administrative) Law, Land Law, Criminal Law, EU Law and the Law of Trusts. The QLD has remained unaffected by the result of the June 2016 referendum on EU membership.

Figure 10.2 Solicitors' qualification routes: graduates and CILEx

10.2 Solicitors

10.2.1 Organisation

The following information is taken from the Law Society's webpages, including the annual statistical reports and key fact charts, all available at www.lawsociety.org.uk:

- As at 31 July 2015, there were 168,226 solicitors on the Roll, an increase of nearly 5 per cent on the year before.

- At the same date, 133,367 solicitors held practising certificates (79.2 per cent of those on the roll), an increase of 2.3 per cent on the previous year. [Section 1A of the Solicitors Act 1974 requires that any solicitor employed in connection with the provision of legal services in England and Wales will need a practising certificate (pc). They cost £290 each in 2016.]

- The number of solicitors working in private practice firms registered in England and Wales declined for the fifth year in a row to 9,403.

- Over 5,000 commerce and industry organisations employed practising solicitors in 2015, an increase of 4.4 per cent on 2014.

- Solicitors working in-house made up 21.6 per cent of practising solicitors in 2015, up from 15 per cent in 2000. This proportion is expected to grow further over coming years.

- In 2015, excluding those whose ethnicity was unknown, solicitors from BME groups represent 15.5 per cent of all solicitors with practising certificates. There were 18,547 practising solicitors from minority ethnic groups in 2015 – up from 5,009 in 2000.

- Women now account for 48.8 per cent of solicitors with practising certificates. The proportion of female practising solicitors has risen from 40.5 per cent in 2005.

- More than a fifth of all practising solicitors in England and Wales now work in the City of London.

ACTIVITY

Self-test question

What trends on the composition and size of the profession are indicated by the statistics above?

Solicitors in private practice are generally regarded as more accessible to the public than barristers, solicitors' firms being found in the high streets of every town. Clients can employ the services of a solicitor directly, which was never the case with barristers (but now see 10.3.3 below). Solicitors are also able to advertise their services (within the limits of the professional rules), and this enables potential clients to select a practitioner with experience of their particular legal problem.

Region	Population (000s)	Total number of solicitors	Number of solicitors per 1,000 population
City London	11.5	20,245	1,760
Rest of inner London	3,049.5	23,543	8
Greater London	4,692.4	43,788	9
South East	8,435.7	12,112	1
Eastern	5,766.6	7,330	1
South West	5,231.2	5,660	1
West Midlands	5,431.1	7,847	1
East Midlands	4,451.2	4,466	1
Yorkshire and Humberside	5,258.1	7,652	1
North West	6,897.9	12,293	2
North East	2,584.3	3,087	1
Wales	2,999.3	3,683	1
Total	54,809.1	117,862	2

Figure 10.3 Location of solicitors and number of solicitors per 1,000 population in 2010

ACTIVITY

Self-test question

Geographically, which areas are best served in terms of numbers of solicitors compared with the percentage of the population, and which areas are worst? Why do you think these areas have such a high/low proportion of solicitors' firms?

10.2.2 Education and training

First, refer back to Figure 10.2. That table shows the most common routes for entry to the solicitors' profession, but there are in fact seven routes to qualification as a solicitor:

- law graduate;
- non-law graduate;
- via the CILEx route;
- overseas lawyer (transfer);
- barrister (transfer);
- Scottish/Northern Irish lawyers (transfer);
- justices' clerk (a Magistrates' Court clerk who passes the Legal Practice Course and has at least five years' experience as a clerk).

Most newly admitted solicitors (approximately 42 per cent in 2010/11) are law graduates. The remainder are either graduates of another discipline who have undertaken a conversion course in law (the Common Professional Examination or the Graduate

Diploma in Law: in 2010–11, 14 per cent of newly admitted solicitors came by this route) or have qualified through the CILEx's route (approximately 2 per cent). The remaining 30 per cent were qualified lawyers who transferred to become solicitors.

The academic stage

In 2014, 31,800 people applied to study law at undergraduate level in England and Wales, out of whom 21,775 were accepted on to courses. A total of 16,116 students graduated with a Law degree in the summer of 2014. In the year ending 31 July 2015, 6,077 individuals were admitted to the roll. Of these, 61 per cent were women, 907 solicitors admitted were from minority ethnic groups and 62.8 per cent of those admitted from minority ethnic groups were female. The average age of those entered on to the roll in 2014–15 was 29.5 years. The average age of males was slightly higher than that of females.

In terms of content, all students must study the seven foundation subjects (see the note below Figure 10.2). Research data gathered by the LETR in 2013 indicated that practising lawyers as well as academics were not universally in support of those seven subjects being more important, or necessarily more of a foundation, over others. For example:

QUOTATION

'2.56 The majority of the key stakeholders, including, for example, the Council of the Inns of Court, the Law Society and the Society of Legal Scholars, share the view that the existing Foundation subjects remain a good proxy, albeit with some qualification.

2.57 … there were suggestions for additions to the Foundation subjects. The range of subjects proposed was diverse, including professional ethics, company or commercial law, (these being the most common suggestions) international law, comparative law, information technology law, and also, on the private plight side, some pleas for more emphasis on "social welfare" areas such as housing law …

4.67 A majority of respondents took the view that ethics and professionalism need to be developed throughout the continuum of education and training. This view is accepted and underpins a number of the final recommendations in this report.

4.68 LETR research data … highlighted the significance of commercial awareness to clients and suggested that this includes:

- awareness of the sector and the clients' business; having an interest in the sector so as to be able to communicate with clients;
- an ability to recognise clients' commercial objectives rather than proposing "pure law" solutions;
- wider knowledge of commercial and financial subjects: understanding relevant financial products; corporate structures; markets and sectors;
- numeracy and ability to interpret financial data;
- understanding of law as a business: that firms (etc) are profit-making entities; marketing and networking; how law firms and chambers are run.'

The contents of the law degree (and Common Professional Examination (CPE)/Graduate Diploma in Law (GDL)) are likely, therefore, to change to reflect these recommendations.

The vocational stage

After the academic stage, all potential solicitors must complete a professional course, the Legal Practice Course, which prepares them for the practical aspects of the work. Students on the Legal Practice Course study property law and practice, business and litigation plus professional conduct and ethics, solicitors' accounts, advocacy and drafting, as well as taking options in their chosen fields of specialism (for example family, welfare, legal aid, commercial, property, corporate law).

The training contract – the practical stage

Fellows of CILEx are exempt from the practical stage because they will have been working in a law firm for at least three years. However, all other students must serve a prescribed period of training (usually two years) attached to a practising solicitor. At this stage, the trainee solicitor is in effect serving an apprenticeship. The trainee will be salaried during the term of the training contract (there used to be a minimum salary set by the Law Society, but in 2012 the decision was made to abolish the trainee minimum wage from 2014, although trainees will receive at least the *national* minimum wage). Obtaining training contracts is not easy and competition is fierce. In the year ending 31 July 2015, 5,457 new traineeships were registered with the SRA. Of the new trainees registered, 62.8 per cent were women.

The SRA published an Equality Impact Assessment when consulting on abolishing the trainee solicitor minimum wage. That assessment included some of the following observations:

QUOTATION

'the majority of trainee solicitors are based in large firms. Only 5% of TCs [training contracts] are provided by sole practitioners and 14% take place in firms with between two and four partners ... the majority (62%) of trainees are paid more than 10% above the minimum level stipulated by the SRA. Under a third of trainees are paid the minimum level [however] women and BME groups are both underrepresented in the higher paid groups. [T]here are effectively two distinct "markets" for TCs:

- A prime market paying high training contract rates (salaries falling within the range £34k–£42k). This market currently accounts for around 37% of total TCs and is dominated by large city and national firms.
- A lower tier market paying at or just above the minimum level (salaries falling within the range £16k–£22k). This market currently accounts for 42% of all TCs and includes a significant proportion of trainees in small firms.'

ACTIVITY

Self-test question

Discuss what factors may influence the average starting salary of trainee solicitors.

10.2.3 Work

Solicitors are largely occupied in providing legal services to clients on a face-to-face basis, or by telephone or letter. They have direct personal contact with clients and therefore need to employ personnel to assist in providing this service.

Increasingly, solicitors tend to specialise in their work in order to gain expertise in particular areas of the law. Within a firm in private practice, therefore, you may find different departments specialising in, for example, criminal matters, family law, probate (i.e. dealing with the property of those who have died), land law matters and civil cases such as personal injuries. Figure 10.4 shows the categories of work undertaken by solicitors in England and Wales, and is drawn from research carried out by the Law Society in July 2010, based on responses from solicitors on renewal forms for their practising certificate.

ACTIVITY

Self-test question

In which areas do most of the solicitors renewing their practising certificates work? Do the statistics surprise you?

Administrative and public law	3,814	Immigration and nationality	3,579
Advocacy	6,961	Insolvency and bankruptcy	3,591
Agricultural law	912	Insurance	4,094
Aviation	528	Intellectual property	6,570
Banking law	5,410	International law (non-EC)	1,269
Business affairs	20,696	Landlord and tenant – residential	11,131
Chancery	840	Libel and defamation	817
Charity law	2,073	Liquor licensing/gambling	3,196
Children law	5,695	Litigation – commercial	16,681
Civil liberties/human rights	1,757	Litigation – general	21,937
Commercial property	20,176	Maritime/shipping/admiralty	1,151
Common law	1,254	Media/entertainment law	2,440
Computer and IT law	3,890	Mediation – civil/commercial	1,965
Construction/civil engineering	2,705	Mediation – family	810
Consumer problems	2,998	Medical negligence	3,260
Conveyancing residential	17,828	Mental health	1,654
Corporate finance	8,327	Mergers and acquisitions	7,713
Crime – general, motor, juvenile	10,942	Neighbour disputes	2,128
Debt and money advice	3,563	Personal injury	13,094
Education	1,011	Planning law	2,477
Employment	12,591	Professional negligence	3,561
Energy and natural resources	1,727	Taxation	4,550
Environment law	2,351	Transport road and rail	1,089
European Community (EU) law	2,211	Travel and tourism	316
Family	13,633	Trusts	6,187
Financial and investment services	4,063	Welfare benefits	1,689
Fraud	2,844	Wills and probate	13,685

© 2010, The Law Society

Figure 10.4 Categories of work undertaken by solicitors, 2010

The Courts and Legal Services Act 1990

A significant change in the work solicitors were permitted to do occurred in the CLSA 1990. This Act was introduced with the specific aim of developing and improving the way in which legal services were offered to the public. Section 17(1) made it clear that the 1990 Act was an attempt to strike a balance between the desire to ensure that justice was administered properly and the wish to allow people other than members of the two main professions to carry out some of the work which had hitherto been reserved for barristers and solicitors alone. This meant, for the first time, they were faced with competition for their clients. The hope of those drafting the legislation was that this element of competition would lead to better services being offered to the public, for more realistic fees.

Conveyancing

Previously, solicitors had enjoyed a complete monopoly in matters of conveyancing (i.e. transferring ownership in land from one person to another) but, in 1985, the first significant change in the work of solicitors occurred. Despite the fact that many solicitors were financially dependent on the income produced by conveyancing, there had been criticisms of the low quality of the work and the relatively high charges for it. So the Administration of Justice Act 1985 (Part II) introduced a system of **licensed conveyancers** which allowed non-solicitors to carry out work for members of the public and s37 of the CLSA 1990 ensured that non-solicitors involved in conveyancing work would be suitably qualified, accountable and insured against the risk of loss to the client. There had been considerable pressure from banks and estate agents to open up the market to enter into competition with solicitors.

Rights of audience

So solicitors lost their monopoly on conveyancing, but at the same time practice rules of the courts ensured that only barristers had the right of advocacy in the High Court, Court of Appeal and House of Lords. Barristers also had a virtual monopoly in the Crown Court. In 1979, the (Benson) Royal Commission on Legal Services examined the exclusivity of the work of solicitors and barristers and, although it recommended that no change should be made in the rights of audience in the courts, solicitors challenged the position whereby they enjoyed advocacy in the Magistrates' and County Courts and not the higher courts. Solicitors who, for example, had carefully prepared a case for Crown Court trial were frustrated that they had to hand over the case to a barrister (who would be less acquainted with it) for presentation at court. Over time, barristers' monopoly on higher courts advocacy has also been lost.

Section 27 of the CLSA 1990 established a new system for the professional bodies to grant rights of audience before the courts subject to the requirements of those bodies. Thus, since 1993, the Law Society and now the SRA, has been able to grant a Certificate of Advocacy to those solicitors who have met the necessary training requirements. Solicitors with Higher Rights Certificates are called solicitor-advocates.

There are three categories of Higher Rights qualification:

- **Higher Courts (All Proceedings).** The solicitor can exercise rights of audience in all proceedings before all the higher courts in England and Wales.

- **Higher Courts (Civil Proceedings).** The solicitor can exercise rights of audience in all civil proceedings in the higher courts of England and Wales, including judicial review proceedings in any court arising from any civil cause.

- **Higher Courts (Criminal Proceedings).** The solicitor can exercise rights of audience in all criminal proceedings in the higher courts and judicial review proceedings in any court arising from any criminal cause in England and Wales.

Approximately 6,000 solicitors have higher rights. All senior advocates, and this includes solicitor-advocates and barristers, can be appointed as Queen's Counsel (QC). Appointments are made by the Queen on the advice and recommendation of the Secretary of State for Justice and Lord Chancellor, but despite the implication in the title, QCs do not advise the Queen; rather it is the 'gold star' of advocacy (and a mark of quality) and a very big step on the ladder to high judicial office. The role and controversy surrounding QCs is examined in more depth in section 10.3.3.

Alternative business structures

Whilst we are discussing solicitors' work, now is a convenient time to introduce ABSs, although as you will soon see, ABSs are *not* limited to solicitors. There is a growing culture for what is often referred to as a 'one-stop shop'. This means one professional service provider who is able to provide all of the relevant services for a particular range or type of transaction(s). Consumers are believed to want access to one professional; for example, an estate agent to show them properties, advise them on finance and mortgages and convey the relevant land, without having to use, unless they wish, three different advisers.

The Legal Services Act 2007 was enacted to continue the change started by the CLSA 1990, and, it is suggested, go further in terms of opening legal services to even wider competition. Section 1(1) of the Legal Services Act 2007 refers to eight regulatory objectives:

SECTION

'(a) protecting and promoting the public interest;
(b) supporting the constitutional principle of the rule of law;
(c) improving access to justice;
(d) protecting and promoting the interests of consumers;
(e) promoting competition in the provision of services within subsection (2) [defined as services such as are provided by authorised persons (including services which do not involve the carrying on of activities which are reserved legal activities)];
(f) encouraging an independent, strong, diverse and effective legal profession;
(g) increasing public understanding of the citizen's legal rights and duties;
(h) promoting and maintaining adherence to the professional principles.'

For our purposes, the Act introduced three major changes to the legal system:

- it created a new body, the Legal Services Board (LSB), which oversees the regulation of legal services by the approved regulator (see Figure 10.1);

- it created the Office for Legal Complaints (OLC), to deal with consumer complaints arising from legal services provided by all lawyers (considered below); and

- it extended a new business model for commercial entities offering legal services. This is the ABS.

An ABS is a regulated organisation consisting of legal professionals with other kinds of professionals who may be non-lawyers. Who might wish to join forces with the solicitors in such a venture? Accountants, tax consultants, estate agents, barristers, legal executives, paralegals, intellectual property specialists, surveyors, commercial/business experts, risk assessment managers, insurance companies ... the list is probably endless because law infuses so much of a professional person's life. Merging law with other professional services is not illogical.

Historically, the Law Society and Bar Council restricted the forms of business model that solicitors and barristers could use, but the ABS means that non-lawyers are able to manage or own a solicitors' firm. The aim has been to integrate legal and professional services into a single entity, so clients with multiple business and legal needs will be able to get assistance from a single professional firm. That's why it is called the 'one-stop shop' or, more commonly now, 'Tesco-law', drawing a parallel to the self-service supermarket where all different types of commodities are available in one place.

Arguments in favour of ABSs

- ABSs allow direct access for clients to a range of specialists all under one roof.
- There is a demand for convenient one-stop shopping.
- ABSs would be better for the client because of the free market competition.
- Clients could have choice of a traditional firm or an ABS.
- With safeguards, a solicitor's independence does not necessarily have to be lost and other rules on conflict of interest can be provided.
- Solicitors should have the choice of how to practise.

Arguments against ABSs

- The legal profession must be independent in order to maintain its role of protecting individuals' liberties.
- All the best lawyers would be in one firm, reducing client choice.
- There would be an increased risk of conflict of interest.
- There would be problems of client confidentiality, legal professional privilege, protection of client funds and professional indemnity.
- There would be problems regulating solicitors' and non-solicitors' professional conduct.

The first ABSs were licensed in March 2012 (more information is available on the SRA's website) and the new licensed businesses all paid testament to the flexibility of the new arrangements in terms of being responsive to the market and attracting external investment and/or management.

ACTIVITY

Self-test questions

1. What is the name of the representative body of solicitors?
2. How many solicitors are there in England and Wales?
3. What percentage are women?
4. What is a practising certificate?
5. How long does a training contract last?
6. Name the seven foundation subjects.
7. Summarise the effect of the CLSA 1990 on (i) conveyancing and (ii) rights of audience.
8. What is an ABS?

10.2.4 Complaints

In-house schemes

The first port of call for a client with a complaint is the firm itself. Each solicitors' firm must be able to deal with the complaint in-house first and the SRA regulates the form and nature of the in-house system by the Solicitors' Code of Conduct 2011.

First, each solicitor must comply with the ten core *principles* which are:

QUOTATION

'You must:
1. uphold the rule of law and the proper administration of justice;
2. act with integrity;
3. not allow your independence to be compromised;
4. act in the best interests of each client;
5. provide a proper standard of service to your clients;
6. behave in a way that maintains the trust the public places in you and in the provision of legal services;
7. comply with your legal and regulatory obligations and deal with your regulators and ombudsmen in an open, timely and co-operative manner;
8. run your business or carry out your role in the business effectively and in accordance with proper governance and sound financial and risk management principles;
9. run your business or carry out your role in the business in a way that encourages equality of opportunity and respect for diversity; and
10. protect client money and assets.'

In respect of complaints in particular:

QUOTATION

'Acting in the following way(s) may tend to show that you have achieved these outcomes and therefore complied with the principles:

Complaints handling
IB(1.22) having a written complaints procedure which:

(a) is brought to clients' attention at the outset of the matter;
(b) is easy for clients to use and understand, allowing for complaints to be made by any reasonable means;
(c) is responsive to the needs of individual clients, especially those who are vulnerable;
(d) enables complaints to be dealt with promptly and fairly, with decisions based on a sufficient investigation of the circumstances;
(e) provides for appropriate remedies; and
(f) does not involve any charges to clients for handling their complaints;

IB(1.23) providing the client with a copy of the firm's complaints procedure on request;
IB(1.24) in the event that a client makes a complaint, providing them with all necessary information concerning the handling of the complaint.'

The SRA

Concerns about compliance with the Solicitors' Code of Conduct are dealt with by the SRA, and, where necessary, the SRA can take regulatory action, such as reprimanding the solicitor, or even closing down solicitors' firms. It can also refer solicitors to the Solicitors Disciplinary Tribunal (SDT) (below). All solicitors have to make an annual financial contribution to the Compensation Fund (between £50 and £300 p.a.) which is held by the SRA and used to compensate for the acts/omissions of dishonest solicitors.

Solicitors Disciplinary Tribunal

The SDT is a statutory tribunal whose function is to adjudicate upon allegations of professional misconduct or breaches of professional rules by solicitors. The SDT's powers arise from the Solicitors Act 1974 (as amended). Members of the public or the SRA can bring alleged misconduct to the attention of the SDT. The Tribunal has the power to:

- strike a solicitor off the Roll;
- suspend a solicitor for a fixed or indefinite period;
- reprimand a solicitor;
- fine a solicitor (fines are payable to HM Treasury);
- ban a solicitor's employee from working in a law practice without the consent of the Law Society (under s43 Solicitors Act 1974).

Legal Ombudsman

The Legal Ombudsman was established by the OLC, under the Legal Services Act 2007. The Legal Ombudsman is independent and impartial, and has the power to deal with complaints about any of the lawyers mentioned in Figure 10.1. As is explained in its Annual Review 2015, its role is to provide a single and free gateway for consumers of legal services to channel their complaints but at the same time to drive systemic improvement by feeding back to the profession information and methods to improve, in accordance with the regulatory objectives of the Legal Services Act. In 2015, the ombudsman resolved around 7,500 complaints about lawyers in England and Wales. If, when the case has gone to an ombudsman, the ombudsman agrees that a lawyer's service is unsatisfactory, the lawyer can be ordered to take action to put things right for the consumer. That can include apologising, returning documents, doing remedial work, reducing or refunding fees (without limit), or paying up to £50,000 compensation. In 2014, the cases were resolved as follows:

- resolved informally, 39 per cent;
- Ombudsman decision, 37 per cent;
- complaint withdrawn by complainant, 8 per cent;
- complainant failed to respond or was unable to continue, 6 per cent;
- Ombudsman's decision to dismiss/discontinue, 10 per cent.

Actions against solicitors for negligence

See Actions against Barristers for Negligence at section 10.3.4.

ACTIVITY

Self-test question

You are working for your university's free legal advice clinic. A member of the public asks you for information about how to make a complaint about his solicitor. It appears that the client feels he was overcharged by his solicitor and the solicitor will not return his calls or respond to his letters. What advice can you give the client about how to proceed?

10.3 Barristers

You have already examined much of the work of barristers indirectly as a result of the discussion about solicitors above. What we have not considered, however, is why there is a divided profession in England and Wales. This division has its roots in history and although critics point out that the system can result in duplication of effort, increased costs and sometimes confusion for the public, suggestions that there should be fusion (i.e. one single profession of 'lawyer') have never been accepted by either branch of the profession. Perhaps in view of the changes in the work done by each branch, fusion is no longer the issue it once was. The abolition of the traditional monopolies has blurred the line of demarcation between solicitors and barristers.

10.3.1 Organisation

From as early as the fourteenth century, the Bar has been organised around the four Inns of Court. These are the Inner and Middle Temple, Lincoln's Inn and Gray's Inn. Since the seventeenth century, it has been necessary to belong to one of the Inns in order to be a barrister. The Inns are responsible for the 'call to the Bar', part of the procedure by which students become qualified barristers. The General Council of the Bar of England and Wales, commonly referred to as the Bar Council, is the representative body of the profession. The BSB is the regulatory body, with responsibility for setting the education and training requirements for becoming a barrister, the Code of *Conduct of the Bar of England and Wales* (currently in its eighth edition, 2004), monitoring the service provided by barristers to assure quality and handling complaints against barristers.

In 2015 there were 15,899 practising barristers, 12,757 of whom were self-employed and there were 409 sets of chambers. The profession currently comprises 64.4 per cent men and 35.6 per cent women and, of those asked, 11.9 per cent expressed they were a member of a BME minority. The low representation of women has been slowly but steadily changing since the first edition of this textbook when women were only 32 per cent of all barristers. In 2015, 48.7 per cent of new barristers (this is called being 'Called to the Bar') were women.

Fears that the Higher Rights Certificates available to solicitors would dramatically reduce the number of barristers have not materialised; entry to the Bar has *increased* since Higher Rights Certificates were introduced.

Barristers used to be very limited on the business structures from which they could work, and until 2013 were barred from forming partnerships. However, barristers have been licensed, under the Legal Services Act 2007, to operate ABSs (page 297). In fact, for now at least, most barristers are self-employed, taking tenancies in 'chambers', many of which (just under 50 per cent) are in London. From an economic point of view, it makes sense for self-employed barristers to share expensive resources, such as premises, secretarial support, library facilities and, most importantly, a clerk who acts as a business manager. When a solicitor sends instructions (known as a 'brief to counsel') to chambers for the attention of a barrister, unless a particular barrister has been named on the brief, the clerk will allocate it to a member of the chambers and will also arrange the fee. The clerk is therefore able to control the amount of work each barrister receives.

In June 2013, the SRA licensed a barristers' chambers to operate as an ABS. This meant both the individual barristers are regulated (by the BSB) and the business entity is regulated (by the SRA). It has also allowed the business to develop a career structure for its employees as well as a management structure including non-lawyers.

10.3.2 Training

Most barristers are graduates but, as you know, it is not necessary to have a degree in law to have a career as a legal professional. Conversion courses are available for graduates of other disciplines (the CPE or GDL mentioned above). After taking a QLD, or a non-QLD and a CPE/GDL, a Bar student must become a member of one of the Inns of Court, eat a certain number of dinners there (known as 'keeping terms') as admission to an Inn is required before registration on the Bar Professional Training Course (BPTC).

Many undergraduates in fact join an Inn before this stage in order to participate in the activities, use the library or start dining. A student's choice of Inn does not affect the area of law in which he wishes to practise or his choice of pupillage or tenancy – it is a matter of personal choice. The BPTC has units of study on:

- Case Preparation;
- Legal Research;
- Written Skills;
- Opinion-writing (that is giving written advice);
- Drafting (of various types of documents);
- Conference Skills (interviewing clients);
- Negotiation;
- Advocacy (court or tribunal appearances).

The subject-specific knowledge taught on the BPTC is:

- Civil Litigation and Remedies;
- Criminal Litigation and Sentencing;
- Evidence;
- Professional Ethics;
- Optional subjects, for example commercial law.

Pupillage

Once the examination stage has been successfully completed, the student is called to the Bar and can then undertake the next stage in the process, known as 'pupillage'. In 2014/15, there were over 1,500 students taking the BPTC, but only 422 pupillages.

This is the practical stage of training and, without it, a barrister is not able to practise. The newly called barrister has to find an established barrister who will take him as an 'apprentice' for one year. Pupillage is divided into two parts: the non-practising six months during which pupils shadow their pupil master and the second practising six months when pupils, with their pupil master's permission, can undertake to supply legal services and exercise rights of audience. Once pupillage is completed, the barrister can look for a place in chambers from which to work (a tenancy), or a partnership or ABS. Competition for such places is extremely fierce.

Because of the need for students to become acquainted with the customs and etiquette of the Bar, the requirement that they keep terms by dining at their chosen Inn for a specified number of times helps them to discover how the Inns work and the type of conduct which is expected. However, this does involve a certain amount of expense in addition to the fees required for attending Bar School. Although a limited number of scholarships and bursaries are available, students generally have to support themselves, usually by means of loans, during their training period. However, in March 2002, the Bar Council approved changes relating to pupillage funding, stating that pupils must be paid not less than £12,000 a year plus reasonable travel expenses where applicable, although awards of £25,000 to £40,000 per annum are not unheard of.

10.3.3 Work

If asked to describe the work a barrister does, most people would think of a man or woman in gown and wig, using their skills of advocacy in the courtroom. However, almost 3,000 barristers are employed rather than self-employed; working in commerce, industry, government or for a solicitors' firm. Even for self-employed barristers, advocacy is not their only work, for they also spend a lot of time researching points of law and giving advice to solicitors (known as 'counsel's opinion'). All barristers, like solicitors, must have practising certificates. The cost of the certificate is calculated on income and for 2016/17 the fee ranged from £110 (for those earning under £30,000 a year) to £1,652 (for those earning over £240,000 a year).

Access to barristers

An historically striking distinction between solicitors and barristers was that the latter were only permitted to take instructions from 'professional clients', a term which was carefully defined by the Bar Council's Code of Conduct. In practice this meant they always received instructions through a solicitor and were not approached directly by the individual who needed their services.

During the 1990s, a pilot scheme called BarDIRECT was set up by the Bar Council to give certain professionals and organisations (such as trade unions, police force and doctors' defence agencies) direct access to barristers through a licensing arrangement without having to use a solicitor. In June 1998, the Lord Chancellor published a consultation paper which suggested that the general public should be allowed direct access to barristers in order to instruct them, and direct access should not be restricted to professional clients. Following a report from the Office of Fair Trading in 2002, the Bar Council adopted rules which would allow any member of the public to instruct a barrister directly. This is called 'Public Access'.

One of the advantages from the point of view of the lay and the professional client in allowing direct access to the barrister is that this often reduces the costs of litigation. Instead of having to pay a solicitor to instruct a barrister, the client can seek the advice of the barrister direct and cut out the 'middle man'. A disadvantage is that the client will not have the experience to select the most appropriate chambers from which to seek advice.

The cab-rank rule

Paragraphs 601 and 602 of the Code of Conduct explain the cab-rank rule as:

QUOTATION

'601. A barrister who supplies advocacy services must not withhold those services:

(a) on the ground that the nature of the case is objectionable to him or to any section of the public;

(b) on the ground that the conduct opinions or beliefs of the prospective client are unacceptable to him or to any section of the public;

(c) on any ground relating to the source of any financial support which may properly be given to the prospective client for the proceedings in question (for example, on the ground that such support will be available as part of the Community Legal Service or Criminal Defence Service).

602. A self-employed barrister must comply with the "Cab-rank rule" and accordingly ... he must in any field in which he professes to practise in relation to work appropriate to his experience and seniority and irrespective of whether his client is paying privately or is publicly funded:

(a) accept any brief to appear before a Court in which he professes to practise;

(b) accept any instructions;

(c) act for any person on whose behalf he is instructed;

and do so irrespective of (i) the party on whose behalf he is instructed (ii) the nature of the case and (iii) any belief or opinion which he may have formed as to the character reputation cause conduct guilt or innocence of that person.'

The rule is called the 'cab-rank rule' because an analogy is drawn with customers queuing for a hackney taxi cab. The taxi driver cannot refuse to carry a passenger just because he does not like the look of them; this is contrary to the rules governing what are known as Hackney Cabs. Barristers are governed by a similar rule.

Queen's Counsel

Barristers who achieve prominence through their success at the Bar are eligible to 'take silk', that is apply to become a QC. All barristers who are not 'silks' are known as 'junior barristers', irrespective of age or experience, and a number of them apply each year to be made QC.

Why become a QC? First, QCs wear distinctive dress in court, including a silk gown. This has resulted in the nickname 'silk', given to QCs. Second, QCs sit in the front row of the court and are traditionally invited to speak first. Third, QCs tend to specialise more than juniors and take on more weighty or complex cases. They will usually be accompanied by a junior barrister who will share the work of the case. It is also regarded as a mark of distinction to be appointed as a QC and it is from the ranks of the QCs that most High Court Judges are appointed, so further promotion is possible for those who take silk. There is also evidence that QCs charge rather more for cases than juniors.

ACTIVITY

Critiquing the law – thinking points

Remind yourself of the statistics on entry to the legal professions of women and ethnic minorities, above. Why does it matter whether solicitors and barristers are predominantly white and male? Surely the most important thing is that the individuals working in the profession are qualified and competent, not whether they are representative of society?

The 2001 Report of the Office of Fair Trading ('Competition in Professions'), raised questions about the need for the post of QC and whether the title brings any benefit to the public. The Office of Fair Trading Report especially questioned whether it was appropriate for the Queen to bestow the title on members of a particular profession where the rank brought such benefits, particularly financial. The selection process (informally known as 'secret soundings') consisted of the Lord Chancellor consulting other legal professionals and judges, but who said what about whom was not revealed. The lack of transparency caused concerns. The government issued a Consultation Paper in 2003 querying whether the rank of QC should continue and, if not, how senior advocates should be appointed, if indeed there was any need for a 'senior' rank. The consultation paper did not express a governmental preference concerning the retention or abolition of the rank, but it did say that the old system had to be justified on the ground of public interest if it was to be retained. In their responses, the Office of Fair Trading and the Law Society both called for the system to be abolished. The Law Society preferred to see an accreditation scheme for senior advocates.

By the end of 2004, a new process for the award of QC was agreed and took effect from Easter 2005. The system of applications and appointment was changed and is operated by the QC Selection Panel, a wholly independent and self-financing body. The process involves taking up references and conducting face-to-face interviews with the applicants. It is expensive; it costs each applicant **£2,160** to enter the 2016–17 competition, with a further fee of **£3,600** for those who are successful. The system is open both to barristers and to solicitors.

ACTIVITY

Self-test questions

1. What are the names of the representative and regulatory bodies of barristers?
2. How many barristers are there in England and Wales?
3. What percentage are women?
4. How long does pupillage last?
5. Name the four Inns of Court.
6. If solicitors work in firms, what is the equivalent term for barristers?
7. What does the term 'brief to counsel' mean?
8. What does the phrase 'keeping terms' mean?
9. What does the phrase 'Queen's Counsel' mean? Why might a solicitor or a barrister wish to become a QC?
10. Why was there call for the post of QC to be abolished?

10.3.4 Complaints

The Code of Conduct of the Bar of England and Wales regulates the conduct of barristers, whether employed or in independent practice. For example, under Part III: Fundamental principles:

CLAUSE

'r 301 A barrister ... must not:

(a) engage in conduct whether in pursuit of his profession or otherwise which is:

   (i) dishonest or otherwise discreditable to a barrister;
   (ii) prejudicial to the administration of justice; or
   (iii) likely to diminish public confidence in the legal profession or the administration of justice or otherwise bring the legal profession into disrepute;

(b) engage directly or indirectly in any occupation if his association with that occupation may adversely affect the reputation of the Bar or in the case of a practising barrister prejudice his ability to attend properly to his practice.'

Because the majority of lay clients access barristers through a solicitor in the first instance, the initial step in a complaint is to discuss the situation with the solicitor to try to obtain a resolution. Thereafter, concerns should be raised with the barrister, but if the complaint cannot be resolved, the BSB will look into complaints about any aspect of a barrister's professional work. The BSB investigates the complaint and decides how serious it is. The complaint may involve professional misconduct (a serious error or misbehaviour by a barrister which may well involve some element of dishonesty or serious incompetence) or inadequate professional service (service towards the client falling significantly below that which would normally be expected of a barrister).

Depending on how serious it is, the BSB has a number of penalties. These range from simply requiring the barrister to apologise to a client, to disbarring the barrister (i.e. so that he ceases to be a barrister). The penalties also include suspending for a period of time, a fine or an order to repay fees.

Legal Ombudsman

See above under 10.2.4 Complaints (against solicitors).

Actions against barristers for negligence

There was an ancient immunity from actions in negligence, given, for a variety of reasons, to barristers for acts concerned with the conduct of litigation. Initially, one of the reasons for the immunity was the dignity of the Bar, but this ceased to be recognised as a valid reason in *Rondel v Worsley* [1967] 3 All ER 993. That a barrister does not enter into a contract with either the solicitor or the client ceased to be recognised as a reason in *Hedley Byrne v Heller* [1963] 2 All ER 575. However, it was made clear in *Rondel* (1967) that as the primary duty of the barrister is to the court, it would make barristers unwilling or even unable to carry out that duty properly if clients were allowed to sue in negligence. In addition, the reluctance of the courts to allow a client to re-litigate cases and the 'cab-rank' rule were reasons for the immunity.

In *Saif Ali* [1978] 3 All ER 1033, Lord Diplock further recognised that it was not in the public interest to allow a court decision to be challenged by collateral (second) proceedings (i.e. a negligence suit against the barrister). The scope of the immunity was extended by s62 of the CLSA 1990. Section 62 provided solicitor-advocates with the same immunity as barristers. However, despite the fact that barristers and solicitors are professionals, no other profession has ever been granted such immunity. Accordingly, the immunity was seen in *Arthur J S Hall v Simons* [2000] 3 All ER 673 to be an anomaly (out of line with the other professions).

CASE EXAMPLE

Arthur J S Hall v Simons [2000] 3 All ER 673

In three cases of negligence brought against solicitors, the solicitors relied on the immunity of advocates from negligence suits and at first instance the claims against the solicitors were struck out as being unsustainable. The Court of Appeal subsequently reversed those decisions, finding that there was no public policy reason for allowing immunity. The clients had contended that there was no longer a justification for the immunity which deprived a client of a legal remedy where he had suffered loss as a result of professional negligence of his legal representatives.

The main arguments for the immunity had been:

1. that the lawyer would experience a conflict of duties between that to the court and that to his client and might be exposed to vexatious litigation by a disgruntled client;
2. the 'cab-rank' rule obliged barristers to accept clients for whom they might otherwise have refused to act and exposed them to vexatious actions;
3. the position of legal representatives was analogous to that of witnesses who could not be sued for what they said in court; and
4. the lack of exemption would encourage the re-litigation of cases.

The solicitors appealed and the issue of immunity fell to be considered by the House of Lords. Their Lordships abolished the immunity. Their reasons included:

1. Even though barristers are bound by the cab-rank rule, solicitors are not. Immunity could therefore not be justified on the ground that an advocate must have immunity in a situation where he cannot choose whether to accept his client or not. Other professionals are not shielded from 'tiresome or disgusting [or] … vexatious [clients]' (per Lord Hoffmann), so there is no valid argument for protecting barristers.
2. The advocate's overriding duty to the court, far from providing a reason for the immunity, provides a strong reason against it – if an advocate carries out his duty to the court, he has nothing to fear from a negligence action, because he will not have been negligent. It could be argued that the immunity actually harmed the profession and that actions against negligent advocates would help the public have more faith.

3. While immunity from suit in a civil case could not be justified on the ground of limiting a person's 'right' to re-litigate, their Lordships had some difficulty in deciding whether or not to lift the immunity in criminal cases on this point. The problem lay in permitting a civil court to review the conviction of a defendant passed in an earlier criminal case in an action by the defendant against his advocate. The problem centres on the different standard of proof in civil (balance of probabilities) and criminal (beyond reasonable doubt) cases. It is clear that a convicted person who is able to establish, on a balance of probabilities, that he was wrongly convicted (but nevertheless convicted beyond reasonable doubt) as a result of counsel's negligence would cause untold damage to the legal system as a whole. Unless the conviction was quashed, the defendant would be entitled to damages, but not his freedom. To prevent this situation, Lord Hope felt it wise to continue the immunity in criminal cases as, he felt, abolishing it would damage the advocate's independence. Nevertheless, the majority of their Lordships recognised that a civil action against an advocate, which was in fact an appeal against conviction by another name, would be struck out as an abuse of process.

10.4 The legal profession – the future?

Fusion

A common examination question on the legal professions is to consider the nature of the divided professions and the question of fusion, although England and Wales is far from unique in separating and demarking legal work according to job role and title (for example, the French system does).

In 1979, the Benson Commission on Legal Services received some of the following written submissions in favour of fusing the profession. Employing a solicitor and a barrister was inefficient. The inefficiencies were caused by failures of communication, delay and the return of briefs from barristers who were double-booked or whose previous cases overran. This resulted in a loss of client confidence and a feeling that barristers were too remote and insufficiently prepared. It was also submitted that it was more expensive. A client was paying for two lawyers rather than one. The logic behind these arguments is not in doubt, but nevertheless the Law Society and the Bar Council strongly oppose a fused profession and thus no changes were made.

Subsequently, in the response to the Consultation Paper 'Review of the Regulatory Framework for Legal Services in England and Wales' in May 2004, the Bar Council insisted:

QUOTATION

'The existence and structure of the Bar has the following very substantial public advantages:

Barristers develop expertise in advocacy and in specialist areas of the law which enables them to provide expert advice and services to solicitors (and other professional clients). This is of vital importance to the 80% of solicitors' firms with five partners or fewer, which are spread throughout the country and provide the point of access to legal services for the majority of the general public. Such firms cannot have their own expertise in every branch of the law, nor in advocacy.'

The response continues that a divided profession is best for the consumer because it generates a free market and competition keeps costs down.

QUOTATION

'It also promotes competition among solicitors because it gives smaller solicitors' firms access to the full range of expertise and enables them better to compete with the larger firms. It also promotes access to justice because it enables the smaller solicitors' firms based in local communities to provide a much higher quality and range of services to their clients than would otherwise be possible, and thereby goes some way to redressing the advantages enjoyed by the wealthy and experienced in obtaining legal advice and effective representation.'

KEY FACTS

Solicitors and barristers

	Solicitors	Barristers
Representative body	Law Society	Bar Council
Regulatory body	SRA	BSB
Key statistics	168,226	15,899
Vocational training	Legal Practice Course	BPTC
Practical Stage	Training contract (articles) – 2 years	Pupillage (1 year)
Work	Front-line lawyers, with an increased tendency to specialise	Written opinions and advocacy
Independent practice	Partnerships (firms)/ABSs	Tenancy in chambers/ Partnerships/ABSs
Former monopolies	Conveyancing	Advocacy in the higher courts
Changes by CLSA 1990 and since	Lost conveyancing monopoly; gained opportunity for higher rights of audience	Public access

The cab-rank rule also provides an advantage in a separated profession because it requires barristers to fulfil their obligation to:

QUOTATION

'accept the instructions addressed specifically to you, irrespective of:

a.   the identity of the client;
b.   the nature of the case to which the instructions relate;
c.   whether the client is paying privately or is publicly funded; and

any belief or opinion which you may have formed as to the character, reputation, cause, conduct, guilt or innocence of the client.'

The Bar Standards Board Handbook (2nd edn, December 2016) r 29

Changes to the work and organisation of the two professions since the mid-1980s have blurred the lines of demarcation to such an extent that a law student with any oral advocacy skill has a more difficult career choice than one without – each side of the profession offers advocacy and increased client contact. Formal fusion is unlikely – the energy of the debate has diminished and the fight has left many of the antagonists as a result of the changes made, especially by the CLSA 1990. However, discussion continues in the background, especially in light of the Office of Fair Trading report in 2001; but it did not recommend abolition of the dual professions either, rather it called for an examination of the organisation and regulation of the governing bodies.

SAMPLE ESSAY QUESTION

'The debate about the future of the legal profession is not about fusion but alternative regulation of new business structures.' Discuss.

You need a clear introduction explaining the nature of the legal professions (you could mention all eight of the regulated professions, but the main focus of the answer is on solicitors and barristers and how they will operate in future so do not waste words).

You should spend at least one paragraph on solicitors and at least one more on barristers, explaining the operation, governance and regulation of each profession.

Now move on to dealing with the fusion debate; include points made by the 1979 Benson Commission, changes made to the traditional monopolies on the work of solicitors and barristers by the CLSA 1990 and the Office of Fair Trading report in 2001.

The Legal Services Act 2007 introduces ABSs. Explain what this term means and give some of the arguments in favour of and against ABSs in the legal profession.

CONCLUDE

Figure 10.5 Essay map on the legal profession

SUMMARY

- There are eight regulated legal professions.
- The representative body of Chartered legal executives is CILEx and the regulatory body is ILEX professional standards.
- The representative body of solicitors is the Law Society and the regulatory body is the SRA.
- The representative body of barristers is the Bar Council and the regulatory body is the BSB.
- In 2015 there were 168,226 solicitors and 15,899 barristers.

There are three stages to the training involved in becoming a solicitor or barrister:

- the academic stage (law degree or other degree and a conversion);
- the vocational stage (Legal Practice Course or BPTC);
- the practical stage (training contract or pupillage).

Most solicitors and barristers work in independent practice: solicitors in firms (partnerships) and barristers in chambers, but licensing of ABSs will change the nature of legal services provision.

Former monopolies have all but disappeared (solicitors losing the monopoly on conveyancing, and barristers their exclusive higher rights of audience).

The essence of complaint handling is self-regulation and each branch of the profession has a Code of Conduct and a complaints system, overseen by the Legal Ombudsman.

The future of the legal professions will be directed by the Legal Services Act 2007.

Further reading

Articles

Ames, J, 'Coping with the alternatives' [2008] 81 *Euro Law* 12.

Ames, J, 'Old profession: new frontier' [2008] 81 *Euro Law* 20.

Davies, M, 'The demise of professional self-regulation? Evidence from the "ideal type" professions of medicine and law' [2010] 26(1) *PN* 3–38.

Hopper, A, 'An uncertain future' [2013] 163(7544) *NLJ* 30.

Ramage, S, 'The Legal Services Act 2007 raises issues of criminality by persons qualified or unqualified, incompetent, unregistered, unlicensed or licensed, or negligent' [2009] 189 *Crim Law* 4–7.

Seneviratne, M, 'Legal profession; negligence: the rise and fall of advocates' immunity' [2001] 21(4) *LS* 644.

Stephen, FH, 'Regulation of the legal professions or regulation of markets for legal services: potential implications of the Legal Services Act 2007' [2008] 19(6) *EBL Rev* 1129.

Steyn, Lord, 'The role of the bar, the judge and the jury: winds of change' [1999] *UKPL* 51.

Underwood, K, 'The Legal Services Bill: death by regulation?' [2007] 26 *CJQ* 124.

Young, S, 'A class Act' [2008] 158 *NLJ* 10.

Internet links

Bar Standards Board at: www.barstandardsboard.org.uk

Chartered Institute of Legal Executives at: www.cilex.org.uk/

For information about public access to barristers, see: www.barcouncil.org.uk/using-a-barrister/public-access/

General Council of the Bar at: www.barcouncil.org.uk

Law Society at: www.lawsociety.org.uk

Legal Education and Training Review Report 2013 'Setting Standards: the future of legal services education and training regulation in England and Wales' at: www.letr.org.uk/the-report/index.html

Legal Ombudsman at: www.legalombudsman.org.uk/

Legal Services Board at: www.legalservicesboard.org.uk/index.htm

Notaries Society of England and Wales at: www.thenotariessociety.co.uk

Solicitors Regulation Authority at: www.sra.org.uk

11

The judiciary

AIMS AND OBJECTIVES

After reading this chapter you should be able to:

- Describe the historic and the modern constitutional roles of the Lord Chancellor
- Explain the main effects of the Constitutional Reform Act 2005
- Identify the courts in which the inferior and senior judiciary sit
- Analyse the composition of the judiciary
- Describe and comment on the systems for appointing, disciplining and removing judges
- Evaluate the real and the apparent bias rules whereby judges recuse themselves for conflict of interest

11.1 Introduction

Judges are the arbiters of disputes. They hear the cases tried before a court. They make decisions concerning the law and also make decisions concerning the facts of cases. (See Chapter 8. Most law students believe that the decisions on facts are made by juries alone, but you will see from the small number of cases where juries are used that the majority of fact-finders are judges.) Judges may hear trials and may also be appointed to hear appeals.

What makes a good judge?
Lord Judge, the Lord Chief Justice, speaking at Equality in Justice Day, October 2008:

QUOTATION

'[When taking the judicial oath, judges and magistrates swear] "To do right to all manner of people after the laws and usages of this realm without fear or favour, affection or ill-will." Ponder the words. I hear them frequently, and they still send a shiver up my spine. It binds my conscience, as it binds the conscience of every judge who takes it. Many qualities are required of a judge … He or she must of course know the law, and know how to apply it, but the judge must also be wise to the ways of the world. The judge must have the ability to make a decision. Decisions can be profoundly unpleasant: for example, to say to a mother that her children can be taken away from her, or to say to an individual that he is going to go to prison for the rest of his life. Judges must have moral courage – it is a very important judicial attribute – to make decisions that will be unpopular with the politicians or the media and the public, and indeed perhaps most importantly of all, to defend the right to equal treatment before the law of those who are unpopular at any given time. … But however you draw up the list, and in whatever order, gender, colour of your skin, religious belief, and social origins are all utterly irrelevant. It is you who is the judge.'

11.1.1 The Lord Chancellor

All judges are appointed by the Queen, but she is given advice on whom to appoint. Traditionally it was for the Lord Chancellor to give this advice. The most dramatic change to the judiciary since the turn of the century has been concerned with the post of the Lord High Chancellor. Historically, the UK has operated its constitution on the basis of the Rule of Law and the independence of the judiciary (refer to Chapter 1). Essentially, the latter principle is rather loosely based on something called the separation of powers doctrine, which provides that the legislature (Parliament) has the exclusive power to legislate (enact Acts of Parliament) and the judiciary (the judges) has the exclusive power to apply the law; to decide what is legal and what is not. The third body, the executive, is the government and has the exclusive power to administer the leadership of the country. The separation of powers doctrine states that these three bodies (the legislature, judiciary and executive) should be separate and independent from each other. The role of the Lord Chancellor in particular breached this doctrine. Until the Constitutional Reform Act 2005, the various and overlapping roles of the Lord Chancellor were often best represented pictorially, as in Figure 11.1.

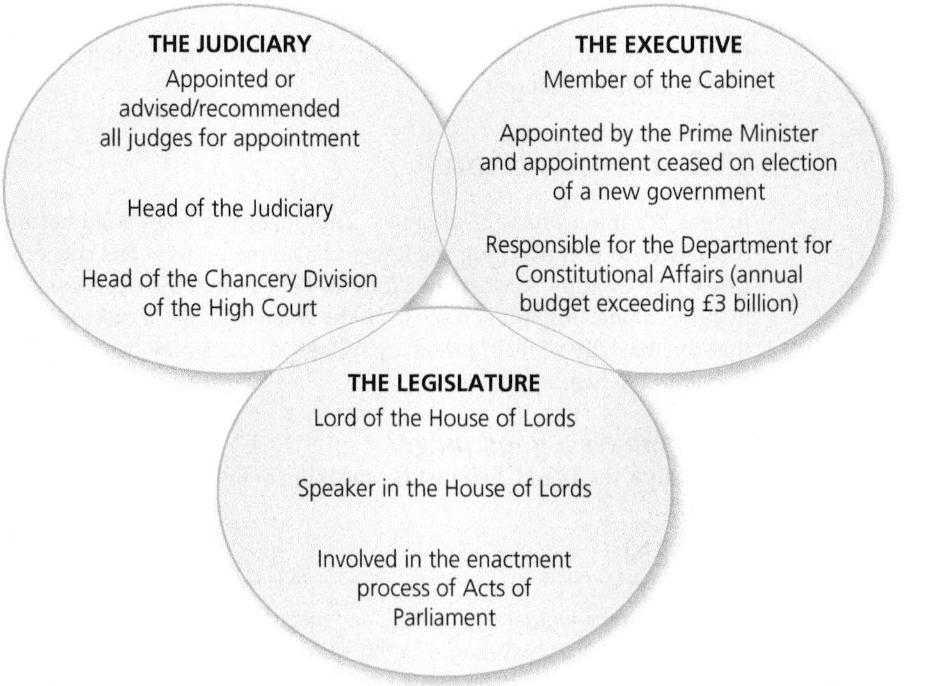

THE JUDICIARY
Appointed or advised/recommended all judges for appointment

Head of the Judiciary

Head of the Chancery Division of the High Court

THE EXECUTIVE
Member of the Cabinet

Appointed by the Prime Minister and appointment ceased on election of a new government

Responsible for the Department for Constitutional Affairs (annual budget exceeding £3 billion)

THE LEGISLATURE
Lord of the House of Lords

Speaker in the House of Lords

Involved in the enactment process of Acts of Parliament

Figure 11.1 The historic roles of the Lord Chancellor

11.1.2 The Constitutional Reform Act 2005

The multiple roles of the Lord Chancellor were untenable. The government's response was to attempt to abolish the role entirely and allocate the functions across different government and judicial post-holders. What was the Lord Chancellor's Department became the Department for Constitutional Affairs in 2003, and the Constitutional Reform Bill 2004 contained further proposals to reorganise governance of the judicial and courts systems. However the Bill was delayed in the House of Lords for a number of political reasons, and fearful that it would run out of time, the government agreed to retain the post of Lord Chancellor, but restrict his functions. The Act received Royal Assent in March 2005.

While these changes were occurring, the Home Office had come under increasing media and public pressure over a number of high-profile errors. The then Home Secretary, John Reid, admitted that the Home Office was too big and unwieldy. So, some of the Home Office's activities were transferred to a newly created Ministry of Justice which also took over the Department for Constitutional Affairs in its entirety. The head of this new ministry, the Secretary of State for Justice, is also the Lord Chancellor. In 2012, Chris Grayling MP was appointed Secretary of State for Justice and Lord Chancellor. He was the first Lord Chancellor since 1672 not to be a qualified lawyer. This trend has continued. Michael Gove MP (who has no legal background), took over the office in May 2015, and Elizabeth Truss MP (the first female Lord Chancellor, and who is also not a lawyer) became Lord Chancellor in July 2016.

Figure 11.2 summarises what the Lord Chancellor did do, still does and now does for the first time under the Constitutional Reform Act 2005.

What the Lord Chancellor used to do but no longer does	Head of the Judiciary.	This has been taken over by the Lord Chief Justice. Judicial appointments are dealt with (on the whole) by the JAC.
	Judge in the House of Lords (and the Chancery Division).	–
	Speaker in the House of Lords (legislative).	This has been taken over by the Lord Speaker, an elected post.
What the Lord Chancellor used to do and still does	Responsible for the operation of the courts system (but now through the Ministry of Justice).	
	Member of the Cabinet (executive) and appointed by the Prime Minister.	
What the Lord Chancellor does now and did not do previously	Can be appointed from either the House of Commons or the House of Lords.	The Secretary of State for Justice and Lord Chancellor. Jack Straw MP was the first ever Lord Chancellor not to sit in the House of Lords.

Figure 11.2 The changing roles of the Lord Chancellor

The Constitutional Reform Act 2005 expressly provides for the independence of the judiciary. This is set out in s3 of the Act:

'3 Guarantee of continued judicial independence

(1) The Lord Chancellor, other Ministers of the Crown and all with responsibility for matters relating to the judiciary or otherwise to the administration of justice must uphold the continued independence of the judiciary.

...

(4) The following particular duties are imposed for the purpose of upholding that independence.

(5) The Lord Chancellor and other Ministers of the Crown must not seek to influence particular judicial decisions through any special access to the judiciary.

(6) The Lord Chancellor must have regard to –

(a) the need to defend that independence;

(b) the need for the judiciary to have the support necessary to enable them to exercise their functions;

(c) the need for the public interest in regard to matters relating to the judiciary or otherwise to the administration of justice to be properly represented in decisions affecting those matters.

(7) In this section "the judiciary" includes the judiciary of any of the following –

(a) the Supreme Court;

(b) any other court established under the law of any part of the United Kingdom;

(c) any international court.'

11.1.3 The Supreme Court

Subsection (7) above refers to the Supreme Court. Part 3 of the Constitutional Reform Act 2005 provides for the establishment of a new court to replace the House of Lords.

SECTION

'23 The Supreme Court

(1) There is to be a Supreme Court of the United Kingdom.

(2) The Court consists of 12 judges appointed by Her Majesty by letters patent.

24 First members of the Court

On the commencement of section 23 –

(a) the persons who immediately before that commencement are Lords of Appeal in Ordinary become judges of the Supreme Court.'

These sections provide for the abolition of the old Appellate Committee of the House and its replacement with the new Supreme Court of the United Kingdom, with the same judges presiding in the first instance. The Supreme Court's jurisdiction is similar to that of the old Appellate Committee, but it also took over devolution issues from the Privy Council. The new court opened in October 2009 and is located in the Middlesex Guildhall building in Parliament Square, London.

The rationale for the change from House of Lords to Supreme Court was to ensure judicial independence from the other two branches of state; the law lords were no longer able to sit as members of the House of Lords in its legislative capacity. However, unlike some other countries which have a Supreme Court, the UK Court is not a constitutional court with the power to strike down legislation. That, it seems, would be pushing judicial independence too far and sacrificing parliamentary sovereignty.

ACTIVITY

Self-test questions

1. Explain the reasons for changing the role of the Lord Chancellor.
2. Outline the main changes introduced by the Constitutional Reform Act 2005.
3. What are the reasons behind the establishment of a UK Supreme Court?

11.2 The judicial hierarchy

Just as the court system is based on a hierarchy, so too is the judiciary. Judges are grouped into inferior and senior judges. Inferior judges preside, on the whole, in the inferior courts (the Magistrates' Court, the County Court and the Crown Court). Senior judges preside, on the whole, in the senior courts (the High Court, the Court of Appeal and the House of Lords).

Judicial title	Full-time or part-time?	Main court in which the judge presides	Salary 2016–17
DJ(MC)	FT	Magistrates' Court	£107,100
District Judge	FT and PT	County Court	£107,100
Recorder	PT	Crown and County	Pro-rata Circuit Judge
Circuit Judge	FT	Crown and County	£133,506

Figure 11.3 Inferior judges

Judicial title	Full-time or part-time?	Main court in which the judge presides	Salary 2016–17
High Court Judge	FT	High and Crown (and Court of Appeal if invited)	£179,768
Lord or Lady Justice of Appeal	FT	Court of Appeal	£204,695
Heads of Division	FT	Court of Appeal	£222,470 to £249,583 (Lord Chief Justice)
Justice of Supreme Court	FT	Supreme Court (and Privy Council)	£215,256

Figure 11.4 Senior judges

11.3 Training

Judicial training is provided by the Judicial College. The Judicial College was created in 2011 by bringing together separate arrangements that had previously existed for training judicial office-holders in the courts (the Judicial Studies Board) and Tribunals Service (through the Tribunals Judicial Training Group).

The Judicial College's activities fall under three main headings:

1. initial training for new judicial office-holders and those who take on new responsibilities;

2. continuing professional education to develop the skills and knowledge of existing judicial office-holders;

3. delivering change and modernisation by identifying training needs and providing training programmes to support major changes to legislation and the administration of justice.

A fundamental principle underlying the work of the Judicial College is that the training is for judges by judges. This supports judicial independence. In the main, training is designed and delivered by judges but they are assisted in this by advisers and administrators.

11.4 A note about judicial appointments

The old system of judicial appointments was variously referred to as the 'tap on the shoulder', the 'old boys' network' and the 'secret soundings' where the 'tap' came from the Lord Chancellor. The changes to his role were discussed in section 11.1.1 above. The JAC was created by the Constitutional Reform Act 2005 in order to remove the responsibility for selecting candidates for judicial office from the Lord Chancellor alone and making the appointments process clearer and more accountable. Instead, the JAC advertises the vacancies, short lists and interviews the candidates, and makes a recommendation to the Lord Chancellor who can reject that recommendation (but he is required to provide his reasons to the JAC).

Appointment is solely on merit:

QUOTATION

'The JAC has identified the following qualities and abilities which are assessed against evidence showing relevant knowledge and experience.

The five generic qualities and abilities listed below may be tailored for specific posts. The final qualities and abilities for each post are published on the website page for each exercise.

For more senior roles, the fifth generic quality and ability (Efficiency) is replaced by that entitled Leadership and Management Skills.

QUALITIES AND ABILITIES – GENERIC

1. Intellectual capacity

   - High level of expertise in your chosen area or profession
   - Ability quickly to absorb and analyse information
   - Appropriate knowledge of the law and its underlying principles, or the ability to acquire this knowledge where necessary.

2. Personal qualities

   - Integrity and independence of mind
   - Sound judgement
   - Decisiveness
   - Objectivity
   - Ability and willingness to learn and develop professionally
   - Ability to work constructively with others.

3. An ability to understand and deal fairly
   - An awareness of the diversity of the communities which the courts and tribunals serve and an understanding of differing needs
   - Commitment to justice, independence, public service and fair treatment
   - Willingness to listen with patience and courtesy.

4. Authority and communication skills
   - Ability to explain the procedure and any decisions reached clearly and succinctly to all those involved
   - Ability to inspire respect and confidence
   - Ability to maintain authority when challenged.

5. Efficiency
   - Ability to work at speed and under pressure
   - Ability to organise time effectively and produce clear reasoned judgments expeditiously. (including leadership and managerial skills where appropriate)

QUALITIES AND ABILITIES – LEADERSHIP AND MANAGEMENT
For posts requiring particular leadership skills, the efficiency quality is replaced by:

5. Leadership and Management Skills
   - Ability to form strategic objectives and to provide leadership to implement them effectively
   - Ability to motivate, support and encourage the professional development of those for whom you are responsible
   - Ability to engage constructively with judicial colleagues and the administration, and to manage change effectively
   - Ability to organise own and others time and manage available resources.'

11.5 The inferior judges

Eligibility for all judicial posts is subject to statutory eligibility based on professional qualification. Historically, eligibility was based exclusively on minimum years as a solicitor or barrister, but the Tribunals, Courts and Enforcement Act 2007 widened this to include members of the legal services regulated professions (see Figure 10.1) for appointment to District Judge. Appointments are all made on merit by the Queen, on the recommendation of the Lord Chancellor, following assessment of the candidates by the JAC.

11.5.1 District Judge (Magistrates' Court)
The first inferior judges for our consideration are DJ(MC) who, obviously, preside in the Magistrates' Courts. It is usual to have sat part-time as a deputy District Judge before being considered for the position of District Judge.

11.5.2 District Judge (County Court)
There is a larger number of District Judges who do *not* work in the Magistrates' Court than who do. District Judges, formally known as Registrars, have civil jurisdiction and work in the County Court. The JAC will normally consider only applicants who have been serving as Deputy (part-time) District Judges for two years. Before sitting alone, all newly appointed deputies have to attend a three- to five-day residential induction course arranged by the Judicial College and complete a period of 'sitting-in' with an experienced District Judge for at least five days. After the 'sitting-in' there is a mentor and appraisal system to guide and support the judge during his first three months of sitting.

11.5.3 Recorder

Recorders are part-time judges who have mainly criminal jurisdiction in the Crown Courts, but under s5(3) of the County Courts Act 1984, may also sit in the County Courts. Appointments are for five years and will normally be automatically extended for further successive terms of five years, subject to the retirement age of 70. To become a Recorder the applicant has been qualified as a barrister or solicitor and has gained experience in law for at least seven years.

Recorders also benefit from an induction training run by the Judicial College. Very intensive residential courses have to be completed before a Recorder can sit in his own Crown Court. Emphasis is placed on practical exercises such as sentencing, directions to the jury and summing up. The newly appointed judges must also sit in for at least a week with an experienced judge and they must also visit local prisons and the Probation Service.

11.5.4 Circuit Judge

Recordership is a step on the ladder to appointment as a Circuit Judge. The applicant must have been qualified as a barrister or solicitor and must have gained experience in law for at least seven years or to be a Recorder, or to be the holder of one of a number of other judicial offices of at least three years' standing in a full-time capacity. Circuit Judges are permanently assigned to a particular area, or circuit, on appointment. There are seven circuits: Midland, North Eastern, Northern, South Eastern, Western, Wales and Chester and the European Circuit, which comprises barristers working in Europe, as well as barristers in England and Wales whose work focuses on European law. Each circuit also has two presiding judges who are High Court Judges.

11.6 The senior judges

The Constitutional Reform Act 2005 governs eligibility and the appointment processes for the senior judges.

11.6.1 High Court Judge

The first senior judge to be considered is a High Court Judge, but this title does not denote the only court in which he presides. Obviously a High Court Judge does work in the High Court and he is assigned to one of the three divisions of the High Court on appointment, but he also has important jurisdiction in the Crown Court and may sit in the Court of Appeal if requested.

In order to be eligible to be appointed as a High Court Judge it is necessary either to have been qualified as a barrister or solicitor and have gained experience in law for at least seven years or to have been a Circuit Judge for at least two years. High Court Judges, as with other judges, are appointed on the basis of open competition. In practice, appointments are made from the ranks of QC, particularly from QCs who have sat as a Deputy High Court Judge and/or Recorder. QC was once the exclusive domain of the Bar, but is no longer (see Chapter 10) because of the progression now available from a solicitor to a solicitor-advocate and then a High Court Judge.

High Court Judges are appointed by the Queen, on the recommendation of the Lord Chancellor, who is in turn recommended by the JAC. The provisions governing the selection and appointment process for all inferior judges (considered at section 11.4 above) and High Court Judges are ss85–93 of the Constitutional Reform Act 2005 and are summarised in Figure 11.5.

The Courts Service or the Tribunals Service or the Ministry of Justice makes a 'Vacancy Request' to the JAC.

↓

The vacancy(ies) are advertised by the JAC.

↓

The JAC receives the application forms and sifts them for eligibility and good character. The JAC then shortlists potential candidates by reviewing the submitted paperwork which may include a 'qualifying test'.

↓

The JAC will take up references, both from the referees named by the applicant and from others (the JAC draws up a 'tailored' list of referees for each vacancy and the list of names is available to applicants).

↓

Shortlisted candidates are invited to a 'selection day' which will involve an interview and may also involve role-play. The interviewing panel will report back to the JAC.

↓

The JAC will send summary reports on candidates likely to be considered for selection to the Lord Chief Justice and to another person who has held the post or has relevant experience. Their response will be taken into account in the final selection.

↓

The JAC makes a final report to the Lord Chancellor.

Figure 11.5 Appointments process for judges up to and including the High Court

11.6.2 Lord Justice of Appeal

There are 39 Lords Justices of Appeal who are appointed by the Queen, acting on the advice of the Lord Chancellor. The Lord Chancellor is advised by a selection panel of the JAC (ss76–84 of the Constitutional Reform Act 2005). Lords Justices of Appeal, broadly speaking, preside in the Court of Appeal. They must have been qualified as a barrister or solicitor and have gained experience in law for at least seven years or to have been an existing High Court Judge. In recent times all Lords Justices of Appeal have been appointed from existing High Court Judges. Section 63 of the Courts Act 2003 repealed s2(3) of the Senior Courts Act 1981, which required a judge of the Court of Appeal to be termed a 'Lord Justice of Appeal' whatever their gender. The first woman to be appointed to the Court of Appeal, Elizabeth Butler-Sloss, was called 'Lord' before the law was changed. It had not originally been envisaged that a woman would rise to such high judicial office.

11.6.3 Head of Division

In addition, with the same statutory qualification requirements as the Lords Justices of Appeal, and also appointed by the Queen, there are five Heads of Division. The five are the Lord Chief Justice who is also the most senior judge in England and Wales and is also head of the judiciary (currently Lord Thomas CJ), the Master of the Rolls (Lord Dyson), the President of the Queen's Bench Division (Sir Brian Leveson), the President of the Family Division (Sir James Munby) and the Chancellor of the High Court (Sir Terence Etherton). The Heads of Divisions are appointed from among the Justices of the Supreme Court or Lords Justices of Appeal. Sections 67–75 of the Constitutional Reform Act 2005 govern the appointment of the Heads of the Division.

11.6.4 Justice of the Supreme Court

At the top of the judicial hierarchy are the 12 Supreme Court Justices. The President of the Supreme Court is Lord Neuberger. The statutory qualification for appointment as a Justice of the Supreme Court is either to have been the holder for not less than two years of one or more of the high judicial offices described in the Appellate Jurisdiction Act 1876, as amended, or has been a solicitor of the senior courts of England and Wales or a practising barrister for 15 years.

Most Justices of the Supreme Court have been appointed from among the experienced judges of the Court of Appeal in England and Wales, the Court of Session in Scotland and the Court of Appeal in Northern Ireland. In 2012 Lord Sumption was appointed to the Supreme Court having been a QC for many years but having never sat as a judge on the Court of Appeal. It is yet to be seen whether this is the start of a trend away from appointing senior judges to the Supreme Court, or an exceptional case. The Justices' biographies are on the Supreme Court website at www.supremecourt.uk/about/biographies-of-thejustices.html.

Appointments to the Supreme Court are made by the Queen, acting on the advice of the Prime Minister, but the effective voice is, again, that of the Lord Chancellor.

The Constitutional Reform Act 2005 sets out the different processes that must be followed for appointments above High Court level; see Figure 11.6.

The Lord Chancellor consults the Lord Chief Justice to invite the JAC to set up a committee to make a selection. For appointments to the Supreme Court, the Lord Chancellor convenes the committee.

The selection panel comprises senior judges (e.g. for appointment as a Head of Division, the panel consists of the President of the Supreme Court and the Lord Chief Justice, and for appointments to the Court of Appeal, the panel consists of the Lord Chief Justice and a Lord Justice of Appeal), plus the Chairman of the JAC and a lay member of the JAC.

The panel determines the process it will follow, makes a selection and reports to the Lord Chancellor, who can then accept the selection, reject it or require the panel to reconsider.

Figure 11.6 Appointments process for senior judges

ACTIVITY

Self-test questions

1. Name two inferior judicial posts.
2. Name two senior judicial posts.
3. Who appoints:
   - Lords Justices of Appeal?
   - High Court Judges?
   - Recorders?
4. What are the titles for the five Heads of Division? Name the current appointees.
5. How many Supreme Court Justices are there?
6. Explain why the Lord Chancellor's role in judicial appointments was regarded as controversial.
7. What is the role of the JAC?
8. What were 'secret soundings'? When were judicial appointments made on this basis?

11.7 The composition of the judiciary

The composition of the judiciary has been criticised. Some of the common criticisms are that the judiciary is predominantly elderly, male and white. Lord Denning was 83 when he retired, although, as he was appointed before the Judicial Pensions Act 1959, he has been the exception rather than the rule in the last 20 years. What about the accusations of 'male and white'? The accusations are certainly, and for at least the present time, true.

Compare the statistics in Figures 11.7 and 11.8. This is an opportunity for you to track the changes in the composition of the judiciary over 15 years. To help you focus on the key developments, consider these questions:

ACTIVITY

1. In 2001 and 2016, how many of all judges (senior and inferior) were women?
2. In 2001 and 2016, how many of all senior judges were women?
3. In 2001 and 2016, how many of all inferior judges were women?
4. Have there been any changes over that time period? Are these changes significant, and, if so, of what?
5. In 2001 and 2016, how many of all judges (senior and inferior) were (or stated they were) of an ethnic minority background?
6. In 2001 and 2016, how many of all senior judges were (or stated they were) of an ethnic minority background?
7. In 2001 and 2016, how many of all inferior judges were (or stated they were) of an ethnic minority background?
8. Have there been any changes over that time period? Are these changes significant, and, if so, of what?
9. A final question – why did the judiciary start to track percentage non-barrister (that is, chartered legal executives or solicitors or other regulated legal service professionals) becoming judges?

	Post	Total	Female number	Female %	Of ethnic minority origin number	Of ethnic minority origin %
Senior judiciary	Lords of Appeal in Ordinary*	12	0	0	0	0
	Heads of Division	4	1	25	0	0
	Lords Justices of Appeal	33	2	6.1	0	0
	High Court Judges	99	8	8.1	0	0
Inferior judiciary	Circuit Judges (inc. Technology and Construction Court)	570	45	7.9	4	0.7
	Recorders	1,370	168	12.3	35	2.6
	District Judges (inc. Family Division)	427	70	16.4	7	1.6
	Deputy District Judges (inc. Family Division)	760	151	19.9	9	1.2
	DJ(MC)s	98	17	17.3	2	2
	Deputy DJ(MC)s	162	35	21.6	9	5.6
	Total	3,535	497	14.1	66	1.9

* Now Justices of the Supreme Court.

Figure 11.7 Extract from the Annual Judicial Statistics, as at 1 April 2001

	Appointment name	Total in post	Female number	% Female	BME number	% BME	% Non-barrister
Senior judiciary	Justices of the Supreme Court	12	1	8.3	0	0	8.3
	Heads of Division	5	0	0	0	0	0
	Lords Justices of Appeal	39	8	20.5	0	0	0
	High Court Judges	106	22	20.7	5	4.7	0.9
Inferior judiciary	Circuit Judges	626	160	25.5	23	3.7	11.0
	Recorders	1,035	203	19.6	62	6.0	6.6
	District Judges (County Courts)	430	153	35.5	34	7.9	78.6
	Deputy District Judges (County Courts)	627	231	36.8	35	5.6	68.9
	DJ(MC)s	133	44	33.1	7	5.3	65.4
	Deputy DJ(MC)s	101	31	30.7	6	5.9	65.3
	Grand total	3,202	882	27.5	174	5.4	34.7

Figure 11.8 2016 judicial diversity statistics – gender, ethnicity and profession

ACTIVITY

Critiquing the law

Look at the statistics for judicial diversity again in Figures 11.7 and 11.8, and consider the long-term trends which you can see emerging between 2001 and 2016. When looking at this data, consider the following thinking points:

- Why does it matter if the judiciary is predominantly elderly, male and white?
- Think about the common law system of precedent (see Chapter 2) and the judicial role in statutory interpretation (Chapter 3). Do judges make law?
- If so, where do they draw their influences from when making decisions?

Research carried out by University College London and the National Centre for Social Research ('The Paths to Justice') in November 1999 found that two out of every three people think judges are out of touch with ordinary people's lives. They are also seen as anachronistic, inconsistent in the sentences they hand down and given to inexplicable utterances on rape and other subjects (Clare Dyer, 'A very public wigging', *The Guardian*, 22 November 1999).

Further:

QUOTATION

'The intellectual isolation of appellate judges who resolve "hard cases" with reference to notions of social justice and public policy which they are singularly (and collectively) ill-equipped to understand … remains a deeply worrying feature of our judicial process.'

G Drewry [1984] 47 MLR 380

11.8 Dismissal and judicial independence

Retirement

Under the terms of the Judicial Pensions and Retirement Act 1993 all judges appointed after March 1995 must retire on their 70th birthday.

The rules governing judicial pensions have recently been changed. To qualify for a full pension, a judge has to have served 20 years on the Bench instead of 15. This means that younger lawyers who wish to become judges will be going to the Bench earlier than perhaps they would have done. While this will result in a younger judiciary, many QCs take a substantial drop in salary (often half) when appointed to the Bench and, under the new rules, would have to make judicial appointment by their 50th birthday. This change may backfire and suitable potential judges may refuse to apply or be appointed as a result.

Dismissal and judicial independence

One way in which the independence of the judiciary is protected is through the principle of 'security of tenure during good behaviour'. This means that the Heads of Division, Law Lords, Lords Justices of Appeal and High Court Judges can only be removed by the Queen after a vote to that effect by both Houses of Parliament. This security of tenure derives from the Act of Settlement 1701, but is now governed by the Senior Courts Act 1981. No English judge has ever been removed in this way, and probably never will be, given the creation of the Judicial Conduct Investigations Office, below.

Inferior judges may be dismissed on the grounds of incapacity or misbehaviour by the Lord Chief Justice and he does not need approval from Parliament. The only occasion on which that power has been used against a full-time judicial office-holder was in 1983, when a Circuit Judge was removed from office when the judge concerned pleaded guilty to several charges of smuggling.

On 12 April 2000 the Lord Chancellor announced new terms of service for those judges appointed on fixed-term contracts, such as Deputy District Judges. To ensure a degree of judicial independence from the Executive, the judges are appointed for terms of five years and the only grounds for non-renewal of such contracts are:

- misbehaviour;
- incapacity;
- persistent failure to comply with sitting requirements (without good reason);
- failure to comply with training requirements;
- sustained failure to observe the standards reasonably expected from a holder of such office;
- part of a reduction in numbers because of changes in operational requirements; and
- part of a structural change to enable recruitment of new appointees.

Judicial Conduct Investigations Office

The Constitutional Reform Act 2005 gave the Lord Chancellor and the Lord Chief Justice joint responsibility determining complaints about the personal conduct of all judicial office-holders. Any complaint is investigated by the Judicial Conduct Investigations Office, but the complaint does also have to be upheld by the Lord Chancellor and the Lord Chief Justice who have the power to agree to advise, warn or remove a judge for misconduct. In April 2009, Judge Margaret Short was dismissed in this way, for 'inappropriate, petulant and rude' behaviour.

Judicial impartiality

In addition to being as independent as possible from the Legislative and the Executive, a judge must remain independent from the parties to the case he is hearing.

CASE EXAMPLE

R v Bow Street Metropolitan Stipendiary Magistrate and others, ex parte Pinochet Ugarte (No 2) [1999] 2 WLR 272

Pinochet was the former head of state of Chile who was on a visit to London for medical treatment. He was arrested under extradition warrants issued by a Spanish court alleging various crimes against humanity, including murder, hostage-taking and torture, committed during his period of office in the 1970s and for which he was knowingly responsible.

Before the main hearing, Amnesty International, a human rights body which had campaigned against Pinochet, obtained leave to intervene and was represented by counsel in the proceedings. Pinochet claimed diplomatic immunity in an attempt to quash the warrants, but his claim was rejected by the House of Lords by a 3–2 majority, including Lord Hoffmann in the majority. However, Pinochet's advisers then discovered that Lord Hoffmann, although not a member of Amnesty International, was an unpaid director and chairman of Amnesty International Charity Ltd; one of the objects of which was to procure the abolition of torture, extrajudicial execution and disappearance. Lord Hoffmann had neither withdrawn from the case nor declared his interest in Amnesty International (he may have thought that the parties knew, or that the opposition to torture was a commonly held belief and as such he was no different from the other judges).

Pinochet applied for the House of Lords to set aside its previous decision on the ground of apparent bias on the part of Lord Hoffmann, and the House did so. Lord Browne-Wilkinson held that, as regards the appearance of judicial bias, the fundamental principle that a man may not be a judge in his own cause was applicable if the judge's decision would lead to the promotion of a cause in which he was involved together with one of the parties. Therefore, in order to maintain the absolute impartiality of the judiciary, there had to be a rule which automatically disqualified a judge who was involved, whether personally or as a director of a company, in promoting the same causes in the same organisation as was a party to the suit; and that, accordingly, the earlier decision of the House would be set aside.

In *Locabail Ltd v Bayfield Properties* [2000] 1 All ER 65, the Court of Appeal heard five conjoined appeals alleging bias in the judiciary.

In the first two, the application concerned a Deputy High Court Judge, Lawrence Collins QC (interestingly, he was only the second solicitor to have been appointed to the High Court). As a partner in a law firm's litigation and arbitration department and a judge, he became aware that his firm had acted for a company which had claims against one of the defendants (the applicant's husband). On becoming aware of the issue, he had made immediate disclosure and the parties had done nothing to object. No bias was found. Nor was there in *Williams v HM Inspector of Taxes* [2000] WLR 870; [2000] 1 All ER 65; [2000] IRLR 96, where the applicant asserted that the Chair of the Industrial Tribunal, having worked for the Inland Revenue, should not have chaired her unfair dismissal case against the same party (many years later). Nor was there even the appearance of bias in *R v Bristol Betting and Gaming Licensing Committee, ex parte O'Callaghan* [2000] QB 451, even though the judge was a director of a company which owned property of which one of the businesses in the case was a tenant.

However, in *Timmins v Gormley* [2000] QB 451 the judge was an author of a number of articles on personal injury claims in which he criticised some defendant insurers. The issue was not the fact that Mr Recorder Braithwaite was the author of the articles, but of their tone. The Court of Appeal held that there was a real danger that he might have leaned unconsciously towards the claimant. The Court also issued guidance on judicial bias:

JUDGMENT

'There can be no objection to a judge on the grounds of ethnic or national origin, religion, gender, age, class or sexual orientation. Nor can there be objection on the grounds of social, educational or employment background, or that of his family or membership of bodies such as the Freemasons.'

JUDGMENT

'A judge should recuse himself if aware he is in a situation like that involved in Pinochet, or where he has a financial interest in the outcome of the case, or he should make disclosure as soon as he becomes aware he is in such a situation. If the parties do not object following appropriate disclosure in the latter case, that party cannot later complain of a real danger of bias.'

The appointment, composition and independence of the judiciary

Inferior Judges	DJ(MC)	Appointments are operated by the JAC
	District Judge (Civil Court)	Vacancies are advertised
	Recorder	Referees are consulted
	Circuit Judge	Interviews are held
Senior Judges	High Court Judge	Lord Chancellor retains last word in appointment
	Lord Justice of Appeal	
	Justice of the Supreme Court	
Heads of Division	Lord Chief Justice	The Heads of Divisions are appointed from among the Justices of the Supreme Court or Lords Justices of Appeal
	Master of the Rolls	Sections 67–75 of the Constitutional Reform Act 2005 govern the appointment of the Heads of the Division
	President of the Queen's Bench Division	
	President of the Family Division	
	Chancellor of the High Court	
Women	Count for 27% of the total judiciary and less than 20% of the senior judiciary	
Members of an ethnic minority	Count for approximately 5% of the total judiciary but only 3% of the senior judiciary	
Retirement	For first appointments after March 1995, retirement age of 70, but need 20 years on the bench for a full pension	
Dismissal	Senior judges have security of tenure Inferior judges on grounds of incapacity or misbehaviour	
Impartiality	*R v Bow Street Metropolitan Stipendiary Magistrate and others, ex parte Pinochet Ugarte (No 2)* [1999] 2 WLR 272 *Locabail Ltd v Bayfield Properties* [2000] 1 All ER 65	

SAMPLE ESSAY QUESTION

Critically consider the constitutional role of the Lord Chancellor and comment on the way(s) his role has changed over the past decade.

> You must start with an historic overview of the role. He was head of the judiciary, could sit as a judge in the House of Lords, had the major say in the appointment of judges, and was also a member of the executive and of the legislature.

> Develop that explanation further by explaining the doctrine of the separation of powers and its purpose. Show how his role conflicted with the doctrine.

Summarise the constitutional reforms in the Constitutional Reform Act 2005. Include a reference to the Supreme Court, but focus on the transfer of many judicial responsibilities to the Lord Chief Justice, and the creation of the JAC and Judicial Conduct Investigations Office.

Point out that the Lord Chancellor retains some power (for example, he may reject candidates put forward by the JAC for judicial appointment; he also has the final say, with the Lord Chief Justice, on dismissal under the Constitutional Reform Act 2005).

CONCLUDE

Figure 11.9 Essay map on the role of the Lord Chancellor

SUMMARY

- The judiciary is a collective term for the judges of England and Wales.
- There are inferior and senior judicial posts, which may be full-time or part-time.
- Judicial appointments used to be shrouded in secrecy. Now all vacancies are advertised and appointments are recommended by the JAC although the last word is with the Lord Chancellor. The Queen makes the final appointment.
- The judiciary is often criticised for the poor representation of women and members of ethnic minority groups.
- Judges may be removed from office for misconduct and the Constitutional Reform Act 2005 created a new body with the power to investigate judicial behaviour, the Judicial Conduct Investigations Office.
- Judicial impartiality is an important part of the separation of powers doctrine and the rule of law.

Further reading

Books

Hunter, R, McGlynn, C and Rackley, E, *Feminist Judgments: From Theory to Practice* (Hart Publishing, 2010).

Hutchinson, AC, *Laughing at the Gods: Great Judges and How They Made the Common Law* (Cambridge University Press, 2012).

Articles

Blackwell, M, 'Old boys' networks, family connections and the English legal profession' [2012] *PL* 426–444.

Etherton, T, 'Liberty, the archetype and diversity: a philosophy of judging' [2010] *PL* 727–746.

Gee, G, 'Guarding the guardians: the Chief Executive of the UK Supreme Court' [2013] *PL* 538–554.

Wilson, S, 'Judicial diversity: where do we go from here?' [2013] 2(1) *CJICL* 7–15.

Woodhouse, D, 'The office of Lord Chancellor' [1998] *UKPL* 617.

Woodhouse, D, 'The Constitutional Reform Act: defending judicial independence the English way' [2007] 5 *IJCL* 153.

Internet links

Judicial Appointments Commission at: www.judicialappointments.gov.uk

Judicial College at: www.judiciary.gov.uk/training-support/judicial-college

Judicial Conduct Investigations Office at: http://judicialconduct.judiciary.gov.uk/

Judiciary at: www.judiciary.gov.uk

Supreme Court Justices at: www.supremecourt.uk/about/biographies-of-the-justices. html

12

Sentencing

AIMS AND OBJECTIVES

After reading this chapter you should be able to:

- Understand the purposes of sentencing
- Describe the types of sentences that can be passed by the courts on adults
- Describe the types of sentences that can be passed by the courts on young offenders
- Understand the factors taken into account by the courts when passing sentence

12.1 Introduction

Whenever a person pleads guilty, or is found guilty of an offence, the role of the court is to decide what sentence should be imposed on the offender. Judges and magistrates have a fairly wide discretion as to the sentence they select in each case, although they are subject to certain restrictions. Magistrates can normally only impose a maximum of six months' imprisonment for one offence or a fine of £5,000 (and could also impose a fine of £20,000 for some offences committed by companies, such as a breach of health and safety laws). Under the LASPO 2012, magistrates now have the power to issue unlimited fines for some more serious offences. This change in the law came into force in 2015, and applies to offences committed after this date only. Judges in the Crown Court have no limits on sentencing; they can impose up to life imprisonment for some crimes and there is no maximum figure for fines. As well as custody and fines, the courts have a wide range of community orders which they can impose and they can also give an offender an absolute or conditional discharge.

Figure 12.1 shows the different use of sentences in the Magistrates' Courts and the Crown Court. The Crown Court deals with the more serious offences and this is reflected in the type of sentences imposed.

12.1.1 Maximum sentences

However, there are other restrictions, both in the Magistrates' Court and in the Crown Court. Each crime has a maximum penalty for that type of offence set by Parliament. For example, the crime of theft has a fixed maximum of seven years' imprisonment, so that

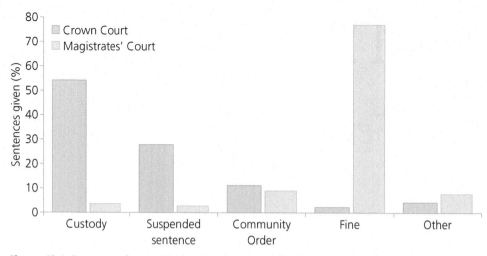

Figure 12.1 Sentences given at Magistrates' Courts and the Crown Court in the 12 months to December 2015

no matter how much has been stolen, the judge can never send an offender to prison for longer than this. Some offences have a maximum sentence of life imprisonment; these include manslaughter and rape. In such cases the judge has discretion when sentencing; the offender may be sent to prison for life or given a shorter prison sentence or a non-custodial sentence may, in exceptional cases, be thought appropriate. Murder is the exception as it carries a mandatory life sentence; in other words the judge has to pass life imprisonment; there is no other sentence available. The judge does, however, set the minimum period which the offender should serve before he can be considered for release on licence.

12.1.2 Minimum sentences

Although Parliament has set down maximum sentences for all offences, there are only two offences for which minimum sentences have been set down. Minimum sentences apply only to repeat offenders who have committed a third (or further) offence and are for:

- burglary (minimum of three years' imprisonment);
- Class A drug trafficking offences (minimum of seven years' imprisonment).

There is also a minimum sentence of five years' imprisonment for anyone convicted of possession of prohibited firearms, even if they have no previous convictions.

For these offences the courts must impose at least the minimum level unless there are particular circumstances relating to the offender which would make it unjust to do so.

12.1.3 Dangerous offenders

The Criminal Justice Act 2003, as amended by the LASPO 2012, makes special sentences available to the Crown Court when the offender is a dangerous offender. The first is a life sentence for public protection. This is imposed where the court is of the opinion that there is a significant risk to members of the public of serious harm through the offender committing further offences. In these circumstances the court can impose a life sentence, but only for offences which carry a maximum of a life sentence.

The second type of sentence is an extended sentence for certain violent or sexual offences. This allows the court to impose the appropriate custodial sentence for the actual offence plus an extension period during which the offender is subject to a licence. The total period cannot exceed the maximum term of imprisonment for the offence. An extended sentence can only be used where the court is of the opinion that there is a significant risk to members of the public of serious harm through the offender committing further specified offences.

12.1.4 Young offenders

In addition, for offenders under the age of 21, both the Magistrates' Courts and the Crown Court have to comply with the current legislative rules on what sentences are available for young offenders. This is an area where there have been frequent changes over the last ten years or so. It is an area which is constantly under review and it is possible that government policy will bring further changes. The sentences currently available for young offenders are considered briefly at section 12.5.

12.2 Purposes of sentencing

When judges or magistrates have to pass a sentence, they will not only look at the sentences available, they will also have to decide what they are trying to achieve by the punishment they give. These purposes or aims of sentencing are now set down by statute in the Criminal Justice Act 2003. Section 142 states the purposes which apply to offenders aged 18 and over:

SECTION

's 142 Any court dealing with an offender in respect of his offence must have regard to the following purposes of sentencing –

(a) the punishment of offenders,
(b) the reduction of crime (including its reduction by deterrence),
(c) the reform and rehabilitation of offenders,
(d) the protection of the public, and
(e) the making of reparation by offenders to persons affected by their offences.'

Section 142A of the Act sets out the purposes which apply to offenders under the age of 18. This section was inserted by the Criminal Justice and Immigration Act 2008. These are almost the same as for older offenders:

SECTION

'(a) the punishment of offenders,
(b) the reform and rehabilitation of offenders,
(c) the protection of the public, and
(d) the making of reparation by offenders to persons affected by their offences.'

However, the court must also have regard to the principal aim of the youth justice system which is to prevent offending by children and other persons aged under 18. The court must also consider the welfare of the offender in accordance with s44 of the Children and Young Persons Act 1933.

The Sentencing Guidelines Council pointed out in their guidelines, 'Overarching Principles: Seriousness' (2004):

QUOTATION

> '1.2 The Act does not indicate that any one purpose should be more important than any other and in practice they may all be relevant to a greater or lesser degree in any individual case – the sentencer has the task of determining the manner in which they apply.'

One of the problems in relation to these purposes of sentencing is that some of them may be in conflict in particular cases. For example, the sentence which is most suitable for reforming an offender may not be the same sentence which would be imposed if the judge merely considered the purpose of punishment. In most cases the judge is performing a balancing act but always keeping in mind the need to reduce crime. Also, although there are five purposes of sentencing set out here, academics have always considered that there are six aims of sentencing. The additional one not covered in s142 is denunciation. Each of these aims of sentencing will be examined in turn.

12.2.1 Punishment

This aim is also referred to as retribution. It is based on the idea that punishment should be imposed because the offender deserves punishment for his or her acts. It does not seek to reduce crime or alter the offender's future behaviour. This idea was expressed in the eighteenth century by Kant in *The Metaphysical Elements of Justice* when he wrote:

QUOTATION

> 'Judicial punishment can never be used merely as a means to promote some other good for the criminal himself or for civil society, but instead it must in all cases be imposed on him only on the ground that he has committed a crime.'

Retribution is therefore concerned only with the fact that the offence was committed and making sure that the punishment inflicted is in proportion to that offence. The crudest form of retribution is seen in the old saying 'An eye for an eye and a tooth for a tooth and a life for a life.' This was one of the factors used to justify the death penalty for the offence of murder. The offender had taken a life and so had to forfeit his own life. In other crimes it is not so easy to see how this principle can operate to produce an exact match between crime and punishment. For this reason sentencing guidelines are produced to help judges in deciding an appropriate punishment.

Sentencing guidelines

Under the Criminal Justice Act 2003, the Sentencing Guidelines Council was given responsibility for producing such guidelines. When drafting guidelines, it received advice from the Sentencing Advisory Panel and this Panel consulted widely before tendering its advice. In 2010 both of these bodies were replaced by the Sentencing Council.

The Sentencing Council has responsibility for:

- developing sentencing guidelines and monitoring their use;
- assessing the impact of guidelines on sentencing practice;
- promoting awareness amongst the public regarding the realities of sentencing; and
- publishing information regarding sentencing practice in Magistrates' and Crown Courts.

The Sentencing Council has more powers than the previous Sentencing Guidelines Council. In particular the courts are now under a duty to impose a sentence which is within the offence range set out by the Council. The courts should only depart from the range when it is in the interests of justice to do so.

The Sentencing Council has issued guidelines for different types of offence. In their guidelines they divide each offence into levels of seriousness. Then for each level of seriousness they set out the starting point for sentence and the maximum sentence. This results in an overall 'offence range' of sentence from the starting point for the lowest level of seriousness to the maximum for the highest level of seriousness. It is this 'offence range' within which judges should normally set the sentence.

Figure 12.2 shows extracts of the Sentencing Council's guidelines on sentencing for assault occasioning actual bodily harm. All sentencing guidelines can be found on the website of the Sentencing Council at www.sentencingcouncil.org.uk.

STEP ONE Determining the offence category

The court should determine the offence category using the table below.

Category 1	Greater harm (serious injury must normally be present) and higher culpability
Category 2	Greater harm (serious injury must normally be present) and lower culpability; or lesser harm and higher culpability
Category 3	Lesser harm and lower culpability

The guidelines then give factors which indicate higher or lower culpability. They also give factors to help decide the level of harm.

STEP TWO Starting point and category range

Having determined the category, the court should use the corresponding starting points to reach a sentence within the category range below. The starting point applies to all offenders irrespective of plea or previous convictions. A case of particular gravity, reflected by multiple features of culpability in step one, could merit upward adjustment from the starting point before further adjustment for aggravating or mitigating features, set out below.

Offence Category	Starting Point (Applicable to all offenders)	Category Range (Applicable to all offenders)
Category 1	1 year 6 months' custody	1–3 years' custody
Category 2	26 weeks' custody	Low level community order – 51 weeks' custody
Category 3	Medium level community order	Band A fine – High level community order

Figure 12.2 Extracts from the Sentencing Council's guidelines on assault causing actual bodily harm

All guidelines produced must include a starting point for sentencing and a range for the offence. The courts have to impose a sentence which is within the offence range set by the Council. The only exceptions will be where the case before the court does not sufficiently resemble any of the cases in the guidelines.

When producing guidelines the Council also has to produce a resource assessment of the effect of the guidelines. This means that it has to identify whether the guidelines are likely to increase the numbers being sent to prison or if there will be an effect on the probation service. The intention behind this is to allow the government to forecast more accurately the requirements of the prison and probation services.

While this system upholds the aim of punishing offenders and leads to consistency in sentencing, it is more difficult for courts to impose sentences aimed at reforming offenders. The guidelines appear to leave very little discretion in sentencing with the judges. The guidelines are nearer to the system of tariff sentences which operates in some states in America. These often have a very rigid system in which each crime has only a narrow range of sentences which the judge can impose.

The objections to such a system are that it does not allow sufficient consideration of mitigating factors, and may produce a sentence which is unjust in the particular circumstances. The concept of retribution and giving the offender his 'just desserts' should not be so rigid as to ignore special needs of the offender.

However, the Sentencing Council's Crown Court Sentencing Surveys show that although most sentences are within the offence range, judges do deviate from the guidelines, sometimes giving lower sentences and sometimes higher. For example, the guidelines for causing grievous bodily harm (s18 Offence against the Person Act 1861) give three years' imprisonment as the bottom of the offence range and 16 years as the top of the offence range. In 2014, 2 per cent of sentences for this offence were above the 16-year guideline, whilst 7 per cent of sentences fell below the three years' imprisonment bottom of offence range guideline.

12.2.2 Deterrence

This can be individual deterrence or general deterrence. Individual deterrence is intended to make sure that the offender does not re-offend through fear of future punishment. General deterrence is aimed at preventing other potential offenders from committing crimes. Both are aimed at reducing the future levels of crime.

Individual deterrence

There are several penalties that can be imposed with the aim of deterring the individual offender from committing similar crimes in the future. These include a prison sentence or a suspended sentence, electronic tagging or a heavy fine. It is noticeable, however, that prison does not appear to deter, as about 60 per cent of adult prisoners re-offend within two years of release. With young offenders custodial sentences have even less of a deterrent effect as the re-offending rate is even higher.

Critics of the theory of deterrence point out that it makes an assumption about criminal behaviour that is not borne out in practice. It assumes that an offender will stop to consider what the consequences of his action will be. In fact, most crimes are committed on the spur of the moment and many are committed by offenders who are under the influence of drugs or alcohol. These offenders are unlikely to stop and consider the possible consequences of their actions.

It is also pointed out that fear of being caught is more of a deterrent and that while crime detection rates are low, the threat of an unpleasant penalty, if caught, seems too remote. Fear of detection has been shown to be a powerful deterrent by the success rate of closed-circuit televisions used for surveying areas. In one scheme on London's District Line of the Underground system there was an 83 per cent reduction in crime in the first full year that surveillance cameras were used.

General deterrence

The value of this is even more doubtful as potential offenders are rarely deterred by severe sentences passed on others. However, the courts do occasionally resort to making an example of an offender in order to warn other potential offenders of the type of punishment they face. This will usually be where there is a large increase in a particular type of crime. General deterrence also relies on publicity so that potential offenders are aware of the level of punishment. It is in direct conflict with the principle of retribution, since it involves sentencing an offender to a longer term than is deserved for the specific offence. It is probably the least effective and least fair principle of sentencing. The Sentencing Guidelines Council in its guidelines, 'Overarching Principles: Seriousness' (2004), recognised this and pointed out:

QUOTATION

'1.38 The seriousness of an individual case should be judged on its own dimensions of harm and culpability rather than as part of a collective social harm. It is legitimate for the overall approach to sentencing levels for particular offences to be directed by their cumulative effect. However, it would be wrong to further penalise individual offenders by increasing sentence length for committing an individual offence of that type.'

12.2.3 Reform and rehabilitation

Under this the main aim of the penalty is to reform the offender and rehabilitate him into society. It is a forward-looking aim. The hope is that the offender's behaviour will be altered by the penalty imposed so that he will not offend in the future. It also aims to reduce crime in this way. This principle of sentence came to the fore in the second half of the twentieth century with the development of sentences such as probation and community service orders. The Criminal Justice Act 2003 has extended the range of orders that can be made within a community sentence. The details of this are examined at section 12.4.

Reformation is a very important element in the sentencing philosophy for young offenders, but it is also used for some adult offenders. The court will be given information about the defendant's background, usually through a pre-sentence report prepared by the probation service. Where relevant the court will consider other factors, such as school reports, or job prospects, or medical problems.

Individualised sentences

Where the court considers rehabilitation, the sentence used is an individualised one aimed at the needs of the offender. This is in direct contrast to the concept of tariff sentences seen in the aim of retribution. One of the criticisms of this approach is, therefore, that it leads to inconsistency in sentencing. Offenders who have committed exactly the same type of offence may be given different sentences because the emphasis is on the individual offender. Another criticism is that this aim tends to discriminate against under-privileged people. Offenders from poor home backgrounds are less likely to be seen as possible candidates for reform.

Persistent offenders are usually thought less likely to respond to a reformative sentence.

12.2.4 Protection of the public

Protection usually involves incapacitating the offender in some way. That is, the offender is made incapable of re-offending. Of course, the ultimate method of incapacitation is the death penalty. In some countries the hands of thieves are cut off to prevent them from re-offending. Another controversial method of incapacitation is the use in some American states of medical means to incapacitate sex offenders and thus ensure that they cannot re-offend.

Incapacitation is also thought of as protecting society from the criminal activities of the offender, so today in Britain this is achieved by removing dangerous offenders from society through the use of long prison sentences. This is shown by the Criminal Justice

Act 2003 where dangerous offenders may be given a life sentence or an extended sentence in certain circumstances. Also, the use of minimum sentences for persistent offenders is aimed at protecting the public from their repeated criminal activities.

There are other penalties that can be viewed as incapacitating the offender. For example, in driving offences, the offender can be banned from driving. There is also a move to using community-based sentences that will incapacitate the offender in the short term and protect the public. These include exclusion orders under which an offender is banned from going to the place where he offends, usually a pub or a football ground, and **curfew orders** which order an offender to remain at a given address for certain times of the day or night. There is also the provision of electronic tagging to help supervise curfew orders.

curfew order
An order that an offender must stay at home during certain times

12.2.5 Reparation

This is where the offender has to make reparation to the victim or community who have suffered as a result of the offence. At the lowest level this may be done by compensating the victim of the crime. This is usually by ordering the offender to pay a sum of money to the victim or to make restitution, for example by returning stolen property to its rightful owner. The idea that criminals should pay compensation to the victims of their crimes is one that predates the Norman Conquest to the Anglo-Saxon courts. In England today, the courts must consider ordering compensation to the victim of a crime in addition to any other penalty they may think appropriate. Under s130(2) of the Powers of Criminal Courts (Sentencing) Act 2000, courts are under a duty to give reasons if they do not make a compensation order.

The concept of restitution also includes making reparation to society as a whole. This can be seen mainly in the use of unpaid work requirements in a community sentence when offenders are required to do so many hours' work on a community project under the supervision of the probation service.

Reparation is now often viewed in the wider concept of restorative justice. This has two aims. The first is to prevent the offender from re-offending through an understanding of the trauma the crime has caused to the victim. At the same time the offender will be expected to make reparation. A widely accepted definition of 'restorative justice' is:

QUOTATION

'A process whereby all the parties with a stake in a particular offence come together to resolve collectively how to deal with the aftermath of an offence and the implications for the future.'
T Marshall, 'Restorative Justice: An Overview' (Home Office, 1999)

The trend today is towards more focused reparation in which the offender is brought face to face with the victim and there have been pilot schemes bringing offenders and victims together, so that the offender may make direct reparation. A series of Home Office studies evaluated three schemes operating in different areas of England and Wales. The first study, 'Implementing Restorative Justice Schemes (Crime Reduction Programme): A Report on the First Year' by Shapland et al. (Home Office Report 32/04, 2004), found that setting up schemes had taken more time and funding than expected. The second study was about management and is not relevant here, but the third report, 'Restorative Justice: The Views of Victims and Offenders' (Ministry of Justice Research Series 3/07, 2007) found high victim and offender satisfaction in the process, especially where offending-related problems such as drug or alcohol abuse were also addressed in the meetings.

The fourth report, 'Does Restorative Justice Affect Reconviction?' (Ministry of Justice Research Series 10/08, 2008) found that in all three schemes, those offenders who participated in restorative justice 'committed statistically significantly fewer offences' than offenders in the control group. However, in two of the schemes, the severity of the new offences committed was no different from the control group. The third scheme, operating in Northumbria, showed a large impact on the reduced likelihood and severity of re-offending.

Reparative justice is used in youth justice. Youth Offending Panels/Teams often use it as part of the package in the contract for a young offender's future behaviour.

12.2.6 Denunciation

This is society expressing its disapproval of criminal activity. A sentence should indicate both to the offender and to other people that society condemns certain types of behaviour. It shows people that justice is being done. Denunciation also reinforces the moral boundaries of acceptable conduct and can mould society's views on the criminality of particular conduct. For example, drink-driving is now viewed by the majority of people as unacceptable behaviour. This is largely because of the changes in the law and the increasingly severe sentences that are imposed. By sending offenders to prison, banning them from driving and imposing heavy fines, society's opinion of drink-driving has been changed.

The ideas of retribution and denunciation were foremost in the concepts behind the Criminal Justice Act of 1991, as shown by the government White Paper on Crime and Punishment (1990) which preceded the Act. However, in the 2003 Criminal Justice Act denunciation was not included as one of the purposes of sentencing in s142.

KEY FACTS

The purposes of sentencing

Purpose	Explanation	Suitable punishment
Punishment	Punishment imposed only on ground that an offence has been committed also known as retribution	Tariff sentences Sentence must be proportionate to the crime
Protection of the public	Society is protected from crime by making the offender incapable of committing further crime	Death penalty for murder Long prison sentences Tagging
Deterrence	Individual – the offender is deterred through fear of further punishment General – potential offenders warned as to likely punishment	Prison sentence Heavy fine Long sentence as an example to others
Reform and rehabilitation	Reform offender's behaviour	Individualised sentence Supervision requirement Unpaid work requirement
Restitution	Repayment/reparation to victim or to community Restorative justice	Compensation order Unpaid work requirement Reparation order
Denunciation	Society expressing its disapproval Reinforces moral boundaries	Reflects blameworthiness of the offence

12.3 Custodial sentences

This book does not seek to give a detailed examination of all the sentences available, but merely to examine briefly the different categories of custodial sentences, community-based sentences, fines and discharges. A custodial sentence is the most serious punishment that a court can impose. Custodial sentences range from 'weekend' prison to life imprisonment. They include:

- mandatory and discretionary life sentences;
- fixed-term sentences;
- suspended sentences.

12.3.1 Life sentences

Mandatory life sentence

The only penalty available where an offender aged 21 or over pleads guilty or is found guilty of murder is life imprisonment. This is, therefore, a mandatory sentence where the judge has no discretion in sentencing. However, the judge does state the minimum term that should be served before the offender is eligible for release on licence. This minimum period used to be set by the Home Secretary but this procedure was held to be a breach of the ECHR, since it gave the Executive power over sentencing. There was also a challenge as to whether having a mandatory life sentence for murder was a breach of human rights, but it was ruled in *R v Secretary of State for the Home Department ex p Lichniak and others* [2001] 3 WLR 933 that it was not incompatible with Articles 3 and 5 of the Convention.

The minimum term to be served in a life sentence is now governed by s269 and Sch 21 to the Criminal Justice Act 2003, as amended. This gives judges clear starting points for the minimum period to be ordered. The starting points range from a full life term down to 12 years. A whole life term should be set where the offence falls into one of the following categories:

- the murder of two or more persons, where each murder involves a substantial degree of premeditation or planning or the abduction of the victim or sexual or sadistic conduct;
- the murder of a child if involving the abduction of the child or sexual or sadistic motivation;
- a murder done for the purpose of advancing a political, religious or ideological cause;
- a murder of a police or prison officer in the execution of their duty; or
- a murder by an offender previously convicted of murder.

Cases which have a starting point of 30 years include murders using a firearm or explosive or the sexual or sadistic murder of an adult or a murder that is racially or religiously aggravated. Any offence of murder which is not specifically given a starting point of a whole life term or 30 years has a starting point of 15 years, although where the offender was under the age of 18 at the time of the offence this period is 12 years.

Aggravating and mitigating factors

Once the judge has decided on the starting point, any aggravating or mitigating factors must then be considered. Aggravating factors which can increase the minimum term ordered by the judge include the fact that the victim was particularly vulnerable because of age or disability or any mental or physical suffering inflicted on the victim before death. Mitigating factors include the fact that the offender had an intention to cause grievous bodily harm rather than an intention to kill, a lack of premeditation or the fact that the offender acted to some extent in self-defence (though not sufficient to give him a defence). Where there are mitigating factors the judge can set a minimum term of less than any of the starting points.

Where the offence carries a discretionary life sentence and the judge decides that a life sentence should be imposed, then again the judge must set a minimum term to be served before the offender can be released on licence. However, there are no statutory guidelines for such cases and the judge may select the term he thinks appropriate.

Life sentence for public protection

This sentence may be imposed under s225 on any defendant who is convicted of a serious offence and where the court is of the opinion that there is a significant risk to members of the public of serious harm caused by further offences by the defendant.

When the court imposes such a sentence the judge will set a minimum period which must be served before the defendant can be considered for parole. The intention was that prisoners serving such sentences would be offered rehabilitation courses, such as an anger management course, while in prison in order to make it safer to release them.

Between 2003 and 2012, s225 allowed the courts to give an indeterminate sentence for public protection. This was used so much that one in ten of those in prison were serving such a sentence. There were also human rights issues with such a sentence, particularly where rehabilitation courses were not available to prisoners. This lack of provision meant that prisoners were unable to apply for parole as they had not attended courses. In 2012 the sentence was changed to a life sentence for public protection and the range of offences for which it can be imposed has been reduced to only those where the maximum sentence for the offence is life imprisonment.

12.3.2 Fixed-term sentence

A fixed-term sentence is one for a definite period, for example six years' imprisonment. Under the Criminal Justice Act 2003, all offenders serving fixed-term sentences of 12 months or more are released on licence after they have served half their sentence. They remain on licence until the full term of the sentence and if, at any time during the licence period, they breach their licence condition, they can be recalled to prison. It is also possible for offenders to be released up 135 days before the half-way stage of their sentence under a curfew condition.

There is considerable debate as to the use of short prison sentences for non-dangerous offenders as just under 50 per cent of adults released from prison re-offend within one year of being released. The rate for those serving short sentences is worse than for those who have served longer sentences.

12.3.3 Suspended sentences

A suspended sentence of imprisonment is one where the offender will only serve the custodial period if he breaches the terms of the suspension. The length of prison sentence can be for up to two years. The period of suspension can be between six months and two years. The idea is that the threat of prison during this period of suspension will deter the offender from committing further offences. If the offender complies with the requirements of the suspended sentence he will not serve the term of imprisonment. The suspended sentence can be given on its own or combined with any of the requirements used in a community order (see section 12.4). If the offender fails to meet the requirements the suspended sentence may be 'activated'. That is, the offender will be made to serve the term of imprisonment. Prior to the Criminal Justice Act 2003, a suspended sentence could only be combined with a fine or a compensation order, leaving the offender unsupervised. As a result, a suspended sentence was seen as a 'soft option' and rarely used by the courts. As it can now be combined with any order the court thinks appropriate, it is used more often, especially in the Crown Court where it is used in about 20 per cent of sentences.

12.4 Community orders

Prior to the Criminal Justice Act 2003, the courts had individual community sentences which they could impose on an offender. They could combine some of these sentences, in particular unpaid work with a supervision order. Also, they could add requirements about treatment and residence to a supervision order, but they could not use a whole range of orders. The Halliday Report recommended:

QUOTATION

'6.1 To ensure that a non-custodial sentence reduces the likelihood of re-offending, courts should have the power to impose a single, non-custodial penalty made up of specific elements – which would replace all existing community sentences. These elements would include:

- treatment for substance abuse or mental illness;
- curfew and exclusion orders;
- electronic monitoring;
- reparation to victims and communities;
- compulsory work;
- attendance at offending behaviour programmes.'

Halliday Report, 'Making Punishments Work: A Review of the Sentencing Framework for England and Wales' (2001)

This was brought into effect by the Criminal Justice Act 2003 and there is now a community order available to the courts which is a customised community sentence combining any requirements which the court thinks necessary. These requirements include all the previous existing community sentences which became available as 'requirements' and can be attached to the sentence. There are also new 'requirements' available. The sentencers can 'mix and match' requirements allowing them to fit the restrictions and rehabilitation to the offender's needs. The sentence is available for offenders age 16 and over. The full list of requirements available to the courts is set out in s177 of the Criminal Justice Act 2003, as amended.

SECTION

'177(1) Where a person aged 18 or over is convicted of an offence, the court by or before which he is convicted may make an order imposing on him any one or more of the following requirements:

(a) an unpaid work requirement
(b) an activity requirement
(c) a programme requirement
(d) a prohibited activity requirement
(e) a curfew requirement
(f) an exclusion requirement

(g) a residence requirement
(h) a mental health treatment requirement
(i) a drug rehabilitation requirement
(j) an alcohol treatment requirement
(k) a supervision requirement, and
(l) in the case where the offender is aged under 25, an attendance centre requirement.'

Each of these is defined within the Criminal Justice Act 2003. Most are self-explanatory from their name, such as drug rehabilitation and alcohol treatment. Much crime is linked to drug and alcohol abuse and the idea behind these two requirements is to tackle the causes of crime, hopefully preventing further offences. Mental health treatment is also aimed at the cause of the offender's behaviour. The main other requirements are explained briefly below.

12.4.1 Unpaid work requirement

This requires the offender to work for between 40 and 300 hours on a suitable project organised by the probation service. The exact number of hours will be fixed by the court and those hours are then usually worked in eight-hour sessions, often at weekends. The type of work involved will vary, depending on what schemes the local probation service has running. The offender may be required to paint school buildings, help build a play centre or work on conservation projects. When Eric Cantona, the French footballer, was found guilty of assaulting a football fan, the court ordered that he help at coaching sessions for young footballers. Also, Leeds footballers Lee Bowyer and Jonathan Woodgate were ordered to do unpaid work after they were convicted of assault.

12.4.2 Activity requirement

The offender has to take part in set activities on certain days for up to a maximum of 60 separate days. The activities can include activities for the purpose of reparation, including contact between the offender and the victim.

12.4.3 Curfew requirement

Under a curfew requirement an offender can be ordered to remain at a fixed address for between two and 16 hours in any 24-hour period. This order can last for up to six months and may be enforced by electronic tagging under which the offender has to wear a tag which sends signals of his whereabouts to a central monitoring system. This is usually via a radio receiving unit connected to a telephone line. Tagging is also used when prisoners are released early on a home detention curfew. There have been worries that curfews are not being properly monitored and that offenders have continued to offend even though they were tagged.

Initially tagging appeared to be a successful method of preventing re-offending. However, a report in 2007, 'Satellite Tracking of Offenders: A Study of the Pilots in England and Wales', showed that 58 per cent of offenders broke the terms of their tagging order. More than one-quarter committed further offences while tagged. However, the use of electronic tagging has increased (its use doubled between 2005 and 2012) even though the failure rate has not improved.

A report in 2012 by the Chief Inspector of Probation showed that over half of offenders ordered to wear an electronic tag broke the terms of their curfew. Twenty per cent were minor violations where the offenders were warned and then successfully completed their order. However, in 37 per cent of cases there was a serious violation which required further action by the courts.

12.4.4 Exclusion order

Under s205 of the Criminal Justice Act 2003 courts may order that an offender be banned from entering a specified place or places. It can be just for certain days or it can be a complete ban. Such an order can be for up to two years. An exclusion requirement may be used for a variety of offences: for example banning football hooligans from attending at certain football clubs or persistent shoplifters from entering certain shops. Tagging and satellite technology is also being piloted as a way of monitoring whether an offender is keeping out of the excluded area.

12.4.5 Supervision requirement

This places the offender under the supervision of a probation officer for a period of between six months and three years. During this time the offender must attend appointments with the probation officer or another person determined by the probation officer. A supervision requirement will be made for the purpose of promoting the offender's rehabilitation.

12.5 Young offenders

12.5.1 Custodial sentences

Custodial sentences are viewed as a last resort for young offenders. When a custodial sentence is imposed young offenders are kept separate from adult offenders and there is a considerable emphasis on education and training. Despite this, statistics show that custodial sentences are not effective in preventing young offenders from re-offending as about 70 per cent of young offenders given custodial sentences re-offend within one year of being released.

Detention at Her Majesty's Pleasure

Any offender aged 10–17 who is convicted of murder must be ordered to be detained during Her Majesty's Pleasure. This is an indeterminate sentence which allows the offender to be released when suitable. The judge in the case can recommend a minimum number of years that should be served before release is considered. This must be in accordance with the guidelines set out in the Criminal Justice Act 2003 (see section 12.3.1). The sentence will be initially served in a special unit for young offenders. When an offender reaches 21 he will be transferred to an adult prison.

Detention for serious crimes

For very serious offences the courts have additional power under s53 of the Children and Young Persons Act 1933 to order that the offender be detained for longer periods. For 10–13 year olds this power is only available where the crime committed carries a maximum sentence of at least 14 years' imprisonment for adults or is an offence of indecent assault on a woman under s14 of the Sexual Offences Act 1956. For 14–17 year olds it is also available for causing death by dangerous driving or for causing death by careless driving while under the influence of drink or drugs. The length of detention imposed on the young offender cannot be more than the maximum sentence available for an adult.

Young offenders' institutions

Under s91 of the Powers of Criminal Courts (Sentencing) Act 2000 offenders aged 15–20 can be sent to a young offenders' institution as a custodial sentence. The minimum sentence is 21 days and the maximum is the maximum allowed for the particular offence. If the offender reaches the age of 21 while serving the sentence, he will be transferred to an adult prison.

Detention and training orders

Under s100 of the Powers of Criminal Courts (Sentencing) Act 2000 the courts can make a detention and training order in relation to an offender aged 12–21. The sentence is for a specified period with a minimum of four months and a maximum of 24 months. Half the sentence is spent in custody and the second half in the community. For offenders under the age of 15 an order can only be made if they are persistent offenders.

12.5.2 Youth Rehabilitation Orders

These simplify sentencing for young offenders as various requirements can be attached to such an order. This brings the sentencing structure into line with that for adults where a community order can contain a variety of requirements.

The requirements which can be attached to a youth rehabilitation order are:

1. an activity requirement;
2. a supervision requirement;
3. in a case where the offender is aged 16 or 17 at the time of the conviction, an unpaid work requirement;
4. a programme requirement;
5. an attendance centre requirement;
6. a prohibited activity requirement;
7. a curfew requirement;
8. an exclusion requirement;
9. a residence requirement;
10. a local authority residence requirement;
11. a mental health treatment requirement;
12. a drug treatment requirement;
13. a drug testing requirement;
14. an intoxicating substance treatment requirement; and
15. an education requirement.

In addition a youth rehabilitation order may also impose an electronic monitoring requirement. Also a rehabilitation order may be combined with intensive supervision and surveillance or with fostering of the offender.

12.6 Fines and discharges

As seen at the beginning of this chapter a fine is the most common way of disposing of a case in the Magistrates' Court. In the Crown Court only a small percentage of offenders are dealt with by way of a fine. One of the problems is the number of unpaid fines. This has two bad effects: it makes the punishment ineffective, and it leads to defendants being imprisoned for non-payment. The level of fine payment has improved in recent years.

Discharges are used at the lowest level of sentencing seriousness. They may be either conditional or absolute. A conditional discharge is the one more commonly used by the courts. It means that the offender is discharged on the condition that no further offence is committed during a period set by the court, which can be up to three years. It is intended to be used where the court is of the opinion that punishment is not required and also that the offender is not in need of supervision. If an offender re-offends within the time limit the court can then impose another sentence in place of the conditional discharge as well as imposing a penalty for the new offence. Conditional discharges are widely used by Magistrates' Courts for first-time offenders who have committed minor offences.

An absolute discharge means that effectively no penalty is imposed. This type of discharge is likely to be used where an offender is technically guilty but morally blameless. An example could be where the tax disc on a vehicle has fallen to the floor. It is technically not being displayed and an offence has been committed. So, in the unlikely situation of someone being prosecuted for this, the magistrates, who would have to impose some penalty, could decide that an absolute discharge was appropriate.

12.7 Sentencing practice

There has been considerable concern over the inconsistencies in sentencing in both the Magistrates' Courts and Crown Courts in different areas of the country. In the White Paper 'Justice for All', Cm 5563 (2002) which preceded the Criminal Justice Act 2003, the government gave the following examples of inconsistency:

- only 21 per cent of those convicted of driving while disqualified are sent to prison in Neath and Port Talbot (South Wales) against 77 per cent in mid and north Essex;
- of those convicted of receiving stolen goods, 3.5 per cent were jailed in Reading against 48 per cent in Greenwich and Woolwich in South London.

The Lord Chancellor again stressed the problems of inconsistency in a speech on Penal Policy to the Howard League for Prison Reform in September 2004. He pointed out that in 2002, 30 per cent of those convicted of theft offences in West Yorkshire were given a custodial sentence but only 19 per cent in Merseyside for the same sorts of crimes.

In order to try to prevent such inconsistencies the Criminal Justice Act 2003 set down various points which the court should consider in deciding what sentence to impose. In addition, the Sentencing Guidelines Council was created to give more detailed guidance on the levels of sentencing. Now the Sentencing Council of England and Wales has replaced the Sentencing Guidelines Council and the courts normally are obliged to impose sentences within the offence range set by the Council. This should lead to a much higher level of consistency in sentencing.

12.7.1 Seriousness

The first point to be considered in what type of sentence should be given is the seriousness of the offence. In s143(1) the 2003 Act states:

SECTION

'In considering the seriousness of any offence, the court must consider the offender's culpability in committing the offence and the harm, or risk of harm, which the offence caused or was intended to cause.'

This shows that in considering seriousness there are two factors to be taken into account:

- culpability; and
- harm.

There are certain factors which the Criminal Justice Act 2003 or the Powers of Criminal Courts (Sentencing) Act 2000 set out as being aggravating factors. These include committing an offence when on bail, having previous convictions and failure to respond to previous sentences. In regard to previous convictions s143(2) of the Criminal Justice Act 2003 states:

SECTION

'Previous convictions are an aggravating factor if the court considers this to be so in view of the relevance to the present offence and the time which has elapsed since the previous conviction.'

So, previous convictions which are recent and for similar offences to the one charged will clearly be an aggravating factor. Under ss145 and 146 other aggravating factors can lead to an increase in sentence where the offence was committed because of the victim's:

- race;
- religion;
- disability; or
- sexual orientation.

There are many other factors which make the culpability of the offender greater. These are referred to as aggravating factors. The Sentencing Guidelines Council guidelines in 'Overarching Principles: Seriousness' (2004) included such points as a high level of profit from the offence, an attempt to conceal or dispose of evidence and an abuse of trust. Also the offender's culpability is greater if an offender deliberately causes more harm than is necessary for the commission of the offence or where the offender targets a vulnerable victim, for example, because of their old age or their youth or a disability.

There can also be factors which indicate a lower level of culpability. The Sentencing Guidelines Council in its guidelines gives the following factors:

- an exceptional degree of provocation;
- mental illness or disability;
- youth or age where it affects the responsibility of the individual defendant;
- the fact that the offender played only a minor role in the offence.

In deciding on an appropriate sentence, it is necessary to consider both aggravating and mitigating factors.

The overall approach given in the guidelines, 'Overarching Principles: Seriousness' (2004) points out:

QUOTATION

'1.3 The sentencer must start by considering the seriousness of the offence, the assessment of which will:

- determine which of the sentencing thresholds has been crossed;
- indicate whether a custodial, community or other sentence is the most appropriate;
- be the key factor in deciding the length of a custodial sentence, the onerousness of requirements to be incorporated in a community sentence and the amount of any fine imposed.'

12.7.2 Reduction for a guilty plea

On the other hand, the 2003 Act allows for a reduction in sentence for a guilty plea, particularly where made early in the proceedings (s144). This provision was previously included in s152 of the Powers of Criminal Courts (Sentencing) Act 2000. The Sentencing Guidelines Council has suggested that the reduction for a guilty plea at the first reasonable opportunity should attract a reduction of up to one-third, whereas a plea of guilty after the trial has started would be given only a one-tenth reduction. The amount of reduction is on a sliding scale, as shown in Figure 12.3.

Figure 12.3 Reduction for guilty plea

The concept of reducing the level of sentence imposed on a defendant just because he has pleaded guilty has caused controversy. Many people believe that if someone has 'done the crime, they should do the time'. However, in its guidelines, the Sentencing Guidelines Council gave its reasons for allowing discounts in sentences for guilty pleas as:

QUOTATION

'A reduction in sentence is appropriate because a guilty plea avoids the need for a trial, shortens the gap between charge and sentence, saves considerable cost, and, in the case of an early plea, saves victims and witnesses from the concern about having to give evidence.'

Following objections to offenders whose guilt was 'overwhelming' being given a reduction in sentence for pleading guilty, the Sentencing Guidelines Council issued revised guidelines on sentencing discounts for a guilty plea. These state that where the prosecution case is overwhelming, the appropriate reduction for a guilty plea at the first reasonable opportunity should be 20 per cent. The Sentencing Guidelines Council carried out a further public consultation in 2016, asking for views on the levels of reductions which should be available, and the principles on which the reduction for a guilty plea would be based. The outcome of the consultation has not been released at the time of writing.

12.7.3 Thresholds

The idea of thresholds comes from the Criminal Justice Act 2003. In relation to custodial sentences, s152(2) provides:

SECTION

'The court must not pass a custodial sentence unless it is of the opinion that the offence, or the combination of the offence and one or more offences associated with it, was so serious that neither a fine alone nor a community sentence can be justified for the offence.'

How this is to be applied is suggested by the Sentencing Guidelines Council in its guidelines, 'Overarching Principles: Seriousness' (2004), where it stated:

QUOTATION

'1.32 In applying the threshold test, sentencers should note:

- the clear intention of the threshold test is to reserve prison as a punishment for the most serious offences;
- it is impossible to determine definitively which features of a particular offence make it serious enough to merit a custodial sentence;
- passing the custody threshold does not mean that a custodial sentence should be deemed inevitable, and custody can still be avoided in the light of personal mitigation or where there is a suitable intervention in the community which provides sufficient restriction (by way of punishment) while addressing the rehabilitation of the offender to prevent future crimes.'

There is a similar threshold test for a community sentence in s148(1):

SECTION

'A court must not pass a community sentence on an offender unless it is of the opinion that the offence, or the combination of the offence and one or more offences associated with it, was serious enough to warrant such a sentence.'

However, although there is a seriousness threshold for the offence, it is also necessary for the court to consider previous convictions and sentences of the offender. On this the Sentencing Guidelines Council points out:

QUOTATION

'1.35 In addition, the threshold test for a community sentence can be crossed even though the seriousness criterion is not met. Section 151 Criminal Justice Act 2003 provides that, in relation to an offender age 16 or over on whom, on 3 or more previous occasions, sentences had been passed consisting only of a fine, a community sentence may be made (if it is in the interests of justice) despite the fact that the seriousness of the current offence (and others associated with it) might not warrant such a sentence.'

Where the court decides that the threshold test for a community sentence has not been crossed and there is no other reason for imposing a community sentence, then the court can impose on the offender a lesser penalty such as a fine or a discharge.

12.7.4 Pre-sentence reports

In deciding whether the threshold for either a custodial sentence or a community sentence has been crossed, the court can also take into account information in a pre-sentence report on the offender. Section 156 of the Criminal Justice Act 2003 makes it obligatory for such a report to be obtained and considered before passing a custodial sentence or a community sentence, unless the court is of the opinion that such a report is not necessary. Thus, for an adult offender, the court can decide that a report is not necessary where the offence is very serious, such as an armed robbery, so that only a custodial sentence is justified. However, for offenders under the age of 18 the court *must* consider a pre-sentence report.

Such a report must be submitted by a local probation officer or, for an offender under the age of 18, by a social worker or member of a youth offending team. It will give information about the defendant's background and also his suitability for certain types of requirement in a community order.

Where a defendant is, or appears to be, mentally disordered, then the court must also obtain a medical report in respect of the defendant.

There is now also provision for pre-sentence drug testing of offenders aged 14 and over. This will be relevant only where the court is considering imposing a community sentence or a suspended prison sentence. The test is to ascertain whether the defendant has been using Class A drugs. Such a test is helpful as, if there is evidence of drug abuse, the court may wish to make a drug rehabilitation requirement as part of a community sentence.

ACTIVITY

Critiquing the law

The Criminal Justice Act 2003 makes clear that any court dealing with an offender in respect of his offence must have regard to the following purposes of sentencing:

1. the punishment of offenders;
2. the reduction of crime (including its reduction by deterrence);
3. the reform and rehabilitation of offenders;
4. the protection of the public; and
5. the making of reparation by offenders to persons affected by their offences.

Are all these purposes consistent with each other, or do some contradict with others? Is it possible to take into account all of these purposes in every case? Which of these do you prefer, and why?

12.8 Prison statistics

There has been concern that the number of people in prison (known as the prison population) has risen rapidly in recent years. In fact, the increase has been going on for the past 50 years, as is shown by Figure 12.4.

From Figure 12.4 it can be seen that the prison population doubled between 1951 and 1991. It then nearly doubled again between 1991 and 2016.

It can be argued that the population of England and Wales has increased during this period and so some increase should be expected. However, the population increase has not been that great and looking at the rate of number of prisoners per 100,000 of the general population confirms that there has indeed been a great increase in the number of people sent to prison. In 1951 there were only 50 per 100,000 of the population in prison; by 2001 this had risen to 136. By 2004 the UK had the highest rate of prison population per 100,000 in the whole of Europe.

The other worrying factor is that just under 50 per cent of all prisoners and about 70 per cent of young offenders are re-convicted within one year of release. One of the

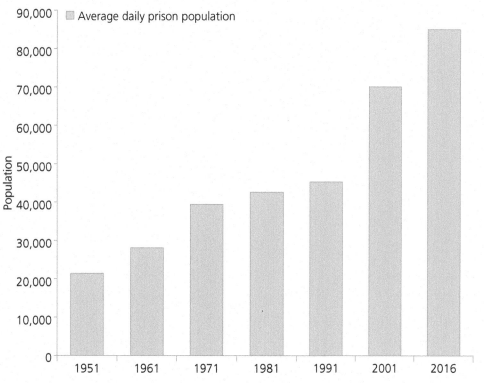

Figure 12.4 Average daily prison population for England and Wales, 1951–2016

reasons for this is that many of those in prison have poor education, poor home backgrounds and weak work skills. A parliamentary briefing paper giving statistics on prisoners showed:

- Over 25 per cent of prisoners had been taken into care as a child compared to 2 per cent of the population.

- Eighty-one per cent of prisoners were unmarried prior to imprisonment, rising to 85 per cent since imprisonment. Almost 10 per cent had been divorced. These figures are twice as high as those found in the general population.

- One-half of male and one-third of female sentenced prisoners were excluded from school. One half of male and seven out of ten female prisoners have no qualifications.

- Two-thirds of prisoners have numeracy skills at or below a level expected of an 11 year old. One-half have a reading ability and 82 per cent have writing ability at or below this level.

- Two-thirds of prisoners were unemployed in the four weeks before imprisonment.

- Around 70 per cent of prisoners suffer from two or more mental disorders. In the general population the figures are 5 per cent for men and 2 per cent for women.

- Prisoners are more likely to be abusers of illegal drugs and alcohol than other sectors of the community.

(Taken from Prison Population Statistics, House of Commons Library, 24 May 2012.)

SAMPLE ESSAY QUESTION

Consider the aggravating and mitigating factors and what would be a suitable sentence in the following cases.

Kevin, aged 22, has been found guilty in the Magistrates' Court of assault on a police officer in the execution of his duty. The facts are that he kicked a police officer who was trying to arrest a friend of his. Kevin has two previous convictions for assault. For the first offence he was fined £400. For the second offence he was given a community sentence with an unpaid work requirement. Kevin is employed as a car mechanic. He is single and lives with his mother.

Lola, aged 28, has pleaded guilty at the Crown Court to possessing cocaine. She has a previous conviction for shoplifting for which she was given a conditional discharge. She is an unemployed single mother caring for two children, aged seven and five.

Niall, aged 24, has been found guilty at the Crown Court of an assault causing grievous bodily harm. He committed this offence while on bail for an offence of taking and driving a car without the owner's consent. He has a previous conviction for causing criminal damage for which he was fined and another previous conviction for burglary for which he was imprisoned for six months. He was released from prison eight months ago. He is single and unemployed and was living in a bail hostel at the time of the offence.

Explain what mitigating and aggravating circumstances are and how they impact on sentencing:

- Summarise the different sentences available to the Crown Court and Magistrates' Court – custody, suspended sentence, fine, community order.
- Connect the discussion of mitigating and aggravating circumstances to the different purposes of punishment:
  - the punishment of offenders;
  - the reduction of crime (including reduction by deterrence);
  - the reform and rehabilitation of offenders;
  - the protection of the public;
  - the making of reparation by offenders.

Kevin's case:

- Note the sentencing powers of the Magistrates' Court.
- Aggravating factors include:
  - two previous convictions;
  - Kevin has assaulted a police officer.
- A mitigating factor is:
  - Kevin is employed.
- Reach a conclusion as to what sentence you would hand down in this case and for what reasons.

Lola's case:

- Mitigating factors for Lola include:
  - the offence is a non-violent drug offence;
  - she is a single mother caring for two children.
- Aggravating factors include:
  - the fact that she has prior convictions.
- Reach a conclusion as to what sentence you would hand down in this case and for what reasons.

Niall's case:

- Aggravating factors include:
  - the fact that Niall committed the offence whilst on bail;
  - that he has prior convictions for assault and taking a motor vehicle without consent.
- Mitigating factors could include the fact that he is unemployed and living at a bail hostel.
- There are high re-offending rates for ex-prisoners, so could the court look to a sentence which would be more effective at preventing re-offending?
- Reach a conclusion as to what sentence you would hand down in this case and for what reasons.

CONCLUSION

In your conclusion you should summarise what you think a suitable sentence in each scenario would be and explain why you have come to that conclusion.

Figure 12.5 Essay map on sentencing

SUMMARY

Purposes of sentencing

- The punishment of offenders. **Punishment** is based on the concept of retribution with sentencing ranges being imposed on the courts.

- The reduction of crime (including reduction by deterrence). **Deterrence** can be aimed at an individual or it can be general making an example of an offender in order to warn other potential offenders of the type of punishment they face.

- The reform and rehabilitation of offenders. **Reform**: the hope is that the offender's behaviour will be altered by the penalty imposed so that he will not offend in the future.

- The protection of the public. **Protection of the public** usually involves incapacitating the offender in some way so that he cannot re-offend.

- The making of reparation by offenders. **Reparation** is where the offender has to make reparation to the victim or community for his offences.

Types of sentences

- custodial (adults):
    - mandatory and discretionary life sentences;
    - fixed-term sentences;
    - suspended sentences;

- custodial (young offenders):
    - detention at Her Majesty's Pleasure;
    - young offenders' institutions;
    - detention and training orders;

- community orders/youth rehabilitation order (under 18) with requirements attached;

- fines;

- discharges.

Sentencing practice

- consider seriousness of offence – aggravating and mitigating factors;

- reduction for guilty plea;

- consider pre-sentence report;

- consider any mental health problems of offender.

Further reading

Book
Keating, H, Kyd Cunningham S, Elliott T, Walters, M, *Criminal Law: Text and Materials* (8th edn, Sweet & Maxwell, 2014) Part III of Ch 1.

Articles
Ashworth, A, 'Coroners and Justice Act 2009: sentencing guidelines and the Sentencing Council' [2010] *Crim LR* 389.

Lewis, P, 'Can prison prevent reoffending?' [2003] *NLJ* 168.

Robinson, P and Darley, J, 'Does criminal law deter? A behavioural science investigation' [2004] 24 *OJLS* 173.

'Story of the prison population 1995–2009: England and Wales' [2009] Ministry of Justice Statistics Bulletin.

Young, W, 'The effect of imprisonment on offending: a judge's perspective' [2010] *Crim LR* 3.

Internet links
Annual sentencing statistics and prison population at: www.justice.gov.uk

Youth Justice Board including Youth Offending Teams at: www.gov.uk/government/organisations/youth-justice-board-for-england-and-wales

Index

Page numbers in **bold** denote figures.